Information Systems for Management

Information Systems

Robert J. Mockler

St. John's University

for Management

Charles E. Merrill Publishing Company
A Bell & Howell Company
Columbus, Ohio

168478

To my colleagues and students
at St. John's University

Published by
Charles E. Merrill Publishing Company
A Bell & Howell Company
Columbus, Ohio 43216

Library of Congress Catalog Card Number: 73-89660

International Standard Book Number: 0-675-08844-5

Printed in the United States of America

1 2 3 4 5 6 7 8 9 10—78 77 76 75 74

Preface

The purpose of this book is to help managers and potential managers learn how to work effectively with systems technicians in developing management information systems or (where necessary) how to develop these systems on their own.

Management information systems are just what the name implies—systems which provide managers with information needed to get their jobs done. Managers always play a key role in developing these systems. Because they perform the management job, they know its information requirements better than anyone else. Because they are the ones who will use the systems, they are in the best position to evaluate their usefulness to management.

Systems technicians (systems analysts and data processing technicians) can also play a significant role, although they are not always involved in developing management information systems. For example, in small companies, a manager may be entirely on his own. Even in large companies, some managers may develop their own systems for gathering information in those areas not serviced by centralized data systems. Given today's technologically-oriented business environment, however, managers can anticipate working with systems technicians and computerized data systems at some time during their career.

While an understanding of data processing systems and how information systems are developed is important to a manager, this does not mean that a manager has to be a systems technician. It does mean knowing enough about data processing systems to be able to define information requirements in a way that will facilitate effective use of available systems technology. In addition, in situations where a manager is without technical assistance, it means knowing enough to be able to design and develop his own information system.

The ability to define information systems requirements in a way that anticipates and takes advantage of a data system's capabilities is necessary in systems work. A manager cannot depend on someone else to do this job of definition, since he knows his own needs better than any systems technician could. Unfortunately, defining information requirements in a way that effectively bridges the gap between technology (or technicians) and managers is not an easy job for a manager to learn.

This book is designed to make that difficult learning job easier. Since a manager needs to understand the tools he'll be working with, some technical aspects of data processing systems are covered; but this is not a technician's book. Rather, it is an introductory learning and teaching guide intended for managers or those who will be managers someday, and for present and potential systems technicians who want to better understand the manager's role in systems development.

The first three chapters of the book give a brief introduction to information systems and data processing, and describe an approach to developing management information systems. Chapters 4 through 10 discuss the development of basic information systems in several familiar areas of management: finance and accounting; marketing; operations; and project management. Chapters 11 through 13 cover simulation techniques, advanced information systems, and organizing and implementing systems development efforts.

The discussion of each information systems area is patterned after the systems approach. First, management jobs and the decisions required to get those jobs done are analyzed. The next focus is the way in which these management decision needs guide systems development. Throughout the book, basic information systems technology is introduced at points where it can be used to solve management information problems.

Entire chapters and major sections of chapters are devoted to examples of the development of information systems in different kinds of management situations. Numerous case study problems are included to give the reader practice in developing information systems.

As a final note, I want to thank my many friends in business and those at St. John's University who read parts of the book and made constructive suggestions on ways to improve it. I also wish to thank my students who stimulated the writing of this book, and my research assistants, Martin Bree and Basil Katsamakis, who did background research for several chapters.

Robert J. Mockler

Contents

Chapter 1 Information Systems for Management 2

A Key Concept: Meeting Manager Information Requirements, 3
Translating Information Requirements into Information Systems, 4
Information Systems Needed by Managers, 7
Management Information Systems and Operational or Application
Systems, 10
Systems Theory, 11
Conceptualizing a Management Information System, 16
Text Discussion Questions, 18
Case Study Exercises, 18
    The Neuman Consulting Company, 18
    The Little Publishing Company, 19

Chapter 2 An Approach to Developing 22
               Information Systems

Situation Diagnosis and Concept Design, 23
System Development, 30
Implementation of the System, 32
Putting the Systems Approach to Work, 33
Summary Conclusion, 35
Text Discussion Questions, 36
Case Study Exercises, 37
    Sunrise Motels, 37
    Management Information Systems at Domby Publishing
    Company, 39

Chapter 3 Data Processing Systems 46

Kinds of Data Processing Systems and their Function, 46
Manual Systems, 48
Punched-Card Systems, 51
Computer Systems, 53
Developing a Computerized Data Processing System, 61

Converting a Data System for Operations to a Management Information System, 73
Data Bank Management, 74
Types of Computer-Based Applications, 78
Summary Conclusion, 80
Text Discussion Questions, 80
Case Study Exercises, 82
    Hollis Corporation, 83
    Ajax Manufacturing Company, 87

Chapter 4   Financial Information Systems   92
                   for Corporate Management

Managing Company Assets, Income, and Expenses, 93
Questions to be Answered, Decisions to be Made and Information to be Provided, 94
Supporting Information Systems: An Overview, 95
An Expanding Concept of Financial Information Systems for Management, 115
Text Discussion Questions, 119

Chapter 5   Developing Accounting and Financial   120
                   Information Systems

Income and Asset Reporting: The Overman Laundry, 120
Corporate Financial Budgetary Systems: Video Productions Company, 126
Cost Accounting Systems: Bajar Industries, 129
Responsibility Accounting Systems: Barker Company, 132
Profitability Accounting and Analysis Systems, 137
Summary Conclusion, 139
Case Study Exercises, 139
    Consumer Gas Company, 139
    Manley Company, 142
    Gilray Corporation, 145
    New England Spring Company, 147
    FAD Limited, 151

Chapter 6   Marketing Management Information Systems   156

Marketing Management, 156
Supporting Information Systems, 159
Information Systems Used in Overall Marketing Planning, 160
Sales Forecasting, 162
Profitability Analysis for Marketing, 165

Information Systems for Operational Planning, Control and
Administration, 173
Summary Conclusion, 196
Text Discussion Questions, 197

Chapter 7   Developing Marketing Management   200
                     Information Systems

Overall Marketing Planning: Enright Company, 200
Sales Forecasting: A Telephone Company and a Consumer Products
Company, 210
Profitability Analysis for Marketing: Gizmo Novelty Company, 214
Sales Management: Correspondence Schools Unlimited, 218
Advertising: Bedrock Products Company, 222
Customer Service: H. R. Watson Company, 226
Summary Conclusion, 231
Case Study Exercises, 232
        Photom Corporation, 232
        The Austin Company, 236
        The Francine Candy Company, 240
        National Petroleum Company, 242
        Wolman Carpet Company, 254
        Chase Department Store, 258

Chapter 8   Information Systems for   262
                     Operations Management

Operations Management, 262
Supporting Information Systems, 266
Production Planning and Control, 266
Inventory Management, 274
Materials Management, 278
Quality Control Management, 286
Maintenance Management, 295
Facilities Management, 302
Text Discussion Questions, 305

Chapter 9   Developing Systems for   308
                     Operations Management

Production Planning and Control: Hughes Aircraft Company, 308
Inventory Management: The Handpower Company, 314
Materials Management: Bantom Pharmaceuticals Company, 318
Quality Control: General Dynamics Corporation, 323
Maintenance Management: Port Authority of New York, 327

Facilities Management: Condor Foods Corporation, 335
Summary Conclusion, 338
Case Study Exercises, 339
    Supreme Gear Manufacturing Company, 339
    Meany Motors, Inc., 343
    Mickle Aircraft Company, 344
    Barton Company, 349
    American Manufacturing Company, 352

Chapter 10   Information Systems for Project Management   356

Project Management, 356
Questions to be Answered, Decisions to be Made, and Information
Needed, 358
Project Management Information Systems, 360
Developing Specific Systems, 370
Summary Conclusion, 378
Text Discussion Questions, 378
Case Study Exercises, 379
    Beelow Merchandising Company, 379
    Robernal Company, 380
    Kerner Company, 380

Chapter 11   Simulating Management Decisions   382

Operational Planning under Conditions of Certainty: The Richman
Company, 384
Operational Planning under Conditions of Risk or Uncertainty: The
Power Company, 391
Summary Conclusion, 398
Text Discussion Questions, 399
Case Study Exercises, 400
    Cardone Brothers Company, 400
    All-Purpose Tire Store Simulation, 401
    Korman Toy Company, 408

Chapter 12   Advanced Management Information Systems   410

Advanced Management Decision-Supporting Systems, 410
Larger-Scale, More Fully Integrated Management Information Systems,
435
Total Information Systems?, 447
Summary Conclusion, 448
Text Discussion Questions, 449

Case Study Exercise, 450
    The Sun Oil Company (A), 450
    The Sun Oil Company (B), 457

Chapter 13   Organizing and Implementing   462
                        the Development Effort

Organization of the Data Processing and Information Systems Development Functions, 462
The Impact of Systems Development and Implementation on Company Organizations, 470
Human Factors, 473
Planning and Developing an Information System: Guidelines for Overcoming Some Typical Problems, 475
A Summary Overview: The Systems Approach at Work, 484
Text Discussion Questions, 487
Case Study Exercises, 488
    Domby Publishing Company, 488
    The City of Dalton, 488
    Avco-Everett Research Laboratory (A), 496
    Avco-Everett Research Laboratory (B), 500
    Midwest Apparel, Inc., 507

Index   513

OTHER BOOKS BY ROBERT J. MOCKLER

The Business Management Process: A Situational Approach

Business Planning and Policy Formulation

Circulation Planning and Development for the National Observer: A Research Study on Business Applications of Management Planning and Control Principles

Guidelines for More Effective Planning and Management of Franchise Systems (with Harrison Easop)

The Management Control Process

Management Decision Making and Action in Behavioral Situations

Management Decision Making in Today's Social Environment

New Profit Opportunities in Business Publishing (editor and contributing author)

Putting Computers to Work More Effectively in Business Publishing (editor and contributing author)

Readings in Business Planning and Policy Formulation (editor and contributing author)

Readings in Management Control (editor and contributing author)

Information Systems for Management

Information Systems for Management

MANAGERS NEED INFORMATION TO GET THEIR JOBS DONE. THIS INFOR-
mation might be on product costs, production schedules, salesmen's
activities, inventory levels, probable demand, personnel turnover, the
projected profitability of alternative courses of action, or any other area
which may affect planning, control, or operational decision making in the
management situation under study.

A manager gets his information in a variety of ways and forms. Much of it
will come piecemeal, from daily conversations and correspondence with
subordinates and superiors, through chance meetings with associates, in
special study reports, in memos and reports on current or planned operations,
from professional publications, through negotiations with suppliers, and from
other similar business data sources.

While such random, piecemeal information sources are useful, they cannot
meet the full range of a manager's information requirements. Managers also
need some systematic way of obtaining the information needed to make key
decisions. Management information systems are the means of systematically
structuring the flow of business data to managers.

2

1

A Key Concept:
Meeting Manager Information Requirements

Since management information systems are designed to help a manager get his job done, developing these systems begins with defining this job and its information requirements. This definition covers the kind of operation managed, a manager's major responsibilities, critical decisions he must make, and information needed to carry out those responsibilities and make such decisions.

In many cases, managers have difficulty defining information requirements. In one systems development situation, for example, the managers in the marketing area were asked to prepare a two-page summary of key decisions they made to get their jobs done, questions raised in making these decisions, and information needed to answer the questions. They were also asked to draw up a two-page description (or, if they preferred, a flowchart) of how their business operations worked and critical events in the business flow.

All of the managers exhibited difficulty in describing comprehensively, yet concisely, the operation they managed and the way they managed (although they knew their jobs intimately, almost instinctively). Some of them openly resented making this analysis. And curiously, very often the better the manager in the group, the less likely he was to be able to give a succinct outline of the essential decision points and decision processes in the business operation he managed.

Without exception, the lists of critical decisions made to manage their operations were incomplete. It was only after these managers had spent some time back at their jobs (during which time they were asked to check, refine, and develop their summaries) that anything like an adequate summary of critical decisions and the information needed to make these decisions was developed.

Defining management information requirements is more difficult in situations where a manager is taking on new job responsibilities. One manufacturing manager, for example, had spent most of his time in the past handling the very complex scheduling required in his department. When a systems group, as the first stage of their study, developed a computerized mathematical technique for doing the scheduling, the manufacturing manager was faced with the task of defining all the jobs he would now have time to do. Since he had devoted very little time and attention in the past to these jobs (such as equipment upgrading and replacement, employee development, community relations, improved quality control, and the like), months of study and experience were necessary before he could define with any precision the new decision activities required in his job.

Systems analysts who are assigned the job of developing information systems for operating managers encounter even greater difficulties, since they do not actually work at the management job. In defining management information requirements, a systems analyst must depend, in large part, on what the operating managers tell him, or what his own study of the managers' jobs reveals, and, at times, on what he himself uncovers in imaginatively recreating the work situation and management activities.

As is evident from the above discussion, a sound basis for developing management information systems cannot always be established by just asking a manager what information he requires. It is more likely that management decision activities, as well as the operation itself, may have to be studied and restudied in depth before an adequate definition of management information requirements can be developed.

Translating Information Requirements into Information Systems

While managers need not be systems technicians, they need to know enough about systems technology to state their information requirements in terms compatible with available data systems. They must also set their requirements within equipment, manpower, and cost limitations of the data processing system to be used.

The data processing and information system design areas of most concern to a manager are: the nature and availability of the basic data needed, the kind and size of data storage, the form and content of the information reports, the timing of information flows, and the processing costs and capabilities of available data systems.

During the design of a marketing management information system at one company, for example, the marketing manager was asked to help design the customer identification number to be carried in the computerized customer account file. His task was to specify what data should be contained in a twelve-digit customer identification number, in light of the information reports he wanted.

Since the file was also used by the controller for accounting reports and for customer billing and payment processing, the first five digits were assigned to zip codes, which were used for city and state identification. The zip code was useful to the marketing manager, since it could tell him not only where the customer was located, but also which salesman (where the account was not sold by mail) and which warehouse serviced the customer (there was no more than one salesman and warehouse assigned to each city). The sixth digit was assigned to type of customer (industrial firm, institution, individuals segregated into alphabetical groups, and so on). The seventh digit would indicate the type of products normally bought by the customer (the company sold three product lines). The eighth digit would tell the type of media through which the customer was sold (direct sales, mail-order advertising, wholesaler, and so on). The ninth digit would show the customer's credit rating. The tenth through twelfth digits would be a unique customer number (there were less than one thousand customers in each customer category in each zip code area).

The final identification number of one customer thus might be 10028-2641-125, which would give the following information:

10028	New York City, upper east side of Manhattan
2	Educational institution
6	Customer normally purchased product lines B and C
4	Direct sales account (A salesman called on the account)
1	Top credit rating
125	Customer number

Initially, the company controller in this situation had wanted to use the first six digits for state and city (using an IBM standard geographical location numbering system) and the seventh through twelfth for a unique customer identifying number. Only after carefully reviewing the decisions the marketing manager made, the new marketing information reports the manager requested, and the analysis of potential use of the customer account file to produce these reports, did the analyst develop alternative numbering patterns and create the new identifying number described above.

The new number enabled a wider range of customer analysis reports and greater use of the data now carried for marketing information reports in the customer account file (on purchases, payments, delinquencies, and the like). It would now be possible, for example, to analyze customer activity by area and type of customer, determine the purchasing preferences of different groups of customers, plan sales efforts more effectively, control distribution and salesman performance more efficiently, measure the effectiveness of different advertising media, and the like.

The marketing manager in this situation worked with the systems analyst in translating information requirements into a detailed definition of one segment of the data bank (the customer identification number in the customer account file), within the restraints of the data processing system (twelve digits) and other demands placed on the system (the controller's reports and customer account maintenance and processing).

In many systems development situations, a manager may find it necessary to reevaluate his information requirements because of the costs involved in proposed information processing systems. In one situation studied, for example, a personnel manager initially listed several kinds of information "it would be nice to have." One of the reports he wanted, a list of the foreign-language qualifications of all personnel in the company, was found to be needed only fifteen or twenty times a year, at those times when the personnel manager was searching for people to fill specific job openings in the company. Rather than going to the cost of gathering, entering, and carrying language-proficiency data in the computer system, the manager found that it would be cheaper (and just as effective) to insert a small notice of the job's availability in employee pay envelopes each time such a job opening occurred.

Effectively translating information requirements into actual information systems is, therefore, not always a simple and straightforward job. At times, modification of existing data systems and extensive programming may be needed to meet manager information requirements. At other times, technical restraints and data processing costs will set limits on and lead to adjustments in the information requirements, and in the reporting format and timing. At all times, plain common sense and ingenuity are needed to meet manager information requirements with the most economical and effective data processing system possible.

Information Systems
Needed by Managers

Management information systems can be classified by the management jobs they support. The management jobs (and related information systems) discussed here range from those of the president and board of directors to those of the major operating managers within a company. The discussion is limited to those management job areas discussed in Parts Two and Three of this book.

Corporate Management: Financial Information Systems

A company's president and board of directors are responsible for managing the capital invested in their company. Financial information systems are, therefore, among the most important (and most familiar) kinds of information systems within a company. These systems provide corporate managers with historical information on earnings (income statements) and on assets and liabilities (balance sheets)—information which is also required by the company's investors—as well as information on costs (cost and responsibility accounting). Through the budgetary process, they also provide information for planning and control of profits, costs and assets (including cash). Because of the investor orientation of these systems, return-on-investment (ROI) is used as a planning and control standard throughout financial information systems.

Such systems are also used by operating managers for planning and control. However, as is seen in later discussion in this book, financial information systems are limited in their capacity to meet all operating managers' information requirements.

Marketing Management Information Systems

Marketing involves selling and distributing a company's products. In managing the sales and distribution activities, a marketing manager develops an overall strategy by determining the marketing mix (product, price, place, and promotion), analyzes profitability, develops sales forecasts and operating plans for reaching these forecasts, and monitors marketing activities to insure that results match plans. Marketing managers use a variety of information systems and data sources in carrying out these job responsibilities.

Information systems used in developing overall strategy are less structured than those used in managing day-to-day activities. Economic and market studies, market research studies and market test reports, reports on technological developments, professional journals, suppliers, customers, and other general market data sources can all be used as information sources in planning marketing strategy. And each manager will have his own "system" for tapping these sources to generate strategic planning information, however loosely structured that "system" may be.

Profitability analysis information is also needed by marketing management, in order to evaluate alternative strategies, as well as alternative operating plans, in the light of their projected profitability. In developing these analyses, data is drawn largely from financial records and reporting systems.

Sales forecasts are developed from several data sources, including strategic market information, estimates made by the sales force, and data on past sales results and future plans. Sales forecast information is in turn used in developing specific plans and budgets for such key marketing areas as field selling, product management, advertising, sales promotion, distribution, and customer service. Other information sources used in this detailed planning include external market information (competition, customer, and the like) and internal data on company resources (available money, products, etc.), past marketing results, and corporate objectives and policies.

These detailed plans and budgets are then used as control standards in result reporting systems in marketing, where these systems contain reports comparing actual with planned performance in key marketing areas. Financial budget and result reports and other financial reports (such as profitability analyses) within a marketing information system are used to integrate these systems with overall corporate financial information systems.

Operations Management Information Systems

Operations management involves managing the operations required to produce the products or services which a company markets. In companies which manufacture products, operations management is often called production management. Operations management is, however, a broader concept than production management, since it encompasses management of service-type (such as air transport), as well as production-related, operations.

Planning for operations requires scheduling production or services. Information used in scheduling is drawn from a wide variety of company records and includes data on the available resources—such as plant capabilities, machines, warehousing, and manpower—as well as sales forecast and inventory status information.

Production scheduling information is used in developing detailed operations plans and budgets. These detailed plans and budgets cover such areas as facilities, manpower, equipment, materials purchase, delivery and storage, maintenance, quality control, product and process engineering, costs, and finished product storage and delivery. Operating and financial records and reports are basic data sources used in developing these detailed plans.

In order to provide coordinated control of operations, this planning, budgetary, and scheduling information system is integrated with result reporting systems, just as in marketing. The budget and result reports on costs of operations provide an essential link (usually through the cost accounting and responsibility accounting systems) between operations management and corporate management information systems.

Information Systems for Project Management

Many management situations involve projects, rather than continuing operations. Projects, such as building a new factory or introducing a new product, are specific tasks that are in some ways unique and non-repetitive. A project then is a one-shot affair.

Because of the special characteristics of project situations, the systems developed to provide information for managing projects differ from those described above. Project management information systems are created for a specific project; they contain budgets, records, and reports on a single project's activities, and the costs incurred by these activities. Treating a project as a separate entity enables managers to plan and monitor that project's progress and costs.

In addition to familiar scheduling techniques, such as schedule boards, network techniques are also used in project management. Two of these, PERT (Program Evaluation and Review Technique) and CPM (Critical Path Method), are described in detail in Part Two.

Advanced Management Information Systems

Decision making in many management situations can be improved through using mathematical and statistical analysis information. The techniques used in developing this quantitative analysis information are generally classified as "operations research" techniques.

The decision situations in which these information techniques are used have several distinct characteristics. They all involve planning decisions, both strategic and operational. In some of these situations, the key factors are known or certain: for example, inventory storage and production set-up costs, as well as sales demand or use patterns, can be determined in many inventory management situations. In some situations, there are risk (or uncertain) elements, such as a range of possible sales, a 50-50 chance (or some other ratio) of achieving a specified sales goal and the like. In other situations, key elements are completely unknown (or uncertain): a manager, for example, may not be able to determine expected customer arrival rates and service times at a new service facility with any degree of certainty.

There are, of course, degrees of uncertainty in many business situations, and in practice a manager will attempt to reduce uncertainty as much as possible through sampling, observation, and testing. As a result, very many decision situations can be categorized as situations of varying risk or uncertainty. Another type of management decision situation in which operations research techniques are useful involves competitive elements: for example, questions about where to advertise may involve estimating where competitors will and will not concentrate their advertising.

The information systems or techniques used in these situations are referred to as management decision-supporting systems. These systems make use of complex simulation models (which can assist managers in evaluating alternative courses of action), as well as analytical mathematical formulas (such as economic order quantity formulas which give the best or optimum answer).

Another kind of advanced management information system is the larger-scale, computer-based data processing system which serves the data and information needs of a wide range of managers and departments within a company. These systems make use of a large, central data bank (or data base), as well as advanced computer technology, such as random-access retrieval, on-line direct-access transmission, graphic output displays, etc.

Part Three discusses both advanced decision-supporting systems and larger-scale, computer-based data processing systems used in management decision making.

Management Information Systems and Operational or Application Systems

Data processing systems which perform operating tasks can be distinguished from those which provide managers with information used in managing operations. A data processing system, for example, which maintains inventory records on a current basis and initiates purchase orders, complete with supplier designation and price, is often called an "operational" or "application" system. By this is meant the system "performs" an operation in the manufacturing area (one that might have formerly been performed by several clerks).

Such systems are often an integral part of management information systems. For example, the inventory and purchase-order operating system mentioned in the preceding paragraph might also provide management with information on turnover or supplier efficiency, which is information used in management decision-making in these areas.

Although application systems are frequently a component of a management information system, it is misleading to call a typical application system a management information system—though in practice this is often done. An application system is an independent self-contained entity. It is a closed network of operations designed to carry out a specific function—for example, issue employee paychecks. These operations have definite decision rules, such as percent of payroll deductions for taxes. The data is fed into the system, processed by a well-defined set of operations (very often computer programs) and emerges as some type of output, such as employee checks.

A management information system often contains a network of one or more operational or application systems which (in addition to performing a specific operation) also generate management decision-making information. For example, through creating a twelve-digit customer identification number in the situation described earlier, the systems analyst was able to develop from an application system (customer account maintenance and billing) an information system which could generate reports useful in accounting and marketing management. In this situation, while the conceptual difference between an application system (a clerical function) and a management information system (marketing and accounting reporting) was clear, the two were both parts of a single data processing system.

Using an application or operational system to generate management information can create problems. At times, providing management information reports using an application system can decrease operating efficiency: for example, where getting an operation done must be delayed in order to produce a management information report. At other times, restrictions may be imposed on the processing and output of management information systems: for example, where all available file storage space is used for data needed for operations. The economics of automated data processing nevertheless very often dictate such an integrated approach, so that a systems developer needs to become adept at working imaginatively within the restraints of operating systems and balancing operating and management information requirements when developing management information systems.

Systems Theory

Many of the concepts underlying management information systems are found in systems theory. While an understanding of systems theory is not a prerequisite for learning how to develop information systems for management, it does provide useful insights into the subject.

What is a System?

A system may be defined as an orderly grouping of separate, but interdependent components for the purpose of attaining some predetermined objective.[1] A number of authorities working in diverse fields of specialization, such as Ludwig Von Bertalanffy, Kenneth Boulding, Norbert Wiener and Herbert Simon, have contributed to the development of systems theory.

A biologist, Von Bertalanffy, is considered the originator of general systems theory.[2] Disturbed by the increasing fragmentation and specialization of knowledge in this century, he attempted to find a unifying framework for the separate scientific disciplines. His work led to the development of a general theory of systems, which he felt provided an integrating approach to the study and development of a wide range of scientific disciplines: "The notion of a system being defined as 'any arrangement or combination, as parts or elements, in a whole' applies to a cell, a human being, a society, as well as to an atom, a planet or a galaxy."[3]

Kenneth Boulding carried the general systems theory a step further by defining nine levels of systems, starting with the most static (the anatomy and geography of the universe) and ending with the most dynamic (transcendental systems).[4] He thus conceived of a hierarchical arrangement of separate systems, which are in turn components of a larger system.

Both Boulding and Von Bertalanffy recognized the dangers that result from the increasing fragmentation of science into more and more subgroups and the growing difficulty of communicating among the scientific disciplines. One of the main objectives of their work was to develop "a framework of

---

1. Many variations of this definition exist—e.g., Warren Brown, "Systems, Boundaries, and Information Flow," *Academy of Management Journal,* IX:4 (Dec. 1966), 318, defines a system as "a group or complex of parts (such as people, machines, etc.) interrelated in their actions towards some goal;" and Richard A. Johnson, Fremont E. Kast, and James E. Rosenzweig, *The Theory and Management of Systems,* 3rd edition; (New York: McGraw-Hill Book Company, 1973), p. 4, define a system as "an organized or complex whole; an assemblage or combination of things or parts forming a complex or unitary whole."

2. Johnson, Kast, and Rosenzweig (2nd edition, 1967), p. 6, n. 2, assert that Von Bertalanffy was the first to use this term. For further information on Von Bertalanffy's systems theory, see his *Problems of Life: An Evaluation of Modern Biological and Scientific Thought* (London: C. A. Watts and Company, Ltd., 1952), and his *General Systems Theory* (New York: George Brailler, Inc., 1968), as well as a series of papers by Von Bertalanffy, Carl G. Hempel, Robert E. Bass, and Hans Jonas, published as "General Systems Theory: A New Approach to Unity of Science," in *Human Biology,* XXIII:4 (Dec. 1951), 302-361.

3. Von Bertalanffy, "General Systems Theory," 303.

4. Kenneth E. Boulding, "General Systems Theory—The Skeleton of Science," *Management Science,* II:3 (April 1956), 197-208.

general theory to enable one specialist to catch relevant communications from others."[5]

Since systems theory focuses on the dynamic interrelationships and interaction of entities, information and communication theory are important to the development of systems theory. In his study of information theory and communication, Norbert Wiener drew many parallels between the communication process in living beings and the newer communication machines, such as computers. Both have special apparatuses for collecting information from the outside world, storing it, and using it as a basis for action. Through this mechanism, both human beings and information processing machines have the capacity to compare actual performance to expected performance and to correct any deviations by "the sending of messages which effectively change the behavior of the recipient."[6] Thus, Wiener saw communication and information theory as a basis for understanding and explaining the planning, control, and decision-making processes.[7]

Herbert Simon, in his study of business management, extended the scope of Wiener's information and communication theory and Von Bertalanffy's general systems theory by applying them to business operations, where they could be viewed as vehicles for effectively achieving corporate objectives. Simon saw the business organization within which a manager works as a decision-making information system, and he considered "decision making" and "management" as synonymous.[8]

From a systems theory viewpoint, therefore, a business organization can be viewed on one level as an integrated decision-making system designed to achieve some specific objective, such as producing automobiles or paper products. On another level, this internal business system can be viewed as a component or subsystem of a larger system—the economic, social and competitive environment within which the business operates.

Components of a System

Every system (including management information systems) has common basic components. These include an *input* (that which is to be processed by the system), a *processor* (the component which manipulates input in some predetermined way to produce output) and *output* (what results from the

---

5. *Ibid.,* p. 199.

6. Norbert Wiener, *The Human Use of Human Beings: Cybernetics and Society* (Boston: Houghton Mifflin Company, 1950,), p. 8.

7. *Ibid.,* p. 15.

8. Herbert S. Simon, *The New Science of Management Decision* (New York: Harper and Row, Publishers, 1960), p. 1.

operation of the system). These are termed "systems parameters" and all systems can be described in these terms. Conceptually, therefore, the most rudimentary system can be depicted as follows:

$$INPUT -----\rightarrow \boxed{PROCESSOR} -------\rightarrow OUTPUT$$

An example of a simple system is found in post office operations:

The System: Letter and package handling at a Post Office

Input—all the letters and packages received.

Processor—the sorting, classifying and categorizing of items, for example, separating input into first class, second class or air mail and zip code number categories.

Output—the completely arranged mail sacks ready for shipment.

Unfortunately, most systems have far more complex parameters. Consequently, it is not always an easy matter to identify system parameters exactly, even though the basic components (input, processor, output) remain the same.

Refining System Parameters

In studying a system, it is possible to define it more precisely by specifying additional parameters. The process of doing this is termed *restricting* the system.

For example, the output of a management information reporting system may have many users. Each has different requirements. To be useful, the output must conform to each user's requirements, so that a restriction exists on the output of that system. For instance, one user may be the production scheduling manager and another the controller. The controller needs dollar cost information, while the production scheduling manager needs this dollar information translated into numbers of production units. As a result of these restrictions different kinds of reports must be generated by the reporting system.

These restrictions can be pictured as follows:

$$CONTROL \leftarrow ----- RESTRICTION$$
$$INPUT -----\rightarrow \boxed{PROCESSOR} ------\rightarrow OUTPUT$$

The control of a system may also be effected by the system's feedback. Feedback is that system element which compares output to a predetermined standard to determine if that output is in line with the standard. Control is achieved by taking corrective action on any discrepancy between the output and the standard. The diagram of the concept of a system given below shows the role of feedback as a system parameter.

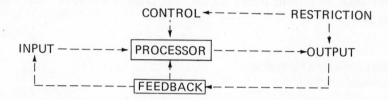

Optner uses the example of a contractor who is bidding on a government contract to illustrate the impact of restraints and feedback within a system:[9]

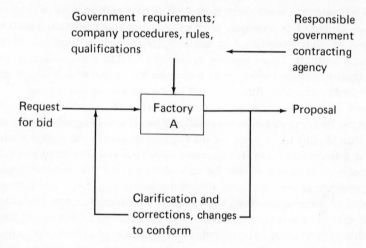

In the situation illustrated above, the government agency not only initiates the bid request, but also gives factory management (the control mechanism) the job and bid requirements (restrictions). These, along with company requirements (other restrictions), control the development of the proposal. The government agency also reviews the proposal and passes along corrections, clarifications, and changes (feedback), which are in turn used as new input.

As seen from this example, defining a system—even a simple one—can be a complex job, especially where larger project or business systems are involved. The purpose of this discussion is not, however, to explore the complexities of

9. Stanford Optner, *Systems Analysis* (Englewood Cliffs, New Jersey: Prentice-Hall International, Inc., 1960), p. 52. For further example see Optner, *Systems Analysis* (2nd edition, 1968), pp. 23-46.

systems theory in depth. Rather, the purpose has been merely to define the basic concept and components of a system, any kind of system, and so establish a basis for studying management information systems. For further information on systems theory see the book listed in footnotes 1 and 2 on page 12.

Conceptualizing a Management Information System

In order to conceptualize a management information system, a manager must visualize a business organization as being comprised of many operating subsystems or series of subsystems. Taken out of company context, each of these subsystems is a complete system of its own with an input, a processor, and an output. For example, production takes raw materials (input) and reworks it with manufacturing facilities (processor) to turn out finished products (output). Taken together as part of a total business enterprise, these independent systems become interrelated, for the output of one system (such as finished products) is often the input to another system (marketing).

Each of these business subsystems also generates an information output which can be construed as an information flow. If well-designed, this information flow should be of value to the decision makers in the organization. If several information flows (for example, sales forecasts, inventory levels, and in-process production) involve the same decision area (for example, production scheduling) and the same time dimensions, they can be considered a network of information flows and called an information system. It should be noted that the limits (or parameters) of an information system do not always coincide with those of an operating system: for example, production scheduling draws information from other operating areas, such as marketing.

If enough information systems exist to cover all areas of decision making, they can be integrated; that is, the output of one may become the input of another. This theoretical situation would yield a *totally integrated management information system,* as shown in Figure 1–1.

In actual business practice, integration of all management information systems in a company is normally neither desirable nor possible. First, management of business activities does not always require it; since many decisions within an operating area can be made without reference to information from other operating areas. Second, there are severe mechanical data collecting, storing, and processing restraints, which can cause the cost of such information systems integration to exceed potential benefits. Nevertheless, considerably more integration of information systems is possible and needed in many companies to enable more coordinated management of operations.

FIGURE 1-1

Concept of a Totally Integrated Management Information System

A business organization is a series of integrated sub-systems.

Each sub-system can be construed as a separate information flow to be used by the decision maker.

Grouping information flows that cover the same:

- Decision areas
- Time dimension
- Requirements for information in the decision process

We have various *networks of information flows* or various *information systems* *

If enough information systems exist to cover all areas of decision making, they may be integrated—i.e., the output of one can be used as the input of another. This situation would reflect *a totally integrated management information system*

Sub-system A ⟶ Information flow A
Sub-system B ⟶ Information flow B
Sub-system C ⟶ Information flow C
Sub-system D ⟶ Information flow D
Sub-system E ⟶ Information flow E
Sub-system F ⟶ Information flow F
Sub-system G ⟶ Information flow G

Network of information flows ① → Information system
Network of information flows ② → Information system
Network of information flows ③ → Information system

① ② ③ → Totally integrated management information system

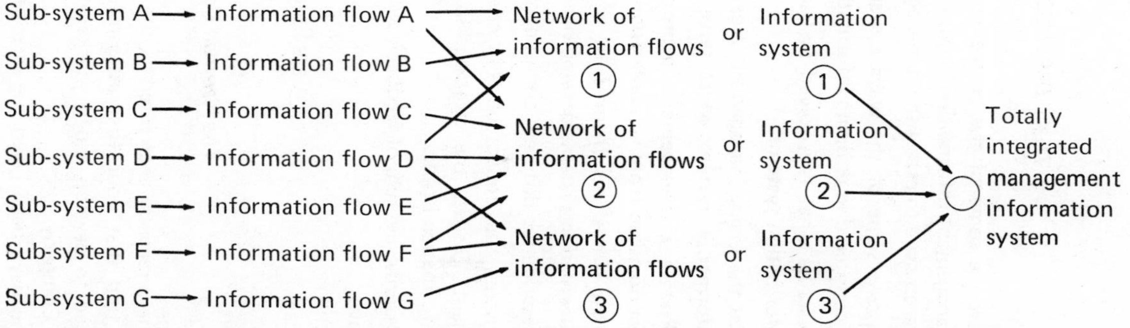

* Note that the organization of information flows does not necessarily conform to the organization of company operations.

17

While the study of systems theory provides a conceptual framework for understanding the basic aspects of management information systems, then the ultimate, ideal theoretical system (as shown in Figure 1–1) is rarely fully achievable in designing information systems for an entire business enterprise.

TEXT DISCUSSION QUESTIONS

1. Describe some of the problems which may be encountered in defining management information requirements. Why are such definitions a major prerequisite to establishing management information systems?
2. Discuss some of the ways a manager might overcome typical problems encountered in defining information requirements.
3. Describe what is involved in translating information requirements into information systems.
4. List the major management areas in a business and describe the kinds of information systems which serve their information needs.
5. What is a management information system? In what way can it be distinguished from an application system? Give specific examples.
6. What is systems theory? In what ways does it relate to management information systems development?
7. Describe the different components of a system and how they interact.
8. Discuss the impact of restrictions or parameters on systems development. Discuss the relationship between restrictions and management information needs.
9. Describe the role of feedback within a system.

Case Study Exercises

The Neuman Consulting Company

You have recently been hired by the Neuman Consulting Company. You have been told that your first assignment will be to work with the consultant assigned to develop a new marketing information system for the Alfa Dog Food Company.

You have been given the client company's annual report which contains the following basic information about the company. The company sells a wide line of canned and boxed dog foods through its own field sales force to wholesalers, large retailers, and institutions in eight midwestern states. The company uses all forms of media (TV, radio, billboards, newspapers, magazines, and point of sales displays) to promote its products. The company also sells a line of expensive dog foods by mail outside its regular eight state marketing area.

At this point, you are wondering how best to prepare for your first assignment which will begin in two days.

Assignment

1. Write out a description of the key activities which might be involved in the marketing operation of the Alfa Dog Food Company.
2. List the key decisions made by the marketing manager in this situation and the information reports which might be helpful in making these decisions.
3. Describe any industry information sources which you used or might use in preparing for this assignment.

The Little Publishing Company

The Little Publishing Company is a medium-size publisher and distributor of educational books.

The company sells three groups of products: basic "programmed" texts—that is, self-teaching books on such subjects as bookkeeping, English, data processing, statistics, operations research, and computer operations, which can be used by the reader working alone or with a classroom group; regular books (without a self-teaching apparatus) on general subjects—such as history, sociology, psychology, anthropology, English literature, and philosophy; and "how-to-do-it" books for the industrial training market—such as foreman training.

The customers for the Little Company's books include educational institutions, public libraries, government agencies, industrial companies, and individuals. Sales are made through company salesmen direct to institutional customers and book wholesalers and through direct mail and newspaper advertising to individual customers.

The company currently has many computerized systems, including one which maintains customer accounts and issues customer bills. Based on conversations with the controller (who manages customer accounts) and the marketing manager, the systems analyst has determined that the information in the customer account file could be used for sales analyses useful to marketing management, through the use of a customer identification number.

It is possible to have a nine-digit customer code on the customer magnetic tape file, within present file-storage limitations. The controller has agreed that any unique number for each customer would satisfy his processing requirements.

The marketing manager during one interview indicated he would like information about what kinds of products each group of customers bought to better direct his advertising and sales efforts. Information on customers located in each area, as well as their credit rating and volume and frequency of purchases (especially institutional customers), would also be useful in assigning salesmen and evaluating their performance. The analyst felt that there were probably even more marketing decision areas which would benefit from the new information system.

The analyst determined that there were less than 9,999 total customers in any given city. He also determined that there were more than one thousand individual customers in many zip code areas and that no zip code area had more than one salesman assigned to it. The customer account file presently carried customer addresses and a record of customer purchases and payments for the past twelve months.

The analyst then began the task of assigning the nine digits in the identification number. He first considered assigning digits one to five in the nine-digit code to a zip code, but then checked and found that all customer addresses in the file carried a zip code in each file. At this point, he was wondering how most effectively and economically to assign the nine digits.

Assignment

1. Define the marketing activity or operation at Little Publishing Company and the job responsibilities of marketing management.

2. List the major decisions the marketing manager might need to make and the kinds of sales analysis information (or information reports) which might be useful in making those decisions.

3. Determine which of these reports can be prepared using the customer account file, if it had the appropriate customer identification number. Explain in detail how the new customer identification number enables use of the existing customer file for marketing management information purposes.

4. Design a nine-digit customer identification number (see text of Chapter One for an example of how this might be done).

5. Specify the additional data which might be added to the customer account file to meet marketing reporting requirements.

6. In what ways is the file now probably used for management reports in the controller's area? Will this capability be affected by the addition of the customer code?

An Approach to Developing Information Systems

FOR ANALYTICAL DISCUSSION PURPOSES, THE APPROACH TO DEVELOP-
ing information systems for management can be divided into three
activity areas:

1. Diagnosing situation requirements, developing the concept (or structure) of the information systems needed, and analyzing existing information and data systems.
2. Developing the information system.
3. Introducing the system.

This chapter gives a brief summary of these activities, as well as some of
the problems which may be encountered in systematically developing information systems for management.

Because of the wide range of possible management situations, more activities are covered in this discussion than a manager would normally need to go
through in dealing with each systems development situation he encounters. In
addition, although the different activities are discussed in a sequential manner, a manager would not necessarily follow such a step-by-step procedural
approach in practice. Rather, a manager may perform several activities at
once, move back and forth among different phases as he works through the

2

situation problems, and in general proceed in the way that best suits his individual working and thinking patterns.

Situation Diagnosis and Concept Design

Several phases of diagnosis and design in systems development situations can be isolated for discussion purposes:

Defining the purpose, scope, and organization of the systems development effort.

Defining the nature of the company's business.

Analyzing the work situation, in order to isolate critical business flows and management job responsibilities.

Defining the key management decisions to be made and the information required to make these decisions.

Analyzing existing information and data systems.

Identifying additional business and human factors which might affect the development, implementation, and use of the system.

Defining the Purpose, Scope, and Organization of the Development Effort

Since systems design is affected by the kind of management job under study, it helps at the beginning to specify or identify the nature of the management situation under study. Management information situations can range from "corporate planning and control" to "advertising planning" or "production scheduling" to any one of thousands of situations encountered by managers. Part Two of this book is organized by management situations.

In addition to identifying the kind of management situation he has encountered, a manager will also be asking himself "What's my job in this particular situation?" For example, in a given situation, the job of an advertising manager might be to assist the systems analyst in defining information requirements and to review and approve the information systems proposal prepared by the analyst; the job of the systems analyst, on the other hand, would be to work with the advertising manager in defining information requirements, design the information system, and supervise the work of programmers. In another situation, an advertising manager in a small company might develop an information system on his own, with a clerk in his department keeping records and producing information reports for him.

A manager's job in a systems development situation is not always clearly defined at the outset of the study. For example, in one situation described later in this book, as the systems study progressed the marketing manager became the informal coordinator of the systems development effort simply because there was a leadership vacuum to be filled. In all systems development projects, each manager has at least the responsibility of defining his information requirements and outlining the general structure of his information requirements.

The formal organization of the systems development function varies widely among business concerns. Sometimes there is a systems development department under the controller, and sometimes it is under a separate systems manager. In other situations, the systems job is divided among several departments. In all cases, operating or staff managers will participate in (if not actually develop) the design of information systems for their area. The subject of organizing the information systems development function is discussed in the concluding chapters of this book.

The Nature of a Company's Business

As an experienced systems developer once put it, "One of the first things to find out is how a company makes a buck": that is, the kind of business a company is in and the key factors which affect profitability.

The kind of business a company is in will affect the systems development effort in many obvious ways. For example, the information systems developed for a consumer finance company will differ greatly from those developed for a fast-food franchising company; because the planning, control and operating jobs are different in each type of company. For this reason, it is necessary to define a company's basic business early in the systems study— even where only departmental information systems are involved. The two study exercises at the end of Chapter One provide concise definitions of relevant overall company factors in those situations.

Surprisingly, the nature of a company's business is not always readily apparent. For example, only after a consultant's review did one manufacturing company which sold its products at a very low markup come to realize that in fact it was a finance company, since almost all its profits came from interest charges rather than product sales.

This phase of definition would also cover the corporate financial, organizational, and management restraints which would affect any systems development work. These restraints set limits not only on the size and scope of the systems which can be developed, but also on the amount of management time which can be devoted to systems development.

The Work Situation: The Operation Managed and Management Job Responsibilities

As was noted at the outset of Chapter One, a manager defines the operation being managed as part of the background study for systems development; since it provides a framework for defining the job of managing the operation.

In a corporate systems study, for example, this phase would include a study of the organization and flow of the entire business operation. For instance, at a large electronics company, after preliminary studies of company plans identified the nature of the company, its markets, and its objective; the flow of business was charted (covering major manufacturing, service, and marketing activities required by the business) and a description developed of the jobs of major management responsibility centers within the business flow.

In another situation discussed later in this book, a production control situation, a flowchart was drawn up of the production process, and of processes which served and were served by the production area. The job responsibilities of key production managers were then described.

In the dog food company study at the end of Chapter One, on the other hand, the consultant merely wrote out a brief description of how the company marketed its products (products marketed, channels of distribution, advertising media used to support different sales activities, different sales methods used in reaching different kinds of customers, etc.) and described the key manager job responsibilities (for example, overall strategic planning and operational planning and control in such key marketing areas as field sales, distribution, advertising, pricing, product development, and the like). Only later in the study, when meeting with company managers, did he draw up more detailed descriptions and flow charts.

The point of this phase is to become familiar enough with the operation being managed not only to be able to identify those aspects which are critical to success and are, thus, key management responsibility areas, but also to be able to describe what the key management responsibilities are.

Management Decisions and Information Required to Make these Decisions

Concurrent with identifying critical aspects of the operation, a systems developer also identifies critical decisions made in carrying out management job responsibilities, as well as the information required to make these decisions and carry out these responsibilities. In a sense, this phase merely extends the general definition of job responsibilities, defining the management job in more detail and specifying the manager's information requirements.

For example, in a mail-order advertising operation, a manager who is responsible for marketing company products makes decisions on which media to use (direct mail, newspapers, radio, etc.), the amount spent in each media, which products to advertise in different media, location of ads, advertising themes to use, and the like. To make these decisions, the manager needs not only strategic planning information on potential customers, markets, and products. He also needs information on the efficiency (how many sales were made per advertising dollar spent) by media, ad or ad group, product and market area. Such information is obtained from past results or market tests.

This phase of the study is a critical one, and one which, as noted at the outset of Chapter One, is a difficult one for managers to do well. There seems to be a natural reluctance to analyze one's job. Yet, no matter how painful an exercise, each decision and its information requirements must be identified— even to the point of formally writing up a list for review—if management information requirements are to be met.

In more complex situations, where more than one level of management is involved, the analysis of key decisions would be made for each level of management. In addition, the systems developer would identify that information useful to more than one level of management, and whether it might be needed concurrently or in the same or a different format. For example, both a general sales manager and a district sales manager might need information on sales; but the district sales manager might need it reported by salesman weekly, whereas the general sales manager might need it reported by district on a monthly basis.

Not only must *all* key decisions and their information requirements be identified, but care should be taken to eliminate non-essential decision requirements. Each proposed information requirement should be reexamined in light of the decisions for which it is needed. For example, "Can we live with the product breakdown quarterly instead of monthly?" "Do we need cost per order information detail in all reports?" "Do we really need daily order counts on each test ad; if so, for how long?" "Who will supply media cost information; and when: at the time of committing for the ad or at the time it is run?"

Such detailed questioning is time-consuming and nerve-fraying at times. And it cannot be done well without the participation of the operating managers who will be using the system. But it is necessary, if an economical, as well as an effective information system is to be developed.

Structuring Information Requirements: The Concept or General Outline of an Information System

As management information requirements are defined in more and more detail, the concept of the information system begins to emerge—as the decision-making activities (and their information requirements) are systematically organized, grouped, and integrated.

This phase generally covers such information areas as: data files; data sources; information report content, format, and timing; and the means of getting and storing data and reporting information. In addition, during this phase, the system developer would also determine, in general terms, the kind of processing system which would best meet management information reporting requirements: manual, punched-card, and computer, or one of the many variations possible for each basic type (Chapter Three gives a detailed explanation of the characteristics and capabilities of each basic type).

The information definition or structure, then, would cover the following aspects of each of the key systems areas:

1. Input
   Sources
   Forms
2. Processing
   General kinds and capabilities of processing system to be used
3. Files
   Data to be stored
   Structure of the file
   Form of storage

4. Program Instructions

How information is to be gathered from sources or drawn from files, how it is manipulated, and how it is reported to managers

5. Output

Content
Form
Timing
To whom reports sent

By defining his information requirements in such a format, a manager is "transforming" his information requirements into a system structure:

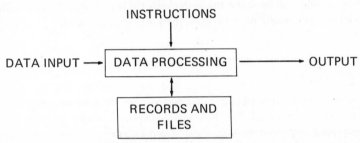

It is a job managers can and should do, but often do not. Such a recasting or restructuring of information requirements is an invaluable aid to a systems technician.

As the manager answers the questions raised, the concept of the information system begins to emerge. For example, during this phase in the mail-order marketing situation described above, the development group began to prepare formal lists of the information reports required and who would receive them, revised their contents and timing, as well as prepared rough layouts of the format of each report. In addition, work began on defining the sources of this information, the basic data files which would need to be kept, and the ways in which the marketing management information systems could be integrated with other management information systems, such as warehousing and materials management. Integration of the management information system with operational systems (such as order processing) also started during this period.

During this phase, very detailed specifications of information requirements may be drawn up. For example, in the I.M. Little Company study (Chapter One), a list might have been prepared of what additional data would need to be carried in the existing customer account file to meet newly-defined marketing reporting requirements.

1. Customer category (individual, library, educational institution, corporate, etc.) identification

2. Kind of product purchased

3. The media through which the sale was made (company salesman, direct mail, newspaper advertising, etc.)

4. Credit rating of customer

In addition to this new file data, the reporting system for marketing would require drawing from the existing file (that is, from the existing data processing system) such financial information as amount and frequency of purchase, name and address of customer, name of purchasing agent (if an institution), and current arrearages.

Before this phase is complete, as is seen in the Little Company example, a study would be made of the existing information and data systems. First, the systems developer needs to know the nature of existing data files, in order to determine if it would be more economical to modify them than to create new files. Second, he needs to know of existing reporting systems to see if existing reports or modifications of them will meet his needs—or whether his requirements can be modified in the light of reports presently available. Third, the system developer needs to know the processing equipment presently available, as well as what additional equipment can be purchased within the financial restraints of the situation.

Analyzing the Existing Information and Data Systems

Except in newly created business operations, there will be existing information and data systems. These systems are studied as part of the situation diagnosis, very often at the outset of the study.

Existing systems can be useful in many different ways depending on the kind of systems development situation under study. In situations where alternatives to an existing information system are being developed, an analysis of the existing system shows the decision now (or at one time in the past) considered critical to management, and the information now (or at one time in the past) used to make these decisions. Such studies also indicate available data banks, and reporting and equipment resources, which—as was seen in the Little Company study discussed earlier—might be drawn upon in the new system. In addition, these studies can give some indication of the extent of changes needed to convert to any new system and the amount of resistance to change which may be encountered.

At times, existing information systems can be roadblocks. They can hinder objective diagnosis of information needs, they can breed employee resistance to change (this will depend on the complexity and age of the existing system and the magnitude of the proposed change), and they can distort evaluation of alternative proposals.

It is possible to overcome many of these problems by a disciplined approach to the diagnosis. At the development meetings between systems analysts and operating managers, for instance, this means constantly reminding each other that the focus is on analyzing management information requirements as if there were no existing system. A typical statement made to operating managers to encourage objective analysis is: "Pretend you have no information system now and imagine all the information you would like to have." If a manager is developing his own information system, he might try doing his diagnosis in another location, away from his daily work environment.

Another useful device in some situations is to treat the existing system as one alternative solution, to be evaluated formally against newly proposed information systems. It is also helpful at times to formally consider (as an additional alternative) modification of the existing information system, where such an alternative is feasible, with one caution: a "let's fix up the old system" approach often limits exploring new and more innovative solutions and leads many managers to consciously or unconsciously favor a modication approach since it is easier.

Additional Factors

Somewhere during the diagnosis, the system developed should also identify the human factors affecting design, implementation, and use of the system. Hopefully, since operating and staff managers who will be using the system participate in this development, human factors at the user end will have been considered. But time does not always permit such involvement at all operating levels; so that special consideration of this human factors area is usually needed, if effective implementation and use of the system is to be achieved.

In larger systems development projects, attention would also be paid to any organizational changes which may be required, any personnel training and indoctrination needed, areas of possible resistance to change (individual and group), and ways in which any of these circumstances might affect the design of the system and its later implementation and use.

The impact of these factors on systems development is discussed throughout Part Two, as well as in the concluding chapters.

System
Development

The development of the new information system extends the work done during the situation diagnosis, when the concept of the information system was developed. The exact nature of this development work will depend on the situation.

At times, where the system under study is relatively simple or when the concept of the system has been developed in considerable detail, this phase may involve merely working out the specific details of the system chosen. At other times, usually where the system is more complex, alternatives will first be developed and evaluated before a decision is made and the final system design and programming undertaken.

For example, in the mail-order marketing study described earlier, a complete system description report was prepared by the systems development group (the group consisted of six operating managers and three. systems analysts, with the analysts assuming the actual job of report preparation). The report—called the "Initial Systems Presentation"—contained a summary description of the present system (a fragmented, computerized system) and three new systems as possible alternatives for handling active customer accounts and generating management reports. The summaries included considerable detail on the proposed systems, along with explanations of the advantages and disadvantages of each.

The three new processing systems proposed differed mainly in the timing of the computer processing (weekly or daily) and the structure of the master file (segmented between active and inactive customers, or arranged in a combined file). All three proposed systems had capabilities for processing new customer orders, checking credit, checking and maintaining inventory records, producing shipping and billing documents, billing customers over a twelve-month period, maintaining customer accounts; producing financial and sales results reports (in total, as well as by customer and by advertising campaign), handling special marketing test programs, and generating a wide range of other management information reports.

The *daily* computer processing of a *combined master file* was the most effective system since it provided the most up-to-date customer account data, but it was also the most costly. However, since the cost difference was small, the most expensive system was judged the best choice of the three proposed customer account systems. Initial projections had also shown that the new system's costs were only slightly higher than those of the existing system. A restudy showed, however, that actual new system costs would run thirty percent higher. In light of the cost difference, it was decided to retain the old system, since anticipated sales volume increases were not considered sufficient to justify the new system for five years, at which time new, more efficient and more economical computer systems would be available.

If a new system had been chosen, the next phase of system development would have involved final selection of equipment and equipment configurations, and the programming of that system. For example, in another situation similar to the one described above, preliminary discussions had been conducted with three equipment manufacturers and with two outside computer service bureaus as part of the evaluation of proposed information systems. In this situation, a decision was made to go ahead with a new system and so detailed bids were requested from the manufacturers and service bureaus.

The evaluation of the two outside service bureau proposals was done by a joint group of computer and systems technicians and operating managers. It was determined that the processing could be done most effectively and economically within the company, by the company's own computer section rather than by an outside computer processing service. At the same time, the equipment proposals were evaluated by systems technicians, and one was selected.

Next, programming was performed in phases. Operating managers were consulted on minor changes which arose during programming. Later, these managers actively participated in the "debugging" phase, when the programs were tested. In all, eighteen months elapsed from proposal to full implementation. Since it took six months to prepare the proposal, two years were needed for the entire project.

More detailed descriptions of the steps involved in developing computer-based information systems are given in Chapter Three.

Not all systems development situations involve computerized information systems and systems development departments, however. For example, a department manager or small company manager may be involved in developing manual systems for planning, control, and administration. The general pattern of diagnosis and evaluation is the same in these situations, as in those described above; but the use of the approach can vary considerably in detail.

Implementation of the System

Any newly developed information system or system change will have to be implemented.

In reality, implementation begins during the diagnosis and development phases. The participation of operating managers (systems users) in developing an information system is the first phase of their orientation and indoctrination into the use of the system. Their familiarity with the system will increase during the "debugging" phase.

User participation in the diagnosis and development phases, then, is a critical first step in implementing an information system. There are, however, limitations on this participation. For example, in the marketing management situations described earlier, only a small number of operating managers participated extensively in the studies, while the other lower-level managers had only limited exposure to the new systems. An effort was made to familiarize these lower-level managers with the new system through document review and consultation, but time and operating constraints prevented anything more than a cursory familiarization.

User training, then, is a key step in implementing management information systems, especially where new systems are complex and differ radically from old ones. The extent of training (as well as staffing changes) needed are determined through reviewing the existing system and studying its relationships with the new system. Plans for any needed organization change would also be developed and carried out during this phase of system development.

Behavioral science skills can be important in administering systems changes. Resistance will inevitably arise, and experience shows that most of this resistance will follow identifiable and predictable patterns. Behavioral science research has identified many of these patterns, and has evolved techniques for handling them. Putting these techniques to work takes foresight, time, and money, and must be planned for and included in systems development plans and costs.

While user acceptance is an important aspect of effective system implementation and use, it is a task which is often neglected. It is very tempting for a system developer to say "since the new system is clearly [to him anyway] the best, everyone will be enthusiastic about it." But, as one manager put it, "It just ain't so." What is best for a lower-echelon manager, in his view, may be to be left alone to finish the job and a half he already has to do, since he has seen "dozens of smart-aleck kids and their bright ideas come and go over the years." Where resistance may be strong or the advantage of new systems hard to perceive, gaining user acceptance may require developing and carrying out a major educational program.

Few management information systems are perfect and few business environments stable, so that refinements and adjustments will be required after a new system is introduced. First, there will be those changes during the early phases of system use which arise simply because some decision situations and work patterns were not anticipated. Second, there will be changes required by changes in business operations or the business environment. Systems development thus can be a continuing job in dynamic business situations. This is frequently a major factor in the establishment of permanent systems development departments.

Putting the Systems Approach to Work

The systems approach is not a rigid procedure. There is, in fact, no one "ideal" step-by-step procedure for developing a management information system—simply because there is such a great variety of systems situations and because individual business organizations and their managers differ in so many significant ways from each other.

For example, there is a natural tendency to start thinking about solutions first when faced with any kind of problem situation in business. One has only to observe a typical management meeting to come to this conclusion. Situation needs are often defined only as someone in the group begins to pull together and summarize the discussion.

In developing information systems, very often there is a similar pattern of analysis. Tentative "concepts" of information systems will begin to emerge early and continue to be developed and refined all the way through a system study. After all, it is easier for a manager to think about the kinds of reports he would like (since reports are concrete) than it is for him to define decision requirements (which are more abstract).

There is, as a result, much overlapping and back-and-forth movement among the different phases of the systems approach. While a manager is searching for the critical factors affecting a situation, for example, he is simultaneously developing alternative solutions built on these premises. Nor does he wait until all the alternatives have been developed before evaluating them, but usually begins evaluating them as they are developed.

This back-and-forth or circular movement continues in the subsequent phases. When a manager begins to evaluate alternatives in a more orderly way, for example, he frequently uncovers key factors which have an important bearing on the decision but were not identified in the earlier diagnosis. And, throughout the process, he will be constantly thinking of the practical roadblocks which may be encountered in implementing and using the system and the effect of these roadblocks on the development and evaluation of alternatives.

The simplified outline of the systems approach likewise gives no hint of the difficulties involved in developing systems alternatives. For example, while logic and experience are important in finding and creating solutions, they are frequently not enough. Experience helps develop judgment and provides a useful starting point in solving many problems; but, just as often, experience can be a wall blocking progress. Creative persons attempt to break through this wall and cut the inhibiting limitations imposed by experience. Creative persons also break patterns of logic by drawing on unusual associations and viewing factors in new ways. For these reasons, creative energies can be destructive, unless harnessed and directed towards constructive, profitable business solutions. Creative energies are needed, however, if a business is to change with its environment; so that while they should be controlled, they should not be suppressed by overreliance on a rational, systematic approach.

Not all situations lend themselves to the broad perspective of the systems approach. Practical considerations often dictate a piecemeal approach to systems development, simply because the time or money may be lacking to do a full-scale study of an operation's total information system. In such situations, a manager often has to work to solve more immediate problems and develop small-scale systems or parts of systems that work, in order to convince company managers larger systems are worthwhile. The systems approach will help in insuring that this piecemeal development will eventually lead to a more integrated, useful information system—instead of a fragmented patchwork system—providing it is adapted to the realities of the situation in question through skillfully reconciling *what ought to be done* with *what can be done.*

The systems approach is not designed to change human nature or restrict creativity, but to help bring some rationality to normal work patterns. While this approach provides general guidance in formally organizing a systems development effort, a manager must also recognize the difficulties in putting the systems approach to work and acquire the management experience and skills required to overcome these difficulties.

Once the general pattern of the systems approach is understood, therefore, the best way to learn it is by practice. For this reason, the treatment of the systems approach in this chapter has been brief and overly simplified. The discussion is designed to give only an overview, a general feeling for the pattern of the systems approach. The chapters which follow are intended to expand the reader's understanding of the approach and increase his skill in putting it to work.

Summary
Conclusion

This chapter has given a brief summary of a systematic approach to developing management information systems. The different activities discussed were grouped into the following categories:

1. Situations Diagnosis
   a. Defining the purpose, scope, and organization of the systems development effort.
   b. Defining the nature of the company's business.
   c. Analyzing the work situation, in order to isolate critical business flows and management job responsibilities.
   d. Defining the key management decisions to be made and the information required to support these decisions.

e. Formulating the concept (or information structure) of the system needed to meet management requirements.

f. Analyzing existing information and data systems.

g. Identifying additional business and human factors which might affect the implementation and use of the system.

2. Developing the information system.

3. Implementing the system.

Each activity was discussed in a separate section, though in practice the activities might be performed simultaneously or in a different order than that presented here. The concluding section described some of the problems encountered in putting the systems approach to work.

This chapter and Chapter One emphasize the diagnosis of management requirements for several reasons. First, managers often have problems diagnosing information requirements. Second, inadequate diagnosis is the greatest cause of lost time and money, and the source of a less than optimum information system. Third, students taking management information systems courses seem to encounter even greater difficulties with situation diagnosis, because of a lack of prior training and business experience. For these same reasons, the early case studies in this book also emphasize situation diagnosis, rather than technique development.

TEXT DISCUSSION QUESTIONS

1. Describe the different activities which may be involved in diagnosing a systems development situation.

2. Distinguish between analyzing a work situation and defining key management decisions. Give specific examples, showing both how they are distinct and how they are related.

3. Explain what is meant by "defining information required to support management decisions," and discuss how this activity relates to developing the "concept" of a management information system.

4. Give some specific examples of "concepts" of different kinds of information systems. Refer to the description of different kinds of information systems discussed in Chapter One.

5. In what ways can external business factors affect the development and implementation of information systems?

6. Describe the differences in the approach used in developing a computerized marketing management information system, a responsibility cost

accounting system, a mathematical decision-making model. In what ways will the basic approach be the same?

7. Discuss some of the roadblocks which might be encountered in implementing an information system.

8. Discuss what is meant by the statement "the systems approach is a flexible process, not a rigid procedure."

9. In what circumstances is it possible to justify a piecemeal approach to systems development in the light of realistic situation restraints?

10. In what ways is a careful diagnosis important in developing management information systems?

Case Study Exercises

Sunrise Motels

Sunrise Motels is a medium-size chain of high-quality motels located primarily in the eastern United States. There are at least two Sunrise motels in every major city east of the Mississippi River; well-traveled rural areas are also prime locations for Sunrise motels in the East. The chain's management is extremely proud of its ability to provide lodging of good quality at a reasonable price.

The Reservations Problem

Four years ago top management of Sunrise Motels met at the corporate headquarters in Baltimore, Maryland, to discuss ways to improve the company's reservation system. Under the reservation system in existence at that time, when a customer in one city (New York, for example) called the local Sunrise motel office for a reservation in a Sunrise motel in another city (Atlanta, for example), the clerk in New York would have to telephone the Atlanta motel office for information regarding availability, size, and price of rooms. If the New York customer (who was holding on the line all this time) was satisfied with the room available in Atlanta, a reservation was made over the telephone. Since this process sometimes took as long as seven or eight minutes by phone, it was expensive and led to numerous customer complaints about the waiting time.

The New System

In an effort to solve these expense and customer complaint problems, a new computerized (IBM System/360) data processing system was developed and installed in special facilities at Sunrise corporate headquarters in Baltimore.

The centralized data banks in the new system stored data regarding occupancy (vacant, not-vacant), size (single, double, suite), and price of the room at each company motel (prices for the same size room varied from city to city). Communication lines were set up connecting the central computer with individual terminals located in each of the company's motels.

Under the new system, when a customer called any motel office in the Sunrise system, the clerk could now use the terminal to make an inquiry about the availability of room desired by the customer at a Sunrise motel in another city. The clerk would input on the terminal keyboard the customer's preference for room size (double room, for example), location (Atlanta, for example), and date when accommodations were needed. The central system would match this input with data in the central data bank on room price and availability at the location desired and send back a message stating the reservation could be made or that the desired room was not available. When the requested room was not available, alternatives would be suggested. The process took only a few seconds.

Updating the data banks took place on a continuous basis. As soon as the reservation was confirmed by the customer, the central data bank would be notified by the clerk and given the name of the customer. In turn, the system would notify the motel where the reservation had been made and update the data bank. In addition, as soon as a guest would check out of a room early or extend his stay beyond the original reservation period (or when a reservation was made locally), the motel clerk would communicate any such changes in room status to the central system through his terminal.

Corporate management of Sunrise Motels was extremely pleased with the operation of the new reservation system. The accuracy, convenience and efficiency of the system had both improved customer relations and reduced costs, by reducing errors and the time required to make reservations. Management also believed that, as a direct result of this system, there had been an increase in total revenue over the past two years, since the system was installed.

Possible Extensions of the New System

Sunrise management felt that the system might be extended to produce information needed for management decision making. At the time of this case study, management information requirements were being studied in an effort to make greater use of the existing computerized reservations system for management information purposes.

Assignment

1. Describe the computerized data processing system presently being used by Sunrise.

2. Describe some of the management information requirements which might be served by an extension of the existing system. Be sure to describe not only the management decisions which could be made using this information, but also the significance of these decisions and the way decision making could be improved by getting information or by getting it faster.

3. Discuss ways in which the existing data processing and communication systems at Sunrise might be expanded to meet the management information requirements described in your answer to Question Two.

Management Information Systems at Domby Publishing Company

General Background

The Domby Publishing Company published three specialized technical periodicals serving the building, chemical, and data processing industries. The major source of income was advertising revenue: each publication generated advertising revenue in excess of $2,000,000 annually, mainly from firms engaged in the sale of industrial goods. The three magazines were distributed free to key managers in companies operating within the industries or industrial areas served by each magazine; such free distribution was called "controlled circulation," a technique also commonly used by competitive magazines.

Success of each magazine thus depended on serving both the needs of readers for information about their special field of interest, as well as the need of advertisers to reach those readers with their message. Competition was severe in the areas served by the three Domby magazines, with over ten competing magazines in each area.

Each magazine had a publisher who reported to the company president and who functioned both as the general manager and sales manager for the magazine. Each publication also had its own sales staff. The chief editor for each magazine, who reported to the publisher, supervised the writing and art preparation activities. Most of the articles were written by the chief editor's own staff writers, while a central staff of artists handled the graphics for all three publications under the overall supervision of each chief editor. Central production and circulation departments also serviced all three magazines.

Corporate Management Financial and Accounting Information Systems

Every fall each publisher prepared a month-by-month projection of expected advertising page sales for the coming year based on historical sales data, salesmen forecasts, orders on hand, the general economic outlook, the outlook for the industry served, and estimates of existing and potential competition from other publications. Each publisher also prepared a promotion budget and circulation projection, and estimated any expected changes in staff and in advertising rates.

The company treasurer used this information to prepare a preliminary financial budget for each publication. First, budgeted sales were calculated based on each publisher's estimate of advertising page sales and advertising rates. Next, expenses were estimated by the treasurer for staff salaries, sales commissions, printing and distribution, promotion, and circulation service, based on reports from the various operating departments. Each publication's contribution to overhead and profit was then calculated, as was overall company projected profit.

In preparing a final budget, these preliminary projections were reviewed with company management and each publisher and operating manager, and adjustments were made in light of overall economic conditions and company profit goals. During this review, for example, the possible impact of increased or decreased expenditures for promotion were studied in light of their effect on total company profits.

Each month during the year, actual expenses and sales were compared with budgeted expenses and sales in a treasurer's report to top management and the operating manager. Any significant variances were investigated by the treasurer. Each publisher, however, retained final authority and responsibility for the profitability of his publication.

Advertising-Sales Management Information Systems

Salesmen had the job of selling advertising pages to both old and new customers. They were responsible for researching their market for potential customer leads, calling on present and prospective customers, and in general seeing that advertising material was received on time and printed to customer specifications. Each salesman had an annual budget to meet and was paid on a salary plus commission basis.

Starting in September, advertising salesmen began soliciting orders for advertising for the following year's issues. At this point, these orders were only statements of intent provided by the customer for planning purposes. On average, actual orders were eventually received for anywhere from one-third to two-thirds of these statements of intent over the following year.

The following reports derived from each publisher's initial forecast of advertising page sales were issued to management during the year.

1. *Issue Control Sheet* (Figure 2–1). Starting three weeks prior to issue deadline (closing), an intensive effort was made by the sales force to firm up orders for ads for the coming issue. All statements of intent on

FIGURE 2-1

Domby Publishing Company
Issue Control Sheet

Publication name
February 1974 issue

Salesman	Advertiser	Will They Run?	Size of Space	Special Instructions	Plate Leased	Plate Received	Insert Order Received	Color	Bleed	Ad Order Sent	Ad Proof Sent
51	A COM Corporation		.9	LHP	1-18	X					
55	B COM Industries		.8		1-18						
50	C COM Company		.6	Spread	1-18	X	X	No	No	1-22	1-23
52	D COM Supplies		1.2		1-18		X				
51	E COM Corporation		1.0		1-18						
52	F COM Manufacturing Co.		.5	Facing editorial	1-18	X					
58	G COM Company		.7		1-18						
56	H COM Corporation		.7	Cover 2	1-18						
55	I COM Equipment		1.2		1-18	X					
51	J COM Company		1.0		1-18	X					
56	K COM Supplies		2.0		1-18						
58	L COM Metals Inc.		1.0	Fold out	1-18	X	X	Red	Yes	1-21	1-22
50	N COM Research Co.		.9		1-18						
50	O COM Supplies		.8		1-18						
51	P COM Company		2.0	Carry over	1-18	X					
58	Q COM Company		.9		1-18		X				
52	R COM Inc.		.7		1-18						
51	S COM Industries		.5	Upper RHP	1-18						
56	T COM Company		1.2	Insert, Back up	1-18	X	X	No	No	1-22	1-23
50	U COM Supplies		.7		1-18						
50	V COM Corporation		.9		1-18						
53	W COM Company		1.0		1-18	X					
52	X COM Firms, Ltd.		.9		1-18						
53	Y COM Inc.		.7		1-18						
54	Z COM Company		1.2		1-18						

hand were listed by customer and salesman, and progress toward closing was noted. Management used the sheet to determine the accounts which needed work and the salesman responsible for the account. In addition, day-to-day comparisons with the status of the prior's year's issue for the same month were prepared for management use.

2. *Current Issue and Year-to-Date Weekly Summary* (Figure 2–2). This report provided management with comparative information on the progress of the current issue, as well as on the magazine's performance for the year to date.

FIGURE 2–2

Domby Publishing Company

Data Processing Monthly*

Current and Year-to-Date Summary—Advertising Pages

Current Issue

Date of Issue	Actual	Budget	Last Year	Date Closed	Report Date
	68				1-17-74
	95				1-27-74
	—				
	—				
3/74	—	116	88	2-9-74	

Year–To–Date

	Advertising Pages by Issue				Cumulative			
Date of Issue	Actual	Budget	Last Year	+ or −	Actual	Budget	Last Year	+ or −
1/74	75	65	56	+19	75	65	57	+18
2/74	90	79	61	+29	176	155	127	+49
3/74		116	88			282	221	
4/74		124	122			417	359	
5/74		91	59			519	428	
6/74		92	79			622	517	
7/74		66	52			699	569	
8/74		79	61			779	640	
9/74		107	108			882	758	
10/74		89	80			976	848	
11/74		91	72			1,002	960	
12/74		88	77			1,150	990	

* A fictitious publication

3. *Monthly Market Share Analysis.* After each issue was published, market share data was gathered by counting the ads appearing in competitive magazines and comparing these to Domby's performance.

4. *Lost and Gained Business Analysis.* An analysis of sales by customer was made at the end of the year and the results compared with the previous year. Significant variations were analyzed to determine the factors affecting the change (general business conditions, industry trends, individual sales effort, etc.).

Editorial Management Information Systems

The editorial management information system relied more on review meetings than on reports, because of the creative and subjective nature of the work.

Monthly Editorial Review Meetings. Fifty days before each issue's closing, the chief editor reviewed the articles planned for the issue with his staff, the publisher, the promotion manager, the art editor, and the production manager. At the meeting, staff editors reviewed the following for each article proposed for the issue: the general content and source of the article; the reader information need it was designed to fill; the article's relationship to the overall objectives of the magazine and to the other articles in the issue; and the general appearance of the article in terms of overall layout, headline and subheadings, and illustrations.

The purpose of the meeting was to review the total content of the issue with all parties concerned. As a result of this review, articles were sometimes revised to highlight different key points, dropped entirely for balance reasons, or replaced with other articles which seemed to fill the readers' information needs better. Changes were also often made to improve an article's visual appearance. In addition to integrating editorial activities for each issue, these meetings served to coordinate the overall efforts of the selling, production, art, and editorial groups.

Annual Editorial Review Meetings. Once every year, each publisher and his chief editor and staff met with top management to review the twelve preceding issues, and the magazine's specific (quantitative where possible) plans for the coming year. The objectives of the annual meetings were: to review the general editorial approach of each magazine; to encourage the publishers and their staff to relate their daily efforts to overall company and publication objectives; to discuss new trends and developments within the industry and their relationship to the planned editorial approach; and to develop specific objectives and programs for the coming year.

The annual review covered the following areas:

1. *Editorial Approach.* First, what were the editorial objectives for the past year? For example: increased emphasis on technical articles relating to data processing; improved balance among the major areas of coverage; and increased emphasis on graphic illustrations (as opposed to text). Second, to what degree were these objectives achieved? For example: five articles were published on advanced developments in random access retrieval systems as compared with one in the previous year; coverage of major areas this year (A-25 percent, B-40 percent, C-35 percent) was better than last year (A-10 percent, B-55 percent, C-35 percent); and there were 15 pages of illustrations per issue this year, as opposed to 10 pages per issue in the previous year.

2. *Review of Competition.* This segment covered such questions as significant moves by competitors and Domby's editorial approach as compared to that of competitors.

3. *Readership Interest.* This segment covered such questions as how well each publication is read by its audience, reader rating of Domby's publications in comparison with competing magazines, and the relationship of this readership data with the stated objectives of the publication.

4. *Operational Planning.* This segment covered such topics as areas for improvement, and specific editorial plans and objectives for the coming year, in terms of areas to be emphasized (percentage balance), editorial costs, layout and illustrations, and overall structure and content of each magazine.

Several criticisms of these annual meetings had been voiced by the editorial staff. Editorial writers unanimously questioned the appropriateness of trying to measure quantitatively a creative activity. They also claimed that about two full weeks of preparations were required, that many editors were not business-management types who could easily address a room full of people under formal conditions, and that the very formal nature of the meetings did not encourage a completely free exchange, since on occasion participants devoted their time to defending past mistakes rather than to objectively discussing basic weaknesses and strengths of a given editorial approach.

Assignment

Answer the following questions:

1. Identify the critical industry, market, and company factors which affect the company's profitability.

2. Briefly summarize the work situation and the management job responsibilities in the three management areas involved in the study: advertising sales management, editorial management, and corporate management.

3. Outline in detail the management decision-making activities and information needed to make these decisions in the same three management areas.

4. Describe the key differences among the three types of information systems needed in each of the three management areas under study.

5. Describe the existing advertising sales management information system. Does it adequately meet sales management's key information requirements, and in what ways could it be improved to better meet sales management's decision-making requirements?

6. Describe the existing financial information system and the ways in which it is used to monitor financial results and integrate advertising sales activities with corporate objectives. Discuss the ways in which the system did and did not meet key corporate management information requirements, as well as ways in which the system could be improved.

7. Describe the existing editorial review system. In what ways did the addition of an annual review meeting enable better integration of editorial activities with corporate objectives and more effective planning and control of editorial activities? Why was it a necessary addition to the system of monthly review meetings? Were the two types of review meetings adequately integrated? Describe the ways in which these review meetings did and did not meet the information requirements of both editorial (operating) and top (corporate) management.

8. Explain why it would be impossible to fully integrate management information systems at the company. Discuss ways in which they might be better integrated.

Alternate Assignment

Write a 1,500 word report covering the following:

INTRODUCTION   Purpose and method of report.
KEY FACTORS
  General Company Background
  Work Situation in Key Operating Areas
  Key Management Decisions and Information Needed
  Concept of the System Needed
  Factors Affecting Implementation and Use
EXISTING SYSTEM
RECOMMENDATIONS FOR IMPROVEMENTS

Data Processing Systems

INFORMATION SYSTEMS ARE LIMITED BY DATA PROCESSING CAPABILITIES. An understanding of data processing systems is, therefore, necessary in developing effective and economical information systems for management.

The purpose of this chapter is to introduce the reader to various methods of storing, processing, and retrieving data in different kinds of data processing systems. The discussion covers what data processing systems are and how computerized data systems and data banks are developed and adapted to supply information for management.[1]

Kinds of Data Processing Systems and their Functions

Data processing systems involve five basic functions or components: collecting and entering data into the system; processing new input data and data already stored in the files; creating and maintaining data files and records;

---

1. Portions of this chapter are adapted from Robert G. Murdick and Joel E. Ross, *Information Systems for Modern Management* (Englewood Cliffs, N.J.: Prentice-Hall, Inc., 1971); Jerome Kanter, *The Computer and the Executive* (Englewood Cliffs, N.J.: Prentice-Hall, Inc., 1968); and IBM technical manuals.

maintaining and using procedures and instructions for data manipulation; and preparing output. These five functions are shown in summary in Figure 3–1. As might be expected, this component breakdown for a data processing system resembles that found in systems in general (see Chapter One).

FIGURE 3–1

Basic Components of a Data Processing System

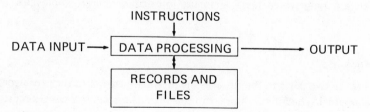

For discussion purposes, data processing systems can be divided into three types: manual, electrical or electromechanical (the most familiar of which are punched-card systems), and electronic (computer). The same five basic components (input, instructions, file storage, processor, and output) are found in manual, electromechanical, and computer data processing systems.

Manual
Systems

The following discussion of the components of manual systems is designed to familiarize the reader with the fundamental concepts of data processing before going on to discussion of more complex machine-based data systems. The example used is a payroll accounting system. Since the system is used for illustrative purposes, only selected aspects of such a system will be discussed. The basic elements of the system which are discussed below are pictured in Figures 3–2 and 3–3.

Input

The initial input device for the manual payroll-processing system shown in Figure 3–3 is the employees' time cards. To prepare these cards for transmission to the payroll clerk, the timekeeper of each department must compute the total amount of regular time and overtime worked and verify any related figures. At the end of the last day of the week, the payroll department collects employee time cards from all departments, and the clerk enters the data into the payroll register.

Processor

The processor in this manual system is made up of three elements: the control element (the payroll clerk's brain), which determines the sequence of operations and maintains the proper relationships among the system components; the arithmetic element (or calculator) which performs the four mathematical functions of adding, subtracting, multiplying, and dividing; and the logic element (again, the clerk's brain) which performs certain functions such as determining which tax rate to use in calculating each employee's deductions.

Storage

There are two parts to the storage: the internal (internal to the processor) and the external. The internal storage in this manual system is the working storage represented by the pencil, scratch pads, or other temporary records, and the data carried in the processor's (or clerk's) memory. The external storage is represented by the individual records and files stored in cabinets. As the payroll clerk needs file data, he will extract the necessary data from these files. The classification and structure of the files are very important to the operation of any system, since they affect the method of retrieving file data,

FIGURE 3–2

A Manual Data Processing System: Payroll Accounting

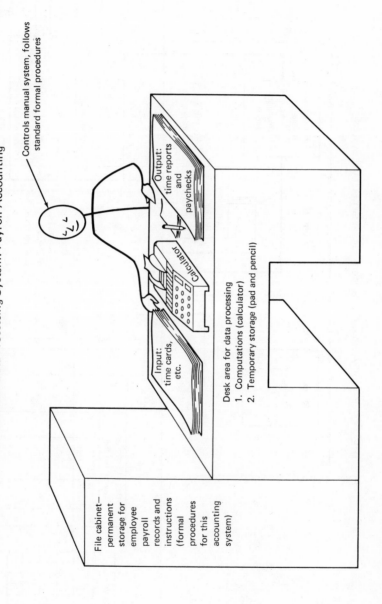

Controls manual system, follows standard formal procedures

Output: time reports and paychecks

Calculator

Input: time cards, etc.

Desk area for data processing
1. Computations (calculator)
2. Temporary storage (pad and pencil)

File cabinet—permanent storage for employee payroll records and instructions (formal procedures for this accounting system)

FIGURE 3-3 Payroll Accounting System Flowchart Manual System

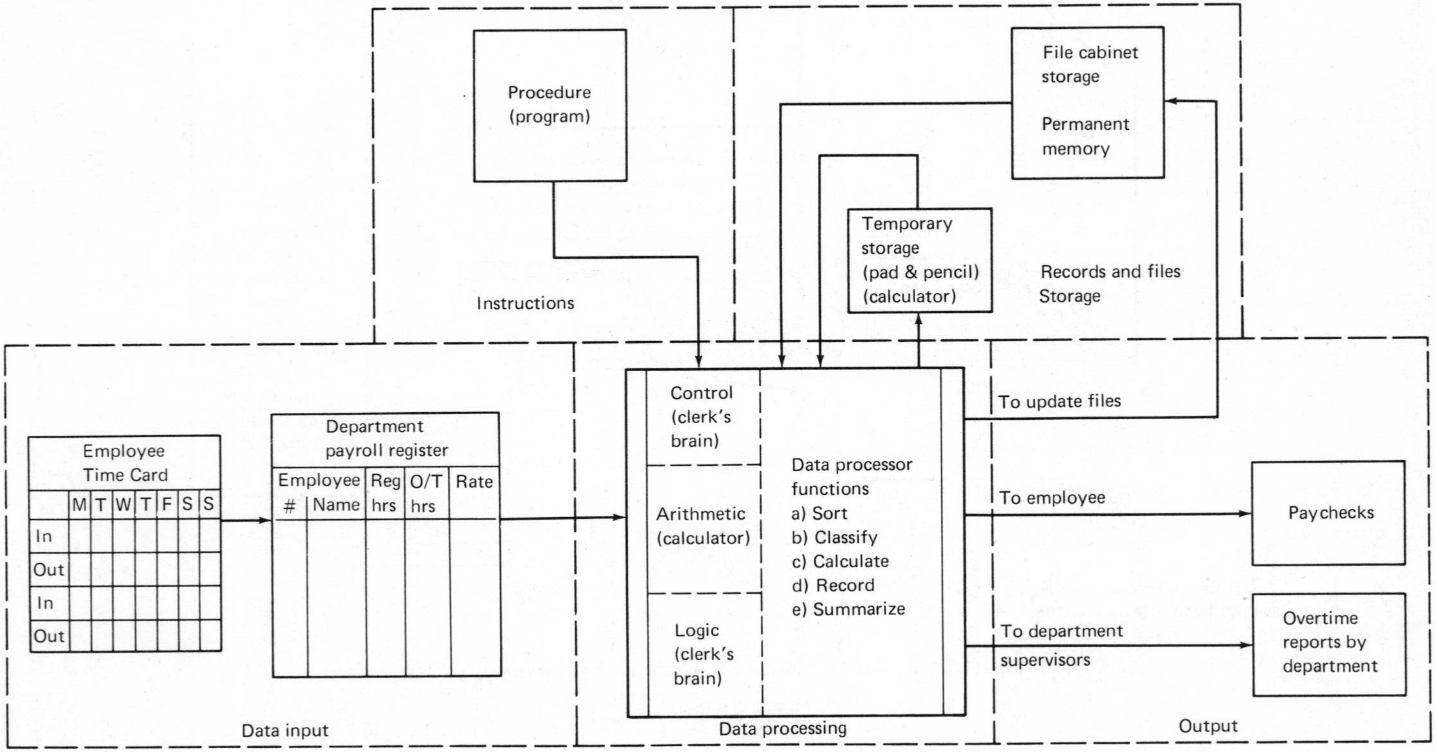

50

as well as determining the time required for that retrieval. In the payroll system, the file is organized by department, by class of worker, and by alphabetic last name sequence within each class—which simplifies processing, since the data which comes to the clerk is also organized by department. Output, such as overtime reports, is likewise organized by department.

Program or Instructions

The program or procedure tells the processor (or clerk) how calculations should be performed or how data should be processed. For example, the overall instructions or program followed by the payroll clerk might be as follows:

1. Retrieve employee payroll file from file cabinet.
2. Multiply hours worked (regular and overtime) by his hourly wage rate for each type of work.
3. Consult tax schedules and other tables for deductions required.
4. Compute net pay by subtracting deductions from gross pay.
5. Enter weekly pay and deductions on employee's payroll file.
6. Prepare payroll check.
7. Prepare report on overtime by department, when checks for each department's employees have been completed.

The clerk would then follow this procedure in processing the input data, updating the payroll file (external storage), and preparing the required output (the paychecks and summary report).

Output

Preparation of output is the final step in a data processing system. The result of the data manipulation is some form of meaningful output. In the case of the phase of the payroll accounting system described above, the outputs are: the employees' pay checks, which were placed in the out-basket for distribution; the updated master payroll files, which are kept in the cabinet; and the summary overtime report, which is sent to management.

Punched-Card Systems

Punched-card systems are the most common type of electromechanical data processing system. In these systems, all data is entered and stored on punched cards (see Figure 3–4 for an example of a punched card). This data includes historical files, as well as new data, such as business transactions (sales,

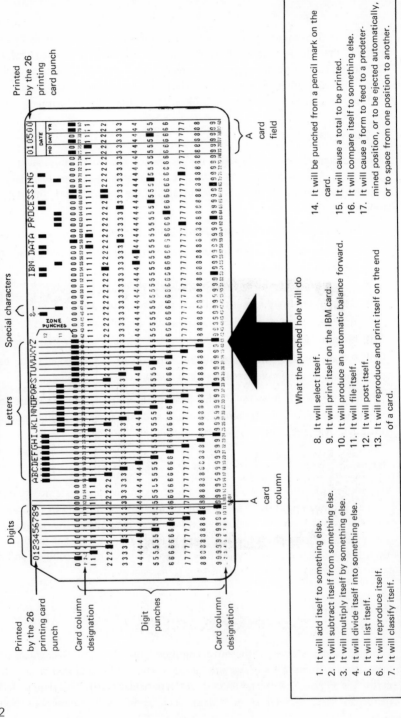

FIGURE 3-4 An IBM Punched Card

What the punched hole will do

1. It will add itself to something else.
2. It will subtract itself from something else.
3. It will multiply itself by something else.
4. It will divide itself into something else.
5. It will list itself.
6. It will reproduce itself.
7. It will classify itself.
8. It will select itself.
9. It will print itself on the IBM card.
10. It will produce an automatic balance forward.
11. It will file itself.
12. It will post itself.
13. It will reproduce and print itself on the end of a card.
14. It will be punched from a pencil mark on the card.
15. It will cause a total to be printed.
16. It will compare itself to something else.
17. It will cause a form to feed to a predetermined position, or to be ejected automatically, or to space from one position to another.

payments, and the like), that is to be entered into the system. New data is placed on punched cards in a predetermined format (coding). The cards are prepared on key-punch machines and are checked on a card-verifier for accuracy.

This input data can then be processed by electrical machines which can read and manipulate the data on cards. Some basic routines which these machines perform are sorting, merging, selecting, matching, reproducing, interpreting, and tabulating. These routines are generally wired into the processing machines and need only be called up or activated by selection at the programming panel. An idea of the capabilities of punched-card data processing systems is given in Figure 3–4.

The output of these data systems is always on punched cards. These cards are sometimes used as updated file cards (such as customer accounts, inventories, receivable records, and the like). At other times, these cards are used to prepare documents used in operations (such as bills, checks, shipping instructions, etc.) or management information reports in tabular form (such as overdue accounts or sales analyses).

A punched-card data system allows some degree of automation over the manual systems described in the preceding section. Punched-card systems have some inherent limitations, however. Since the data in these systems is stored on punched cards, the storage space in these systems is limited by the physical storage space that is available. Retrieval of data from card files requires considerable manual manipulation by the machine operator and mechanical manipulation by a card sorter or a card interpreter. Also inherent in these systems is the need for manual intervention by an operator or a number of operators who must sort, merge, and move the data cards in order to complete the particular operation that is being performed. This manual intervention and the necessity of bulky card storage are serious limitations in developing an economical and effective management information system using a punched-card data system.

Punched-card data systems can nonetheless be an economical tool for smaller companies (or small operations within a company), since they are relatively easy to understand and use. Since electronic data processing (EDP) systems perform all of the functions performed by a punched-card system, this discussion has been limited to a short summary. The following section on EDP systems gives a more detailed explanation of how present-day machine data processing systems work.

Computer Systems

Computers carry the automation of data processing considerably beyond punched-card systems, since computers have much larger storage capacity and memory, and faster processing speeds. They can also make use of a wide range of input/output devices.

The basic concept of a computerized data processing system is no more complex than the manual system just described. The elements involved in data processing as done manually by a clerk were shown in Figures 3–2 and 3–3. Computer or electronic data processing systems have the same five basic functions as the manual system. Figure 3–5 gives an outline of how the components of the manual payroll accounting system given in Figure 3–3 are described when converted to electronic data processing (EDP). Figure 3–6 shows pictures of the components of a computer system currently in use. The following is a discussion of how these components function within a computer-based data processing system.

Input

An input device is used to enter data into a computer system, since the input data must be transformed into a machine acceptable form for storage and use in the system. In order for these input devices to receive data, that data must be transcribed to a medium such as punch cards, punch paper tape, magnetic tape, or special printed matter—or read into the system through keyboard machines. For example, data on the payroll register may be keypunched onto punch cards, which are then fed into a card reader, which in turn transmits the data on the card to the central processing unit in an acceptable electronic form.

Central Processing Unit

Similar to that in a manual system, the central processor in a computer system consists of a control unit, which coordinates the system operation, an arithmetic/logic unit, which performs calculations and comparisons, and an internal memory storage, which may be either temporary or permanent. The control unit directs operations according to instructions contained in programs that are normally maintained in the computer's internal memory storage units. These programs specify the operations that are to be performed and the sequence of those operations. The control unit, using the programs, directs the transfer of data from the input device and to the output device and also coordinates arithmetic calculations with the flow of data to and from storage facilities. The arithmetic/logic unit contains specific programmed sub-routines that may be called up to perform such operations as adding, subtracting, multiplying, dividing, shifting number sequences, or comparing numbers at extremely rapid speed (the speed depends on the EDP system being used).

FIGURE 3–5

Computer Based Payroll Accounting System

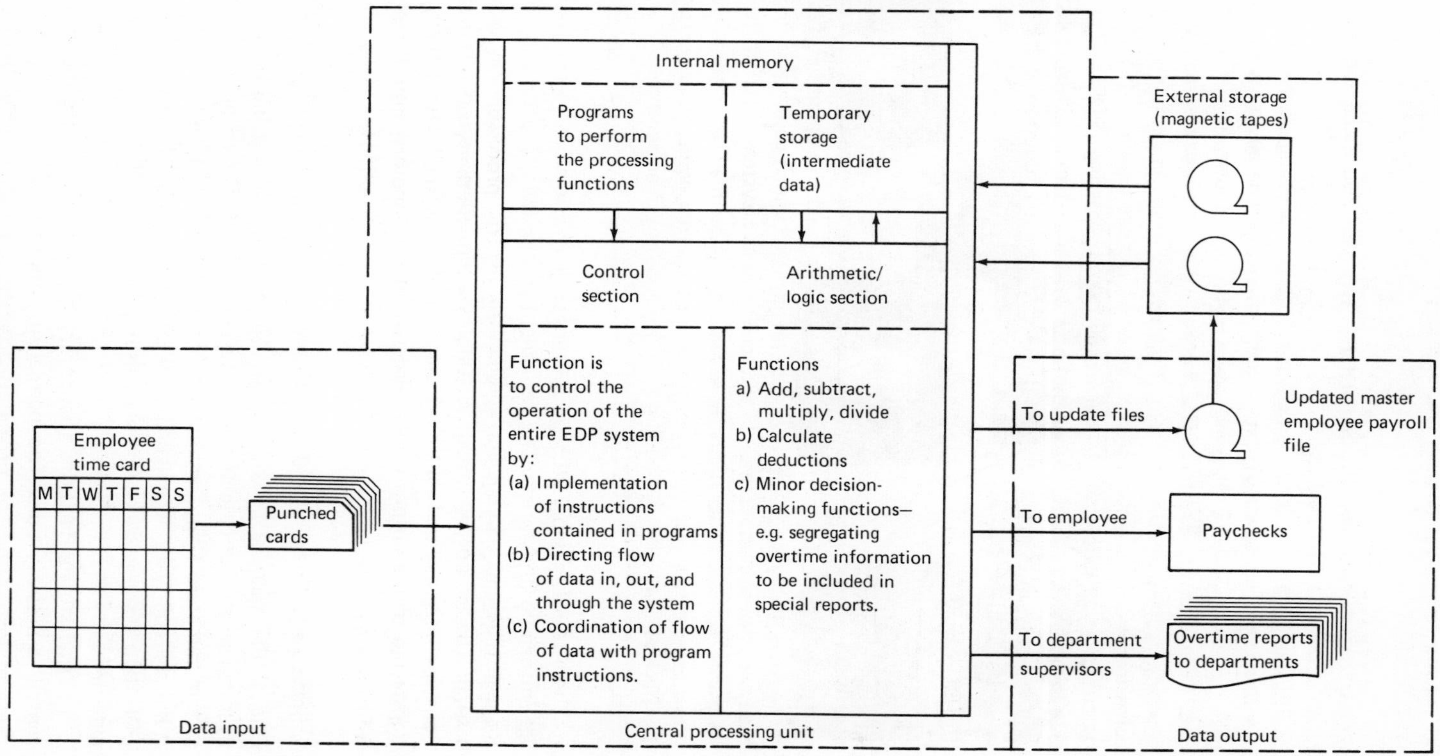

Data input

Employee time card

M	T	W	T	F	S	S

Punched cards

Central processing unit

Internal memory

Programs to perform the processing functions

Temporary storage (intermediate data)

Control section

Arithmetic/ logic section

Function is to control the operation of the entire EDP system by:
(a) Implementation of instructions contained in programs
(b) Directing flow of data in, out, and through the system
(c) Coordination of flow of data with program instructions.

Functions
a) Add, subtract, multiply, divide
b) Calculate deductions
c) Minor decision-making functions— e.g. segregating overtime information to be included in special reports.

External storage (magnetic tapes)

Data output

To update files — Updated master employee payroll file

To employee — Paychecks

To department supervisors — Overtime reports to departments

55

FIGURE 3–6

The Components of a Computer System

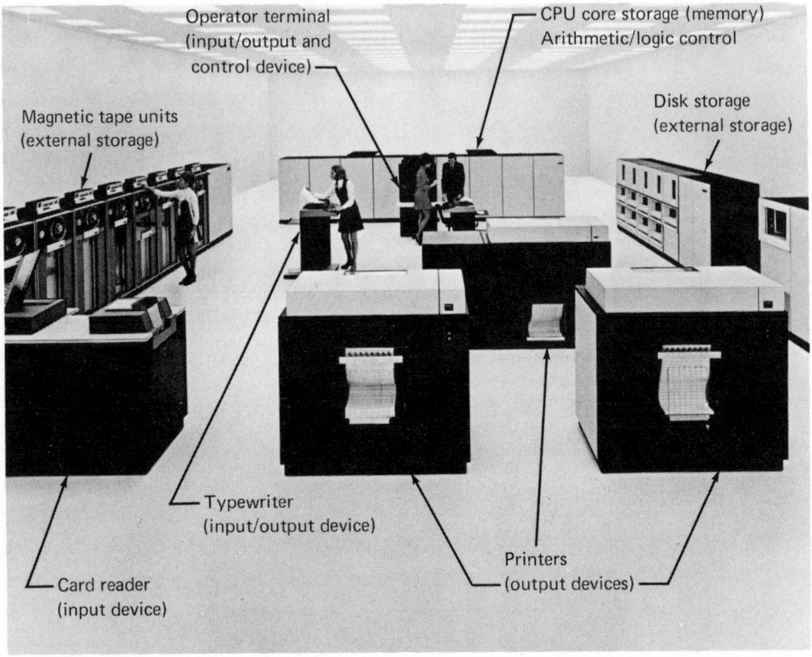

The internal memory storage unit contains two sections: permanent storage and temporary storage. The permanent storage holds program instructions for coordinating, sequencing, and controlling all phases of the data processing. The temporary storage area holds intermediate results of all calculations for later use and will hold pieces of data until all data is ready to be transferred to the output device. Program instructions may also be contained here.

Storage

One of the major advantages of an electronic data processing (EDP) system over other types of data processing systems is its storage capabilities. An EDP system can store a large amount of file data to which it has rapid access, and it has the ability to hold new data in temporary storage for use in processing. EDP data systems generally make use of two types of storage: internal and external.

Internal storage facilities (temporary and permanent) are located in the central processing unit. The permanent storage holds standard hardwired program instructions or procedures, which are called up by the operator through use of a certain code. In addition to the standard hardwired programs, most large EDP systems have facilities for using or trying out new programs. This is accomplished by storing these new programs in the temporary storage area of internal memory. These programs are used in essentially the same way as the standard hardwired programs, but they may be erased and returned to external storage or stored in permanent storage at a later date. The temporary internal storage area is also where input data is temporarily stored until it is called for by the program instructions, where all intermediate data is stored for later use in processing, and where final data is stored until it is moved to output devices. All input data and temporary instructions must be encoded and placed into this temporary storage before they can be processed by the computer.

Almost all internal computer storage memories in use today consist of planes of magnetic cores, as shown in Figure 3–7. The magnetic core, the most common kind of internal computer memory in use today, is a doughnut-shaped ring of ferromagnetic material (iron) the size of a matchhead. Due to the magnetic property of iron, these cores are capable of retaining either of two possible states depending upon which direction an electric current is passing through it. The two states are defined by 0 and 1, depending on the polarity of the magnetized material (that is, the direction of the electric current). Since the cores have only two possible states, all data must be entered in a binary code (one that uses the numbers 0 and 1) and more than one magnetic core is needed to represent a number or letter or symbol.

For example, in order to encode the numbers 0 to 9 the following Binary Coded Decimal (BCD) system may be used:

Decimal Number	BCD Using Four Magnetic Cores
0	0000
1	0001
2	0010
3	0011
4	0100
5	0101
6	0110
7	0111
8	1000
9	1001

Since four cores of four binary digits are used for each number, this coding pattern represents a four-bit (*b*inary dig*it*) word. Other codes than the one represented here could be used, depending on the length of the computer word—that is, the number of bits.

FIGURE 3-7
Magnetic Cores

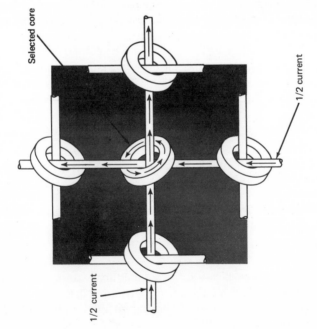

Selected core

1/2 current

1/2 current

(a) Detail view of core positions

(b) One plane of cores

Generally, computer words are defined by the number of bits, and these computer words (or groups of bits) are stored in specific locations in arrays of magnetic cores. Each of these memory locations may be addressed randomly or in sequence, depending on the EDP instructions or data needs. The arrays of magnetic cores are arranged in planes (see Figure 3–7) which are usually plug-in modular assemblies. Each computer word may represent in binary form some constant number or some program instruction. If the EDP system outputs or inputs are to be alphanumeric (as they usually are), the letters or numbers will be sent to or from some typewriting input or output device, which will decode the binary words into the correct symbols (for example, alphabet, decimal number, punctuation, symbol, etc.) or encode the symbols into binary words.

Another type of internal memory that is in use today is the Read Only Memory (ROM), which is used for holding standard programs, procedures, or constant numbers used in common computations. These ROM memories usually are made of electronic integrated circuitry rather than magnetic cores and are built into the central processing unit.

Integrated circuit memories are called monolithic memories and they can do everything that a magnetic core memory can do, although they are slower. One advantage to integrated circuitry is that it needs a much smaller physical space than magnetic core memory. These two storage devices, magnetic core and monolithic integrated circuitry, will be the most frequently used internal memories in the computer systems of the future. Work is also now being done on developing the laser memory (see Figure 3–8) which may also be used for similar internal memory purposes.

External storage will hold all historical data and other file data pertinent to the operation specified. External storage is of two types: direct access and sequential access. The method of "access" refers to the manner in which data is retrieved from the storage device.

In a direct access device, data can be located randomly, without reading each record in the file in sequence. Such access is important if only a few records on the file are needed at any one time. A sequential access device requires that every record on the file be examined in sequence from the beginning, in order to retrieve and read any one.

Direct access devices are magnetic disks, magnetic drums, and magnetic cores. Magnetic tapes are sequential storage devices. These devices are pictured in Figure 3–9. According to IBM, recent technological developments indicate that magnetic disks and magnetic tapes will be the most prevalent type of external storage devices used in the future in computer systems.

Processing According to Program Instructions

In order to process data, a machine operator will specify the program instructions that are to be followed, by either calling them out of permanent

FIGURE 3-8   A Central Processing Unit of the Future Containing
a Laser (Optical) Memory

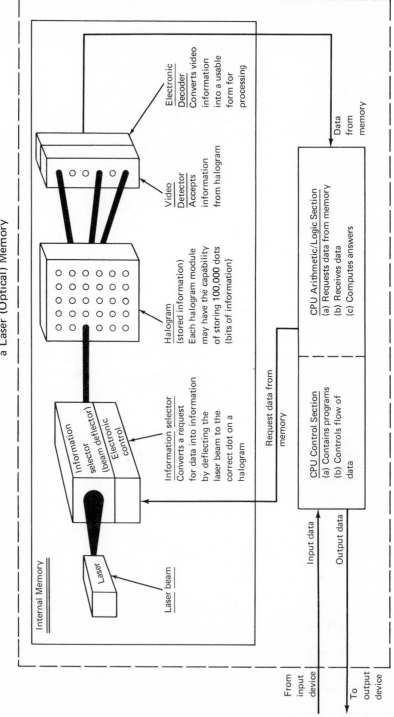

Internal Memory

Laser

Laser beam

Information selector
(beam deflector)
Electronic
control

Information selector
Converts a request
for data into information
by deflecting the
laser beam to the
correct dot on a
halogram

Halogram
(stored information)
Each halogram module
may have the capability
of storing 100,000 dots
(bits of information)

Video
Detector
Accepts
information
from halogram

Electronic
Decoder
Converts video
information
into a usable
form for
processing

Data
from
memory

Request data from
memory

CPU Arithmetic/Logic Section
(a) Requests data from memory
(b) Receives data
(c) Computes answers

CPU Control Section
(a) Contains programs
(b) Controls flow of
data

Input data

Output data

From
input
device

To
output
device

storage or inserting them into temporary memory from an external storage device. The operator also places any historical data file into the input/output devices wired to the central processor, as well as any new input data that is to be processed. All data that is to be processed is moved into temporary storage, as called for by the programs, before it can be processed.

The control unit now sequences through the program instructions, fetching data from temporary internal storage (or transferring it from external storage to internal temporary storage) as the program calls for it and placing the data in another location in the internal memory. Here the data is manipulated according to the sub-routines which are stored in either permanent or temporary internal memory. These sub-routines will perform the calculations called for (for example, take federal tax out of an employee's gross pay in the payroll accounting example earlier). The processed data (either in intermediate or final form) is then stored in other locations in temporary storage for later use as the control unit sequences through subsequent procedures.

When all required procedures have been performed on data, the data that has been stored in temporary storage is moved to the output device and filed or reproduced in the form that has been specified. When data is taken from the temporary storage area, all cores are wiped clean of data unless the program instructions specifically call for the return of the data to storage after printout.

Processing time is a function of the type of calculations performed and the volume of data to be processed. And the maximum storage space and basic complexity of the central processing unit are factors which limit the number and type of instruction that can be performed in any one set of program instructions.

Output

Through output devices the results of the data processing are transferred to punch cards, punched paper tape, magnetic tape, paper printouts, cathode ray tubes, microfilm, or other associated media or storage device. Payroll listings, payroll reports, and pre-printed checks are examples of output from the payroll system described earlier.

Developing a Computerized
Data Processing System

In order to understand a manager's role in developing computer-based information systems, a manager needs to be familiar with how such systems are

FIGURE 3–9

Four External Storage Devices

(a) IBM 2311 Disk storage drive

(b) IBM 2303 Drum storage

(c) IBM 2361 Core storage

(d) IBM 3420 Magnetic tape unit

developed. The following is a description of how the manual payroll account-ing system described earlier might be converted to a computer system. The areas involved in such a conversion are:

1. System description or overall concept design
2. Input documents
3. Output documents
4. File design
5. The program flowchart
6. Computer assembly
7. Computer program
8. Program operation

The following discussion is necessarily simplified to provide a basic intro-duction to the subject. Variations in the approach will inevitably occur in different types of management and business situations, and with different types of computer systems.

System Description or Overall Concept Design

The system description may be in narrative form or in flowchart form or in any combination of the two. The narrative description usually covers the major inputs, outputs, files needed, reports required, and processing opera-tions. The following is a partial description of the payroll accounting system discussed earlier.

The activity involves payroll accounting to compensate employees for work performed, to account for gross pay and all amounts deducted

---

NOTES TO FIGURE 3–9

(a) A magnetic disc is a collection of circular discs, similar to phonograph records, which are stacked one on top of the other on a center column, with enough space between each for the entry of reading arms (with magnetic heads). The discs are coated with a magnetic substance—usually a nickel alloy or iron oxide. The data is engraved onto the tracks of each disc and is a permanent (non-destructive) memory.

(b) A magnetic drum consists of a metal cylinder covered with a magnetic substance (again, usually nickel alloy or iron oxide). The drum is segmented into tracks and data is recorded on the tracks around the outside of the drum in much the way as it is recorded on a tape recorder. This device is also considered a permanent or non-destructive memory.

(c) Described in the text.

(d) Magnetic tape storage is a sequential storage device. It is also a non-destructive, permanent memory. Magnetic tape is similar to that found in home tape recorders, although it is of higher quality. Magnetic tape is the most widely used of the external storage devices, since an unlimited number of tapes may be used on any one input device; whereas with disc, drum, and core memories, data is limited to that which is permanently stored on the disc, on the drum, or in the cores.

from gross pay, to provide payroll data required for internal company use (such as management information reports on overtime incurred in each department) and to maintain payroll records for employees. Each worker's time records are entered onto punched cards, the cards are read, the relevant magnetic tape master record is found and updated, checks are prepared, and a weekly report by department is prepared which indicates the number of overtime hours employees worked during the past week compared to the week before.

During this phase of system description, a manager has the opportunity to shape the system to best meet his requirements—present and future—since he should be participating in preparing the description. He must take the time needed to make certain all his requirements are included in the design description, since a systems analyst cannot be counted on to anticipate and cover all the information requirements of every operating manager.

The flowchart translates the narrative description into symbolic form (see Figure 3–10).

Input Documents

The kind of input format and mechanism used is based on the volume of data, frequency of entry, complexity and kind of data, accuracy and verification required, and the nature of data source documents. In the payroll accounting system example, the time cards and payroll registers (see Figure 3–3) are the data source documents which are used to prepare the input media—punched cards in this situation. The holes in these cards would be interpreted by the input device, a card reader which converts the data into computer readable form to be stored in the computer's temporary memory for processing.

The card input layout for the payroll accounting example is shown in Figure 3–11.

The worker number is represented by a nine-digit numeric field. Every worker is given a number (very often his social security number), since reading and matching a number is faster and more accurate than using names when processing the cards by computer. The name is also included, since the name will have to be printed on the checks and is used in several of the management exception reports. Grade level is needed for the computer to select the correct wage rate, and the hours worked under different classifications (overtime and regular) are listed separately, since each is paid at a different rate. The department number is included, since management reports by department are required.

FIGURE 3-10

System Flowchart, Payroll Accounting System

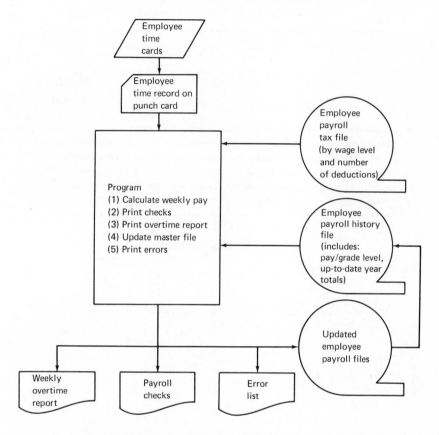

Output Documents

Input equipment translates the data into machine language and transfers it to the computer. Output equipment translates machine language into human language, reversing the process and providing a means of communication between the computer and the outside world. Since it is the output document with which management works in making decisions and taking action, managers should pay particular attention to its design and contents. The layout of the output documents designed in the payroll accounting example, employee checks and management reports on overtime by department, are shown in Figures 3-12 and 3-13.

FIGURE 3–11

Punched Card Layout–Individual
Employee Weekly Time Record

Number	Dept	Name	Grade Level	Reg Hours	O/T Hours	Blank

```
0000000000000000000000000000000000000000000000000000000000000000000000000000000000
1 2 3 4 5 6 7 8 9 10 11 12 13 14 15 16 17 18 19 20 21 22 23 24 25 26 27 28 29 30 31 32 33 34 35 36 37 38 39 40 41 42 43 44 45 46 47 48 49 50 51 52 53 54 55 56 57 58 59 60 61 62 63 64 65 66 67 68 69 70 71 72 73 74 75 76 77 78 79 80
1111111111111111111111111111111111111111111111111111111111111111111111111111111111
2222222222222222222222222222222222222222222222222222222222222222222222222222222222
3333333333333333333333333333333333333333333333333333333333333333333333333333333333
4444444444444444444444444444444444444444444444444444444444444444444444444444444444
5555555555555555555555555555555555555555555555555555555555555555555555555555555555
6666666666666666666666666666666666666666666666666666666666666666666666666666666666
7777777777777777777777777777777777777777777777777777777777777777777777777777777777
8888888888888888888888888888888888888888888888888888888888888888888888888888888888
9999999999999999999999999999999999999999999999999999999999999999999999999999999999
1 2 3 4 5 6 7 8 9 10 11 12 13 14 15 16 17 18 19 20 21 22 23 24 25 26 27 28 29 30 31 32 33 34 35 36 37 38 39 40 41 42 43 44 45 46 47 48 49 50 51 52 53 54 55 56 57 58 59 60 61 62 63 64 65 66 67 68 69 70 71 72 73 74 75 76 77 78 79 80
5081
```

FIGURE 3–12

Employee Paycheck and Check Stub

DALE ELECTRONICS CORPORATION

EARNINGS AND DEDUCTIONS STATEMENT   NOT NEGOTIABLE

		EMPLOYEE NAME	EMPLOYEE I.D.	DESTINATION	PERIOD ENDING		RATE
		John Williams	7876849		1/5/74		4.50/6.75

TYPE EARNINGS	DATE	HOURS	CURRENT	YR. TO DATE AMT.	TYPE DEDUCTIONS	CURRENT	YR. TO DATE	BALANCE DUE
REG PAY		40.0	180.00	180.00	FEDERAL TX	34.76	34.76	
OVERTIME	8/12	6.0	40.50	40.50	NY ST TAX	8.43	8.43	
					N Y CITY	2.19	2.19	
					FICA	14.70	14.70	
					LIFE INSUR	1.75	1.75	
					UNION DUES			
					CRED UNION			
TOTALS		46.0	220.50	220.50			61.83	NET PAY $ 158.67

DALE Electronics Corporation   657142   7-11⁄1234
7 Friendship Court • • • • • • Dayton, Ohio

"Sentry Products"

MO.	DAY	YR.
1	5	74

AMOUNT
158.67

PAY   xxONE HUNDRED FIFTY EIGHT AND 67/100xxxxxxxxxxxx

TO THE

ORDER OF John Williams   7876849

First Commercial Bank
14 Oval Street
New York, New York 10007

John F Henry

NON NEGOTIABLE

FIGURE 3-13

Overtime Report by Department

Weekly Report: Overtime
Manufacturing Operations Departments (2,000)
For week ending 11-26-72

Dept.	Total Reg. time	Total Overtime	Total O/T Prior week	Total O/T Year-to-date (1972)	Total O/T Year-to-date (1971)
2001	600	16	16	4,140	2,760
2002	680	24	16	4,692	3,128
2003	520	12	18	3,588	2,400
2004	480	24	30	3,312	2,210
2005	400	40	20	2,760	1,940
Total	2,680	116	100	18,492	12,438

File Design

File record design layouts specify field by field the contents of each file record to be maintained. In the payroll accounting system, the files to be maintained are the employee payroll history file and the payroll tax file. Figure 3-14 shows these file layouts for the master tape files.

The Program Flowchart

A program flowchart is a detailed outline of the steps which must be performed by the computer in processing the data. It is a graphic representation of operations, decisions, and output that shows the order in which data is to be processed. The chart places emphasis on how the computer is to go about the job, covers operations in detail, and aids the programmer in visualizing the sequence of operations. The flowchart of the payroll accounting system converted from manual to computer processing is shown in Figure 3-15. The flowchart symbols used for both programming and system flowcharting are shown in Figure 3-16.

Computer Assembly

Computer processing units need instructions expressed in machine-readable form (binary numbers) to operate. For example, the instruction to add regular pay to overtime pay might look like this in the computer:

10 100 101 110

The 10 indicates the ADD instruction, the 100 and 101 are addresses of storage locations for the numbers representing regular and overtime pay, and 110 is the location of the sum, total pay.

The "ADD" instruction in binary code calls up a subroutine. Once the

FIGURE 3–14

File Record Layouts

a. Employee Payroll History File (one for each employee)

Employee number	Dept.	Name	Grade level and pay rate	Year to date Reg. hours wages	Year to date O/T hours wages	Number of exemptions	Year to date Federal tax withheld	Year to date State tax withheld	Year to date Local tax withheld	Year to date FICA	Misc. deduct. total to date	Vacation pay (year to date)	Total number of days this year worked	Total number of days this year sick

b. Payroll Tax File (one for each combination of wage level and number of exemptions)

Wage level / Number of exemptions	Total federal tax	Total state tax	Total local tax	Total FICA	X	Wage level / Number of exemptions	Total federal tax	Total state tax	Total local tax	Total FICA

FIGURE 3–15

Program Flowchart

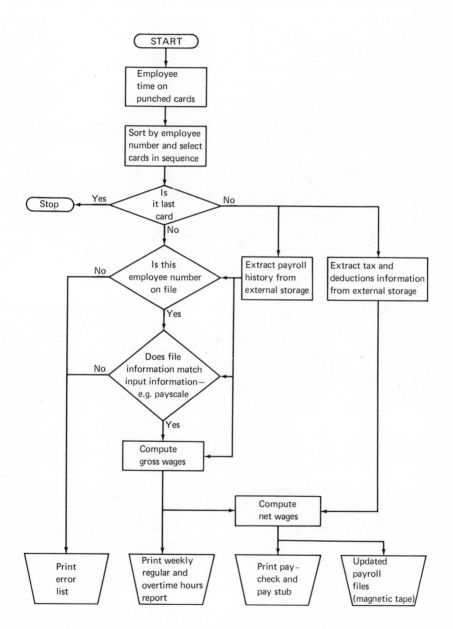

FIGURE 3–16
Symbols Used in Flowcharting

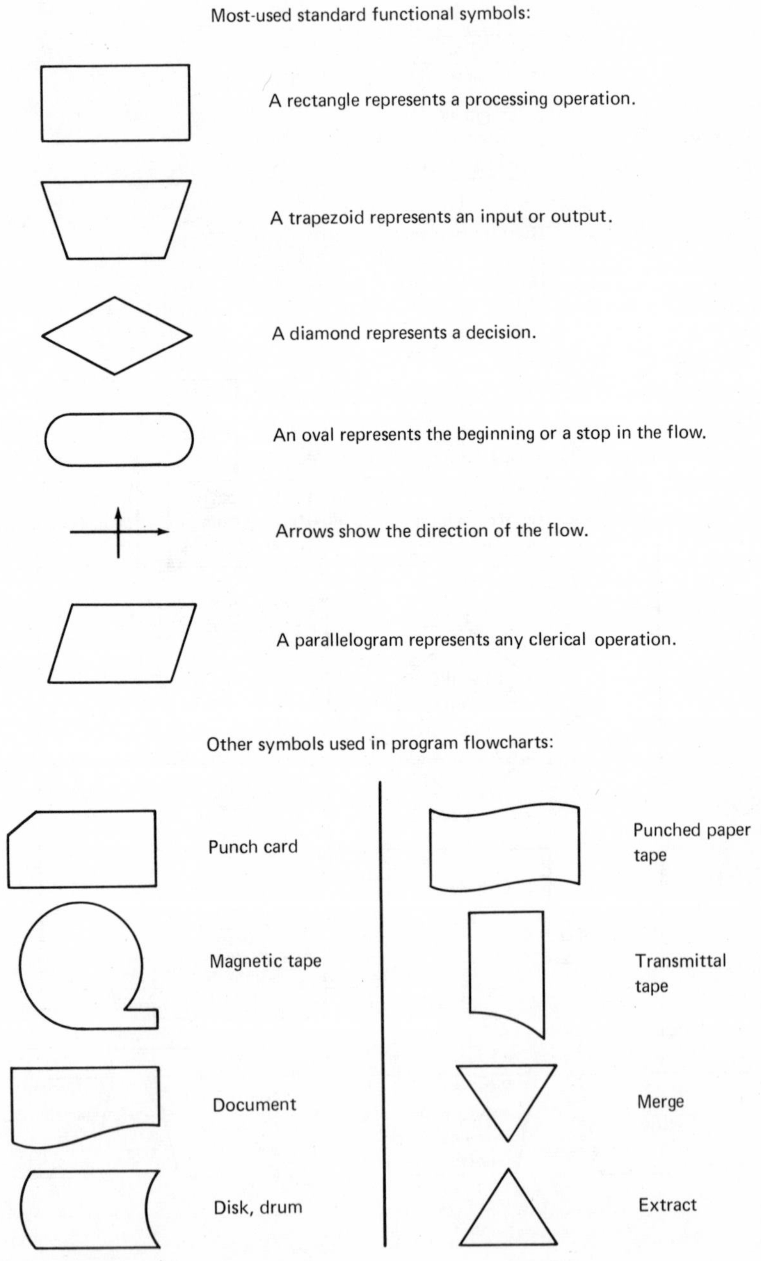

Most-used standard functional symbols:

A rectangle represents a processing operation.

A trapezoid represents an input or output.

A diamond represents a decision.

An oval represents the beginning or a stop in the flow.

Arrows show the direction of the flow.

A parallelogram represents any clerical operation.

Other symbols used in program flowcharts:

Punch card

Punched paper tape

Magnetic tape

Transmittal tape

Document

Merge

Disk, drum

Extract

subroutine has been called up, it searches for data with which to perform the calculation. Here is where the storage locations "100" and "101" come in, for they supply the data for the calculation. When the calculation is finished, the end statement of the subroutine searches for a place to put its answer in temporary memory. Here, the instruction "110" is used, for it indicates the place to store the result of the calculations.

It is often very difficult for a programmer to instruct the computer in binary language; so "assembly" programs are used. An "assembly" program is a basic computer program which translates words like "add" or "subtract," or any other language used by the programmer, into binary form and stores it in designated places in the computer.

Computer Program

A set of instructions or procedures (or "program") must be written in programming language for each computerized data system. For example, the flowchart shown in Figure 3–14 must be translated precisely and in detail into steps or operations involved in the processing of data. Sometimes this set of instructions, which is the program, is called a "source" program to differentiate it from an "assembly" program. These instructions are then run through the assembly process, which converts the source program instructions into machine-readable form (computer binary numbers) and stores them in the computer.

An instruction usually consists of at least two parts:

1. An operation that designates read, write, add, subtract, compare, move data, and so on.
2. An operand that designates the address of the information or device that is needed for the specified operation.

Several instructions from a program in this form could be represented as follows:

Operation	Operand
Select	Tape unit 200
Read	One record into storage positions 1000–1050
Clear and add	Quantity in storage location 1004 in accumulator
Subtract	Quantity in storage location 1005 from contents of accumulator
Store	Result in storage location 1051
Branch	To instruction in storage location 5004

The operation portion of each instruction indicates the operation to be performed. This information is coded according to the type of computer used and the nature of its assembly program. For example, in an IBM System/360, the letter A is interpreted as "add," the letter C is "compare," SIO as "start input/output," and TR as "translate." Other computers use different coding and numbers of characters or positions to define an operation.

The operand further defines or augments the function of the operation. For example, to perform arithmetic, the storage location of one of the factors involved is indicated. For input or output devices, the unit to be used is specified. For reading or writing, the area of storage for input or output records is either indicated or fixed by machine design.

The following are segments of the program for the payroll accounting system discussed earlier. The program is written in FORTRAN for an IBM System/360 computer:

Address	Operation	Operand
00208	Begin	
00210	Open	Time-cards
00212	Call	Subroutine-sort
00214	Open	Payroll history file
00216	Open	Tax and deductions file
00218	Open	Pay-grade level file
00220	Open	Update history file
00222	Read	Card N = XXX, if last card go to stop 242
00224	Read	Employee number, payscale
00226	Call	Match subroutine, if no match go to 232
00228	Call	Comp GR wage subroutine
00230	Call	Comp NE wage subroutine
00232	Print	Error
00234	Print	OT, reg hours worked subroutine 234
00236	Print	Paycheck subroutine 236
00238	Call	Update payroll history subroutine
00240	Go to	Next card step 222
00242	Stop	

Obviously computer programming involves much more than is discussed here, since computer programming is a complex and somewhat technical task. However, the above discussion should give an idea of the general nature of how the computer processor is instructed to perform its operations on the input data in order to produce the output data in the desired form.

Program Operation

After the program has been written and run through the assembly process, it is placed in temporary or permanent internal memory in binary or machine-readable form and is ready when called upon to process the input data, update the master file tape, and print the required reports and other output. The computer will execute the instructions in the program in sequence until the program comes to a halt.

Hardware and Software

In a computer data processing system, *hardware* refers to the actual physical machines—that is, the central processing unit (CPU), input/output devices, graphic display devices, storage units of any type, card reader/card punch devices, etc.; while *software* refers to written programs, the inputs and outputs (punched cards, magnetic tapes, or output documents), sub-routine programs, and all other documentation.

Converting a Data System for Operations to a Management Information System

A data system becomes a management information system when it generates data in a format and at a time useful for management decision making. While it is useful and valid to distinguish between data processing systems (which essentially perform operations, such as check writing or file updating,) and management information systems (data systems which generate information reports used in management decision making), in practice this distinction is not always clear-cut. Very often a manager will find that there are data processing systems already in existence which can be modified and expanded to produce management information reports.

The Little Publishing Company study discussed in Chapters One and Two contains an example of how a familiar existing data system (customer account maintenance) could be adapted and expanded to generate management information reports (sales analyses for marketing management).

Another example is the payroll accounting system described in this chapter, which is used principally for producing payroll checks and updated payroll files, and secondarily for generating a management information report (on weekly overtime expenses in each department.) In addition to the one management information report described here, others could certainly be produced—for example, a report comparing payroll expenses to budget by department and by pay classification monthly. The system would have to have the capacity to isolate and report on different worker level and salary range categories within each department, and to store the budgetary data supplied by management. Expanded coding would be needed, and allowance made for future file expansion and refinement of management reporting. In addition, care would have to be taken not to neglect operating aspects of the system, such as producing payroll checks on time.

In such situations, then, managers must work not only to develop precise definitions of management information requirements, but also to study the restraints and capabilities of the existing data system (input used, file structure, operations performed and their importance, the kind of output and its timing, etc.); if both an economical and effective management information system is to be developed from the existing system and its data bases.

Data Bank Management

Computer systems are capable of storing in a single place data used for a variety of operations and decisions, thus helping overcome the proliferation of duplicate files in those departments which make use of the data. In addition, as an operation grows, the sheer bulk of the files may become overwhelming in manual systems, where file folders, cabinets, and paper are used for recording and storing data. While computer systems may allow more manageable storage of such files, they sometimes make access to the files for retrieving data and updating files more difficult and costly.

The goal in setting up a data bank (or *data base*) then is two-fold:

1. Eliminating or minimizing data duplication, and redundancy.
2. Making file access as economical and efficient as possible.

At times, these can be conflicting objectives, since combining data files in a single data base can sometimes make access more difficult and limited than, for example, if a data file were maintained in the order used in preparing any one information report. For instance, in the manual version of the payroll accounting system the employee records were filed in the cabinet alphabetically by department, which made access for file updating easy (since employee time cards came into the payroll department grouped by department). In the computerized version of the system, on the other hand, the employee files might be maintained in social security number order for the entire company. Such a filing system would necessitate re-sorting the input data or random access to the employee files in order to use data in the data base in preparing department-by-department reports.

The advantages of having a single data base are numerous however. As seen in Figure 3–17, a single data bank can overcome duplication of files in different departments and enable fulfilling many different departments, needs using a single data source. In addition, such coordination of data filing and data reporting often provides new perspectives and insights into how departmental operations which have common data needs can be better integrated. At the same time, this exposure of overlapping operations and responsibilities during systems development work is one of the causes of the resistance of individual department managers to such work. Department managers are also often reluctant to give up control of their data files for other reasons—fearing a more limited access to them and additional restraints on the way they can make use of the files, or anticipating some loss of security of file data.

Effective and efficient multiple use of a data base depends on careful file construction, especially in identifying different kinds of data within each segment of the file. This point was emphasized in the data coding exercise in the Little Publishing Company study in Chapters One and Two, where careful data identification was necessary in order to be able to use the same data base for two distinct sets of departmental operating and reporting requirements: marketing and accounting. If care is not taken to build such multiple capabilities into the data base, department managers will sometimes set up their own duplicate files to avoid any loss of access to information.

In structuring common data bases, compromises are often necessary. Interdepartmental agreement is often needed on what is to be included in a particular file—for example, limits may be set on the number of digits in an identification code, thus requiring the omission of some data from the file. In other words, one department's needs may be superseded by more important needs of another department. Such was the case in the Little Publishing Company study. Compromises may also be needed in the timing of reports; so that departments may have to live with more restricted access to data, in order to achieve a more economical total system. The multiple-use factor also means that any error in the file data is more costly, since the error may be introduced into a variety of reports, instead of being reflected in only one department's reports.

Retrieving data from a single common data source can be a complex and expensive task, especially where the file is large. Very often in today's computer systems individual data files or items are accessed and retrieved directly. Where such direct retrieval is not possible, retrieval is done through scanning a complete file (the most expensive method) or through using a separately maintained *index* to indicate where the data is located or *linked records* to tie one record to another in some logical sequence.

A telephone book serves to illustrate the problems encountered in retrieving data from an integrated data base. A phone book represents a set of records pertaining to telephone users. Each of these records is made up of three or four units (or fields) of data: Name, Business or Occupation, Street Address, and Telephone Number. The name is the key element and the file is, of course, arranged in alphabetic sequence. It is not difficult to envision this file residing in computer random access storage—on disks, for example—and

FIGURE 3–17
Common Data Bank Functions for a Manufacturing Operation

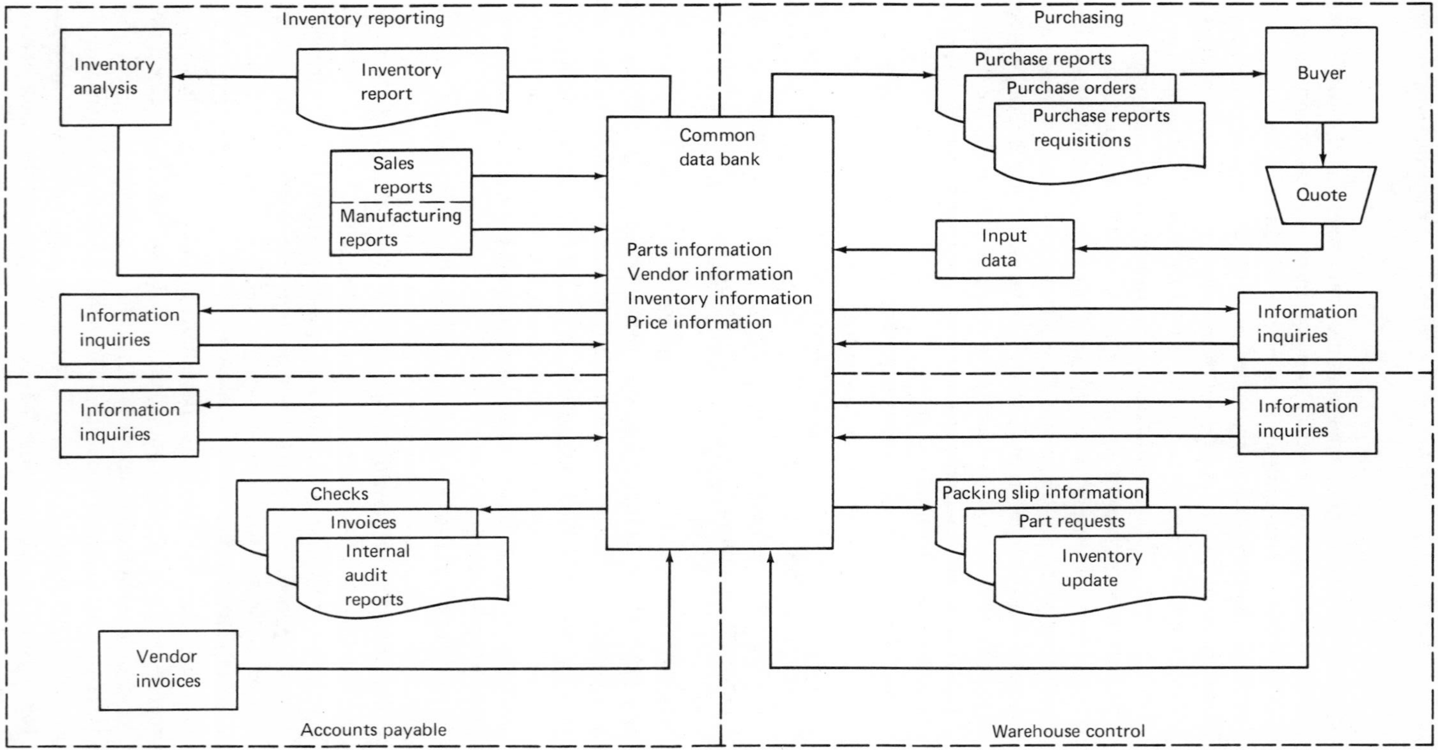

76

to pretend that, in retrieving information from the phone book, an individual acts as a computer program. If a person wishes to learn the telephone number of someone named Morris, he does not begin at the beginning of the book and turn page by page until he comes to Morris. Instead, he breaks the book open somewhere three-quarters from the beginning, since he is familiar enough with the file and its sequence to know approximately where to look for the letter M. From the page he has opened to, he then conducts a partial file scan until the desired line is located.

The logic of this retrieval approach can be programmed for a computer to follow by setting up a subsidiary file, or *index,* which shows the range of phone book pages for each letter of the alphabet. This index would be consulted first and then the appropriate section would be scanned for the name. This kind of retrieval is fairly easy, since the file is arranged or structured alphabetically by name.

A more difficult problem arises when one seeks *imbedded* data from the file, data such as:

1. Whose number is 322-7593?
2. Which names represent restaurants?
3. What are all the names with a 48 street address?

The telephone directory contains all of this information, but how does one locate it short of a total scan? The phone book solves the problem of restaurants by means of yellow pages, which represent a duplicate file of part of the same records organized by a different key or structure—occupation or business. In a computer system, such complete record duplication would be unnecessary, since the occupation or business file would only need to contain the names of the restaurants but no street addresses or telephone numbers, which can be extracted by going back to the name records. This system of reference is called *record linkage* or *chaining,* since the contents of one record point or lead to the location of another record.

If the telephone number were frequently a significant starting point in a search for information, an index to telephone numbers could be constructed; that is, all pages in which the prefix 322 appears could be listed in a separate record, with similar records for all other prefixes. This would create another small subsidiary file to be consulted for purposes of limiting file search. Obviously, a more extensive index would limit the search still further, but at a greater cost for file creation and maintenance. A search beginning with an address could be solved in the same way.

It can be seen that if a file is to serve many uses, including unspecified future ones, many aspects of file organization and data retrieval must be considered. In addition, the objective of eliminating duplications must be compromised to some extent at times so that various indices, new chain fields in existing records, and subsidiary record files must be created.

Someone unfamiliar with computer systems might have the impression that the tremendous speed of a computer enables it to find anything in a file as quick as lightning, so that as long as data are identified there is no need for additional aids. Why then are such retrieval aids needed? Because even microseconds (.000001 second) add up. If a Manhattan phone directory with just under one million names were to be scanned from a disk file, assuming that each record were accessed individually (rather than in blocks of records), the total search time would amount to thirteen hours at fifty milliseconds (.05 second) per access cycle.

To summarize:

1. The scope and costliness of file maintenance in general should not be underestimated.

2. When implementing a single common data base, organizational problems will arise which may have to be resolved by higher management.

3. A compromise or trade-off must be sought between efficiency of file storage and the efficiency of data retrieval.

4. A manager must take the time to study the data base design, if he hopes to have the flexibility to get the reports he needs now or expects to need in the future. If the data needed is not adequately identified in the file or if retrieval aids are not established, he may face insurmountable obstacles in getting the information reports he needs.

Types of Computer-Based Applications

Further insight into data processing systems can be gained from examining the three basic approaches to processing data in computer systems: batch processing, real-time, and decision-making applications.

Batch Processing

Batch processing is the most prevalent type of processing now in use. It involves cyclical processing of input data in batches or groups. For example, in the payroll accounting system, all employee time cards or payroll registers are processed together at the end of the week, so that all data is supplied at one time through the input device. The central processing unit (CPU) sequences through programmed instructions, takes the input data (hours worked) as needed and uses it to compute the output (wages and overtime reports). After the paychecks (output) are printed, all historical employee files are updated (external storage). In other words, the CPU sequences through all the computations for all the data that is supplied at one time, and error lists are printed and corrections are made before the next week's processing is undertaken.

Real Time

Generally, this type of application makes use of a remote terminal connected directly (on-line) with a central data processing unit. An example of this type of processing is an airlines reservation system, which permits an inquiry to be made at a reservations desk while the customer is waiting.

Real-time systems or applications have three characteristics:

1. The data is on-line, that is, on an immediately accessible disc or other type of random access data storage.
2. Data is updated as events happen.
3. The computer can be questioned from remote terminals or other input/output devices at points distant from the central processing unit.

The use of this type of application in business is usually limited to one function, such as the airline reservation system. However, in terms of this one function capability, these systems may make use of both batch processing and real-time processing, while data is entered at the central processing unit or from remote terminals.

Decision-Making Applications

Computer systems can also be used to directly assist management in evaluating alternative courses of action and in making decisions.

The largest decision-making applications in use today are military systems which make decisions using the logic of a computer system to effect the operation of a space vehicle or missile. The Apollo moonshots contain examples of how computer decisions are made to land the moon vehicle or to change the trajectory of the space module in its flight to the moon.

Business has not progressed as rapidly in decision-making applications, since it is not easy to define decision rules and constraints at higher management levels and since other applications provide larger and more immediate payoffs. One type of decision-assisting application used today in business is simulation. Simulation enables a manager to ask the computer "What if. . . ?" questions and so determine the consequences of proposed courses of action more accurately. For example, computer models have been developed of the movement of air traffic in and out of an air terminal. A planner using such a model can sit at a terminal and input changes in schedules or in the number of loading/unloading stations at a terminal to study the impact of each change on waiting time, delays, and the like, as he studies his specific decision problem. Other examples of the use of computer simulation are found in Chapters Eight and Twelve.

Summary
Conclusion

This chapter has discussed data processing systems from manual ones through today's modern EDP systems. The five basic components or functions in each type of system are: input, processing, storage, control or procedures, and output. A summary of the differences in these areas among the three types of data processing systems discussed in this chapter is given in Table 3–1.

Of particular importance to managers involved in information systems development is an understanding of how computerized information systems are developed. Input definition, output design (including specifying report content, format, and timing), and especially file design and structure are all development areas in which a manager can and should participate, if he is to have an information system which effectively meets his decision-making needs.

If left to his own devices, a systems technician may design a system more suitable to the hardware (machines) and software (computer programs) restraints (or to what the technician *thinks* are management needs) than to the actual needs of the manager. The systems analyst cannot be aware of all the daily workings of a particular management function and has to rely on the user (operating management) for direction in his design and development efforts. The user must participate in information systems design, since he is the one who must control and manage the business and since he knows the job best.

Management should use a computer system as a tool for meeting their decision requirements. To do so, they must become involved in developing detail specifications and format design. If this is not done, the computer system may just manage them.

TEXT DISCUSSION QUESTIONS

1. Describe the basic components of a data processing system and their functions.
2. Describe three basic types of data processing systems. Discuss the similarities and differences of the components in each of these types of systems.

TABLE 3–1

Systems Comparison

Component	Manual System	Payroll Application Punched Card (Electromechanical)	EDP System
Input	Time sheet	Punched card	Punch card or remote terminal
Processor	Payroll clerk with calculator	Prewired boards that move data: limited calculation capacity	Central processing unit with built in logic and capacity for complex calculations
Storage			
Internal	Work area	Limited counter storage	Core storage
External	File cabinets	Card files	Disk, magnetic tape
Procedure			
Control	Procedure manual	Operator manual with job steps	Programmed logic in storage
Output	Manual typing of checks Manual check register	Pre-printed checks Tab listings Card files	Pre-printed checks Master file automatically updated

3. Describe the functions of a central processing unit in a computer-based data processing system.

4. Describe the forms which inputs and outputs may take in EDP systems.

5. Describe the functions of internal storage and external storage in EDP systems. What types of devices are used for external storage? What is direct access; sequential access?

6. Describe the function of the program in an EDP system.

7. Outline the steps involved in developing a computer-based data processing system.

8. Discuss the ways in which a manager might become involved in each phase of this development, when the system is to be used to generate management information reports.

9. Discuss the importance of the file design and the program flowchart with respect to the management information system.

10. Describe the two key objectives important in developing data bases or data banks. Discuss the ways in which these two objectives can come into conflict.

11. Why are managers sometimes reluctant to have a single, common computerized data base for data important to their operation?

12. Describe those areas to which a manager should pay particular attention when common computerized data bases are being developed. Why is it so important for a manager to anticipate future information reporting requirements at the time the data base is being developed?

13. Describe the different methods of retrieving data from computerized data bases and the impact they can have on management information reporting.

Case Study Exercises

System Development Exercise

Following the steps outlined in the "developing" section of this chapter, convert the following manual system to a computer-based system. Be certain to include at least the following: system description, system flowchart, input format design, output format design, file design, and program flowchart.

An order is received from a customer or a salesman. The order is registered by a clerk who records the date, order number, name of customer, items ordered, quantities, and price on a sales spread sheet. The order goes to the credit department for a credit check. The order then is passed to an analysis clerk who determines what departments will require working copies to enable the order to be filled. The order is recopied by a typist to a multipart form to provide the required working copies.

When the order has been filled, a shipping department copy (with quantity and weight shipped, freight charges, etc.) is returned to the office for pricing. A clerk checks prices against a price book and writes them in. Another clerk extends cost and selling prices, applies discounts, and calculates the net total of the order.

All the data must now be copied once again by the typist preparing the finished invoice. A seven-part form is used to furnish invoice copies to the customer and to the departments directly affected by the order.

A clerk then prepares an adding machine control tape, totaling the invoice amounts of this and other orders billed during the day. This tape and the accounts receivable copies are sent to the accounting department for posting.

Hollis Corporation

Hollis Corporation is a small chemical company that produces two similar industrial solvents which are made from three raw chemicals in the following proportions:

		Raw Material		
		#1	#2	#3
Solvent	#1	50%	25%	25%
	#2	30%	15%	55%

Process

Raw materials #1 and #2 are solids and #3 is a liquid. There are two phases to the mixing process. First raw materials #1 and #2 are added together by a simple mixing process in the ratio of five to three. The resulting mixture, which is the same for both solvents (called Mix 5:3), is then stored in large bins until ready for phase two. Phase two requires that raw material #3 be heated to a high temperature and then added to Mix 5:3 in the correct proportion called for. Finally, it is moved to another storage unit for one week. After one week, each vat is tested by the Chem lab for the correctness of the mixture. Each product is then ready for shipment and is stored in the warehouse (see Figure 3–18).

FIGURE 3–18

The Manufacturing Operation
of Hollis Corporation

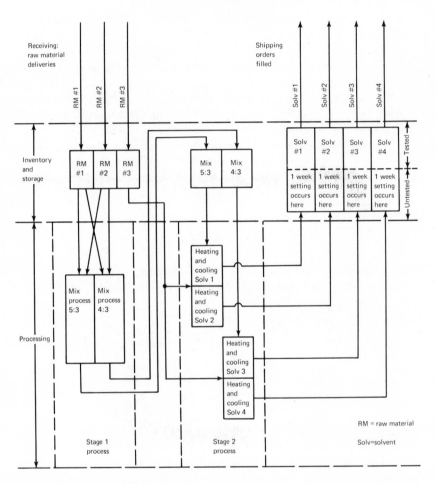

Inventory Control

At present, due to the low volume of business, only one stock clerk is needed for inventory control. He keeps all records in his journal ledger. All shipments in and out of raw materials and finished goods are by railroad cars which unload and load at the warehouse platform. All the records of deliveries and shipments are taken from bills of lading supplied by the railroad. All deliveries for inventory are checked upon receipt and stored in standard storage bins and vats. All shortages and overages are so noted by the stock clerk in his ledger.

The stock clerk is also responsible for the flow of raw materials through the process. Thus, he keeps a separate ledger for partially finished products— e.g. Mix 5:3 and untested solvents #1 and #2. To keep control of these, he makes daily checks in all parts of the warehouse to take an actual physical count. Also, he receives daily reports on all activities of the Chem lab since he cannot tell the difference between untested and tested finished solvents. In addition to this, he also receives a signed requisition from the foreman anytime the foreman takes out of stock any raw material for use in the process. The foreman also reports to him the in-process storage at the end of each phase of the process.

From reports of the foreman of requisitions from stock and in-process inventory, he can calculate the amount of waste, which can occur at stages one and two, or after testing.

The shipping department also sends to him copies of all orders filled and shipped each day.

Sales

Sales of the solvents are made only in orders as large as or larger than a railroad tank car. These are sold to major industrial users on the eastern coast of the United States.

Salesmen are employed at five regional offices. These salesmen provide daily reports concerning new orders. These reports are mailed daily for routine orders and are telephoned in immediately for rush orders. Some typical information that the salesmen will supply is:

1. Order number and date.
2. Salesman and region.
3. Items and quantities.
4. Date required.
5. Method of shipment and route.

This information is made available to the management of Hollis Corporation in order for them to make a profitability analysis. These reports are also made available to the production manager so that he may determine if enough stock of the raw materials is available and whether it is time to reorder.

Production Scheduling

The production manager is responsible for scheduling all production. Thus, he receives from the stock clerk at the end of each day a summary of raw materials inventories, in-process inventories and finished goods inventories. Each day, all new sales orders are also sent to him. He then schedules production runs with the following conditions in mind:

1. New orders may be filled from finished goods or in-process goods which are not allocated to present orders.
2. New orders may be filled by processing raw materials from raw materials inventories; however, he may only mix in quantities greater than one vat and one bin.
3. He must also consider his limited storage space for in-process and finished goods inventories.
4. Largest orders are processed first. Whatever is left over is applied to smaller orders.

Recently, the Hollis Corporation received a large contract to produce solvents #1 and #2 and also two new solvents #3 and #4 which are produced in exactly the same way as solvents #1 and #2, except that proportions are as follows:

		Raw Material		
		#1	#2	#3
Solvent	#3	45%	15%	40%
	#4	60%	20%	20%

The new in-process product at the end of the first phase is called Mix 4:3; at the end of the second phase, these solvents must also remain a week before testing.

Due to the size of the contract and the nature of the control needed, the Hollis Corporation has decided to expand its facilities at its present site and to install a computer-based inventory control EDP system in place of the present manual system.

Assignment

1. Following the steps outlined in the chapter, convert the above manual inventory control system to an EDP system. Be certain to include each of the following in the development of the system.
   a) System description
   b) System flowchart
   c) Input requirements
   d) Output requirements
   e) File design
2. Using the output requirements stated in the previous question, provide a

management information report to the production manager which would detail the daily inventory levels for each step of the chemical process and a weekly sales summary for top management's review. Be sure to provide report formats for each of these two reports.

Ajax Manufacturing Company

The Ajax Manufacturing Co. is a small company which produces relatively few diversified products, which may be grouped into two general categories: electronics subassemblies and mechanical subassemblies. The Ajax Manufacturing Company has recently been bought by a large conglomerate. After evaluating the company for six months, the parent corporation has noted the following:

1) The electronics consist of small transistor subassemblies which are produced for use by a large electronics firm in their equipment. The mechanical subassemblies are metal enclosures which are produced for use by a large power tool manufacturer. There are thirty different transistor subassemblies and fifteen different metal enclosures.

2) The large volume of goods produced lends itself to a totally integrated computer-based EDP manufacturing information and control system.

3) The major stumbling block to this type of system is the fact that the electronics subassemblies are still being hand-tested by technicians and visually inspected by inspectors. The inspectors also must do double duty and inspect the mechanical subassemblies. Each test and inspection must be accompanied by the various paperwork (test procedures and specifications).

4) The parent corporation has received permission from all labor unions involved to install automated testing and inspection equipment for both types of subassemblies. This would require that technicians only test or rework items rejected by the automated system. Inspectors would now only have to inspect the electronics subassemblies before test and mechanical subassemblies when they fail automatic inspection. Other duties would be to write reports only on rejected items.

5) Due to the load on the parent corporation's central data bank, the above system would have to be a separate and distinct information system which could draw information from the central data bank, but would not contribute any information to the data bank. All information and documents used now are already in the data bank.

6) In order to ease the workload on the inspectors and electrical testers, the parent corporation has developed the computer-based inspection and testing information system shown in figures 3–19 and 3–20.

FIGURE 3–19

Flowchart for a Computer-Based Inspection and Testing Information System

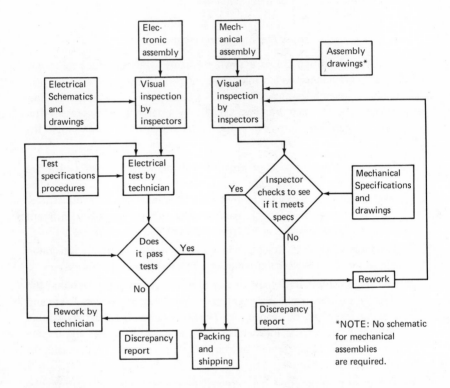

The basic idea of the system would be to automate the testing and the inspections. The inspectors would then be free to inspect only failed items. Technicians would then be free to rework and test only failed items. Of course, all information needed would be fed directly into the CPU for use in the automated system. But where the inspectors and technicians are now operating manually, management feels that they might make use of video terminals to obtain all information needed to inspect or test any item. This information would come from the same data bank that the CPU would be using—i.e., External Storage (Mag-Tape) On-line (see Figure 3–20).

The information needed would be

A. Electrical Subassemblies

   Thirty Drawings—Mechanical Assembly Instructions

   Thirty Schematics—Final Assembly

FIGURE 3–20

A Computer-Based Inspection and Testing Information System

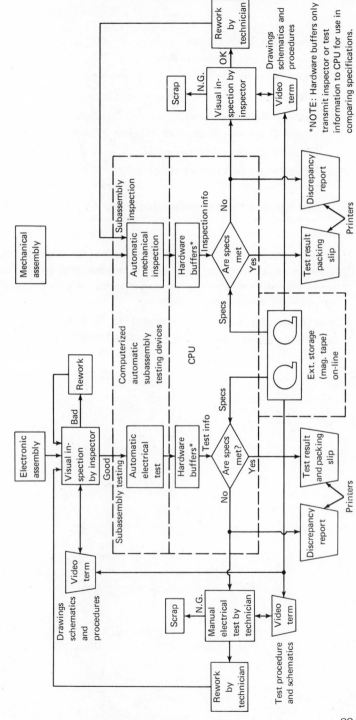

Thirty Test Specifications

Thirty Test and Inspection Procedures

Thirty Part List

One Standard Electronic Components Catalog

B. Mechanical Subassemblies

Fifteen Drawings—Mechanical Assembly Procedures

Fifteen Inspection Requirements

Fifteen Inspection Procedures

Fifteen Parts Lists

One Standard Metal Components Catalog

Assignment

1. Develop a document identification system that could be used by either an inspector or a technician at a remote terminal that would facilitate the acquisition of the above-listed documented information with just the insertion of a single coded number.

2. How could this system be extended to be helpful in manufacturing operations, quality control, and production scheduling?

Financial Information Systems for Corporate Management

A COMPANY'S PRESIDENT IS RESPONSIBLE TO THE OWNERS FOR PRO-
tecting and earning a return on their investment in the company. This
primary financial responsibility accounts for the importance and wide-
spread use of accounting and financial information systems in business, since
such information systems record and provide control over the financial results
of company operations.

Although accounting and finance-oriented information systems are heavily
relied on by corporate management, they are not the only information
systems needed and used by company managers. Corporate managers have
overall responsibility for the operating activities which affect earnings, and
these activities are often planned for and monitored most effectively by
nonaccounting information systems.

These other types of information systems are discussed in later chapters,
where other kinds of management jobs are discussed. This chapter concerns
only accounting and financial information systems, the traditional information systems used in fulfilling basic corporate management responsibilities
and how they can be made more efficient.

4

Managing Company Assets,
Income, and Expenses

In fulfilling primary financial responsibilities to company owners, corporate management must determine how the company did financially in the past period, project future financial results, evaluate manager, product and operations division performance, determine how best to invest capital through evaluating the probable return on proposed courses of action, monitor funds usage, and the like. Accounting and financial management are the management areas traditionally delegated the task of assisting corporate managers in fulfilling their primary financial responsibilities to company owners.

The American Institute of Certified Public Accountants defines *accounting* as "the art of recording, classifying and summarizing in a significant manner and in terms of money, transactions and events which are, in part at least, of a financial character, and interpreting the results thereof."

The accounting job thus can be divided into two areas, financial and management accounting. Financial accounting generally involves the process of keeping a company's books and reporting historical financial data on operating results; whereas management accounting requires estimates of future financial performance—that is, financial budgeting—and then later analysis of actual performance in relation to these budgets or estimates.

Financial management involves providing the funds which the business needs to achieve its objectives, at the most reasonable terms, and monitor the use of these funds within the business. In carrying out this job, a financial manager needs to determine what funds are needed, the ways in which these funds can be obtained (both from inside and from outside the company), and, where necessary, how excess funds are to be invested. He is also responsible for seeing to it that company funds are allocated and used effectively and efficiently.

While accounting and financial managers often have additional, related responsibilities—such as administering insurance—the discussion in this chapter is limited to the basic accounting and financial functions involved in providing information to company managers.

Questions to be Answered, Decisions to be Made, and Information to be Provided

In fulfilling his primary financial responsibilities, a company president necessarily asks the question "How did the company do in the latest period?" The answer is needed in monetary terms, which in general tell the president and owners how much money their company made and what the financial condition of the company is. The information needed to answer this question is historical financial information, and would include sales and expense figures on all operations within the company, as well as data on the status of each company asset and liability.

At the same time, company management will be judging the quality of performance in different areas of operations ("How good were the results?") and searching for ways to improve operations. Such decisions require first, information on standards—estimates of what the cost and sales should have been in the different areas, for example—and second, comparisons between performance results and standards which highlight any performance significant above or below these standards. If the financial estimates or projections are used further to judge individual manager performance, the breakdowns of the financial data will need to conform to key manager responsibility areas.

In studying historical financial information, company management will question in detail why profits and costs were what they were and how they might be improved. Answering these questions requires information breakdowns showing which areas of the operation incurred what costs, which products and product lines earned profits and what those profits were—that is, relevant unit breakdowns of cost, sales and earnings data.

Company managers are also required to answer many "What if?" questions: for example, "What will be the impact on profits and costs of my producing or selling added quantities of specific products?" The answers to such questions, obtained through profitability and cost analyses, provide guidance as to the most profitable courses of action in a manager's operational decision making.

In addition to historical information on past financial results and estimates of future performance, a company manager will also need information on the sources and uses of funds within the company during the latest period, the present cash position, and projections of future cash needs, as well as such external information as current and projected interest rates and the availability of capital. Information is also needed on how capital was employed in producing company earnings, since financial results have to be analyzed to determine the efficiency of capital usage.

Supporting Information Systems: An Overview

A wide range of accounting and financial reporting systems are used by corporate managers in carrying out their basic job responsibilities. The following sections discuss the most commonly encountered systems.

Determining Overall Asset and Income Performance Results

In order to provide the above historical financial information required by corporate management, a basic accounting data collection and processing system is needed. All companies have such a basic accounting system, which begins with the recording of all transactions in the company's *journal,* a chronological record of transactions showing the names of the accounts that are to be debited or credited, the amounts of the debits and credits, and any useful supplementary information about the transaction. These transactions are then recorded or "posted" in the company's *ledger,* which contains a separate account for each item on the balance sheet and income statement. At the end of an accounting period, some adjusting entires must be made and certain accounts closed, so that accounts can be brought up to date and accurate statements may be prepared. A trial balance is run, preliminary income statement and balance sheet work sheets are developed, and the final statements are prepared.

The summary of the current financial condition of a company is called a *balance sheet*. It shows what the company has in the way of assets (cash, accounts due, buildings, machinery, etc.) and what the company owes or is liable for (to suppliers, the government, banks, investors, owners, etc.). The summary of company sales, expenses and earnings is called an *income or profit and loss statement*. Examples of each are given in Figures 4–1 and 4–2.

These two information reports for management (and their supporting documents) will answer company management's primary questions about financial results of operations during the latest period and the financial condition of the company, if the information breakdown is sufficiently detailed and has taken into account the unique operating characteristics of the company.

FIGURE 4–1

XYZ Company

Comparative Income Statement

For the Year Ending December 31, 1973

	Amount		Percent of net sales		Dollar increase (decrease)	Percent increase (decrease)
	1973	1972	1973	1972		
Sales	$700,000	$500,000	100	100	$200,000	40
Less: cost of goods sold	350,000	290,000	50	58	60,000	21
Gross margin on sales	$350,000	$210,000	50	42	$140,000	66
Operating expenses						
Selling expenses						
Salesmen's salaries	70,000	60,000	10	12	10,000	17
Advertising	30,000	20,000	4	4	10,000	50
Delivery expense	10,000	8,000	1	2	2,000	25
Total selling expenses	$110,000	$ 88,000	15	18	$ 22,000	25
General and administrative expense						
General salaries	25,000	25,000	4	5	–	–
Rent of office	5,000	5,000	1	1	–	–
Total general and administrative expense	$ 30,000	$ 30,000	5	6	–	–
Total operating expenses	$140,000	$118,000	20	24	$ 22,000	19
Gross operating profit	$210,000	$ 92,000	30	18	$118,000	128
Less: depreciation	5,000	5,000	1	1	–	–
Net operating profit	$205,000	$ 87,000	29	17	$118,000	136
Other income: rent	20,000	–	3	–	20,000	–
Gross income	$225,000	$ 87,000	32	17	$138,000	159
Other expenses: interest	5,000	5,000	1	1	–	–
Profit before income taxes	$220,000	$ 82,000	31	16	$138,000	168
Provision for income taxes	110,000	36,000	15.7	7	74,000	206
Net income	$110,000	$ 46,000	15.7	9	$ 64,000	139

FIGURE 4–2

ABC Company
Balance Sheet
January 31, 1974

ASSETS	Actual	Budget	Over (Under)
Current assets:			
Cash on hand and in banks	$ 229,340	$ 245,360	($16,020)
Accounts receivable	358,300	373,000	(14,700)
Allowance for doubtful accounts	(21,788)	(22,400)	612
Inventories at standard cost:			
Direct materials	238,600	219,000	19,600
Finished parts	100,400	100,400	
Work in process	54,400	54,400	
Finished product	559,870	544,200	15,670
Prepaid expenses and deferred charges:			
Insurance			
Excess of standard cost in finished product inventory over current standard	3,150	3,500	(350)
Deferred advertising	4,500	4,500	
Total current assets	$1,526,772	$1,521,960	$ 4,812
Mixed assets:			
Machinery and equipment	$1,000,000	$1,000,000	
Depreciation taken to date	(210,000)	(210,000)	
Buildings	800,000	800,000	
Depreciation taken to date	(102,000)	(102,000)	
Land	100,000	100,000	
Total fixed assets	$1,588,000	$1,588,000	
Total assets	$3,114,772	$3,109,960	$ 4,812
LIABILITIES			
Current liabilities:			
Accounts payable	$ 287,500	$ 271,500	$16,000
Dividends payable			
Accrued sales commissions	17,682	18,600	(918)
Federal income tax accrued	227,995	233,130	(5,135)
Real estate taxes accrued	21,300	21,300	
Accrued interest on mortgage	5,000	5,000	

FIGURE 4-2 (*Continued*)

LIABILITIES	Actual	Budget	Over (Under)
Mortgage payable, current installment	12,000	12,000	
Accrued interest on demand note			
Note payable			
Total current liabilities	$ 571,477	$ 561,530	$ 9,947
Long-term debt, mortgage payable	$ 228,000	$ 228,000	
Total liabilities	$ 799,477	$ 789,530	$ 9,947
CAPITAL			
Capital stock, 20,000 shares, common, par $100	$2,000,000	$2,000,000	
Retained earnings	315,295	320,430	($ 5,135)
Total capital	$2,315,295	$2,320,430	($ 5,135)
Total liabilities and capital	$3,114,772	$3,109,960	$ 4,812

Because companies differ in the ways they are organized and the kinds of business environment in which they operate, the details of income statements and balance sheets will vary in form and content from company to company, even though their overall pattern remains the same. For example, magazine publishers may show as money owed subscribers (a liability) subscription payments for magazine copies to be delivered the following year. In addition, within the same company, income statements and balance sheets will vary according to the management information purposes they serve. For example, the income statement for tax purposes may show different depreciation expense figures from that prepared for stockholders, in order to have the lowest possible tax expense, but still show a more realistic earnings picture to stockholders.

When used to explore the question of how good the performance reported on was, these basic financial accounting reports are often developed in greater detail, and combined and compared with other reports.

One of the most familiar kind of comparisons is that found in company annual reports—comparisons to the prior year's performance. These comparative reports often present both a horizontal and a vertical analysis. Figure 4-1 gives an example of such a comparison. The vertical analysis translates the figures for any given year into percentages to give the relative importance of each item. The horizontal analysis provides information on trends from period to period, by showing both the dollar amount of change and the relative increase or decrease in importance of the item. Both vertical and horizontal comparative analyses are used in all types of financial reports for management, where it appears they will facilitate the manager's job. Managers, however, rarely use historical standards as the sole yardstick against which to judge performance.

Planning and Controlling Financial Performance: The Budgetary System

Rather than studying comparisons of historical figures, managers focus on comparing performance against a planning standard—that is, a figure based on planned expectations of what management feels should happen. Budgets (quantified plans) are the most familiar kinds of financial planning standards.

Budgets can be made for all aspects of a company's operations. Those budgets prepared for overall income and asset reporting are called *pro forma* income statements and balance sheets and take the form of projections of the accounts in these statements for as many years into the future as desired. An example of a comparative report based on a *pro forma* (budget) balance sheet is given in Figure 4—2. In this report, horizontal analysis is used to study the variances of performance results from standards.

Budgets are not, however, limited to income statements and balance sheets. As is seen later in this section, *pro forma* cash flow statements are needed, along with supporting capital outlay budgets, for financial management; cost accounting information systems make use of estimates of expected costs against which to measure performance; and profitability and responsibility accounting systems for management require budgetary cost and sales projections, if the performance evaluations are to be meaningful.

In preparing budgets, a balance is struck between setting goals that are too easily attainable and establishing those that are too difficult to achieve. If budget standards are not reasonably attainable, there may be inefficient and frustrating employee performance. On the other hand, budget standards that are too easily attainable are also inefficient, since they can lead to lower performance than is possible. Both these extremes cause the budget to lose much of its effectiveness as a planning and control tool. In order to obtain efficient and productive performance, budget goals should be attainable and yet challenging.

One method for achieving this balance is the use of a flexible budget. Under a fixed budget, goals become meaningless as soon as the operating level varies from the one assumed in preparing the budget. A flexible budget is intended to provide attainable goals regardless of the operating level, by setting different budget figures for different levels of operation. For example, a department might establish budget figures for operations at 100 percent of capacity, 95 percent of capacity, 90 percent of capacity and so on. Figure 4—3 gives in summary form a flexible budget for manufacturing costs for the ABC Company under different levels of production.

FIGURE 4–3

ABC Company
Manufacturing Cost Budget

Number of items produced	*100,000*	*150,000*	*175,000*	*200,000*
Manufacturing costs:				
Materials	$ 50,000	$ 75,000	$ 87,500	$100,000
Direct labor	25,000	37,500	43,750	50,000
Supervision	10,000	12,000	14,000	16,000
Maintenance	5,000	6,000	6,500	7,000
Depreciation	20,000	20,000	20,000	20,000
Other overhead	10,000	10,000	12,000	13,000
Total manufacturing costs	$120,000	$160,000	$183,750	$206,000
Cost per item produced	$1.20	$1.07	$1.05	$1.03

Budgetary review practices vary from company to company. Budgets for individual operations may be reviewed quarterly, monthly, or even weekly; but whatever the time period, budget revision should be kept at a minimum, since frequent changes in standards undercut their validity and create the feeling that all company standards are poorly conceived and so valueless criteria for measuring performance. Budgets are not immutable, however, and budgetary practices should be reexamined constantly, for it is possible that continual variances from budget may be caused by poor budgeting rather than by below standard operating performance.

While there are general ground rules for budget preparation, no two companies seem to develop their overall budgets in exactly the same way. In many large companies, major departments and divisions are asked to submit five-year budgets, with supporting plans, to a control section every year. These five-year budgets and plans are broken down into yearly segments, except for the first year which is broken down into monthly or quarterly segments. The control or planning section normally provides managers with information needed for preparing these budgets, such as anticipated economic and market changes, overall sales forecasts, restrictions on spending, and overall corporate objectives and policies. There is usually considerable interaction between the control section, the various planning managers and the planning director concerning major factors affecting the plan and its budget, and many adjustments are made on the basis of this exchange of information.

This first developmental stage results in a plan and budget which the department or division manager believes are reasonable, and which he believes the managers above him will find reasonable. Then, another round of development occurs, as pressures come from higher management to reach for higher sales goals, cut costs, or change the direction of a unit's efforts. A final plan and budget are agreed upon at this point.

There are many variations in this process. In some companies, the control section and higher management develop plans and their budget quantifications in more detail for sub-managers, and sub-managers are given less freedom to do their own planning. In general, this practice will hurt planning and budgeting, but it may be justified by the particular corporation's circumstances. Many companies ask for one-year instead of five-year plans and budgets, others revise current budgets quarterly and five-year plans annually, and still others vary the requirements by level of management.

Whatever budgetary process is followed, it is important that there be an interaction in the preliminary stages between the budget manager and the managers who are developing and carrying out the budgets. Through this interaction, the budgets created will be more realistic and will have a greater utility to the entire company.

Other Types of Comparative Financial Reporting Systems

In addition to information on overall company financial results for management, financial and accounting systems also provide detailed information on costs and profits for different product and management areas within a company. The most familiar financial information systems which give management these detailed breakdowns are cost accounting, responsibility accounting, and profitability accounting systems. These systems (or subsystems as they are sometimes called, since they are integral parts of the overall financial and management accounting systems) make use of comparisons of budgetary and actual result information and enable management to analyze variances.

Cost Accounting Systems. A cost accounting information system is concerned with the proper recording, reporting, and analysis of the various costs incurred in the operation of an enterprise. The purpose of cost accounting is to inform management promptly of the cost of producing an article or rendering a particular service.

Cost accounting was first developed and used for finding the unit manufacturing costs of products. The principle aim was to get inventory values for presentation of financial accounting statements. This is still an important aim, for accurate inventory valuation depends on finding a valid unit cost for each type of product. In addition, however, unit costs are important in budgeting, in pricing, and in other management decision areas, so that cost accounting techniques of unit costing are used in calculating costs in many operating areas.

Cost accounting can be divided into *actual* and *standard* cost systems. One deals with costs that have actually been incurred, and the other deals with costs that should have been incurred.

There are two basic *actual* cost accounting systems, job-order costing and process costing. Job-order costing suits industries that manufacture products whose specifications vary from lot to lot or job to job and which do not all pass through the same manufacturing process; whereas process costing suits industries that manufacture uniform products that pass through the same manufacturing process. The job-order cost system, where each job represents different manufacturing specifications, involves the accumulation and attachment of costs (direct materials, direct labor, and manufacturing overhead) to jobs or batches of products. The process cost system, where uniform products are manufactured, involves the collection of production costs for a specified period of time, by the departments, processes, or cost centers through which products flow.

Under the job-order cost system, costs are collected for each job. These costs (material, labor, and overhead) are recorded as the job moves through the various departments in the company. Figure 4–4 gives a simplified example of a job cost sheet for one of the products produced at the XYZ Company.

When each job is completed, the costs are totalled. The total on the job cost sheet is the basis for the entry transferring the product from goods in process to finished goods inventory; and when the product is sold, this same

FIGURE 4–4

XYZ Company

Job Cost Sheet

Job No.	101					Customer			Acme
Item	Machine Tool A					Quantity			1
Date Begun	6/4/74					Date Completed			6/6/74

Materials			Labor			Overhead			
	Req.			Time					
Date	No.	Amt.	Date	Ticket	Amt.	Date	Dept.	Rate	Amt.
6/4	1006	$22.60	6/4	10687	$8.00	6/4	Assem-bly	125% of	$10.00
			6/5	10705	9.00	6/5	Assem-bly	direct labor	11.25
	Total	$22.60		Total	$17.00		Total		$21.25

cost is the basis for the entry transferring the product from finished goods inventory to cost of goods sold.

In the process cost accounting system, emphasis is placed on production for a given period; a day, a week, or a month. This period of time is comparable to the job or lot in a job-order cost system. Material, labor, and manufacturing overhead costs are accumulated and recorded by departments or processes on a time basis, not on a job basis. At the end of the given period of time, all costs are totalled and this total is divided by the number of units produced to arrive at the cost per unit.

Many companies use both job-order and process cost systems for their product costing. For example, a company manufacturing a railway car built according to a customer's specifications uses a job-order cost method to collect costs per railway car. However, the multiple small metal stampings required are manufactured in a department which uses fast and repetitive stamping machines. The costs of these stampings are accumulated by a process cost system.

In an *actual* job-order and process system, product units are charged with the actual costs incurred in their production. Most cost accounting systems, in addition, also calculate the cost of product units that should have been incurred. Such systems are called *standard* cost systems and are used for budgetary comparisons.

Under a standard cost system, standard or estimated costs are established in advance of actual production for such items as direct materials, direct labor, and manufacturing overhead. These standard costs are usually established by the cost accounting department working with operating managers, and are based on historical costs and known future events, such as rises in wage rates and material costs. Both the standard cost and the actual cost of production, as well as any variances between them, are recorded in the cost accounts. The difference between standard and actual costs is called a variance. Figure 4–5 illustrates the recording of standard and actual costs, and the variances. In examining the variances between standard and actual costs and isolating the significant variances, management has guidance in determining where inefficiency and waste may exist and where standards might be changed.

In order for cost accounting systems to be used, a refined coding system is needed for transactions. For example, where management is just interested in having information on overall income and expense (and on the status of assets and liabilities), a simple chart of accounts is adequate. A summary of such a chart is shown in Tables 4–1 and 4–2. As costs are incurred in such a situation, they are entered into these accounts. At the end of each accounting period, the costs within each account (or costs on file which carry that identifying account number) are gathered together manually (or by machine or computer).

FIGURE 4–5

Comparative Cost Analysis
Product A
(Standard Quantity: 100)

Cost Components	Standard Cost	Actual Cost	Variation
Materials			
50 lbs. @ $0.32	$16.00		
52 lbs. @ $0.30		$15.60	$ 0.40*
Labor			
Operation No. 1:			
18 hrs. @ $2.50	45.00		
16 hrs. @ $2.45		39.20	5.80*
Operation No. 2:			
20 hrs. @ $2.40	48.00		
24 hrs. @ $2.42		58.08	10.08#
Operation No. 3:			
10 hrs. @ $2.60	26.00		
15 hrs. @ $2.55		38.25	12.25#
Manufacturing overhead			
48 hrs. @ $0.70	33.60		
55 hrs. @ $0.70		38.50	4.90#
Totals	$168.60	$189.63	$21.03#

*Under standard
#Over standard

With the introduction of a cost accounting system, transactions related to different product, process, or job costs must be further identified through product, process, or job codes, so that these costs can be assembled at a later date when preparing cost accounting reports. For example, when an item is drawn from the materials inventory and used (account #115), and then transferred to cost of goods sold (account #356); under a job order cost accounting system, it is necessary to further code the materials transaction by job number. The same is true for labor and overhead. A detailed example of how cost transactions are segregated and coded within a data file, and later re-sorted and integrated for information reports, is given in Chapter Five.

Information on costs by product, process, or job fills a basic management requirement—since it enables management to price products or jobs, evaluate profitability, control costs, and make such planning decisions as expansion or discontinuation of product lines. A cost accounting information system fills these management needs.

TABLE 4-1

Chart of Accounts for a Manufacturing Business
Balance Sheet Accounts (100–299)

ASSETS (100–199)

Current Assets (100–129)
101	Cash
103	Petty cash
104	Marketable securities
106	Customers' notes receivable
109	Customers' accounts receivable
115	Materials
116	Work in process

Land, Plant, and Equipment (130–159)
130	Land
132	Buildings
135	Machinery and equipment—factory
135.1	Allowance for depreciation of machinery and equipment—factory

Intangible Assets (170–179)
170	Good will
171	Patents

LIABILITIES AND CAPITAL (200–299)

Current Liabilities
201	Notes payable
203	Accounts payable
207	Accrued interest payable
216	Long-term debt (due within one year)

Fixed Liabilities (220–229)
220	Bonds payable
222	Mortgage payable

Capital (250–279)
250	Capital stock
255	Capital surplus
260	Earnings retained in business

Responsibility Accounting Systems. Responsibility accounting information systems are basically a means of relating expenditures to the managers responsible for incurring the expenses. To establish these relationships, financial result reports and budget reports are divided into units of responsibility that correspond to the operating, staff, or profit organizational units for

TABLE 4–2

Income and Expense Accounts (300–899)

Sales (300–349)

301   Sales

Cost of Goods Sold (350–499)

351   Cost of goods sold
356   Materials
366   Labor—rate variance
367   Labor—efficiency variance
372   Applied factory overhead

Factory Overhead (400–499)

400   Factory overhead control
401   Salaries
425   Vacation pay
427   Compensation insurance
434   Fuel—factory
436   Light and power
438   Telephone and telegraph
480   Repairs and maintenance of buildings

Distribution Expenses (500–599)

500   Distribution expenses control
501   Salaries—sales supervision
503   Salaries—salesmen
507   Salesmen's commissions
522   Social security taxes
530   Supplies
565   Advertising
567   Display materials
568   Conventions and exhibits

Administrative Expenses (600–699)

600   Administrative expenses control
604   Salaries—administrative clerical help
630   Supplies
662   Rent of equipment
691   Donations

Other Expenses (700–799)

701   Interest paid on notes payable
703   Interest paid on mortgage

Other Income (800–899)

801   Income from investments
808   Discount on purchases

which individual managers have spending responsibility. In these reports, controllable and non-controllable expenses are normally segregated. In every company, there is a hierarchical structure of authority and responsibility. Responsibility accounting reports are structured around the areas of responsibility specified by a firm's organization structure. Responsibility accounting is based on the theory that the official who exercises the highest authority at each level of the organization should be accountable for the expenses which are under his control.

For example, a company is organized as shown in Figure 4–6. A responsibility accounting reporting system in this situation would provide periodic reports (weekly or monthly, for instance) for each foreman, supervisor, and plant manager and for the V.P. for production which gave a breakdown of controllable and noncontrollable expenses by section, department, plant, and overall operation. An example of the report for the foreman of Section One is given in Figure 4–7.

Such information reports, while making use of basic financial accounting data, differ in purpose and format from financial reports discussed thus far. Their preparation, therefore, requires re-sorting and reclassifying of the data to suit new management needs—monitoring expenses by major responsibility center.

As with cost accounting systems, implementing responsibility accounting systems requires expanding and refining the system of coding transactions. For example, when expenses are incurred—such as labor—each expense must be coded not only by its general category or account (labor) and by its product, job, or process (where a cost accounting system is used), but also by the department or manager that incurred the expense. In addition, it must carry a code which shows whether it was a controllable or uncontrollable (by the manager) expense. Without such identification numbers (and older financial accounting systems often did not have such detailed identification num-

FIGURE 4–6

Organization—XYZ Company

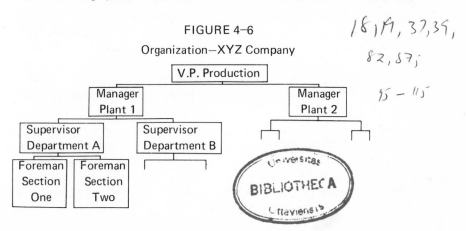

FIGURE 4-7

Section A Costs (July)

	Current Month		Year to Date	
	Actual	(Over) Under Budget	Actual	(Over) Under Budget
Direct materials	$17,000	$(1,000)	$163,000	$(11,000)
Direct labor	4,750	(430)	35,000	(1,130)
Factory overhead				
Foreman's responsibility:				
Supplies	600	(150)	4,200	(150)
Power and utilities	400	—	2,800	—
Maintenance and repairs	600	—	4,200	—
Depreciation—equipment	900	—	6,300	—
Salaries—staff	800	—	5,600	—
Total foreman's responsibility	$25,050	$(1,580)	$221,100	$(12,280)
Other responsibilities:				
Depreciation—plant	400	—	2,800	—
Insurance	150	—	1,050	—
Taxes—real estate	250	—	1,750	—
Total section A costs	$25,850	$(1,580)	$226,700	$(12,280)

bers, since management reports on costs by responsibility center were not asked for), it would be impossible for manual, electromechanical, or computerized sorters to pull all the relevant cost data and re-sort it by section, department, and plant. Examples of how such coding patterns are developed within the master file and used for management reporting follow in Chapter Five.

Responsibility accounting information systems serve management information needs in two important ways. First, they provide a feedback of information on expenses to the responsible manager, showing him the effects of his past decisions and the important areas for future consideration and attention. They thus direct the information to the manager who can take action, the one who has authority and responsibility in the area affected. Second, they enable higher management to better evaluate individual manager performance and take action more quickly, if a situation gets out of hand.

Profitability Accounting and Analysis. Cost information, while important to management planning and control, provides only a partial answer to key questions about profitability raised by corporate managers and individual operating and staff managers.

Profits can be defined in many ways, including profits as a percentage of sales before and after taxes, as contribution to profits and period expenses (expenses not related directly to sales), and as return on investment (ROI). From the owners' viewpoint, the most significant profit measure is profits earned on their investment.

Information on profits as a percentage of sales is needed for formal corporate reporting purposes, as shown earlier. That profit in turn must be compared with the investment required to produce it, in order to have relevant information on earnings on the owners' investment.

At the overall company reporting level, such integration of data is accomplished by combining data in the income statement (profits after taxes) and balance sheet (owners' equity) to come up with an overall return on investment. For example, if the XYZ Company (see Figure 4–1) had capital or owners' equity of $440,000 as of December 31, 1973, their earnings of $110,000 would represent a respectable 25 percent return on the owners' money. Such an ROI information orientation stimulates a company manager to focus on ways not only to cut costs and increase sales, but also to reduce the investment required to produce sales.

At different operating and staff levels within a company, various kinds of information reports and systems can be used which will integrate with and support such an ROI management orientation. As will be seen in the following discussion, such information systems, while financial in nature, do not necessarily follow strict accounting rules. In addition, they are frequently designed to support planning decision making, whereas the cost systems discussed earlier are largely designed for management control purposes.

Where a company is conglomerate, it may be relatively simple to develop profit reporting systems for each major division, since each major division controls all aspects of its business operations and so is, in essence, a separate operating company. Some problems may arise over transfer pricing where one division buys from or sells to another.[1] But, once these isolated problems are resolved, the reporting systems can identify earnings, investment, and return on investment for each operating unit in much the same way as is done at the overall company level.

---

1. In order to maintain the integrity of profit center reporting and accountability, some companies go so far as to have a "hands-off" approach to interdivisional transactions— that is, one division is not required to buy from or sell to another division of the company, if it can obtain more favorable prices outside the company.

Most company operations, however, do not lend themselves to such profit center reporting along traditional accounting lines. For example, the manufacturing division of a company only produces products (not sales) and, as such, earns no profit on its operations. A traditional income statement and balance sheet reporting system, therefore, is not appropriate. In such cases, reports may be made on the manufacturing division's *contribution to profit,* as shown in Figures 4–8.

In this report, the direct expenses are segregated from the period expenses and the percentage contribution is specified. This is done to assist management planning. For example, if the company had limited production facilities and could sell more of all its products, management might want to increase production of product A, since that product contributes more to profits and period expenses—a $50,000 increase in sales of product A and a corresponding $50,000 decrease in product B would increase profits before taxes by $5,000.

Such a reporting system which segregates direct costs is called a "direct"

FIGURE 4–8

Manufacturing Contribution to Period
Expenses and Profit

	Product A	Product B	Total
Unit price	$3.00	$4.00	
Unit cost	1.50	2.40	
Net sales	$300,000	$400,000	$700,000
Direct costs			
Materials	60,000	95,000	155,000
Direct labor	70,000	120,000	190,000
Variable overhead	20,000	25,000	45,000
Total direct costs	150,000	240,000	390,000
Marginal contribution	$150,000	$160,000	$310,000
Sales/cost ratio	50%	40%	
Period expenses			
Manufacturing			$130,000
Administrative			40,000
Marketing			30,000
Total period expenses			$200,000
Variable marketing expenses (5% of sales)			35,000
Pretax profit			$ 65,000

FIGURE 4-9

Manufacturing Return on Investment

	At Present Sales Level	With 10% Increase
Volume	$700,000	$770,000
Pretax profit	$ 65,000	$103,000
Average annual inventory investment	$130,000	$180,000
Rate of return on inventory	50%	60%
Investment in plant and equipment	$650,000	$650,000
Rate of return of plant and equipment investment	10%	16.5%
Inventory turnover	5.4	4.3

costing system and differs significantly from the "absorption" costing systems described above (Figures 4-4 and 4-5), where overhead costs are allocated to (or "absorbed by") each product. The difference arises from management decision needs. The cost accounting reports described earlier (Figures 4-4 and 4-5) answer the question "What were the total costs of making each product?"—this "total" necessarily including overhead costs. The question asked here is "Which product mix will generate the greatest profits in the future?" In other words, the difference is between management control and management planning decision needs.

The report shown in Figure 4-8, however, needs to be expanded, if it is to be integrated with the basic company objective of maximizing return on investment. Information must be added on the portion of the total company investment (or assets) used or managed by the manufacturing department. For example, Figure 4-9 shows the assets managed by the manufacturing division, and the return on those assets. Using traditional inventory turnover figures, as shown in Figure 4-9, a decision to increase inventories excessively (by $50,000) in order to gain additional sales would appear inefficient (reducing turnover from 5.4 to 4.3); whereas, in reality, return on investment would be increased substantially by the decision.

Such profitability-oriented financial information systems can also be developed for other areas of a company's operation. ROI reports, for example, may be prepared for marketing management, as shown in Figure 4-10. This report isolates a key responsibility of the marketing manager, making money on the investment he controls (accounts receivable and inventories). Given this ROI orientation, he might well decide to give additional discounts for prompt payment; if, by reducing his investment in receivables from sixty days

FIGURE 4–10

Marketing Return on Investment

	Actual Monthly	Projected Monthly
Gross sales	$100,000	$100,000
Discounts	10,000	15,000
Net sales	90,000	85,000
Cost of goods sold	50,000	50,000
Commissions	5,000	5,000
Total	$ 55,000	$ 55,000
Gross margin	$ 35,000	$ 30,000
Marketing expenses	5,000	5,000
Profit contribution (monthly)	$ 30,000	$ 25,000
Annual profit contribution (monthly X 12)	$360,000	$300,000
Assets employed		
Accounts receivable		
60-day payment	$180,000	
30-day payment		$ 85,000
Inventories	100,000	100,000
Total assets	$280,000	$185,000
Return on assets	129%	162%

to thirty days (from $180,000 to $85,000) and profit by a 5 percent discount (from $360,000 to $300,000 per year), he would actually increase his return on investment substantially (from 129 percent to 162 percent), as indicated by Figure 4–10.

These abbreviated reports and their analyses obviously do not reveal the whole picture, since other factors may affect the decision and other reports may be needed on these factors. For example, the company may not be short of capital, as assumed in the above illustration, and so might want to make the investment in the additional accounts receivable to save the extra five percent discount. The point is that once the accounting mold has been broken in financial information systems and attention has been shifted to management decision requirements, the way is opened for a wide range of different financial reports tailored specifically to individual company and managerial decision-making needs.

For example, at one mail-order company, an information system was developed which reported projected profitability of orders received (but not yet filled). Such an information system enabled marketing management to act to correct problems and exploit new opportunities two months sooner than had been possible using the profit information given by accounting reports on sales delivered and billed. By extending this same system, the mail-order company was able to analyze the profitability of proposed sales programs— using the same financial analysis group (which was not under the accounting department) that prepared the profit projections of orders received.

Profitability analyses are vital planning tools, since they can be done for a wide range of management decisions, from determining whether or not to run a promotion campaign to deciding on which of two products to produce to setting inventory levels. Additional examples of these and other types of profitability information reports and systems are presented later in Chapter Five.

Cash Flow Information Reporting

The basic method of predicting the amount and timing of future funding needs is through the preparation of a *cash flow forecast* or *cash budget*. The cash flow forecast is a prediction of when and in what quantity cash receipts will come into the company and of when and in what quantity cash payments will be made. Anticipated cash receipts would include such items as cash from the disposal of securities and fixed assets, as well as cash from sales and the collection of accounts receivable. Cash disbursements would include such non-routine disbursements as outlays for equipment, as well as routine payment of wages, accounts payable, taxes, dividends, and so on. Figure 4–11 gives a simplified cash flow budget for the XYZ Company for the six months, January to June 1974.

The cash budget allows management of the XYZ Company to determine approximately how much cash will flow into and out of the company for the first six months of the year. It also serves as a standard or yardstick of performance against which to subsequently measure the actual inflow and outflow of funds.

In order to make this budget comparison, financial management needs to have statements of the flow of funds—the sources from which cash was obtained and the ways in which the money was applied or spent. Figure 4–12 gives an example of such a cash flow statement. Accounting records provide the basic data for the flow statement. Using this information, financial management could then compare actual cash flow with budgeted cash flow to control overall funds movement within the company. For example, a comparison of the numbers in Figures 4–11 and 4–12 shows that the movement of funds in the XYZ Company in January were exactly on budget.

FIGURE 4–11

Summary Schedule of Estimated Cash Flows
XYZ Company—January to June 1974
(in thousands)

	Jan.	Feb.	March	April	May	June	Total
Total net receipts	$25.5	$59.5	$65	$55	$80	$85	$370
Total net payments	40	60	62	65	75	78	380
Net inflow or (outflow)	($14.5)	($ .5)	$ 3	($10)	$ 5	$ 7	($ 10)
Cumulative inflow or (outflow)	($14.5)	($15)	($12)	($22)	($17)	($10)	$10)

FIGURE 4–12

XYZ Company
Statement of Cash Flow
January 1974

Cash provided by:		
Operations		
Net income for period		$11,000
Charges to income not affecting cash		
Depreciation of plant and equipment	$1,000	
Amortization of deferred charges	500	1,500
Total provided by operations		12,500
Reduction of accounts receivable		8,000
Sale of investments		5,000
Total cash provided		$25,500
Cash applied to:		
Purchase of equipment		$20,000
Increase of inventories		11,000
Reduction of accounts payable		4,000
Payment of dividends		5,000
Total cash applied		$40,000
Reduction in cash balance		$14,500
Cash balance January 1, 1974		$50,000
Cash balance January 31, 1974		$35,500

Capital Budgeting

Capital budgeting is a major tool used in planning and controlling the acquisition, allocation, and expenditure of long-term investment funds. The capital budget specifies the projects selected by management which will require investment, together with the estimated cost of and return on each project. Since capital budgets forecast requirements for funds, they enable management to plan in advance to secure whatever additional funds may be needed to finance potentially profitable projects. Capital budgets, like other budgets, can also subsequently be used to monitor the spending on capital projects and the efficiency of capital spending, once they are incorporated into the financial reporting system. An example is shown in Figure 4–13.

An Expanding Concept of Financial Information Systems for Management

The preceding discussion of accounting and financial information systems has ranged from basic accounting data collection systems to individually tailored management decision supporting systems. In some instances—for example, in historical accounting reports—all that is required is re-sorting and reclassifying data; in other instances, additional input data is required, such as budgets, forecasts, prevailing interest rates, and performance of competitors, depending on management decision requirements.

Basic accounting data records are among the first automated when punched card machines and computers are introduced into a company. Since accounting data is necessarily used in such operations as payroll and invoice preparation, customer account maintenance, billing, and similar operations, accounting data recording systems are closely integrated with these operations in computerized data systems (payroll checks and customer account statements are often computer-printed, for example, as are management reports on payroll expenses and accounts receivable, all using the accounting data base). Basic accounting reporting is understandably part of such an automated data processing system, since the required data is already available for performing the operating tasks.

Financial information systems for management which do not conform to traditional accounting molds are not always developed and automated so systematically: sometimes because the requirements can change over a period of time (and so are not as stabilized as in traditional accounting reporting), sometimes because input data from outside the basic accounting system is needed, sometimes because it is more difficult to identify specific managerial information requirements, and sometimes because a company has established

FIGURE 4-13

Stanley Manufacturing Company

Capital Spending Status Report
As of August 31, 1974

Appropriation no.	Description	Work order no.	Actual completion date	Original budget	Outstanding commitments	Actual expenditures to date	Estimated cost to complete	Indicated total cost	(Over) or under original budget
24	Ottawa Avenue plant								
	Buildings and equipment	241		$670,796.52	286,672.84	384,123.68	—	670,796.52	$ —
	Site clearance	242		13,552.86	—	13,552.86	—	13,552.86	—
	Total appropriation 24			$684,349.38	286,672.81	397,676.54	—	684,349.38	—
25	Modifications of overhead conveyor								
	Installation Y building	251		28,353.00	14,533.05	236.39	13,583.56	28,353.00	—
	Others completed as of 7/31			2,990.00	—	4,645.55	—	4,645.55	(1,655.55)
	Total appropriation 25			$ 31,343.00	14,533.05	4,881.94	13,583.56	32,998.55	(1,655.55)
26	Miscellaneous improvements								
	Magnesium pilot line	261	7/31	8,910.00	—	8,551.48	—	8,551.48	358.52
	Wrapping equipment	262	2/28	16,900.00	6.50	14,122.52	—	14,129.02	2,770.98
	Roll mill—design and install— A.C. plant	263		11,680.00	8,944.00	154.00	2,582.00	11,680.00	—
	Intercommunication system	264		24,974.00	4,794.57	20,179.43	—	24,974.00	—
	Move hydraulic press and install in Y building	265	5/31	1,155.50	79.15	926.68	—	1,005.83	149.67
	Design and install air conditioning unit in Y building	266		9,725.00	750.00	8,626.84	348.16	9,725.00	—

	No.	Date						
Changes and modifications in paint room	267		30,115.00	29.89	26,664.06		26,693.95	3,421.05
Buggy scales	268	5/31	11,275.00	212.20	10,158.39	904.41	11,275.00	—
Tote boxes—A.C. plant	269	7/31	3,597.00	340.57	3,198.86	—	3,539.43	57.57
Prepare annealing oven for production use	270		7,700.00	1,290.03	6,202.29	207.68	7,700.00	—
Move electric furnaces to A.C. plant	271		3,585.00	2,989.20	—	595.80	3,585.00	—
Lift truck with exide batteries and battery charger	272		30,486.00	21,670.19	2,737.83	6,077.98	30,486.00	—
Purchase and install 100 HP motor in Y building	273	7/31	4,692.00	424.00	3,701.97	—	4,125.97	566.03
Others completed as of 7/31/			3,701.00	—	2,482.18	—	2,482.18	1,218.82
Total appropriation 26			168,495.50	41,530.30	107,706.53	10,716.03	159,952.86	8,542.64
Aluminum experimental unit	29							
Construction of unit	291		50,000.00	5,533.34	15,385.04	29,081.62	50,000.00	—
Total appropriation 29			50,000.00	5,533.34	15,385.04	29,081.62	50,000.00	—
Grand total			$934,187.88	348,269.53	525,650.05	53,381.21	927,300.79	$ 6,887.09

Issued by Accounting Department—September 5, 1974

117

such systematization as a low priority item for development (basic accounting records *must* be kept, but managers can often make do with incomplete decision information).

For these reasons, breaking the accounting mold in financial information systems has been a slow, piecemeal, and often painful process. Very often this development has had to take place outside of the regular accounting organization. For example, at the mail-order company described earlier, the more current financial analysis reports for marketing management were prepared by a group of analysts reporting to the marketing manager. Such uncoordinated development creates problems of integration. For example, at the mail-order company, there were constant problems encountered in reconciling figures in the early financial analysis reports with figures in the historical accounting reports produced two or three months later.

The accounting mold has gradually been broken, nonetheless, simply because managers need more current information, as well as predictive information, and traditional accounting systems are just not designed to meet such needs. At several companies, the pattern of development has been circuitous: first, an operating manager develops his own financial analysis and reporting systems, which are more current than the accounting reports he receives and which project financial performance based on early results or his own market judgments; second, the traditional accounting and finance department subsequently takes over the administration of these systems (for example, at the mail-order company, the marketing financial analysis group was eventually transferred to the accounting department). In other words, the organization change and system development very often follows, rather than anticipates, the operating management need.

Some accounting and finance managers have been alert to these trends and expanded the scope of their information services. Others have not, and permitted new information needs to be filled by "Information Services Departments," which have grown rapidly in business over the past decade.

There is a growing awareness of the importance of decision-supporting financial information systems to business success. And companies are more and more willing to devote time and money to developing them systematically—analyzing manager decision needs, and adjusting and redesigning existing financial information systems to incorporate new concepts.

A manager approaches the development of management information systems differently from the information technicians or specialists. A manager's concern is with defining information needs and work flows, data file structure, forecasting and predicting models, report content, report format, and the timing of the information flow—that is, the design of the *concept* of the system, not its *mechanics*. The following chapter reviews some common situations in business which illustrate how a manager can participate more effectively in the diagnosis and design phases of accounting and financial information system development.

TEXT DISCUSSION QUESTIONS

1. Describe the major corporate management decision-making needs that financial and accounting information systems fill.
2. Describe the different kinds of accounting and financial systems used in management decision making.
3. Contrast the different ways in which income, balance sheet and cash reports are used in management decision making.
4. Describe what a budgetary system is and how it works. Discuss why budgets and budgetary standards are so important to any financial and accounting information systems used by management.
5. Describe the different kinds of management decision-making needs that responsibility and cost accounting systems fill.
6. Describe the ways in which the financial data file has to be structured through unique coding patterns in order to produce the reports generated by cost and responsibility accounting systems.
7. Describe what comparative financial reports are and the ways in which variance analysis can be used in management decision making.
8. What is profitability accounting? In what ways do profitability accounting information systems differ from more traditional accounting and financial information systems?
9. In what ways is profitability analysis information useful in management decision making?
10. Describe the major basic accounting operations and the ways in which these operating systems (such as payroll, customer billing, accounts receivable, etc.) can provide basic file data for use in management information systems.

Developing Accounting and Financial Information Systems

THIS CHAPTER CONTAINS SELECTED EXAMPLES OF BUSINESS SITUA-
tions involving accounting and financial information systems development. Not all types of financial and accounting information systems
for management are covered, since the purpose of the following discussions is
only to introduce the reader to the general approach to systems development,
not to provide him with a complete introduction to all aspects of financial
and accounting systems.

Income and Asset Reporting:
The Overman Laundry

The Overman Laundry began operations on January 2, 1974. Mr. Overman's
accountant prepared a balance sheet for that date as shown in Figure 5–1.
The accountant supplied Mr. Overman with a record book (or journal) into
which Mr. Overman's secretary-assistant entered all cash transactions during
the year. A summary of these entries for 1974 is shown in Figure 5–2.

FIGURE 5–1

Overman Laundry

Balance Sheet—January 2, 1974

ASSETS		LIABILITIES & CAPITAL	
Cash	$ 1,000	Accounts payable	$ 1,185
Laundry supplies	1,185	Bank loan	12,000
Building & equipment	150,000	Mortgage	56,000
Land	6,000	Capital stock	100,000
Trucks	11,000		
	$169,185		$169,185

Mr. Overman felt the first year had been a good one and was looking forward to the summary results being prepared by the accountant in January 1975. Before preparing a balance sheet and income statement for 1974, the accountant collected the following data from the file of unpaid bills from

FIGURE 5–2

Overman Laundry

Summary of Cash Transactions—1974

CASH RECEIPTS		CASH DISBURSEMENTS	
Cash sales	$ 76,123	Wages	$ 49,412
Collections of accounts		Salaries	8,859
(arising from sale of		Repairs and maintenance	6,228
laundry services)	38,621	Insurance	3,374
		Miscellaneous taxes	1,282
		Property taxes	642
		Heat, light, and power	5,328
		Additional laundry	
		supplies	8,789
		General administrative	
		expense	7,339
		Advertising	2,277
		Other selling expenses	1,593
		Stationery and printing	2,056
		Interest*	720
		Partial payment of bank	
		loan on December 31,	
		1974	6,000
		Payment of accounts	
		payable	1,185
Total cash receipts	$114,744	Total cash disbursements	$105,084

* Interest at 6 percent on the bank loan was payable June 30 and December 31. Interest
payments for 1974 were made when due.

suppliers and unpaid customer accounts and from conversations with Mr.
Overman and his assistant.

1. Salaries were paid monthly on the second of each month for the
   preceding month. Salaries earned during December but not yet paid
   totaled $822 (Information for preparing accruals of income taxes and
   social security taxes has been omitted to avoid undue complications).

2. The yearly depreciation expense on the buildings and equipment was
   figured at $7,500 and on the trucks at $1,375.

3. Wages earned from December 18 to 31 but not yet paid totaled $2,143.

4. Of the total insurance premiums of $3,374 paid in 1974, $1,200
   constituted the full premium on a two-year policy to expire on December 31, 1975.

5. Interest on the mortgage at 4% was payable annually on January 1. No interest had yet been paid.

6. An inventory taken of the laundry supplies at the end of the year revealed a supply on hand costing $1,015.

7. Federal Income Tax on 1974 income was estimated at $1,396.

8. Unpaid bills from suppliers representing purchases of laundry supplies totaled $2,962 and unpaid customer accounts representing laundry services to them totaled $4,421.

The accountant first prepared the income statement using the data in Figure 5–2 and making the following adjustments for the above data:

Sales			
Cash sales		$114,744	
Sales made on credit and not yet paid for		4,421	
Total sales			$119,165
Expenses			
Cash disbursements		105,084	
Less—			
Unused inventory	$1,015		
Bank loan payment	6,000		
Insurance paid for coming year	600	(7,615)	
Plus—			
Unpaid supplier bills	2,962		
Income taxes due	1,396		
Interest due on mortgage	2,240		
Wage payments due	2,143		
Salary payments due	822		
Depreciation expenses	8,875	18,438	
Total expenses			115,907
Profit for year			$ 3,258

Based on this analysis, the accountant prepared the final income statement as shown in Figure 5–3.

The accountant then prepared the balance sheet for January 2, 1975 as shown in Figure 5–4 by adjusting the initial balance sheet in light of transactions during the year.

Mr. Overman reviewed the results with some pride. Besides increasing his cash position substantially and earning about 5 percent on sales, he had an

FIGURE 5–3

Overman Laundry

Income Statement–1974

Gross sales			$119,165
Expenses:			
Selling expenses:			
Advertising	$2,277		
Other selling expenses	1,593		
Total selling expenses		$ 3,870	
General and administrative expenses:			
Wages	51,555		
Salaries	9,681		
Laundry supplies	11,921		
Heat, light, and power	5,328		
Repairs and maintenance	6,228		
Depreciation expense	8,875		
Insurance	2,774		
Property taxes	642		
Miscellaneous taxes	1,282		
Stationery and printing	2,056		
General administrative expenses	7,339		
Total general and administrative expenses		107,681	
Other expenses:			
Interest–bank loan	720		
Interest–mortgage	2,240		
Total other expenses		2,960	
Total expenses			114,511
Net profit before income taxes			4,654
Provision for income taxes			1,396
Net profit			$ 3,258

ample salary from the business. The only troublesome aspect was the low 3¼ percent return on his investment of $100,000. However, with the increased sales he anticipated in 1975, he felt that eventually his return on investment would rise to over 10 percent.

At this phase of his company's growth, Mr. Overman felt his financial information reports and data records were adequate, since he was actively managing the company and the company was small and provided a single service to its customers using a single manufacturing facility. Nor did he feel

FIGURE 5–4

Overman Laundry

Balance Sheet–January 2, 1975

ASSETS

Cash			
Initial	$ 1,000		
1974 receipts	114,744		
1974 disbursements	105,084		$ 10,660
Accounts receivable (from sales made)			4,421
Laundry supplies inventory			
Initial	$ 1,185	(used)	
Year end			1,015
Deferred charges			
Insurance prepaid for 1975			600
Building and equipment	$150,000		
Less depreciation	7,500		142,500
Land			6,000
Trucks	11,000		
Less depreciation	1,375		9,625
			$174,821

LIABILITIES

Accounts payable			
Initial	$ 1,185	(paid)	
Year end			$ 2,692
Accrued wages payable			2,143
Accrued salaries payable			822
Accrued interest payable			2,240
Accrued taxes payable			1,396
Bank loan outstanding			
Initial	$ 12,000		
Payment	6,000		6,000
Mortgage			56,000
Capital stock			100,000
Earnings retained in company			3,258
			$174,821

any account or transaction coding system was needed to retrieve data from the basic files and re-sort it, since the data was used only to prepare the balance sheet and income statement, since no further use of this data for cost or responsibility systems was anticipated in the forseeable future, and since no automated accounting equipment was to be used.

The Overman Company was unique in one aspect—it had no cash problems. Small companies seem continually plagued by cash shortages; so that, in such situations, cash budgeting and reporting is normally an important part of the financial information system. Unlike in the Overman study, in the FAD Limited case study at the end of the chapter, the company's funds are in danger of running out very soon, so that cash flow reporting is probably the single most important financial information need of management.

Corporate Financial Budgetary Systems: Video Productions Company

The Video Productions Company was formed by two men to produce hour-long animated television programs in 1969. In the beginning, the staff consisted of two secretaries and two editors. All creative talent was handled on a contractual basis and all animation production work was contracted to a firm in Japan. The company grew to an annual sales volume of five million dollars with fifteen full-time employees. In early 1974, the two owners sold their interest to a multi-million dollar entertainment company and were retained as President and Vice President of the new subsidiary company.

In the past, the owners had not bothered much with preparing budgets, mainly because they were so closely involved in the details of all operations, had ample borrowing capacity (a generous line of credit with a nearby bank), had no stockholders to account to, and were interested mainly in doing as well as they could each coming year, rather than reaching a specific growth goal. Within the new corporate structure, Video Productions was required to develop a budgetary system to provide the parent company management with estimates of sales, expenses, profits, and cash flow on a monthly basis for the coming year.

The first step was to determine what data was available under the existing system. Before the acquisition, the company maintained a cash receipts and disbursements journal. In addition, a file was maintained for each new production which contained the contracts for the creative talent, production work, and program sales to the networks and which was used for production expense control. Basic financial reports were prepared at year end, using these data files and the cash journal. This had been the extent of the financial and accounting information system at Video Productions.

Since the company's fiscal year was June 1 through May 30, and since the networks firmed up their programming for the coming season each March, a reliable budget could be prepared in March for the forthcoming year. In the contracts with the networks, the sales price was given and the progress payments specified. This data could be used in preparing projected sales and cash flow statements. Once the network contracts for a program were signed, contracts were made with the production company and creative talent. From these contracts, payment schedules could be prepared to complete the disbursement part of the cash flow statement. Historical data was also used, as is seen from the following description of the budgetary system that was developed and implemented.

Sales Budget. This budget was segregated into several sections. First, the properties that the networks had agreed to buy for the current season were listed. Since the networks had already contracted for these programs, the information for domestic sales to networks for the current year could be calculated right from the contracts. Then, the projected sales from properties that were syndicated and sold to independent stations and to stations in foreign countries were listed; these estimates were based on firm contracts, letters of intent, and past experience.

Since older programs were also sold for reruns in domestic and foreign markets (the bulk of foreign sales were made after the first year), the budget next detailed these sales. Projections of these additional sales were made based on the inventory of older programs available, interest expressed in these programs by station outlets, and past experience.

Projections of sales within these three major classifications (initial network sales, initial non-network sales, and rerun sales) were detailed by property by month for the year in the sales budget.

Production Expense Budget. This budget listed the name of each property, the expected total production cost, and the portion of that cost to be written off throughout the budget year. The amount written off within the current year depended on anticipated sales beyond the first year and varied between 50 percent and 100 percent. This budget was prepared from the detailed production schedules for each property which showed such costs as talent, writers, recording, shipping, travel and living, character design, and the cost of animation (which was contracted out). The production budget also included write-offs of previous years' properties, which were also segregated by property by month.

General and Administrative Expenses. This budget covered such items as rent, salaries, supplies, and the like by month for the budget year. It was prepared based upon last year's results and the expansion planned for the coming year. Unlike production expenses, these expenses were charged against sales income at the time they were incurred.

Profit Projections. From the above budgets, a summary budget was prepared which showed projected revenue, expenses, and profits from new productions and from reruns. These profit projections were shown by project to arrive at a net profit after taxes for each new production and for each rerun production. A permanent file was maintained which showed the ultimate profitability of all productions made since the firm began.

Cash Budget. This budget covered expected disbursements and receipts by month for the budget year and was prepared using the same basic data files used for the expense and revenue budgets. This was an important budget because the company received its funds from the parent corporation based upon it.

Budget Comparisons. To determine whether the company was operating as planned, a summary report was prepared each month for the parent corporation management which compared actual revenue, expense, profit, and cash performance against budgets, with major variances explained. In addition, detailed production expense reports were prepared for and used by project managers to monitor individual project performance on a current basis.

The new budgetary system was a considerably more detailed financial information system than anything the company had prepared and used in the past. While the company's founders did not need such an elaborate system, the new owners did, since they were not active in day-to-day management of the company. The new system was tailored mainly to meet the new corporate management requirements introduced with the sale of the company and the change in overall management, though it also proved useful to the operating managers in improving their planning and control of operations.

Because so much of the work in the company was done by project on a contractual basis, basic file data was readily available. New financial records and two new controller's assistants and two new clerks were, however, needed to administer the new budgetary system. Operating managers were required to spend additional time working with the controller's office in preparing budgets. The existing control executives and their staff were otherwise able to handle the expanded budgetary operation.

Review meetings had been held quarterly in the past at which company management and operating managers reviewed plans and past operations. These continued to be held under the new system. In addition, Video Productions' President and Vice President now met with parent company management just after these quarterly meetings to review overall operations and plans. Several special meetings were also held with parent company management when significant variances from budget occurred. In addition, an annual planning meeting was held each May when budgets and supporting plans for the coming fiscal year were reviewed with parent company management.

The form of the reports (for example, project breakdowns), the files maintained, the timing of the reports and the reporting period (for example, a July 1 to June 30 fiscal year), the distribution of reports and similar concerns were thus all dictated by the kind of business Video Productions was in—creative TV production projects—as well as by the new management needs, in light of its unfamiliarity with the operation.

In examining the information generated by the new information system, it became clear that in the past the owner-managers had charged off production costs conservatively (that is, very rapidly) and that there was a large inventory of older productions whose costs were completely written off, but which still generated substantial revenues. These "hidden" assets were one of the major reasons the parent company had bought Video Productions.

As is seen in the following discussion of cost and responsibility accounting and from the study exercises at the end of the chapter, budgetary systems can differ considerably from company to company and from operation to operation. In each situation, the final system will be affected, as at Video Productions, by the nature of the company's business, the needs of management, the operations being managed, and the personnel involved.

Cost Accounting Systems:
Bajar Industries

John Romar, President of Bajar Industries, has engaged a management consultant to study the advisability of developing a new cost accounting system for Bajar. The company has been in business for a number of years producing a standardized high-quality wool thread. Recently, Bajar has accepted an offer from a large distributor to manufacture a line of cloth, in addition to their thread line.

The production process for thread starts with scoured wool, which passes through several different semi-automated production processes. All types of thread pass through the same processes and several types of thread can be produced at the same time at each processing phase. Finished thread is placed in inventory either for sale or for use in the production of cloth. Producing cloth requires drawing a particular type of thread from inventory and then passing it through weaving, finishing, and dyeing processes. Only one type of cloth passes through each process at a time.

Bajar has a computerized accounting system; however, it provides no more information than the company's manual data processing system did prior to the purchase of computers. The present cost accounting system, which was developed when the company manufactured only thread, works as follows:

1. Labor costs are taken from individual worker time sheets which are keypunched; the computer prepares the payroll from these keypunched sheets. Labor is classified as either "manufacturing" or "all other."

2. Material when purchased is recorded in a single inventory account and there is no attempt to determine who or what job is withdrawing it.

3. All other expenses at Bajar are accumulated under a single overhead account.

4. Profitability is calculated by taking total sales (adjusted for finished

goods inventory changes) for a given period (month, quarter, or year) and deducting the labor, material used, and overhead for the same time period.

While the above system was adequate when the company manufactured a fairly homogeneous line of quality threads, which varied only slightly in sales price and manufacturing cost, it cannot provide cost and profit data for the different kinds of cloth now manufactured. The existing system still collects costs on a company-wide basis and does not segregate them by kind or lot of cloth. Such detailed cost and profit information is needed, however, by management in pricing cloth products, and in making decisions on which cloth lines to continue or drop.

The management consultant engaged to review Bajar's financial information system recommended that a two-part accounting system be developed—a process cost system for the thread and a job order system for the cloth. Both systems would make use of standards, which would be used for reporting variances from plan.

As part of the new cost accounting system, the following data would be collected: the direct and indirect costs (labor, material, and overhead) associated with the production of each major type of cloth or lot of cloth; and the costs of making the standardized thread. This data would in turn be used both to prepare cost accounting variance reports for control and to produce profitability analyses for planning.

The method of accumulating costs will remain the same under each system, so that there will be only one source of input into the computer. The input is then re-sorted to meet the differing needs of each system. To enable the system to work, each lot of cloth has to be given a lot number that will identify it from the beginning of production until the final sale.

Labor charges would be accumulated as follows under the new system:

1. Each person involved in manufacturing will be given a weekly time card on which he will record daily the job (for thread) or job and lot (for cloth) he worked on and the number of hours worked.

2. This card will be reviewed by the supervisor weekly and sent to the payroll department. Here the cards will be collected for the whole company, and input into the computer. The computer will prepare the payroll, as well as sort the charges by product and, if the charges are for a cloth product, also by lot number.

3. The wages for people not involved in manufacturing will be charged to a pre-established overhead account. There will be a different account number for factory overhead charges and for administrative expense charges. These cards will follow the same route as the manufacturing time cards.

4. With these weekly time cards, all labor costs for the week will now be segregated by product and/or job lot, factory overhead, and administrative expense.

Raw material will still be purchased against a single inventory account. However, for the finished thread inventory, there will be a perpetual inventory maintained; and, when a withdrawal is made, the cost of the thread material will be transferred from the inventory account to the cloth job lot for which it was withdrawn. With this inventory system, material costs for each cloth lot will be available. Any miscellaneous material (general supplies: paper, cleaning fluids, etc.) will be charged as either factory overhead or administrative expense.

For cloth, the factory overhead will be applied to each job on the basis of labor dollars:

$$\frac{\text{Job XXX Labor \$}}{\text{Total Manufacturing Labor}} = \frac{\text{Job XXX Overhead}}{\text{Total Factory Overhead}}$$

Administrative expenses will be allocated to each job in the following proportions:

$$\frac{\substack{\text{Job XXX Manufacturing Cost} \\ \text{(Labor + Material + Factory Overhead)}}}{\text{Total Manufacturing Cost}} = \frac{\text{Job XXX Administrative Expense}}{\text{Total Administrative Expense}}$$

As for thread, actual labor costs will be collected by process center, overhead charges will be allocated to finished thread on a similar basis to the one used for cloth, and the cost of materials will be calculated in the same way as in the past—based on net changes in raw materials inventory. These actual costs will be used for valuing finished thread inventory.

Standard costs will be established for both thread and cloth under the new system. For thread, historical costs plus adjustments quarterly for changes in labor rates and raw material prices will be used in calculating standards. Variances from standards will be reported montly. For cloth, engineered standards, plus actual thread inventory values, will be used in estimating costs for each cloth lot; and these estimates will be used as standards by accounting in reporting variances from standard on each cloth lot.

With the ability to collect costs against a given job under the new system, Mr. Romar now has the information needed to determine the profitability of different cloth lots. Profitability will simply be the total cost (after adjusting for variances) of a job lot minus its selling price. With this information, Romar will be able to plan pricing policies and to price individual bids in a way that enables Bajar to meet both its profit and ROI objectives for cloth.

The new system also enables more accurate earnings forecasts for the company as a whole, as well as better control of production costs.

The new cost accounting system was developed because the company's business had changed and management needed new kinds of information to make decisions effectively. The new system contained only those changes needed to meet these new management needs and, wherever possible, made use of the existing information system. Some idea of the mechanics involved in developing information systems of this kind are given in the discussion of coding patterns in the following section.

Responsibility Accounting Systems: Barker Company

The Barker Company had some years ago instituted a process cost accounting system which collected costs by process center and reported costs by product line. The company's organization chart is shown in Figure 5–5. Of the company's two product lines, one passed through all processes and departments, while the other passed through only one process.

Recently Mr. Barker had been studying ways to better evaluate individual manager performance and in general improve performance of his operating managers. He felt that if each manager could get a report on the monthly performance in his area as related to costs and that if that performance were

FIGURE 5–5

Company Organization by Management
Responsibility Center*

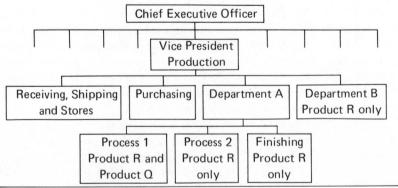

* Represents only selected areas of the organization which are relevant to the text discussion.

compared to some pre-established standard, not only would Mr. Barker be able to more easily measure and control individual manager performance, but the managers themselves would have an objective measure of their performance and would be motivated to better performance. The controller was asked to develop such a cost reporting system by manager responsibility area.

The controller started by examining the organization chart. His task was to develop a series of reports for each management area which would show cost results as compared with a standard. In addition, costs under a manager's control in each area would have to be segregated from other costs in the reports. He also needed reports which integrated with overall financial reports and other cost accounting reports and which could use financial data presently collected and filed.

He first sketched out the kinds of reports he might be able to generate from available financial data files, which would give a fair measure of a manager's performance as regards costs. He started with the foreman's job for process A and prepared a report for August as shown in Figure 5–6. He did the same for each higher level of management, as shown in part in Figures 5–7 and 5–8, until he had a fully integrated responsibility accounting report for the chief financial officer.

As for preparation of budgets, he planned to have operating managers prepare estimates which would be reviewed by the budgeting manager and which after differences were reconciled would become budget standards. Reporting variances from budgetary standards on an exception basis would enable managers to focus their attention on significant variances.

FIGURE 5–6

Process 1 Costs (Foreman)—August

	Current Month		Year to Date	
	Actual	(Over) under budget	Actual	(Over) under budget
Direct materials	$12,000	$(300)	$80,000	$(1,700)
Direct labor	2,000	(40)	13,000	(100)
Factory overhead—foreman's responsibility	900	(50)	3,500	(200)
Total foreman's responsibility	$14,900	$(390)	$96,500	$(2,000)
Factory overhead—other's responsibility	500	–	3,000	–
Total Process 1 costs	$15,400	$(390)	$99,500	$(2,000)

FIGURE 5–7

Department A Costs (Supervisor)—August

	Current Month		Year to Date	
	Actual	(Over) under budget	Actual	(Over) under budget
Supervisor's office	$ 900	$ (50)	$ 6,000	$ (100)
Process 1 foreman's cost	14,900	(390)	99,500	(2,000)
Process 2 foreman's cost	3,000	(100)	21,000	(300)
Finishing foreman's cost	1,400	(50)	11,000	(200)
Total supervisor's responsibility	$20,200	$(590)	$137,500	$(2,600)
Factory overhead—other's responsibility	1,100	—	8,000	—
Total Department A costs	$21,300	$(590)	$145,500	$(2,600)

FIGURE 5–8

Factory Cost Summary
(Vice President-Production)—August

	Current Month		Year to Date	
	Actual	(Over) under budget	Actual	(Over) under budget
Vice president's office	$ 5,000	$ 100	$ 35,000	$ 800
Dept. A supervisor's cost	20,200	(590)	137,500	(2,600)
Dept. B supervisor's cost	17,000	(200)	105,000	(2,000)
Purchasing manager's cost	1,000	100	6,500	(400)
Receiving, shipping, and stores manager's cost	900	—	6,000	—
Total vice president's responsibility	$44,100	$(590)	$290,000	$(4,200)
Factory overhead—other's responsibility	3,000	—	21,000	—
Total factory cost	$47,100	$(590)	$311,000	$(4,200)

The new responsibility accounting reports were integrated with the traditional income statement. For example, the re-sorting of selected detail and summary of detail for income statement preparation is shown in Figure 5–9. Similar re-sorting and reclassifying was done for the cost accounting summary report.

FIGURE 5–9

Income Statement—August

	Current Month		Year to Date	
	Actual	(Over) under budget	Actual	(Over) under budget
Net sales	$110,000	$(2,000)†	$840,000	—
Cost of sales				
Materials*	34,000	(1,100)°	215,000	$(5,000)°
Labor*	9,000	(200)°	80,000	(800)°
Overhead	15,000	(2,000)°	100,000	(1,000)°
Total	58,000	(3,300)°	395,000	(6,800)°
Gross profit	52,000	1,300°	445,000	6,800°
Sales and administrative expenses	34,000	2,000†	260,000	7,000†
Profit from operations	18,000	(700)†	185,000	(200)†
Other income less other expenses	2,000	—	4,000	—
Earnings before taxes	20,000	(700)†	189,000	(200)†
Provision for income taxes	9,000	(350)°	92,000	(100)°
Income after taxes	$ 11,000	$ (350)†	$ 97,000	$ (100)†

* As an illustration of the re-sorting required, these items are aggregate totals of similarly named items that appeared as costs in Figure 5–6 and similar reports on costs for Process 2 and Department B.

† Favorable variance.

° Unfavorable variance.

Several changes in the financial data file were required to enable preparation of the new responsibility accounting reports, the most important of which was the restructuring of the coding pattern, since the re-sorting capability depended on the coding pattern to draw relevant data from the file.

When financial accounting data was initially filed under the new system, this data had to be coded in such a manner that it could be easily reprocessed for preparation of responsibility accounting reports, as well as other financial and accounting reports. To accomplish this, the controller set up a matrix, as shown in Figure 5–10, which showed the general ledger account numbers on one side (these numbers would be used for income statement and general accounting purposes) and across the top organization units and process and product breakdowns (which would enable re-sorting for cost and responsibility accounting information reports).

FIGURE 5-10
Coding Pattern Matrix

| | Code | Foreman Process 1 Prod R | Foreman Process 1 Prod Q | Foreman Process 2 | Foreman Finishing | Supervisor Dept. A Prod R | Supervisor Dept. A Prod Q | Manager receiving, shipping and stores Prod R | Manager receiving, shipping and stores Prod Q | Supervisor Dept. A | Etc. |
		921.1	921.2	922	923	920.1	920.2	910.1	910.2	930	Etc.
Direct materials	471	1	1	1						1	
Direct labor	481	1	1	1	1					1	
Factory supplies	491	1	1	1	1	1	1	1	1	1	
Factory depreciation	400	2	2	2	2	2	2	2	2	2	
Etc.	Etc.										

1 Cost for which manager is responsible.
2 Cost for which manager is not responsible.

136

Based on this analysis, it seemed to the controller that an eight-digit file code would enable him to do all the re-sorting needed for management information purposes. The eight digits would be assigned as follows:

12345678 Eight-digit code

123xxxxx The first three digits would indicate the general ledger account number.

xxx456xx Digits four, five, and six would designate the organization unit to which an expenditure relates or the organization unit that benefits from the expenditure or the organization unit to which an amortization charge relates or benefits.

xxxxxx7x The seventh digit would designate the product for which the cost was incurred.

xxxxxxx8 The eighth digit would designate the characteristic of the cost or amortization charge according to the key presented in Figure 5–10.

The following is an example of one code:

4819211 Direct labor (481xxxxx) that relates to or benefits Process 1 in Department A (xxx921xx), product line R (xxxxxx1x), and for which the Foreman of Process 1 was responsible for costs incurred (xxxxxxx1).

The approach used by the controller was in concept fairly simple, following as it did the basic systems approach. Reporting requirements were first defined: costs by product, costs by responsibility center, and costs for overall income reporting. The data was then restructured (through a new coding pattern) to enable drawing from the file the data required to meet the defined information needs. Additional studies were made to determine the reporting format needs of each manager (not discussed) and programs next were developed to generate the reports at the appropriate time and in the proper form. The responsibility accounting system was throughout structured to conform to the company's organization structure.

Profitability Accounting and Analysis Systems

Developing profitability accounting and analysis information systems requires another kind of re-sorting and reclassification of basic financial data and the accumulation of additional data—by product, product line, profit center, and the like, depending on the kind of information breakdowns required for management decision making.

In the Video Productions Company study described earlier, for example, profits were reported *by project.* This system of profit reporting and analysis was relatively easy to develop in this situation, since the production projects were substantial and limited in number, since costs and income data was collected and filed by project, and since most general administrative and overhead expenses could be identified for each project. The new cost accounting system in the Bajar Industries study was also extended to provide profitability information, in that instance by *job lot,* and while the accuracy of the profit figures depended on the accuracy of the overhead allocations to each lot, the system nonetheless gave a good measure of profits.

While profitability information systems are related to and dependent on cost information systems, they go beyond them and present additional problems. As is seen in the case study exercises which follow, the easiest kinds to construct and the most accurate are those which measure *contribution* to profit and fixed or period expenses—that is, profits after directly variable costs have been subtracted. Calculations of profits after all costs (including allocated overhead, general administrative expenses, etc.) are more difficult to make since it is often necessary to arbitrarily assign or allocate general expenses to individual products or profit centers. The Manly Company study exercise which follows illustrates some of the problems encountered in attempting to calculate profits after all costs by product.

Information on return on investment (profit related to investment), while extremely useful to management, is often the hardest kind of financial information to generate with any degree of accuracy. Because of the complexities involved in developing such systems, space does not permit going beyond the discussion of ROI profitability information systems given in Chapter Four.

Even in less complex situations, profit calculations and projections require many seemingly arbitrary assumptions, and considerable detail work. The FAD Limited study exercise at the end of the chapter presents a problem of projecting potential profits for a newly developed product. Here the analyst is faced with several fixed costs which will be incurred no matter what the sales volume—so that profitability will depend in large part on the sales attained. The analyst's profit projections in this study then not only require segregating fixed from variable costs, but also necessitate calculations of the sales level at which the company will start to earn a profit (the "breakeven" point).

Since the ultimate goal of any company is to earn profits, almost all financial reports are in one way or another profit-related information reports—if they don't actually report directly on some aspect of profit, they invariably report on some aspect of the company's operation which ultimately affects profits. The case study exercises at the end of this chapter provide examples of a wide range of profitability accounting and analysis systems, and how they are developed.

Summary
Conclusion

Financial and accounting information systems development is not a simple matter of learning basic accounting report formats and then applying them to different business situations. Rather, it very often requires careful diagnosing of situation requirements and then developing unique solutions which meet specific management information and work flow needs.

As was seen from the discussions in this chapter, relevant situation factors cover many areas, including:

1. Size of the company and the company's resources.
2. Nature of the company's business.
3. Management decision requirements and processes.
4. The work flow.
5. Organizational and behavioral considerations.

And solutions can range from basic accounting statements to profitability, cost, and responsibility accounting reporting systems.

The study exercises which follow provide practice in such diagnosis and systems development in similar situations, using many of the techniques in this chapter and in Chapter Four.

Case Study Exercises

In addition to the following case studies, the reader may also want to review the Domby Publishing Company study at the end of Chapter Two.

Consumer Gas Company

The Consumer Gas Company serves 415,000 gas customers in four states. A general manager supervises operations in each state, and each state has two divisions, each headed by a division manager. Each division is divided in towns (less than forty-nine per division), each of which has a supervisor in charge of operations. There are 310 town supervisors. The four general managers report to the vice president of operations, who in turn reports to the president.

You have been assigned the job of developing a responsibility accounting system for the company. Besides being used for responsibility accounting reports, the data file is used for preparing an overall annual operating statement for the Federal Power Commission, as well as detailed operating statements for each management unit and an annual financial report to stockholders. The detailed operating statements (requested by the controller) should contain all costs, including allocated general administrative and overhead expenses, and any one general ledger account may contain both direct and amortized charges.

In designing the responsibility accounting system, the controller has requested that the reports segregate those costs which an individual manager has responsibility for incurring. In some areas, it is pointed out, corporate and state managers procure material for the entire company.

Assignment

Develop a coding pattern for the financial data file that will serve all the management reporting requirements specified. Figure 5–11 shows the uniform system of accounts put out by the FPC for regulated gas companies, such as Consumer.

FIGURE 5–11

Uniform System of Accounts
(Selected Detail)

Balance Sheet Accounts—Detail omitted.

Gas Plant Accounts—Detail omitted.

Income Accounts

1.   *Utility operating income*
   400   Operating revenues.
   Operating expenses
   401   Operating expense.
   402   Maintenance expense.
   403   Depreciation expense.
   404.1 Amortization and depletion of producing natural gas land and land rights.
   404.2 Amortization of underground storage land and land rights.
   404.3 Amortization of other limited-term gas plant.
   405   Amortization of other gas plant.
   406   Amortization of gas plant acquisition adjustments.

FIGURE 5–11 (*Continued*)

407.1   Amortization of property losses.
407.2   Amortization of conversion expenses.
408   Taxes other than income taxes.
Etc.
Operating income
412–
413   Income from gas plant leased to others.
414   Other utility operating income.

2.   *Other income*
415–
416   Income from merchandising, jobbing, and contract work.
417   Income from nonutility operations.
Etc.

3.   *Miscellaneous Income Deductions*—Detail omitted.

4.   *Interest Charges*—Detail omitted.

5.   *Earned Surplus*—Detail omitted.

Operating Revenue Accounts

1.   *Sales of gas*
480   Residential sales.
481   Commercial and industrial sales.
Etc.

2.   *Other operating revenues*
487   Forfeited discounts.
Etc.

Operation and Maintenance Expense Accounts

1.   *Production expenses*—Detail omitted.

2.   *Underground storage expenses*
Operation
814   Operation supervision and engineering.
815   Maps and records.
816   Wells expenses.
Etc.

Maintenance
830   Maintenance supervision and engineering.
831   Maintenance of structures and improvements.
Etc.

3.   *Local storage expenses*—Detail omitted.

4.   *Transmission expenses*—Detail omitted.

FIGURE 5–11 *(continued)*

5.   *Distribution expenses*

Operation

870   Operation supervision and engineering.

871   Distribution load dispatching.

872   Compressor station labor and expenses.

873   Compressor station fuel and power.

Etc.

Maintenance

885   Maintenance supervision and engineering.

886   Maintenance of structures and improvements.

887   Maintenance of mains.

Etc.

6.   *Customer accounts expenses*

901   Supervision.

902   Meter reading expenses.

903   Customer records and collection expenses.

904   Uncollectable accounts.

905   Miscellaneous customer accounts expenses.

7.   *Sales expenses*—Detail omitted.

8.   *Administrative and general expenses*—Detail omitted.

Manley Company

The Manley Company, which had not shown a profit for several years, has recently hired a new president, Mr. John Billings, who has been given full authority to make any changes he feels are needed to make the company profitable.

Manley manufactured three industrial products, A, B, and C, which were sold to other industrial companies and used in their manufacturing processes. Sales were made directly to industrial users by company salesmen, who sold all three products and were paid on a straight salary basis. Competitive conditions were such that Manley could not raise or lower its prices unless major competitors did so first.

After a preliminary study, Mr. Billings decided that no immediate drastic action was needed. One of the first reports he requested from his accounting department was a detailed statement of earnings and expenses by products for the year ending December 31, 1973 (see Figure 5–12); a description of the nature of the costs is given in the Note to Figure 5–12. Mr. Billings transmitted copies of the report to the board of directors, who had never received such a report before, for their comments. Upon examining the

FIGURE 5-12

Manly Company

Profit and Loss Analysis by Product

Year Ending 12/31/73

| | Product A | | Product B | | Product C | | Total | Variable | Fixed | Allocation |
	Thousands	Per hundred lbs.	Thousands	Per hundred lbs.	Thousands	Per hundred lbs.	(thousands)	costs	costs	basis
Rent	$ 234	$10.97	$ 182	$ 17.72	$ 154	$ 15.65	$ 570		✓	Area (sq. ft)
Property taxes	24	1.12	19	1.89	15	1.57	58		✓	Area (sq. ft.)
Property insurance	20	.93	15	1.50	20	2.08	55		✓	Equipment value
Compensation tax	32	1.50	22	2.18	17	1.77	71		✓	Direct labor
Direct labor	516	24.20	355	34.52	274	27.81	1,145	✓		
Indirect labor	158	7.41	108	10.54	84	8.56	350		✓	Direct labor
Power	8	.37	9	.92	11	1.17	28		✓	Hours
Utilities	5	.23	4	.44	3	.36	12		✓	Area (sq. ft.)
Facility service	3	.14	2	.25	2	.25	7		✓	Area (sq. ft.)
Materials	390	18.29	111	10.83	114	11.60	615	✓		
Supplies	20	.93	18	1.80	13	1.37	51	✓		
Maintenance	6	.28	5	.53	3	.36	14	✓		
Total	$1,416	$66.37	$ 850	$ 83.12	$ 710	$ 72.55	$2,972			
Selling expense	363	17.03	182	17.73	187	19.00	732		✓	Sales dollars
Administration	137	6.42	51	5.00	70	7.14	258		✓	Sales dollars
Depreciation	65	3.05	50	4.90	65	6.64	180		✓	Equipment value
Interest	20	.93	15	1.50	20	2.08	55		✓	Equipment value
Total cost	$2,001	$93.80	$1,148	$112.25	$1,052	$108.01	$4,201			
Net sales	2,066	96.89	1,038	100.86	1,066	108.06	4,172			
Profit or (Loss)	$ 65	$ 3.09	$ (110)	$ (11.39)	$ 14	$ .05	$ (29)			
Unit sales	2,033,201		1,018,546		953,832					
Selling price	$0.98		$1.03		$1.10					

143

NOTE TO FIGURE 5–12
Manly Company
Explanation of Costs

Cost	Type	Explanation
Rent	Fixed	As stated in lease which runs for fifteen more years.
Property taxes	Fixed	The assessed valuation has remained constant since 1966, with a slightly increasing rate (independent of volume) expected within the next three years.
Property insurance	Fixed	Paid in advance until 1976, under a three-year agreement.
Compensation insurance	Fixed	Five percent of total labor (direct and indirect).
Direct labor	Variable	Workers are paid rate in accordance with industry averages. No unusual increases expected.
Indirect labor	Fixed	Cost is fixed within present range of operations of Manly Company.
Power	Fixed	Long-term contract with public utility company.
Utilities	Fixed	One-third of cost of electricity for light fixed by contract with utility company. Remaining two-thirds of costs consists of heat, which varies slightly with cost of fuel.
Facility service	Fixed	Miscellaneous building supplies, along with cleaning and custodial activities.
Materials	Variable	Average costs shown in Figure 5–12. Purchased at market prices with allowances for waste.
Supplies	Variable	Average costs shown in Figure 5–13. Purchased at market prices.
Maintenance	Variable	Varies with level of production.
Selling expense ⎫ Administration ⎬ Depreciation ⎪ Interest ⎭	Fixed	At normal production levels there is little variation in these costs.

statement, the chairman at the board's March meeting recommended dropping Product B, since he did not see how expenses could be reduced enough to make the product profitable.

Mr. Billings exercised his blanket authority and insisted on continuing production of all three products. He asked his accounting group to temporarily adopt as standard costs the costs per hundred pounds which had been arrived at in analyzing the profit and loss statement shown in Figure 5–12, and asked that a report based on these standards be given him on the first six months operation in 1974 as soon as the figures become available, at which time he would reconsider his decision. This report, as of June 30, 1974, is shown in Figure 5–13 (p. 146).

Assignment

1. Describe in detail the nature of the decision Mr. Billings made and the kind of information he should have to make the decision.
2. Revise Figures 5–12 and 5–13 in order to show cost and profit relationships in a way that you feel will be more useful for management decision making.
3. Was the decision correct in the spring of 1974 not to drop Product B? Explain your reasons, based on the revised figures you have prepared.

Gilray Corporation

The Gilray Corporation is a medium-size electronics company located on Long Island, New York. Its primary source of income is from defense contracts, which are normally written on a cost plus basis. As required under government contracts, Gilray has a highly automated job-order cost accounting system to track costs, both direct and indirect, against a given job.

Recently, Gilray has started to manufacture a "CRT Display Unit," and on-line computer terminal, for commercial sale. From the information available, this display will remain with about the same design and complexity for the next few years. The unit will be manufactured in a manufacturing area separate from other company manufacturing facilities which will consist of several production centers. Four distinct sub-assemblies are first completed and then these four are assembled in the final stages of production. Several of the sub-assemblies are highly technical electronic units.

At the present time, Gilray is considering using their existing job-order cost accounting system to determine costs and profitability of the CRT by production order issue lots. The existing cost accounting system collects actual charges on a job-by-job basis in the following manner:

1. *Labor.* Every individual in the company prepares a weekly time card that indicates how many hours were worked and what jobs the hours are charged to. This information is keypunched and is the basis for computing payroll and calculating job charges.

FIGURE 5-13
Manly Company
Profit and Loss Analysis by Product at Standard
January to June, 1974

	Product A		Product B		Product C		Standard totals	Actual totals	Variance favorable (unfavorable)
	Unit standard	Total (thous.)	Unit standard	Total (thous.)	Unit standard	Total (thous.)			
Rent	$10.97	$109	$17.72	$126	$15.65	$78	$313	$282	$31
Property taxes	1.12	11	1.89	13	1.57	7	31	27	4
Property insurance	.93	9	1.50	10	2.08	10	29	25	4
Compensation tax	1.50	14	2.18	15	1.77	8	37	37	
Direct labor	24.20	241	34.52	245	27.81	139	625	629	(4)
Indirect labor	7.41	73	10.54	74	8.56	42	189	175	14
Power	.37	3	.92	6	1.17	5	14	13	1
Utilities	.23	2	.44	3	.36	1	6	4	2
Facility service	.14	1	.25	1	.25	1	3	2	3
Materials	18.29	182	10.83	76	11.60	57	315	311	4
Supplies	.93	9	1.80	12	1.37	6	27	26	1
Maintenance	.28	2	.53	3	.36	1	6	6	
Total	$66.37	$656	$83.12	$584	$72.55	$355	$1,595	$1,537	$50
Selling expense	17.03	169	17.73	126	19.00	94	389	365	24
Administration	6.42	63	5.00	35	7.14	35	133	127	6
Depreciation	3.05	30	4.90	34	6.64	32	96	87	9
Interest	.93	9	1.50	10	2.08	10	29	25	4
Total cost	$93.80	$927	$112.25	$789	$108.01	$526	$2,242	$2,141	$103
Net sales	$96.89	$965	$100.86	$718	$108.06	$541	$2,146	$2,146	
Profit or (loss)	$ 3.09	$ 38	$(11.39)	$(71)	$ .05	$ 15	$ (96)	$ 5	$101
Unit sales	998,732		711,084		500,123				

146

2. *Material.* Material is ordered, received, and paid for on a job-by-job basis.

3. *Manufacturing Overhead.* These costs are collected in the various accounts and charged back to the jobs on the basis of the percentage of labor dollars on that job to the total manufacturing labor dollars for the company.

4. *General and Administrative Expense.* These costs are collected within various accounts and charged back to the jobs on the basis of the percentage of a job's manufacturing cost (labor, material and overhead) to the total company's manufacturing cost.

The existing system provides an excellent reporting system which provides management with adequate information to assist them in making decisions about their present products and accounting for costs and profits for each government contract.

Assignment

1. Evaluate the existing accounting system and determine its appropriateness for the CRT Unit operation.

2. Would you recommend switching to a process center cost accounting system? Explain your reasons and draw up a sample report form.

3. Describe the advantages and disadvantages of introducing standard costs for labor, materials, and factory overhead. Draw up a sample standard cost report form.

4. In determining profitability for the CRT unit, would you use a contribution to profit system and, if so, what expenses might be treated as general, unabsorbed expenses? Draw up a sample profitability analysis report.

New England Spring Company

Background

The New England Spring Company, which manufactures steel springs, was founded twenty-five years ago by John Daly who is still running the show. Mr. Daly is a self-made man who believes that the best way to get something done is to do it yourself. Although there are functional managers for sales and manufacturing, Big John is the only "real" boss.

John Marino, the sales manager, has been with New England Spring for twenty years. He is so accustomed to Mr. Daly's ways that at times he seems to be totally unaware that some of his salesmen deal directly with Mr. Daly.

This occasionally happens when a particularly good sale has been made and the salesman believes he can get a special bonus from the "boss."

Al Scott runs all the manufacturing areas of the company. He is in charge of everything from raw materials purchasing through finished goods inventory. Al is particularly proud that his factory crew is able to set up new production runs as quickly as any crew he has worked with. Al and Big John are constantly fighting over Big John's interference with production schedules, especially those affecting long-time customers.

Mr. Daly's wife is listed as the corporate treasurer and has to sign some checks and documents for legal reasons. Otherwise, the office and accounting routine is handled by Nancy Jane Lazlo, the head bookkeeper.

Because he has essentially been running a one-man show, Mr. Daly has been able to manage "by the seat of his pants." Slipshod practices and procedures have been overcome by Mr. Daly's thorough knowledge of all phases of the business and his ability to act quickly and decisively.

Sales

There are twenty field salesmen assigned to different geographic areas. The company only advertises in a few industrial magazines on an irregular basis. There is no formal sales forecast or sales budget. John Marino and Mr. Daly usually get together informally to discuss "how things are going" and whether or not this salesman or that salesman is able to "cut it." Pricing of products was based more on "shooting from the hip" than on precise knowledge of costs.

Production

The New England Spring Company produces thirty-five different types of springs, and is able to produce a limited number of additional variations according to customer needs. Production schedules are determined on a weekly basis according to machine availability, chronological listing of orders, and any special considerations.

Financial Reporting

Mr. Daly's first love has always been to run his business, to be the boss, to be active. As long as there's been money in the bank he has not been concerned with "fancy accountant's gimmicks." The financial statements have always been kept simple. The balance sheet and income statement for 1973 are shown in Figures 5—14 and 5—15.

FIGURE 5–14

New England Spring Company
Balance Sheet
As of 12/31/73

ASSETS

Current:

Cash	$ 168,000
Accounts receivable	400,000

Inventories:

Finished goods	139,000
Raw materials & supplies	247,000
Total inventories	$ 386,000
Total current assets	$ 954,000

Fixed assets:

Cost	$1,263,000
Less reserves for depreciation	439,000
Net fixed assets	$ 824,000
Total assets	$1,778,000

LIABILITIES AND CAPITAL

Current:

Accounts payable	$ 153,000
Notes payable-banks	275,000
Total current liabilities	$ 428,000

Fixed liabilities:

Mortgage payable	$ 5,000
Notes payable-banks	33,000
Total fixed liabilities	$ 38,000

Capital:

Common stock (5,000 shares)	$ 160,000
Earned surplus	1,580,000
Total net worth	$1,740,000
Total liabilities & net worth	$1,778,000

Current Situation

Because he and his wife have had serious health problems during the past year, in late 1973 Mr. Daly made an offer to a close relative whereby the relative would buy the company by paying a certain initial amount on 1/1/74

FIGURE 5–15

New England Spring Company
Profit & Loss Statement
Year ending 12/31/73

Gross sales	
Less: returns, allowances, discounts	$3,078,000
Net sales	162,000
Cost of goods sold	$2,916,000
Gross profit	2,082,000
Selling expense	$ 834,000
Selling profit	541,000
General administration expense	$ 293,000
Net income before taxes	193,000
Federal income taxes	$ 100,000
Net profit	48,000
Dividends	$ 52,000

plus an amount to be determined as of 1/1/75 based on a CPA evaluation of the concern. During 1974, Mr. Daly would train his relative, Mr. James Daly, in the business. Mr. James Daly's attorney and the CPA doing the evaluation insist that corporate financial reporting practices be changed, in order that a true and honest analysis which will be fair to both Mr. Dalys can be made at the end of 1974.

Assignment

1. Identify the key factors affecting information system development at New England Spring Company, covering all the areas discussed in Chapter Two.

2. Define the kind of information system you would develop for New England Spring Company. Who would be its major users?

3. Outline, in as much detail as you can, the financial information system which you would recommend for New England Spring Company in light of the changing management situation and the company's business require-ments.

4. Amplify in detail the budgetary process you would recommend for the company.

FAD Limited

Background

June 6, 1959, marked Colonel F. A. Drake's forty-eighth birthday, his retirement from twenty-five years of military service, the graduation of his daughter from college, and the last payment on his retirement home. Mrs. Drake looked forward to returning to their retirement home, and the prospects of having the Colonel undertake some long-delayed home remodeling and landscaping projects. Colonel Drake also looked forward to the years of comfortable living with mortgage payments and college expenses behind him, a modest savings account, a monthly retirement income of $550.00 and time to catch up on his fishing.

The first twelve months of retirement passed quickly with a reasonable balance between home projects and fishing trips. However, during the next six months, Colonel Drake seemed to "get caught up on everything," and began to look for an interesting outlet for his time and energy.

In January, 1961, Colonel Drake received $100,000 in the settlement of a family estate and immediately channeled his activities toward the formation of FAD Limited as a sole proprietorship for the purpose of developing, producing, and marketing "The Twister"—a fad item with an expected short, but highly successful sales life. Colonel Drake had investigated this venture and based his final decision on the following projections. He planned to discontinue any or all phases of operations as soon as financial conditions warranted such action.

Colonel Drake discussed his product ideas with two personal friends who were manufacturers' representatives and relied heavily on their judgment in establishing his sales estimates.

Drawing on his own experiences and that of a neighbor—a retired engineer and production superintendent—Colonel Drake estimated that it would require about twelve months to develop a production model, obtain patent rights, and produce enough inventory to satisfy initial sales demands. He planned to introduce "The Twister" in January, 1962, and expected that his market area would be saturated within eighteen to twenty-four months. If demand for "The Twister" spread, Colonel Drake planned to either sell the patent rights or grant production rights on a royalty basis.

This case was prepared by Professor Earl D. Bennett as a basis for class discussion. It is not intended to illustrate either effective or ineffective handling of the issues in the situation.

In view of the short duration of this venture and the desire to avoid drawing on his savings account, Colonel Drake planned to minimize his capital commitments whenever possible. Figure 5–16 gives his estimates of profitability for "The Twister."

1961 Operations

During the first six months, Colonel Drake was successful in developing a production model in his home workshop at a cost of $12,000, excluding consideration of the value of the time which he devoted to the project. Approximately $6,000 of the total expenditures represented the costs of special jigs and fixtures which would be used on regular production runs.

Patent rights were obtained at a cost of $5,000, while other business formation expenditures totaled $3,000.

After investigating a number of special-purpose machines, Colonel Drake placed an order for a CUSTOM 50 at a delivered and installed cost of $35,000. The contract provided for a payment of $12,000 at delivery on July 1, 1961, and $1,400 per month for eighteen months. The CUSTOM 50 had a rated output of fifty "Twisters" per hour with an expected productive life of 500,000 units. Scrap value would approximate removal costs.

Prior to establishing production schedules for the period 7/1-12/31/61, Colonel Drake took his production model of "The Twister" to his friends to obtain additional marketing and pricing advice. Both manufacturers' agents urged Colonel Drake to accelerate production plans in order to hit the Christmas market with at least 60,000 "Twisters." They also suggested going from a cash price of $5.00 per unit to $6.00 with credit terms of 3/10, net 30 and stated that about 80 percent of their customers, to whom "The Twister" would be sold, usually took advantage of any cash discount deals. They offered to either advance Colonel Drake cash under a contract for 40,000 "Twisters" at $4.75 per unit and handle the rest of his production at the ten percent commission on gross sales, or to go the commission route all the way. Colonel Drake agreed to give them his answer by not later than August 1.

Although available labor supply would have permitted two-shift operations, Colonel Drake decided to start with one shift, with overtime as needed, until production was running smoothly. Then, if conditions warranted, he would add another shift. Initial production schedules were based on 100 ten-hour days at the rated machine capacity of fifty units per hour to provide approximately 50,000 "Twisters" for November 21 delivery. Approximately thirty production days would still be available in 1961, and Mr. Drake tentatively planned to continue the same rate of production unless conditions changed drastically.

Colonel Drake contracted for 100,000 units of material at a delivered cost of $1.00 each, with 60,000 units to be delivered on July 1 and the balance on

FIGURE 5–16

Estimated Revenue:		
January 1–December 31, 1962		
100,000 units @ average price of	$5.00	$500,000
January 1–June 30, 1963		
50,000 units @ average price of	$3.00	150,000
		$650,000
Estimated Cash Outlays:		
Cost of sales:		
Material–150,000 units @ $1.20	$180,000	
Labor–150,000 units @ $0.30		
(Includes a labor rate of		
$1.37 per hour plus estimated		
employee payroll taxes of		
approximately 9½% per		
labor dollar)	45,000	
5% Allowance for estimation		
error (225,000 @ 5%)	11,250	$236,250
Development costs		10,000
Lease of production and raw material storage space		75,000
Special purpose production equipment		35,000
Lease of warehouse for finished product		36,000
Packaging and distribution expense–5¢ per unit		7,500
Sales commission (10% of gross revenue)		65,000
Sales promotion campaign		2,500
Supervisory and administrative expenses		25,000
Business formation and termination expense		10,000
Total		$502,250

October 1. Payment requirements were one-third upon delivery and the balance in four equal monthly installments without cash discount provisions.

Unfortunately, Colonel Drake waited until June 15 before beginning lease negotiations for production and warehouse facilities. Under the pressure for July 1 occupancy, he signed a lease agreement for production and raw material storage space which provided for the deposit of a month's rent (to be returned without interest upon termination of the lease), a monthly rental of $5,000 payable at the beginning of each month, and the right of termination by either lessee or lessor with a thirty-day notice. The lease contract for finished goods storage space contained similar provisions with a monthly rental of $3,000.

On July 14, Colonel Drake completed his first seventy-five machine hours of production with a total output of 3,000 "Twisters." However, his material usage showed a ten percent over-run—i.e., 3,300 units which he attributed to an incorrect machine setting and to hidden flaws in the raw material. Although he could do nothing about the loss from raw material defects, he planned to adjust the CUSTOM 50 over the week-end and expressed the belief that this would cut his material over-run to about 5 percent. In view of this anticipated over-run, Colonel Drake searched for and located an outlet for the scrap material. The potential buyer agreed to pick up the scrap at the Drake plant in 2,000 unit lots *only* and pay $.25 per unit.

Colonel Drake had been able to hire a machine crew of ten for $1.25 per hour, with time and a half above forty hours per week, and two utility men @ $1.00 on a straight time basis for all hours worked. However, he found that the machine crew's low efficiency level and inexperience with his production process, coupled with an inefficient layout for production flows, not only resulted in a twenty-five percent over-run of labor hours (i.e., 750 hours, including 200 overtime hours, to produce 3,000 Twisters) but also in the operation of the CUSTOM 50 at eighty percent of rated capacity. Colonel Drake concluded that a change in production layout, plus some improvement in labor efficiency, would permit future production of 450 units in a ten-hour day.

Colonel Drake had maintained document files and canceled checks for all business transactions since January 1, 1961, although he did not have any formal accounting records other than the minimum to meet payroll requirements. He realized that he would soon need some organized form of accounting data for planning, control, and financial reporting purposes. In addition, Colonel Drake was concerned with the heavy drain on his savings account and was weighing the question of accepting the manufacturers' representatives' offer or seeking short-term bank financing. However, his current production problems fully occupied his time, so Colonel Drake decided to seek your assistance on his information reporting problems.

Assignment

1. Describe the overall business factors relevant to developing an information reporting system for FAD, as well as key organization, marketing, and production restraints.

2. What are the critical problems facing Colonel Drake at this time and what information will he need in making key decisions and solving his major problems?

3. Make two month-by-month cash budgets—one with and one without the 40,000 unit contract. State your assumptions.

Prepare profitability projections under three conditions: taking the 40,000 unit contract at $4.75 (at 40,000 and 150,000 units of sale) and not taking it (at 150,000 units of sale). State your assumptions. Base your cost projections on Drake's actual experience during his first week of production and compare your three projections with his original projection.

Calculate the sales level at which Colonel Drake will break even with and without the contract. State your assumptions.

Project production output under a five-day, ten-hour, one-shift operation and a two-shift operation.

Explain why these reports are the most important ones required by Colonel Drake at this time, based on your answer to Question 2.

4. Should Colonel Drake accept the offer from his friends to buy 40,000 units at $4.75?

5. Was Colonel Drake's original decision to manufacture the "Twister" a good one in light of his experience to date? State your reasons.

Marketing Management Information Systems

O F THE TWO BASIC BUSINESS FUNCTIONS, MARKETING AND PRODUC-
tion (or operations), marketing management is discussed first here,
because information gathered from the marketplace on customer demand
and preference plays a large role in management decision making for operations. The discussion in this chapter covers the nature of marketing management, major marketing management decision areas, and basic marketing
management information systems. Examples of how such systems are developed in specific companies are discussed in Chapter Seven.

Marketing Management

Marketing involves selling and distributing a company's products or services.
The responsibilities of marketing management include (depending on the type
of company and the product or service it provides): developing overall
marketing strategy; sales forecasting; profitability analysis; and planning,
controlling, and administering the different marketing activities.

The *strategic plan* for marketing specifies the overall marketing mix—that
is, the combination of products, prices, customers, markets, distribution

6

channels, and promotions which management thinks will be the most profitable choices for the future in light of company resources and market restraints. Strategic planning for marketing requires gathering and interpreting
market information (market research) to identify market opportunities and
restraints, determining available company resources, analyzing sales and market test results, and developing and evaluating alternative strategies.

Sales forecasting requires estimating for some given time period in the
future (monthly, quarterly, yearly, etc.) both what the total demand for
company products or services will be, as well as what portion of that demand
a company can reasonably be expected to get, given the competitive market
environment and the company's resources and profit objectives. These forecasts may be for varying time periods (very long-term to very short-term) and
may be for the company as a whole, as well as by product, geographic area,
customer type, and the like, as dictated by management decision-making
needs. The sales forecast is the basis for all operational planning within a
company.

Since company sales forecasts and marketing strategies are judged in the
light of expected profitability, *profitability analysis* is a major marketing
management responsibility. Since profitability is affected by sales volume,
price, product mix, investment in marketing assets (distribution, accounts

receivable, etc.), and costs, the impact of these factors are considered in determining past and future profit contributions. Profitability analyses then can range from price/volume and breakeven analyses to product profitability analyses to analyses of the return on investment in different marketing assets.

In addition to overall marketing decision responsibilities, marketing management also involves *planning, controlling, and administering different marketing activities.* These activity areas include sales, advertising, customer service, distribution, and product management.

The sales management job involves, depending on the situation: defining sales objectives and goals (especially by organizational unit) and developing a sales organization; developing sales programs and administering the sales force; planning and administering sales support or sales promotion activities; monitoring overall sales performance; and, in some situations, administering order processing.

Advertising is the paid communication of information about a company's products, services or image, by other than direct personal contact in order to influence the consumer or industrial user, or the public in general, either to buy the product or service, or to accept the idea communicated. Thus, advertising management is concerned with developing an overall advertising strategy, including products to be promoted, relative kind and strength of advertising support to be given each product, and advertising themes which best match product appeals to buyer motivation. This strategy is designed to help achieve the company's overall objectives within realistic cost restraints. Management must also select and schedule the media for each product and develop appropriate advertising messages and advertisements (including copywriting, layout, art and production). Finally, management should monitor the results of the advertising efforts and make changes where needed.

Distribution for marketing involves the physical storage of goods and their movement from various supply points to customers or consumers. Managing distribution involves: overall planning of the distribution system, including number, size, location and type of warehouses, channels of distribution, shipping facilities, and materials handling equipment; establishing procedures for order processing and scheduling of distribution to insure that customer demands are met effectively and economically; administering the distribution activities; and establishing an inventory control system and measuring the effectiveness of the distribution operation.

Customer service involves insuring that the products or services that are sold by a company function as promised. Customer service management involves: developing overall customer service plans and goals through an evaluation of customer and product needs, competition, and company plans and resources; developing warranty service policies and policies for customer service charges; planning and administering such customer service activities as scheduling service and hiring and training of service personnel; and monitoring product and service personnel performance, as well as overall customer service performance in terms of costs, income, and customer satisfaction. In addition, coordination is required with other company operating areas, such as advertising, sales, production and product development.

The product management job involves managing the selling and distribution of one or more specific products from among the full line of products that a company markets. The product manager develops a marketing plan (working with all related departments) and in turn communicates it to those departments that are responsible for making and selling the product, such as advertising and manufacturing. He coordinates all the activities necessary to make the product successful—such as advertising, finance, sales, product development, merchandising, research and manufacturing—reconciles differences and conflicts, stimulates higher performance, monitors results—in short, he is a marketing manager for the product or product line he manages.

The nature and organization of all the marketing tasks discussed here will naturally vary from company to company. For example, a mail-order company sells by mail, whereas a food products company sells through retail grocery stores. As a result, the sales organizations and sales programs will differ markedly at each company—with no salesmen at the mail-order company, but a large organization of order-taking salesmen, store service representatives, and distribution facilities at the food company. The exact responsibilities of each marketing manager, therefore, will depend on the organization and business of the company for which he works.

Supporting Information Systems

In order to provide the information required to carry out these marketing management jobs, a variety of information systems may be needed. These systems can vary from periodic market research studies of consumer psychology, to reporting and review procedures for planning, to profitability analyses and budgets, to results in major marketing activity areas.

As of this writing, it appears that no company had developed a fully integrated marketing management information system—though many are trying (one of these companies is described in the first section of Chapter Seven). In fact, such an integrated system probably cannot be developed, largely because of the diversity of marketing management information needs, especially in the strategic planning area. In addition, because of the complexities involved in developing planning information systems, systems analysts tend to concentrate on financial analysis and historical reporting information systems and neglect other kinds of forward planning information systems.

For example, recently a systems analyst was interviewing the marketing manager of a consumer products division as part of a new information system development project. The analyst at one point asked "What information would you like to have that you are not now getting?" The marketing manager's answer covered information on customer tastes, competitor plans, economic projections, anticipated changes in distribution channels and similar external information essential to marketing planning.

The analyst was visibly surprised. What he had really meant was "What additional breakdowns and analyses of sales results and other operating result information do you want," since the company's internal reporting systems in the past had dealt exclusively with analyzing and reporting on historical information. The subject was never raised again by anyone in the systems development group.

As in so many other situations studied, the analyst here was in reality working to develop an efficient data processing system designed to handle order processing, billing, customer account record keeping, credit screening, shipping, inventory updating, etc. Information for management was considered only a by-product of this system and not its primary function. In fact, it became clear later in the study that the analysts looked upon the requests for management information reports as intrusions, which made their processing system less efficient (for example, longer customer code identification numbers were required to produce additional sales analysis reports, which increased the size of the customer file and so slowed data processing).

Work is nonetheless being done on information systems to support strategic planning for marketing. Such systems, along with more traditional results-oriented marketing management information systems, are discussed in the following sections.

Information Systems Used in Overall Marketing Planning

In fulfilling its responsibilities, marketing management necessarily must first answer questions of overall strategy: what products to sell? where? at what price? to whom? how? through whom? These and similar strategic questions generally constitute the "marketing mix" for the company. The answers to these questions require information from the marketplace on customer need and preference, competition, available distribution channels and advertising media, economic conditions, possible customer reaction to new products and promotions, and predictions of other future trends in the marketplace. Internally generated information on past operating results is also needed, as is information on available company resources.

Every company has a marketing strategy, but it is often no more than a vague concept in top management's mind and, as such, may not be written down in a formal document, but may only be implied in the marketing plans and budgets. Whether formally or informally developed, strategy is a key controlling element in planning, since it provides a single approach to operational planning which presumably is consistent with corporate objectives and so helps coordinate that planning.

In practice, marketing strategies go through many phases of development, evolving from generalized ideas about "good" products or markets for the company to specific strategies, such as the one developed for a small candy company:

> The company will market through independent wholesalers and its own retail outlets both a high quality, medium-priced Perfection boxed candy, as well as other candies, confectionaries, and lower priced non-Perfection boxed chocolates throughout the central United States.

This strategy was further developed as follows:

> The company will continue to serve wholesale accounts only so long as production permits, since its own retail outlets should always have first call on production, and production facilities will be expanded to service wholesale demand only if projected profits from that area justify it.
> New wholesale accounts will be solicited in areas where the company plans to open stores, so that there will be exposure of the Perfection brand name in that area prior to expanding with shops there.
> Wholesalers will be sold Perfection chocolates only in situations where they will not compete with our own stores; other wholesalers will be sold a second, lower-priced line of chocolates carrying another brand name, but only if and so long as demand and profits warrant it.

The process of refining strategies and translating them into plans involves market research. Such research may be extensive and may involve consumer surveys and sampling, special studies of market, competition, and distribution channels, market and product tests, or other kinds of economic and market analyses. Several examples of these kinds of reports are described in the following sections of this chapter and in Chapter Seven.

Simulation is another testing technique that provides information for strategic decision making. Some companies, especially in the oil and air transport fields, have developed simulated planning models which enable computer testing of proposed strategies. Such models, as well as operations research techniques which provide information for assisting marketing management in strategic decision making, are discussed in Part Three.

In addition to information on results of marketing research, information reports on results of past marketing operations can also provide a useful framework for developing and evaluating alternative strategies. For example, information on the first year's operating results led to substantial revisions of marketing strategy for *The National Observer,* Dow Jones newest weekly publication. Initially, management had thought of the publication as competing with local Sunday newspapers. In fact, the new publication competed with national weekly newsmagazines, a market which required an entirely different promotion and distribution strategy. Result reporting systems can thus be considered one of the information systems that support strategic decision making.

The acid test of any strategy is whether it will generate sufficient profits. Proposed strategies are, therefore, ultimately judged in the light of operating budgets and plans built on them. These types of information systems are discussed in the following sections, as are result reports.

While the discussion above covers traditional budgetary and result reporting systems, much of the discussion concerns very different kinds of information systems from the ones discussed in Chapters Four and Five on accounting and finance. Unlike financial and accounting information systems, strategic planning information systems are characterized by heavy reliance on external data reporting, qualitative as much as quantitative information content, sporadic, not regular, timing, and lack of centralized control of data sources. These characteristics lead to lack of standardization from company to company.

It is nonetheless reasonable to speak of an information system for strategic planning in marketing, since it is possible to systematically collect and report on the data used for strategic planning. But developing such systems can be a frustrating job for a systems analyst, who has been conditioned to think of information systems in more conventional terms and whose time is limited. For this reason, strategic planning information systems are often mixed systems, consisting of a combination of information sources, including external market research studies administered by the marketing department, company-wide budgetary and result reporting systems under a central data processing department, and advanced mathematical models, such as those described in Part Three.

Sales Forecasting

In translating marketing strategies into operating plans, a marketing manager needs to answer the question "How much will the company sell?" before he can develop *final* operating plans. In answering this question, a manager must first decide what kind of sales forecast is needed, including time covered by the forecast (one year, five years, ten years, etc.), time intervals used (weekly, monthly, yearly, etc.), type of units forecast (dollar volume, items sold, etc.), who will receive and use the forecast, and the format or layout of the forecasts. These decisions about the kind of forecast needed will be based on the planning for which the forecasts will be used, the nature of the company's business, the resources available for forecast preparation, and other management needs.

Sales forecasts are a combination of two elements: first, estimates of possible company sales based on total market analysis, covering such factors as economic trends, industry and market size and structure, competition, and potential market share for the company; and second, estimates of sales likely to be achieved in light of available company resources. Information is needed, therefore, not only on economic, industry, and market factors affecting company sales, but also on what operating managers feel they realistically can achieve in light of past sales and of available financial, technical, and manpower resources. The sources of this information, then, would also vary—from U.S. Government data on economic trends, industry reports, and market research studies, to company sales records and operating management's estimates of sales—depending on the type of forecast required.

Where longer term sales forecasts are needed, economic forecasts are normally prepared first. Industry forecasts are then prepared within the framework of this projected general economic climate. Government research and statistical services are a major information source used in preparing these forecasts. These services include: basic statistics collected by such government agencies as the Bureau of Census and Bureau of Labor Statistics; statistics assembled as a by-product of other government services, such as the Internal Revenue Service, Social Security Administration, Federal Trade Commission, and the Securities and Exchange Commission; and research and analysis studies conducted by such government agencies as the Federal Reserve Board and the Department of Commerce.[1] Other sources of information are industry associations and publications, research departments of banks and brokerage houses, and independent economic consultants.[2] Economic and industry forecasts are prepared using either non-quantitative methods (such as qualitative appraisals based on the experience and judgment of individual managers) or quantitative methods, drawn from statistics or mathematics.[3]

---

1. For a comprehensive listing of the kinds of information sources useful in economic and industry forecasting see Vernon G. Lippitt, *Statistical Sales Forecasting* (New York: Financial Executive's Research Foundation, 1969), pp. 327-339.
2. William Copulsky, *Practical Sales Forecasting* (New York: American Management Association, 1970), pp. 25-46.
3. See John Chambers, Satinder Mullick and Donald Smith, "How to Choose the Right Forecasting Technique," *Harvard Business Review*, July-August 1971, pp. 45-72, for a comprehensive survey of sales forecasting techniques (and information sources) which are used in preparing sales forecasts.

In preparing overall industry forecasts, potential technological changes may have to be studied to determine their impact on industry and product trends. Industry publications, such as *Drug Topics, Electrical Merchandising, Almanac of Quic‹ Frozen Foods,* and literally hundreds of other magazines, newsletters and special reports, are a major source of this information.

As industry and market forecasts are refined to meet a company's planning needs, estimates are needed of potential customers within different market segments. *Sales Management, Standard Rate and Data Service,* and the marketing division of Hearst magazines are among the many sources of information on the number of potential customers within different marketing areas. Such forecasts can be quite detailed, as shown in Figure 6–1.

FIGURE 6–1

Forecast of Manufacturing Jobs by County: 1965-1985
(in thousands)

	1965	1970	1975	1980	1985	Change 1965–1985 Number	Percent
23-county region	1,972.4	2,030.5	2,061.5	2,070.5	2,074.5	102.1	5.2
New Jersey sector	681.7	730.7	762.2	790.7	815.2	133.5	19.6
Bergen	94.8	101.8	105.8	107.8	109.3	14.5	15.3
Essex	134.7	144.7	149.7	152.7	154.7	20.0	14.8
Hudson	112.1	118.1	122.1	125.1	127.1	15.0	13.4
Mercer	40.9	44.4	46.4	48.4	50.4	9.5	23.2
Middlesex	76.4	82.4	87.4	91.4	95.4	19.0	24.9
Monmouth	18.4	22.4	25.4	29.9	33.9	15.5	84.2
Morris	24.8	27.8	29.3	31.3	34.3	9.5	38.3
Passaic	76.8	79.8	82.8	84.8	85.8	9.0	11.7
Somerset	20.4	22.4	24.4	27.4	29.4	9.0	44.1
Union	82.4	86.9	88.9	91.9	94.9	12.5	15.2
New York sector	1,175.5	1,173.6	1,168.1	1,142.6	1,116.1	−59.4	−5.1
New York City	891.4	871.3	852.6	813.6	775.6	−115.8	−13.0
Bronx	54.2	55.2	56.7	54.7	50.7	−3.5	−6.5
Kings	221.3	224.3	226.3	224.3	216.3	−5.0	−2.3
New York	481.0	458.4	435.2	404.2	387.2	−93.8	−19.5
Queens	126.4	124.4	123.4	118.4	108.4	−18.0	−14.2
Richmond	8.5	9.0	11.0	12.0	13.0	4.5	52.9
Dutchess	23.5	25.5	26.5	28.5	30.0	6.5	27.7
Nassau	107.0	112.0	115.0	117.0	118.0	11.0	10.3
Orange	16.4	17.4	18.4	19.9	21.4	5.0	30.5
Putnam	1.3	1.5	1.7	2.2	2.7	1.4	107.7
Rockland	13.8	15.8	17.8	20.3	22.3	8.5	61.6
Suffolk	47.1	51.1	54.1	58.1	61.1	14.0	29.7
Westchester	75.0	79.0	82.0	83.0	85.0	10.0	13.3
Connecticut sector							
Fairfield	115.2	126.2	131.2	137.2	143.2	28.0	24.3

Source: *The Next Twenty Years* (New York: Port of New York Authority, 1966), p.19.

As the forecaster attempts to determine the share of the total market his company can expect to gain (for different products in different marketing areas), competition is studied. Gathering information on future competitor plans is extremely difficult, and there are no readily available sources from which this kind of information can be systematically gathered, outside of salesmen's reports on competitor tests. What information that can be gathered on planned competitor moves is combined with information drawn from company plans relating to new products, marketing programs, facility development, and available financial resources in estimating the company's market share.

As shorter-term, more specific company sales forecasts are developed product by product and region by region, information is often gathered from sales personnel. This information would reflect sales management's view of local market trends and competitor moves which might have an impact on company sales forecasts. In many companies, this is a major source of local market data. Other areas of marketing management would also be consulted for information on short-term plans and programs which might affect the sales forecast.

Within the framework of these forecasts, specific short-term sales plans or budget forecasts are developed. For example, at *The National Observer* the sales plan (which was called a sales budget) was broken down by selling media and by month. The plan also included information on cancelled subscriptions and showed the impact of planned sales on total circulation, since the ultimate goal of subscription and newsstand selling was to increase total circulation (see Figure 6–2). Other commonly used ways to break down sales in the sales plan are by product, by manufacturing region, and by sales territory. Dollar sales, instead of unit sales, are frequently shown.

The format used for the sales plan will depend on the type of business and management decision-making needs. For example, *The National Observer* is a single product operation which sells through mail-order media and newsstands, and the report was for sales planning and control use. A multiproduct company, on the other hand, might require several different sales information breakdowns. For instance, the field sales manager might need a report on unit sales by selling region to plan and monitor the work of his salesmen; production management could use unit sales by product to develop forecasts of production requirements; and top management needs a dollar summary by product.

Profitability Analysis
for Marketing

In developing and evaluating marketing strategies and operating plans, forecasts and budgets, a marketing manager analyzes such areas as what products

FIGURE 6-2

The National Observer—Circulation Department
Estimated Subscription Sales and Circulation—1964*

	Jan.	Feb.	March	First quarter	April	May	June	Second quarter	July	August	Sept.	Third quarter	Oct.	Nov.	Dec.	Fourth quarter	Year
Subscription circulation (paid) beginning of period	100,000	100,000	109,600	100,000	127,600	150,200	148,800	127,600	146,400	114,000	86,400	146,400	95,600	115,000	131,600	95,600	100,000
Additions																	
Subscription sales																	
Direct mail	26,200	35,600	39,000	100,800	12,800	2,000	2,000	16,800	4,000	14,000	32,400	50,400	25,200	18,000	12,400	55,600	223,600
Advertising	10,000	17,000	15,000	42,000	8,400	1,200	1,200	10,800	2,000	4,000	12,800	18,800	6,000	2,000	400	8,400	80,000
House ads in DJ publications	800	800	800	2,400	600	600	600	1,800	600	600	600	1,800	400	400	400	1,200	7,200
Development and testing	1,200	3,600	2,200	7,000	200	200	200	600	200	1,600	3,600	5,400	3,600	1,200	200	5,000	18,000
Community and phone	1,000	1,200	1,200	3,400	2,000	2,000	2,000	6,000	2,000	2,000	2,000	6,000	2,000	2,000	2,000	6,000	21,400
Subscription agency	200	200	200	600	200	200	200	600	200	200	200	600	200	200	200	600	2,400
Education and clergy	1,600	1,200	600	3,400	–	–	–	–	–	–	1,000	1,000	6,000	3,000	1,000	10,000	14,400
Regular and Christmas gift	200	200	200	600	200	200	200	600	200	200	200	600	200	200	5,800	6,200	8,000
Over the counter, employee and institutional	1,800	1,800	1,800	5,400	1,200	1,200	1,200	3,600	1,400	1,400	1,400	4,200	1,400	1,200	200	2,800	16,000
Solicitation of home delivery expires	2,000	–	–	2,000	–	–	–	–	–	–	–	–	–	–	–	–	2,000
Total subscription sales	45,000	61,600	61,000	167,600	25,600	7,600	7,600	40,800	10,600	24,000	54,200	88,800	45,000	28,200	22,600	95,800	393,000
Renewals																	
Long-term	8,000	10,000	4,000	22,000	4,000	10,000	14,000	28,000	8,000	6,000	6,000	20,000	8,000	6,000	6,000	20,000	90,000
Short-term	14,000	14,000	12,000	40,000	–	–	–	–	16,000	20,000	16,000	52,000	6,000	2,000	2,000	10,000	102,000
Total additions	67,000	85,600	77,000	229,600	29,600	17,600	21,600	68,800	34,600	50,000	76,200	160,800	59,000	36,200	30,600	125,800	585,000

Losses

Long-term expires	15,000	24,000	9,000	48,000	5,000	17,000	20,000	42,000	12,000	10,000	8,000	30,000	10,000	10,000	10,000	30,000	150,000
Short-term expires	44,000	42,000	40,000	126,000	—	—	2,000	—	51,000	63,600	51,000	165,600	23,600	5,600	5,600	34,800	326,400
Education and gift expires	2,000	—	—	2,000	—	—	2,000	2,000	4,000	—	—	16,000	—	—	4,000	4,000	8,000
Credit stops	6,000	10,000	10,000	26,000	2,000	2,000	2,000	6,000	4,000	4,000	8,000	16,000	6,000	4,000	2,000	12,000	60,000
Total losses	67,000	76,000	59,000	202,000	7,000	19,000	24,000	50,000	67,000	77,600	67,000	211,600	39,600	19,600	21,600	80,800	544,400
Net subscription gain (or loss) for period	—	9,600	18,000	27,600	22,600	(1,400)	(2,400)	18,800	(32,400)	(27,600)	9,200	(50,800)	19,400	16,600	9,000	45,000	40,600
Subscription circulation (paid) end of period	100,000	109,600	127,600	127,600	150,200	148,800	146,400	146,400	114,000	86,400	95,600	95,600	115,000	131,600	140,600	140,600	140,600
ABC grace carried	12,000	10,000	6,000	6,000	6,000	6,000	4,000	4,000	6,000	6,000	6,000	6,000	6,000	6,000	6,000	6,000	6,000
Total ABC subscription circulation end of period	112,000	129,600	133,600	133,600	156,200	154,800	150,400	150,400	120,000	92,400	101,600	101,600	121,000	137,600	146,600	146,600	146,600
Other ABC circulation end of period																	
Newsstand and home delivery	16,000	16,000	16,000	16,000	16,000	16,000	16,000	16,000	17,000	17,000	17,000	17,000	18,000	18,000	18,000	18,000	18,000
Young salesmen program	3,600	3,800	4,000	4,000	4,200	4,400	4,700	4,800	5,000	5,200	5,200	5,200	5,800	5,800	6,000	6,000	6,000
Total ABC circulation end of period	131,600	149,400	153,600	153,600	176,400	175,200	171,100	171,100	140,800	114,400	123,800	123,800	143,600	161,400	170,600	170,600	170,600

* All figures have been disguised. However, the general relationships among the various components of the flow plan have been maintained.

to sell or give emphasis to, what price to charge, how to allocate advertising expenditures to products and regions, which distribution channels to use, the effectiveness of marketing asset use, and the quality of the marketing operation's overall performance.

In making decisions on what price to charge, the manager needs information on the impact of price changes on total sales volume and profits. In evaluating existing product lines, he must examine the costs and relative profitability of these products, while evaluating new product proposals in light of anticipated profits. In making advertising or distribution decisions, the marketing manager needs information on the anticipated profits of alternative advertising or distribution programs. Overall marketing performance is judged in light of total profits and return on investment in marketing assets.

Several kinds of profitability analyses are used to provide marketing management with this information, including product line or product profitability, price/volume analysis, new product profitability analysis, advertising allocation analysis, and analysis of return on investment in marketing assets. Financial data is required for all phases of profitability analyses. As was pointed out in Chapters Four and Five, this data may be obtained from inventory control, shipping records and sales invoices and from cost accounting reporting systems which provide product cost and marketing and administrative expense data.

Pricing and Product Decisions

Table 6–1, an analysis of product line profitability at a company with three product lines, shows the profit contribution of each product line after

TABLE 6–1

Analysis of Product Line Profit Contribution

| | Product Line | | | |
	A	B	C	Total
Sales	$500,000	$300,000	$200,000	$1,000,000
Variable costs	350,000	180,000	100,000	630,000
Gross profit contribution	$150,000	$120,000	$100,000	$ 370,000
% to sales	30%	40%	50%	37%
Specific programmed costs	100,000	36,000	14,000	150,000
Net profit contribution	$ 50,000	$ 84,000	$ 86,000	$ 220,000
% to sales	10%	28%	43%	22%
General programmed costs				40,000
Fixed costs				120,000
Operating profit before tax				$ 60,000
% to sales				6%

deduction of only variable costs and after deduction of advertising and other programmed costs. Management's attention is drawn to product line A, which accounts for half of dollar sales, but which has a low profit contribution. For simplicity, assume that product line A consists of a single product with planned sales of 5,000 units at a price of $100 each.

In searching for a way to improve the profitability of product line A, management may first want to estimate the effect of different prices on sales and total profits for the line. Two questions need to be answered: with no change in marketing expense, what volume of A could be sold at a 10 percent higher price and what volume at a 10 percent lower price? Management estimates that the present sales volume of 5,000 units would decrease by 20 percent at the higher price and increase by 40% at the lower price. Based on these estimates, a comparison of estimated profitability of the two price alternatives and of the present price is developed, as shown in Table 6–2. Although this analysis indicates that the higher price offers the most profitable alternative, management may well decide the difference does not justify the risk inherent in the price change.

In examining the risk involved, management might study essentially the same pricing question in a somewhat different way, by determining the volume required with the 10 percent higher and lower prices to cover fixed or programmed costs and to produce the same amount of profit contribution as at present. These types of profit contribution analyses are most clearly presented to marketing management graphically. Figure 6–3 shows these two kinds of breakeven analyses. In the first graph, the intersection of each price line with the horizontal line at zero dollars indicates the breakeven volume at

TABLE 6–2

Effect of Alternative Prices on Profit

	Present price	10% Higher price	10% Lower price
Unit sales	5,000	4,000	7,000
Unit price	$100	$110	$90
Variable unit cost	$ 70	$ 70	$70
Sales	$500,000	$440,000	$630,000
Variable costs	350,000	280,000	490,000
Gross profit contribution	$150,000	$160,000	$140,000
% to sales	30.0%	36.4%	22.2%
Specific programmed expense	100,000	100,000	100,000
Net profit contribution	$ 50,000	$ 60,000	$ 40,000
% to sales	10.0%	13.6%	6.5%

FIGURE 6-3

Breakeven Analyses

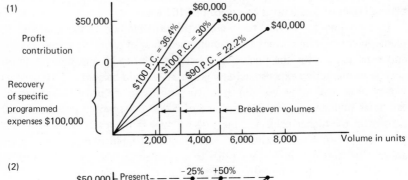

(1)

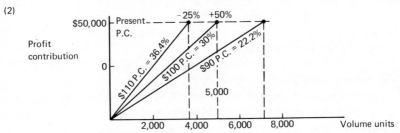

(2)

which the profit contribution covers the product's programmed expenses. Vertical distances above the zero line indicate the profit contribution after breakeven is reached. The second graph shows the volumes required at the new prices to maintain the existing level of profit contribution. Based on just these breakeven analyses, the 10 percent higher price would again seem to be the best choice, though other competitive and market factors might offset this advantage.

New Product Evaluation

In addition to being useful as an aid to pricing and product line evaluation, profitability analysis can assist in evaluating new products. One kind of new product profitability analysis is given in Table 6-3. As shown in Column 1, if idle plant capacity is available, the profit contribution is 20.9 percent of sales and 50.3 percent of investment, a substantial profit. If additional equipment is required, the return on investment is reduced to 17.5 percent, as shown in Column 2, a good but not exceptional return.

TABLE 6–3

Evaluating New Product Profitability
under Various Production Conditions

	1	2
	Make New Product	
	Have idle capacity	Need new equipment
Profit		
Sales (price @ $3.00)	$300,000	
Material	66,000	
Direct labor	48,000	
Variable overhead	123,200	
Total variable costs	237,200	
Profit contribution	$ 62,800	$ 62,800
% to sales	20.9%	20.9%
Less depreciation	-0-	20,000
Less tax at 50%	31,400	21,400
Profit after tax	$ 31,400	$ 21,400
% to investment	50.3%	17.5%
Investment		
Cash	$ 5,365	
Accounts receivable	30,000	
Inventory		
—Material	2,750	
—In-process	25,270	
—Finished	9,850	
Total current assets	73,235	
Less—accounts payable	8,835	
Less—accrued payroll	1,900	
Net working capital	$ 62,500	$ 62,500
Fixed assets (average value)	-0-	60,000
Total investment	$ 62,500	$122,500

With new products, the risk is high because of the money invested and the difficulty in forecasting sales. Breakeven analysis can again be used to estimate how many units of a new product would have to be sold in order to recover costs (the number of units required to do this is called the breakeven volume). This and other kinds of profitability analyses used in new product

TABLE 6–4

Alternative Advertising and Distribution Programs

Mix no.	Price (P)	Adv. (A)	Distr. (D)	Breakeven Volume (Q_B)	Expected Volume (Q)	Q-Q_B	Profit (Z)
1	$16	$10,000	$10,000	9,667	12,400	2,733	$16,398
2	16	10,000	50,000	16,333	18,500	2,167	13,002
3	16	50,000	10,000	16,333	15,100	-1,233	-7,398
4	16	50,000	50,000	23,000	22,600	-400	-2,400
5	24	10,000	10,000	4,143	5,500	1,357	18,998*
6	24	10,000	50,000	7,000	8,200	1,200	16,800
7	24	50,000	10,000	7,000	6,700	-300	-4,200
8	24	50,000	50,000	9,857	10,000	143	2,002

evaluation are discussed in more detail in the *Gizmo Novelty Company* study in Chapter Seven.

Advertising and Distribution Decisions

An example of a profitability analysis report useful to marketing management in determining the best mix of advertising and distribution expenditures is shown in Table 6–4. Sales of the product are forecasted for various advertising and distribution programs and the profit for each alternative is calculated. From the table, it is seen that marketing mix number 5 has the best projected profit.

As in the new product example, this is again only one of the many ways to calculate the "profitability" of the marketing decisions under study. As was pointed out in the text of Chapter Four and in the *FAD Limited* study in Chapter Five, the actual format and content of the profitability analysis will be dictated by the management decision situation. In addition, it should be kept in mind that the analysis is only as good as the assumptions on which it is based and is only an *aid* to decision making, since the profit projections must be weighed with other business considerations.

Return on Investment Analysis

Profitability analysis techniques used in calculating the profit contribution from alternative investments in marketing assets being considered were discussed in Chapter Four, in the section on profitability analysis in general.

Information Systems for Operational Planning, Control and Administration

Information systems are needed for management of all major marketing activities. The following discussion gives a brief review of some of the information commonly used in sales, advertising, distribution, and customer service.

Sales Management

Because selling is the basic marketing job, questions of overall sales strategy are for the most part answered when developing overall marketing strategy. Planning for sales management, then, usually begins with developing specific sales forecasts, goals or budgets (by area, customer, product, salesman, or some other category important to sales management) and determining the kind of sales organization needed. The information sources used include: overall company sales forecasts, which were described earlier in the chapter; analyses of overall market trends; and analyses of local market conditions, salesmen's capabilities, individual customers, planned promotions, and other specific external and internal factors affecting sales by area, customer, product, or salesman.

The National Observer sales budget shown in Figure 6–2 is an example of one company's sales forecast. This forecast was based mainly on the availability of profitable advertising media, on company financial restraints, and on projections of past profit performance, adjusted for anticipated changes in the economy. A portion of another company's sales budget is shown in Figure 6–5. This forecast, by region and by salesman, was developed first by taking the overall company sales forecast and distributing it to districts based on the percent of company sales in each district last year. Next, changes in

FIGURE 6–5

Sales Budget—Pittsburgh District

Salesman	Jan.	Dec.	Total
Abernathy	$33,776	$25,841	$387,491
Bristol	18,823	14,384	196,822
Caldwell	21,131	16,468	227,391
etc.	·	·	·
	·	·	·
	·	·	·
Total	$1,139,896	$827,297	$11,981,492

the number of customer accounts and in individual customer activity were analyzed, as was the past performance of each salesman and the number of salesmen in the district, and estimates made of the likely sales to be achieved by each man in each district. Since the total of these "likely to be achieved" sales turned out to be slightly below the overall company sales forecast, individual salesmen's goals were all raised 8 percent.

Management also needs detailed information on customers (past, present, and future) and customer activity to develop sales programs to meet budgeted goals. An example of customer analysis reporting and the files needed to generate these reports was given in the *Little Publishing Company* study in Chapters One and Two. In that situation, sales management developed a system for getting reports on products purchased by different groups of customers, customer potential in each sales area, relative credit rating (that is, sales potential) of individual customers, and the like. This information was in turn used in assigning accounts to salesmen, determining what products to promote to each customer, and developing other aspects of the sales program.

Buyer or customer studies are not limited to present customers. As is seen in the following section on advertising systems, market research studies are often made of buyer motivation or buying habits, as shown in Figure 6–9. These and other similar market research studies are used by management to determine where sales efforts should be concentrated, what products to emphasize in selling, how large the sales force should be, what kind of sales promotion literature should be used, and what other aspects of the sales program should be examined or altered. An example of how such studies led to specific changes in selling programs is given in the *Bedrock Company* study in Chapter Seven.

In addition to buyer studies, market studies are also needed on the competition. Surveys of competitors' sales in any given market are available from such research companies as Albert Sidlinger Company and Time Inc.'s market research division. Or, they can be done by the company, as in the *Enright Company* study in Chapter Seven. An example of a segment of one of these reports is given in Figure 6–10 in the following section.

A major source of market information on customers, industry trends, competitors, and local market conditions is the field sales staff itself. At times, this information is gathered informally, with salesmen being encouraged to pass along to sales management any information uncovered on significant changes in the customer, market, or competition. Other companies use more formal reporting systems, such as weekly written reports from each salesman to sales management covering this type of information. In some situations, where large customer accounts are involved, some salesmen go so far as to do profile analyses on each customer. An example of customer information files and reports prepared and maintained by salesmen is given in Chapter Seven in the *Domby Publishing Company* study.

All this market information, combined with information on company factors, is used not only on a regular basis for sales forecasting and sales program development, but also periodically for revisions in the organization of the sales operation. Such revisions may occur both when significant changes take place in company products, competitor strategies, or customer needs, as well as when the performance of the sales force has consistently not met budgeted goals or when selling costs rise disproportionately to sales.

Information used in monitoring sales performance can come from a variety of sources. For example, salesmen's call reports, such as the one shown in Figure 6–6, are used to monitor selling activities. Other kinds of "activity" control reports used by sales management are summary reports on orders of intent (planned customer purchases) and new accounts added or old accounts lost, as well as summary reports on salesmen's time utilization. Extreme care is required in constructing any type of "activity" control reporting system where the source of information is the salesman himself, since there is a tendency for a salesman to tell management what it wants to hear, rather than report the facts accurately.

In monitoring selling activities, reports are also needed on sales results, by appropriate budgetary categories. In comparing actual sales for each salesman or district to budgeted sales, for example, a sales analysis report can either report on all salesmen or on an exception basis (that is, only on those

FIGURE 6–6

Number __12__   Daily Call Report

Name __Doe, John__   Location __Major City, U.S.A.__ Date __Mar. 6__

Scheduled calls	Purpose of call	Results of call
Joe's S.S.	Clean-up station	Done
6th + Main	Set up new TBA display	Dealer will order $500; shelves clean, rearranged
7th + Olive	Arrange spring promotion	Dealer won't sign; will call again
Art's Super	Improve records + bookkeeping	Set up National's Dealer Accounting System
Three D Truck	Sell 12 cases of antifreeze	Sold 6

salesmen who did not meet their budgeted sales figure by more than a certain percentage). An example of such an exception report is given in Figure 6–7. The left-hand column of this report identifies the salesmen in the Pittsburgh district (and their identification number) whose sales were under budget by a significant amount—in this case more than 5 percent—and so alerts sales management to potential areas of improvement.

Other types of sales result reports are also used in monitoring sales activities. For example, where several distribution channels are used (retail and wholesale, for instance) or different sales methods (coupon advertising and salesmen, for instance) reports are needed on sales through each distribution or sales channel. Reports on overall costs of selling activities are also needed, along the lines of the financial reports discussed in Chapter Four.

In administering the sales force (hiring, firing, and training), sales management makes use of more than the call reports and sales performance reports described above. Sales management also needs some sort of file on the sales staff. This file would contain basic personnel information (address, age, sex, data on hiring, etc.). At times, this file may be integrated with performance evaluation reports and files, which are used in making sales personnel decisions, as well as in developing individual salesmen's budgets. Such an integrated system was used by a large housewares company, which sold its products through some 3,000 part-time salesmen and women around the country. The file was used to produce information on the numbers of salesmen per region, much as inventory files would be used. In addition, by computer, reports on sales by salesmen (compared to budget), analyses of successful salesmen profiles, and commission reports and checks were also prepared using these files.

Order processing administration is also often part of sales management's responsibilities. An outline of the data flow within one company's order processing and billing system is given in Figure 6–8. The bottom of each column contains a management analysis of each phase of the operation.

Advertising Management

In developing an overall advertising strategy, an advertising manager first reviews overall marketing planning to determine the role or objective of advertising in his company. In addition, he would review specific marketing plans for information on products to be promoted, their unique features and appeals, and the kind of advertising support each product or product group will require; new product plans; geographic areas of sales concentration; total market potential for different products and product groups; channels of distribution; the nature of buyers of different products or product groups; competition and competitors' advertising strategies; and sales forecasts. These

FIGURE 6–7

Salesman under Budget 5 Percent or More Year to Date
District Pittsburgh
(Current Month and Year to Date)

Description	Salesman No.	Actual Sales	Current Month Under or (over) budget Amount	%	Actual Sales	Year to Date Under or (over) budget Amount	%
Performance satisfactory		$ 827,432	($112,610)	(15.8)	$4,623,096	($497,830)	(12.1)
Under budget performance							
Abernathy	2609	32,016	1,760	5.2	102,600	6,300	5.8
Bristol	2671	17,433	1,390	7.4	61,080	4,270	6.5
Caldwell	2685	19,811	1,320	6.2	70,100	4,600	6.2
Fischer	2716	24,033	1,470	5.8	84,390	5,090	5.7
Gordon	2804	8,995	480	5.1	31,600	1,810	5.4
Inch	2827	27,666	1,820	6.2	97,010	5,930	5.8
Long	2982	4,277	600	12.3	15,020	900	5.7
Mather	3007	39,474	3,800	8.8	138,400	8,540	5.8
Owens	5066	43,189	4,400	9.6	151,800	9,080	5.6
Subtotal		216,894	17,040	7.3	752,000	46,520	5.8
District Total		$1,044,326	($ 95,570)	(10.1)	$5,375,096	($451,310)	(9.2)

FIGURE 6–8   Diagram for Analyzing Order Booking, Processing, and Billing Procedure

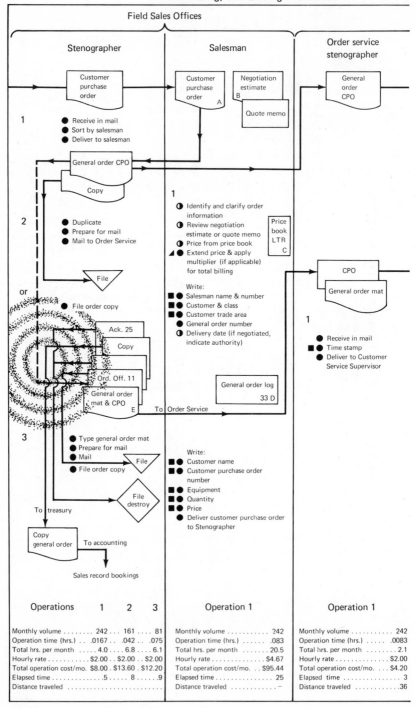

Field Sales Offices

Stenographer | **Salesman** | **Order service stenographer**

Customer purchase order | Customer purchase order A — Negotiation estimate B / Quote memo | General order CPO

1
- Receive in mail
- Sort by salesman
- Deliver to salesman

General order CPO / Copy

1
- Identify and clarify order information
- Review negotiation estimate or quote memo
- Price from price book
- Extend price & apply multiplier (if applicable) for total billing

Price book LTR C

2
- Duplicate
- Prepare for mail
- Mail to Order Service

File

Write:
- Salesman name & number
- Customer & class
- Customer trade area
- General order number
- Delivery date (if negotiated, indicate authority)

CPO / General order mat

1
- Receive in mail
- Time stamp
- Deliver to Customer Service Supervisor

or
- File order copy

Ack. 25 / Copy / Ord. Off. 11 / General order mat & CPO E

To Order Service

General order log 33 D

3
- Type general order mat
- Prepare for mail
- Mail
- File order copy

File

File destroy

Write:
- Customer name
- Customer purchase order number
- Equipment
- Quantity
- Price
- Deliver customer purchase order to Stenographer

To treasury

Copy general order   To accounting

Sales record bookings

Operations	1	2	3
Monthly volume	242	161	81
Operation time (hrs.)	.0167	.042	.075
Total hrs. per month	4.0	6.8	6.1
Hourly rate	$2.00	$2.00	$2.00
Total operation cost/mo.	$8.00	$13.60	$12.20
Elapsed time	.5	8	.9
Distance traveled			

Operation 1	
Monthly volume	242
Operation time (hrs.)	.083
Total hrs. per month	20.5
Hourly rate	$4.67
Total operation cost/mo.	$95.44
Elapsed time	25
Distance traveled	–

Operation 1	
Monthly volume	242
Operation time (hrs.)	.0083
Total hrs. per month	2.1
Hourly rate	$2.00
Total operation cost/mo.	$4.20
Elapsed time	3
Distance traveled	.36

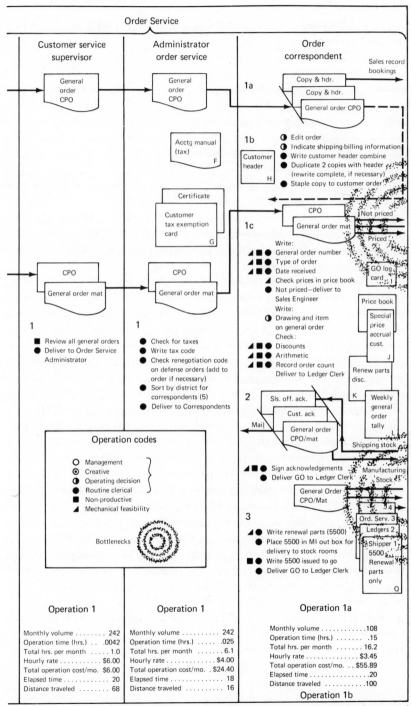

Source: Reproduced by permission of *Harvard Business Review*, Marshall K. Evans, and Lon R. Hague from "Master Plan for Information Systems," *Harvard Business Review* (Jan.–Feb., 1962), p. 111.

strategic definitions of general advertising directions (media mix, advertising themes, product emphasis, and the like) in turn provide the information framework within which specific advertising programs are developed.

Overall advertising budgets are formulated within the context of overall company financial plans and marketing budgets, as well as advertising strategy. In some instances—for example, in mail-order advertising where the advertising generates sales directly through coupon replies—the decision on the size of the advertising budget is dictated by an analysis both of how much sales can be generated economically by advertising and of the company's general financial, order-processing, and product resources. Normally, a mail-order company will spend as much as it thinks it can spend profitably. In most companies, however, a decision is more likely to be based on the amount of money corporate management feels can be allocated to advertising in light of projected economic conditions, past allocations of funds to advertising, competitive conditions, available funds, sales forecasts, and other related general planning data.

In developing specific advertising plans within this general strategic and budgetary framework, an advertising manager would study his customers, both present and potential. For example, he might first make a *customer* survey to determine the characteristics of past and present buyers (age, sex, occupation, income and the like, their buying habits, their response to the products and product features advertised, their reasons for buying and using the products, the product characteristics which appeal to them most, their reading and listening habits, etc.). For instance, at one mail-order company where customers had supplied considerable information to open charge accounts, an analysis was made of the types of customers who bought different company products, and a selected random sample of buyers were interviewed. These surveys enabled advertising management to develop new advertising themes and to select media more appropriate to both the products and the customers involved. Another example of such a customer analysis study was described in the *Little Publishing Company* study in Chapters One and Two.

A survey may also be made of a representative sampling of the general consumer market for a company's products. Figure 6–9 shows a segment from a report on the results of such a survey made by an insurance company. Additional examples of such customer surveys are given in the *Bedrock Products Company* and *Wolman Carpet Company* studies in Chapter Seven. As is seen from these companies' studies, such general consumer surveys (or market research studies) very often provide information useful not only in advertising management, but also in product development, product design, and sales and distribution management, as well as in developing overall marketing strategy.

FIGURE 6-9

Selected Study Questions Which Dealt with Why and How
People Buy Automobile Insurance*

Question 6a: How did you first get in touch with your present company—
that is, how did you hear about it?

46%—Through a friend, neighbor or relative

23%—Know the agent (good friend, neighbor, relative)

8%—Don't remember

4%—Through car dealer or person who sold respondent the
car

4%—Saw or heard company's advertising and called company

3%—Agent called on respondent

3%—Other agent recommended it

2%—Friend or relative worked for the company

2%—Carried other kinds of insurance with company

1%—Through bank or loan company where car was financed

7%—Other sources

Question 6b: The last time you bought auto insurance did you "shop
around"—that is, did you get prices from different companies?
(Yes or no)

18%—Did shop

82%—Did not shop

Question 6c: (If "yes" to previous question) How did you go about finding
the names of companies to contact?

8%—Friends, relatives, neighbors

2%—Phone book

2%—Advertising

3%—Went to different insurance offices

2%—Other

3%—Don't remember

Question 6d: What reasons were most important to you in choosing the
company you did: . . . any others? (Probe)

24%—Save money, cheaper

18%—Good company, reputable, reliable, good service

17%—Agent is a friend, relative, neighbor, etc.

17%—Heard about company through friends, relatives

12%—Better coverage, different types

12%—No reason given

* All percentages are State Farm members. Comparable figures for all insured car owners
and for other companies are not shown here.

FIGURE 6–9 (*Continued*)

9%—Settle claims promptly, fairly
2%—Insured through finance company—no choice
2%—Conveniently located
2%—Heard about agent through friends
1%—Insurance in connection with job
1%—Offered payment plan
1%—Wanted all insurance with one company
6%—Other reasons

Question 8a: Do you think there is a big difference in what different companies would charge you for the same kind and amount of auto insurance, or a small difference, or do you think that they all charge about the same?

38%—Insurance charges are about the same
24%—There is a big difference in insurance charges
21%—There is a small difference in insurance charges
17%—Don't know

Source: Reproduced with permission from Hansen, *Marketing: Text, Techniques, and Cases* (3rd ed.; Homewood, Ill.: Richard D. Irwin, Inc. 1967), p. 282.

In developing advertising programs, information is also needed on what the competition is doing, covering both the advertising themes they are using and the kind and amount of media they are using. This information can be obtained periodically (for example, quarterly) internally or through the company's advertising agency through a manual check of the printed media reaching consumers or through such data services as Media Records, Inc. and Leading National Advertisers, Inc., if broadcast media is used widely. Surveys of competitor sales by market area are also used in studying where to concentrate advertising expenditures (see Figure 6–10).

Drawing upon this market information, combined with information on the product to be advertised, advertisements are created and very often tested. Testing information is obtained in a variety of ways. For example, ads can be shown to a consumer panel before they are run and the reaction of the test audience studied. Or, an ad can be run in a test market (for instance, a medium-size city) and then a telephone survey made of consumers to study their recall of the ad or their reaction to it. Or, sales in the area before and after the ad is run may be analyzed and evaluated in relation to some historical standard. In mail-order advertising, where coupons are used in the ad, the circulation of a newspaper may be divided into two equal parts, with a different ad appearing in each part. The coupon replies from each will show a comparative measure of the relative effectiveness of each ad.

In selecting the media to be used, information on the media available and the audience of each media is needed, in addition to information on con-

FIGURE 6-10

Consolidated Consumer Analysis Shows Variations in Brand Preferences
(Milwaukee Journal and Cooperating Newspapers)

Tooth Paste

City	Percent of use (bought within 60 days)			Crest		Colgate		Gleem		Pepsodent		Macleans		Ipana	
	1964	1963	1962	Place	%	Place	%	Place	%	Place	%	Place	%	Place	%
Denver	89	89.4	90.5	1.	38	2.	22	3.	15	4.	9	5.	6	7.	3
Duluth-Superior	86	86.6	87.0	1.	44	2.	22	3.	13	4.	4			6.	2
Indianapolis	94	89.3	91.8	1.	58	2.	13	3.	12	4.	7			5.	4
Long Beach	87	87.0	88.6	1.	38	2.	19	3.	14	4.	8	7.	3	5.	5
Milwaukee	90	91.4	89.5	1.	31	2.	26	3.	20	4.	7	5.	4	7.	2
Omaha	90	89.8	91.1	1.	29	2.	25	3.	19	4.	7	6.	4	6.	4
Pensacola	93	90.3	90.4	1.	32	2.	30	3.	20	4.	6			5.	4
Phoenix	91	92.1	93.6	1.	33	2.	28	3.	16	4.	5	5.	3	5.	3
Providence	92	94.6	94.2	1.	34	2.	33	3.	15	5.	4			4.	5
Salt Lake City	90	90.9	90.2	1.	45	2.	24	3.	13	5.	4	4.	5	7.	3
St. Paul	89	89.5	90.4	1.	39	2.	22	3.	13	5.	5	7.	2	7.	2
West Palm Beach	81	86.2		1.	44	2.	22	3.	12	4.	6			5.	4
Wichita	93	93.8	92.3	1.	43	3.	15	2.	18	4.	9			5.	2

Source: Reproduced with permission from Zacher, *Advertising Techniques and Management* (Homewood, Ill.: Richard D. Irwin, Inc., 1967), p. 79.

sumer reading and listening habits and competitive use of the media. Advertising agency media departments are the most commonly used source of information on available time or space in broadcast and print media, the number of viewers, listeners, or readers in each, and the cost per thousand audience members. The agency, the media itself, or independent market researchers are sources of information on the characteristics of each media's audience (for example, their income, age, sex and the like). Other kinds of information would be needed, naturally, where other advertising media is used, such as direct mail or billboard displays.

This external information is then combined with information drawn from past sales records, customer surveys, product and distribution channel analyses, and actual sales and special promotion plans in developing the final media schedule.

As with advertisements, the effectiveness of media can also be tested. For example, in mail-order advertising the cost per order from different media tests may be compared to determine which media generates orders at the least advertising cost per sale. An example of a report form for such a test is shown in Figure 6–11.

Information is ultimately needed on the overall effectiveness of advertising in obtaining sales. Specific yardsticks can be used where sales can be traced directly to advertising expenditures, as in mail-order advertising or in special promotions; an example is Figure 6–12, which measures the sales impact of special in-store promotions. Similar reports could be prepared for a special TV or newspaper advertising campaign for a specific product in a selected geographic area. More general measures of effectiveness (such as long-term correlations between advertising and sales) must be used in most advertising management situations, however, because of the lack of such a direct relation-

FIGURE 6–11

January Test Results—Columbus

Media used	Cost	Orders	Initial cost per order	Payments & renewals	Final cost per order
Direct mail					
Local TV station XXX					
Local radio station XXX					
Regional Sunday supplement					
Sunday magazine —XXX paper					
Daily newspaper ads —XXX journal					

FIGURE 6–12

Comparison of Sales

Normal Sales vs. Use of Displays

	Display unit sales	Normal unit sales	% Increase	Display $ sales	Normal $ sales	% Increase
Coffee, tea, cocoa	4,904	879	458%	$ 4,303	$ 891	383%
Crackers & cookies	13,112	2,226	489	4,677	781	494
Deserts	5,466	301	1,716	576	41	1,296
Jams, jellies, spreads	3,761	288	1,206	1,219	173	603
Paper products	4,937	1,064	364	1,426	345	314
Prepared foods	16,026	944	1,598	1,914	177	979
Salad dressing, mayonnaise	1,919	379	406	866	168	415
All displays (without price changes)	57,587	10,052	473%	$18,832	$3,581	425%

Source: *Progressive Grocer*

ship between sales and advertising expenditures. It is because of this lack of direct measures of the effectiveness of consumer advertising that budgets are often developed based on past expenditures, funds available, and other business planning factors.

Distribution Management

One of the first questions to be answered in distribution management is "What kind of distribution system is best for the company and the amount and kind of facilities needed within the system?" Decisions on distribution channels to be used (wholesalers, retailers, direct-to-customers), distribution methods (trucks, rail, air) and whether these are to be company owned, rented, or provided by outside services, the number, location and size of warehouses and whether these are to be leased or owned, and the merchandise handling equipment are all involved in answering long-range planning questions.

In developing overall distribution plans, distribution management would study overall company marketing plans, especially those segments relating to product and sales plans and sales forecasts. Based on this analysis and an analysis of available distribution facilities and competitors' distribution systems, a review would be made of the adequacy of the company's distribution system and appropriate changes made in the company's distribution strategy. For example, while Sears and Roebuck sells extensively by catalogue throughout the United States, as residential areas developed, more and more Sears stores have been opened—because as the number of competitive stores increase in an area, people tend to shop in stores instead of by catalogue. As this expanded network of stores became a significant part of Sears business, the company shifted from a centralized warehouse system to a system of regional warehouses and distribution to support local stores.

Within the general strategic planning framework, forecasts are drawn up of longer-term distribution facility needs. A simplified example of such an overall summary forecast is given in Figure 6–13, which shows a three-year forecast of distribution facilities requirements (warehouse space, materials handling equipment, and delivery trucks), segregating additions needed to present facilities, and whether they will be leased or company owned.

The decision to own or lease facilities and equipment is based on both cost analyses and analyses of business needs. While the purchase of facilities is

FIGURE 6–13

Long-range Planning—Distribution Facilities

Years of 1974–77	1st year	2nd year	3rd year	4th year
Sales by product in units	185,000	203,500	223,850	246,230
Warehouse capacity needed (in sq. ft.)	200,000	220,000	242,000	266,000
Available—rented	75,000	75,000	95,000	95,000
Available—owned	125,000	125,000	125,000	175,000
Additional rent needed	-0-	20,000	-0-	-0-
Additional purchase needed	-0-	-0-	50,000	-0-
Materials handling mach.				
Available	500	500	550	605
New quantity needed	-0-	50	55	-0-
Trucks: Standard delivery size				
Available	10	10	11	12
Needed	-0-	1	1	2
Rental cost (for one year)	-0-	$ 3,000	$ 5,500	$ 8,000
Purchase	-0-	$ 7,600	$ 7,700	$ 15,600
Truck life 3 years—purchase				

more expensive the first year, the cost of leasing will generally be greater over a longer period of time. In making the decision, once this difference in cost is calculated, it is then weighed in some kind of formal analytical report, against other factors, such as available capital, the size and kind of distribution system planned, and the risk of obsolesence.

As the planning for distribution gets more detailed, for example in determining the location and design of warehouses, information as to projected regional patterns of sales by product, as well as information on new product plans, is needed. This same information is used in determining the amount and kind of materials handling and delivery facilities needed. A more detailed discussion of information system used for these kinds of decisions is given in the section on facilities management in Chapters Eight and Nine.

Short-term operational decisions involve such areas as processing of orders, scheduling the use of facilities in storing and moving goods, and controlling inventories. Operational planning for order processing and scheduling and for inventory control requires information on anticipated sales, kind of orders anticipated (phone, mail, salesman), location and kind of customers and distribution channels, types of products, inventory status and movement, and available distribution facilities. Administering the actual order processing and scheduling activities requires such data as the orders themselves, scheduling summaries, and information on the availability of products and facilities.

In developing order processing procedures, the flow of orders, including order generation, order receipt, scheduling of the order, delivery, and acknowledgment of deliveries must be identified or established, based on information about the amount of orders and the pattern of ordering. This analysis would be the basis for developing a data and information system for handling distribution order processing and scheduling, such as the one developed for sales management shown in Figure 6–8 above.

The initial order can be handled in several ways, depending on the type of situation. For example, the sales department may forward orders to distribution or customers may order directly from the distribution center. Based on these orders, schedules are prepared for delivery. For example, Figure 6–14 shows a monthly schedule by day of the number of orders on hand to be delivered, the delivery trucks needed each day, and the change in inventory levels anticipated. The lower part of the figure relates warehouse space to shipments made and production delivered daily to inventory.

In order to schedule deliveries, information is needed on the current availability both of delivery equipment and inventory. Figure 6–15 gives an example of a report on availability of delivery equipment. Column one shows the truck number, and the following columns the days of the month. Under the days column is indicated whether the truck is scheduled for maintenance or, if it is available, what orders are assigned to it. Several examples of

FIGURE 6–14

Items to be Scheduled for Delivery

Day	1st	2nd	3rd	4th	etc.
	Month of _____ 197__				
Orders to be delivered	373	415	600	513	
Trucks needed	10	10	15	13	
Inventory items	105	98	305	200	
Warehouse space					
Needed	0	0	0	320	
Still available	427	460	480	550	
Daily production anticipated	0	0	0	1,000	

inventory reports which might be used are given in Chapters Eight and Nine in the sections on inventory and material management.

Monitoring distribution requires information on the status of orders and equipment. For example, Figure 6–16 shows one kind of shipping control report. In this report, the performance of a truck and its driver is monitored using such criteria as number of orders delivered, miles driven, wages paid, and units broken. Depending on the situation, many other kinds of operational control reports may be used. For example, reports may be required on the status of orders by order number, the location of delivery equipment, the status of in-transit shipments, the location of delivery equipment, the load per truck, breakdowns of equipment, and other areas of concern to distribution managers.

The overall peformance of the distribution system is measured against three criteria: delivery performance (delays, breakage, and the like); equipment and warehouse usage (amount of idle equipment, unused warehouse space, etc.); and overall costs of and investment in the distribution system. Overall summary reports are needed, therefore, covering these three criteria.

FIGURE 6–15

Truck Availability and Assignment Schedule

Days	1st	2nd	3rd	4th	etc.
			Month of _____ 197__		
Truck 1	AM maintenance	Order #'s	etc.	Order #'s	
Truck 2	Order #'s	AM maintenance	etc.	etc.	
Truck 3	Order #'s	Order #'s	P.M. maint.	etc.	
Truck 4	PM maintenance	Order #'s	etc.	etc.	

FIGURE 6-16

Month of_____, 197___

Truck #	Number of orders delivered		Breakage	Delivery Expense			Driver
	Orders	Units	Units	Wages	Fuel	Mileage	
1	35	726	12	$600	80 gal.	400 mi.	Name
2	40	501	7	640	75 gal.	360 mi.	Name
etc.							

The preceding discussion has only given selected examples of information reports used in distribution management. Because of the wide range of distribution operations found in different companies, arising from the varying needs of different businesses and the variety of transportation methods available, information systems for distribution management also vary widely from company to company. The overall information flows within a typical distribution system can nonetheless be identified, as shown in Figures 6-17(a) and (b). The actual distribution management information systems developed in specific company situations to facilitate the required information flows will naturally vary with the size and complexity of the distribution system.

Customer Service

The first questions to be answered in customer service management are "What are the overall objectives of the customer service operation, the number and kind of facilities needed, and the overall manpower requirements?" The information needed to make these decisions comes from overall marketing plans or planning. Sometimes, there will be formal marketing plans, while at other times such planning information must be gathered informally. Regardless of the source, this information should cover new product plans, policies regarding the expected contribution of customer service to the overall sales and marketing effort, analyses of competitors' customer service activities and anticipated changes in their operations, operating budgets for the customer service area, the present customer service organization, facilities and manpower, short- and long-term sales forecasts, and the anticipated level of customer service activities.

Specific plans and controls for customer service activities are developed within the framework of these overall customer service plans. The decision areas covered would include determining warranty and service charge policies, personnel hiring and training, scheduling of services, maintaining the spare parts inventories needed to meet customer service requirements, and monitor-

190

FIGURE 6–17

(a) External Information Flow

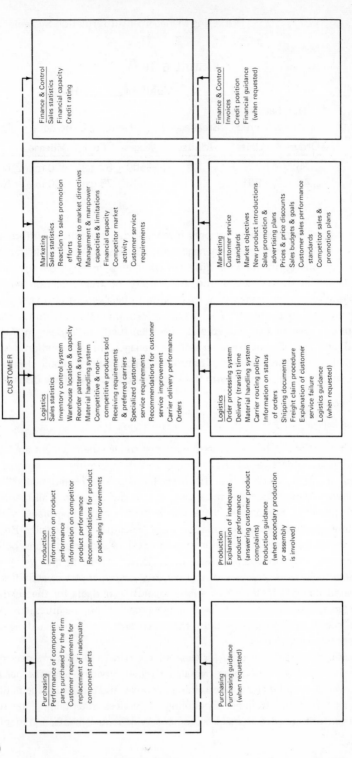

CUSTOMER

Purchasing
Performance of component parts purchased by the firm
Customer requirements for replacement of inadequate component parts

Production
Information on product performance
Information on competitor product performance
Recommendations for product or packaging improvements

Logistics
Sales statistics
Inventory control system
Warehouse location & capacity
Reorder pattern & system
Material handling system
Competitive & non-competitive products sold
Receiving requirements & preferred carriers
Specialized customer service requirements
Recommendations for customer service improvement
Carrier delivery performance
Orders

Marketing
Sales statistics
Reaction to sales promotion efforts
Adherence to market directives
Management & manpower capacities & limitations
Financial capacity
Competitor market activity
Customer service requirements

Finance & Control
Sales statistics
Financial capacity
Credit rating

Purchasing
Purchasing guidance (when requested)

Production
Explanation of inadequate product performance (answering customer product complaints)
Production guidance (when secondary production or assembly is involved)

Logistics
Order processing system
Delivery (transit) time
Material handling system
Carrier routing policy
Information on status of orders
Shipping documents
Freight claim procedure
Explanation of customer service failure
Logistics guidance (when requested)

Marketing
Customer service standards
Market objectives
New product introductions
Sales promotion & advertising plans
Prices & price discounts
Sales budgets & goals
Customer sales performance standards
Competitor sales & promotion plans

Finance & Control
Invoices
Credit position
Financial guidance (when requested)

Source: Robert M. Ivie, "Information Systems for Logistics Management," in *Business Logistics*, eds. Norman E. Daniel and J. Richard Jones (Boston: Allyn & Bacon, 1969), pp. 310 and 311.

(b) Internal Information Flow

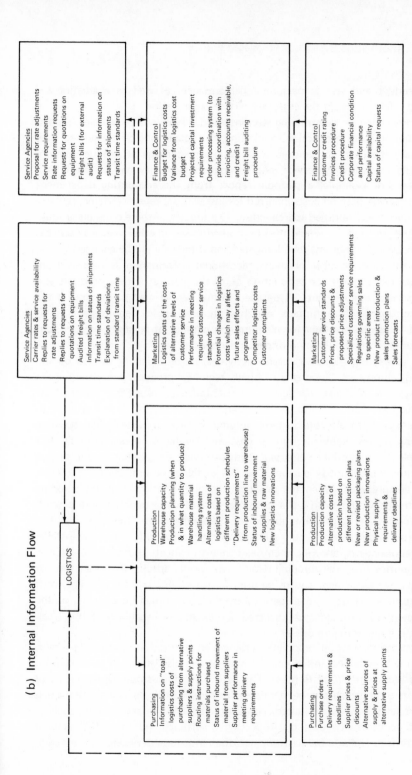

Source: Robert M. Ivie, "Information Systems for Logistics Management," in *Business Logistics*, eds. Norman E. Daniel and J. Richard Jones (Boston: Allyn & Bacon, 1969), pp. 310 and 311.

ing product and service personnel performance, as well as evaluating the overall effectiveness of the customer service organization.

In reviewing or determining warranty and service charge policies, reports are required from production, marketing, and accounting on product services required, the costs of required services, the percentage of product margins available for warranty service, and competitor warranty and service charge policies. For example, a periodic report from the accounting department might provide data on costs incurred for installation, repair servicing, replacement parts, and returned merchandise. The impact of these costs on product sales and profitability would then be studied to see whether warranty services were costing more or less than budgeted and if they should be changed.

In the case of new products, additional information is needed from product development or production as to the nature of new products and their service requirements. A detailed formal report may be required if the product involved is complex and has unusual service requirements. This report is needed not only for planning the number of personnel needed, but also for determining the kind of personnel needed.

In scheduling customer service activities, current data is needed on impending shipments. Shipments of highly technical products will often require the presence of a customer service representative to insure that the products are installed and perform as promised. In the case of products such as appliances which are sold in large volume and require installation services, shipping orders would be sent to customer service on a regular basis. For example, if a product sold will require service installation, order service personnel would notify customer service at the same time shipping instructions are prepared. When the product is about to be shipped, the shipping department would notify the customer service department, where a work order/call report might be prepared for the service man. The initial notification from order service would alert customer service to forthcoming installation requirements, allowing them lead time to allocate personnel; the subsequent notice from the shipping department would specify the exact time of the service requirement and so be used for scheduling service calls. The work order/call report would then be used by the service man in reporting on the services performed and costs incurred. An example of such a work order/call report is given in Figure 6–18.

Several information reporting systems can be used in monitoring service personnel's activities. Initial control may be exercised through an evaluation of the Work Order/Call Reports. The nature of the customer service activity prevents establishing precise standards for service performance against which performance may be evaluated. However, a supervisor familiar with specific service requirements can, by inspecting a sufficient number of completed work orders, evaluate the performance of an individual serviceman—for example, simply by noting whether the man took excessive time to perform standard installation jobs.

Additional control of service personnel may be exercised through the use of spot checks by immediate supervisors. An example of a report form used for such a spot check inspection is given in Figure 6–19.

FIGURE 6–18

Work Order Customer Call Report

Item description _TV/ Console_ Date of purchase _May 20, 1974_
Code number _8623_ Check box if first purchase ✔
Warranty number _8H26_ Delivery date requested _6-1-74_
Customer name/address Action to be taken:
Mr. Frank Smith _Supervise installation_
Kent, Conn. Assigned Service Personnel:
    L. Jones / 4C5

Action Taken

Description	Classification	Charges	
		Warranty	Non-warranty
Supervised installation	_Service_	$15.00	

Date and time of service _June 1, 1974_ Employee signature _L. Jones_

FIGURE 6–19

Service Personnel Inspection Summary

Service person in assigned location? _Yes_
Service person in command of situation with knowledge of problem and required corrective action? _Yes_
Service person conveying the image of the company in an appropriate manner? _Yes_
All parts and services are charged for and recorded? _Yes_
Customer is satisfied with service provided? _No_ _L.J._
EXPLANATION: All no answers are to be discussed in detail below and initialed by service man in question

Serviceman signature _L. Jones_
Supervisor signature _T. Peters_ Date of check _June 1, 1974_

FIGURE 6-20

Product Service Requirement Summary				
			Coverage period 12/11/7- through 12/23/7-	
Item/number	Problem Categories			
	Mfg. defect	Delivery damage	Action required	Parts req.
Kitchen appl. Washer/W-1428	15 x	12	Replace door	lea-#685P
Audio-visual appliances TV/Z-8623	8	14 x	Replace cabinet	lea-#236C

In addition to monitoring the performance of its own personnel, customer service management also monitors the performance of the products serviced. The information needed for this evaluation can be summarized and reported on in a periodic Product Service Requirement Summary Report, as shown in Figure 6-20, a form used to show the services required and their causes by product. This report serves to pinpoint product quality and performance problems. In addition, it indicates spare parts usage and so serves as a guide in determining spare parts inventory levels required. The information needed to prepare this report is obtained from the Work Order/Call Reports. Such a report helps the product development and quality control departments improve product quality and performance, and also serves as an indicator of future service requirements—by highlighting the products or product lines

FIGURE 6-21

Product Service Cost Summary					
Week ending 12/23/7-					
Item Categories	Tot sales	Tot svc cost	Warranty	Non-warranty	NW Inc.
TV/Radio	6,000	600	250	350	525
Console	2,000	300	200	100	150
Portable	4,000	300	50	250	375
Color	3,200	250	250	0	0
Black + white	2,800	350	0	350	525
Parts					
Total					

FIGURE 6–22

Customer Complaint Summary					
Department __TV/ Radio__		Week ending __12-23-7-__			
Total customer complaints __62__		Total sales __6,000.00__			
Nature of Complaint	Corrective Action Taken				
	Phone Call	Letter	Visit	Other	_Level of_
Poor service __31__	20	6	5	0	_customer_
Faulty product __28__	8	8	12	0	_satisfaction_
Other __3__	0	0	0	0	_acceptable_ _R.S._

requiring the most service and the nature of the major product breakdown and service problems. This report serves as the basis for the Product Service Cost Summary shown in Figure 6–21, which is used to reevaluate warranty policies.

Customer service activities are also monitored through the use of Customer Complaint Summaries (Figure 6–22). These reports serve as a means of evaluating, in general terms, the effectiveness of the customer service department; they also serve to indicate whether major complaints are product or service-oriented. This report may be supplemented with one indicating the speed with which service calls were answered.

Overall evaluation of the customer service operation is accomplished through studying total operating costs and general customer satisfaction. Overall cost information can be gathered and reported on as shown in the Customer Service Department Cost Summary in Figure 6–23. This report

FIGURE 6–23

	Customer Service Dept Cost Summary						
	Month ending 12/30/7-						
	Current			Last Month		Last Year	
	Budget	Actual	% Var	Budget	Actual	Budget	Actual
Total CS cost	$8,000	$8,950	.118	$8,000	$7,650	$7,000	$7,800
Warranty	3,000	4,000	.333	3,000	3,650	2,500	3,000
N-warranty	3,500	3,500	-0-	3,500	3,000	3,500	3,300
Admin.	1,500	1,450	(.033)	1,500	1,000	1,000	1,200
Total sales*	$ 160	$ 178	.112	$ 160	$ 155	$ 140	$ 148
Total CS income	$8,000	$8,200	.025	$8,000	$7,300	$7,000	$7,400
Svc income	5,200	5,200	-0-	5,200	4,500	5,200	4,800
Parts sales	2,800	3,000	.071	2,800	2,800	1,800	2,600

* Sales values are in thousands of dollars.

FIGURE 6-24

Customer Survey Questionnaire

1. The date of last visit or contact with us? _____

2. The average number of contacts or visits per month _____

3. The date and amount of last purchase _____

4. The product of last purchase _____ (include brand name)

5. What do you feel to be our greatest feature? _____

6. What do you feel to be our weakest feature?_____

7. Have we been improving since the last questionnaire?_____

8. Do you feel we are sufficiently responsive to customer demands?_____
   If no, how do you feel we can improve?_____

9. How would you rate the overall operation in terms of service
   provided?_____ If unsatisfactory, please explain
   why. Be specific _____

10. If you have had a specific complaint which you have reported, has
    it been rectified?_____ If no, what is its present status?_____
    _____Describe the specific nature of the complaint
    and please be specific. Include time, location, brand names, etc.

compares actual customer service costs and income, as well as total product sales, to the budget and to earlier periods.

A Customer Survey Questionnaire is also sometimes used to evaluate overall customer service performance. An example of one used in an institutional/industrial sales situation is shown in Figure 6-24. This report serves not only to indicate customers' opinions of past performance, but also to gather information on future requirements. As such, it is an important tool in predicting the future environmental conditions within which the customer service activity will have to function.

Summary
Conclusion

It is possible to integrate information systems in marketing to some degree. The *Enright Company* study in Chapter Seven gives an example of a highly integrated marketing management information system. As is seen there and in the discussion of information systems for strategic planning, however, it is difficult to conceive of a fully integrated information system for marketing management.

The marketing information systems and reports discussed in this chapter were chosen to illustrate a wide range of such systems and reports. The examples illustrate how information reports are designed to meet the specific needs of the situation (some marketing activity) and the decision maker (some level and area of marketing management). They also illustrate different kinds of data sources, report contents, formats and timing, and data collection and processing.

These examples do not cover all types of marketing information systems, for each company's marketing operation will require variations to meet its own individual requirements. They merely give an overview of marketing information systems. The next chapter describes how marketing information systems are developed for marketing in different types of work situations and at different management levels.

TEXT DISCUSSION QUESTIONS

1. Describe the overall marketing management jobs, and the principal marketing activity areas managed.

2. Discuss the ways in which the information needs for strategic planning and operational planning and control in the marketing area differ. Pay particular attention to data sources, file structure and updating, and the timing, form, and content of information needs.

3. Describe some of the difficulties encountered in developing marketing management information systems which meet the wide range of marketing management responsibilities.

4. Discuss the ways in which the information systems used in overall marketing management reflect the strategic planning job needs.

5. Discuss the different ways in which profitability analyses and sales forecasts are used in overall market planning and operational planning in such areas as field sales and advertising. In what ways will these analyses and forecasts differ, depending on how they are to be used?

6. Describe the types of information systems used for operational planning and control in sales management. Discuss the ways in which these systems will differ in a consumer products and in an industrial products company.

7. Describe the different marketing management needs at different levels of marketing management in a large consumer products company. In what ways will the timing and content of reports for different management levels vary?

8. Discuss some of the ways in which a single computerized data bank will increase or decrease the effectiveness and economics of a marketing

management information system. Refer to the section on data banks in Chapter Three in your discussion.

9. The statement is frequently made that information systems differ from company to company and business to business. Describe two advertising, sales or customer service situations with which you are familiar and discuss the ways in which the supporting information systems differ because of different business requirements.

10. Discuss some of the difficulties involved in integrating marketing information systems. What impact do the differences in the timing of information needs, the data sources, and the nature of the data itself have on such integration efforts? Refer to Figure 1—1 at the end of Chapter One in your discussion.

11. Discuss the ways in which the structure of the discussion in this chapter reflects the systems approach described in Chapter Two.

Developing
Marketing Management
Information Systems

THE SITUATIONS COVERED IN THIS CHAPTER DESCRIBE HOW MAR-
keting management information systems are developed. The exercise
studies at the end of the chapter give the reader practice in developing
such systems.

Overall Marketing Planning:
Enright Company

Dr. Robert Hagen, Director of Marketing Information at Enright Company,
was reviewing the company's marketing information system in early 1974.[1]

Dr. Hagen believed that the starting point in designing an information
system was to study the decisions made by the managers using the system. He
felt that the greatest problems with contemporary marketing information
systems was that they provided a continuous stream of financial data about
internal company operations, but only sporadic data about the external

---

1. Adapted from Robert D. Buzzell, Donald F. Cox, and Rex V. Brown, *Marketing
Research and Information Systems* (New York: McGraw-Hill Book Company, 1969), pp.
39-66.

environment—even though a marketing manager's major need was for a continuing flow of data about his market environment.

Dr. Hagen had attempted to overcome this deficiency in designing the marketing management information system for Enright Company, but was still not satisfied his system could not be improved.

Background

Enright Company was a division of a large consumer products company. Enright's principal products were health foods, baby cereal, and other special market foods. Enright's annual sales were around $60,000,000.

The market for Enright's products was volatile (many occasional users), highly competitive (over 100 significant competitors), and seasonal. Major competitors had large sales forces which sold directly to supermarket chains, products which were equal in quality to Enright's, and marketing expertise which was, in several ways, superior to Enright's (major competitors had been in business longer and had broader product lines than Enright).

The market vice president, who reported to Enright's president, was responsible for all marketing activities. Reporting to him were four product managers (each of whom was responsible for a major Enright product line), a sales manager (responsible for selling all products), a new product manager, and a marketing information manager (Dr. Hagen).

Sales were made principally through food brokers and drug wholesalers to food and drug stores. The sales organization consisted of five regional managers who supervised the work of thirty area managers. The area managers worked with brokers and wholesalers to insure distribution of Enright's products to all stores in their area, and were responsible for stimulating sales and checking stores to see that adequate shelf position, display, promotional support and the like was obtained.

The product managers were responsible for overall planning and promotion of their product line and for coordinating the sales efforts with the promotional activities. The marketing decisions made by product managers covered such areas as: product characteristics, product line (variation in size, color, flavoring, etc.), packaging, advertising (themes, mix, etc.), promotion (coupon sampling, recipe booklets, contests, etc.), pricing, in store displays, and trade selling terms (trade discounts, advertising and display allowances). Since product managers were responsible for overall planning and marketing for each product, they prepared sales, expense and profit budgets for their products each year and were accountable for meeting these budgeted goals.

Data Input for the Current Marketing Information System

The marketing information system was designed to help the product and sales managers make decisions and carry out their jobs.

Sales personnel were the source of a considerable amount of marketing data, as is seen from the list of their reports in Figure 7–1. Additional data was obtained from a variety of external and internal sources.

For example, to measure consumer reaction Dr. Hagen's department had quarterly surveys done by an outside market research agency of 5,000 consumers (called a "consumer panel"). These surveys covered both existing products and new product proposals, and measured such factors as buyer characteristics; number of consumers using company and competitors' products; consumer awareness of and attitudes towards major products; user habits (how they started using the product and how much they use it); product experience; and buying intentions. Since these surveys were done on a regular basis, comparative trend data was also available.

In addition to buyer data, data on actual purchases was gathered in two ways. First, A. C. Nielson Company supplied bi-monthly reports (based on a 3,000 store sample survey) on sales, retail prices, percentage of stores stocking item, and stores out of stock—covering both Enright's and major competitors' products. Second, Dr. Hagen's department surveyed 120 stores in six key cities to verify the Nielson results and to gather data on market tests of products, promotions, prices, and advertising.

FIGURE 7-1

Required Field Sales Reports

Subject	Information needed	Report submitted	Frequency	Where information goes
Distribution company products	1. Retail Distribution	Broker, Wholesale Evaluation	Annually	V-P Sales, Sales & Promotion, Product Management
	2. New products	Area Manager Call Report	Weekly	V-P Sales, Product Management, President, Sales Service
		Special	As needed	
		Area Manager Call Report	Weekly	
	3. Back orders	Special	As needed	V-P Sales, Director Finance, Management, Sales Service
		Area Manager Call Report	Weekly	
	4. New accounts	New Account Form	As needed	V-P Sales, Sales Service, Finance, Distribution
	5. Termination of accounts	Special	As needed	V-P Sales, President, Sales Service, Sales & Promotion
	6. Fringe distribution channels	Region Manager Report	Weekly	V-P Sales, Product Managers, Asst. V-P Sales, Sales & Promotion
		Special	As needed	
		Area Manager Call Report	Weekly	
		Military Contact Report	As needed	
	7. Warehouse inventories	Special	As needed	V-P Sales, President, Sales Service
	8. Sales forecast	Sales Forecast Worksheet	Quarterly	V-P Sales, Sales Service
	9. Orders	Order Form		Sales Service, Distribution
	10. Product adjustment	Adjustment Record		Sales Service, Finance
	11. Free trade	No Charge Order		Sales Service, Distribution

FIGURE 7–1 (*Continued*)

Subject	Information needed	Report submitted	Frequency	Where information goes
Market Conditions	1. Economic conditions	Region Manager Report	Weekly	V-P Sales, Sales & Promotion, Product Management
		Area Manager Call Report	Weekly	V-P Sales, Sales & Promotion, Product Management
	2. Opportunities	Region Manager Report	Weekly	V-P Sales, Sales & Promotion, Product Management
		Special	As needed	
		Area Manager Call Report	Weekly	
	3. Problems	Region Manager Report	Weekly	V-P Sales, Sales & Promotion, Product Management
		Special	As needed	
		Area Manager Call Report	Weekly	
	4. Catastrophic loss	Statement Catastrophic Loss	As needed	V-P Sales, Sales Service, Director Finance, Management
		Area Manager Call Report	Weekly	
Competitive Developments	1. New products	Region Manager Report	Weekly	V-P Sales, Sales & Promotion, Product Management
		Special	As needed	
		Area Manager Call Report	Weekly	
	2. New distribution existing products	Region Manager Report	Weekly	V-P Sales, Sales & Promotion, Product Management
		Special	As needed	
		Area Manager Call Report	Weekly	
	3. Special programs	Region Manager Report	Weekly	V-P Sales, Sales & Promotion, Product Management
		Special	As needed	
		Area Manager Call Report	Weekly	
	4. Pricing–packaging	Region Manager Report	Weekly	V-P Sales, Product Management
		Special	As needed	
		Area Manager Call Report	Weekly	

Effectiveness—Company programs	1. Training programs	Region Manager Report	Weekly	V-P Sales, Sales Training Manager
		Area Manager Call Report	Weekly	
		Special Report	As needed	
Effectiveness—Company programs	2. National promotions (products A, B, C, & D)	Region Manager Report	Weekly	V-P Sales, Product Management
		Special Report	As needed	
		Area Manager Call Report	Weekly	
	3. Special promotions (products A, B, C & D)	Region Manager Report	Weekly	V-P Sales, Product Management
		Special Report	As needed	
		Area Manager Call Report	Weekly	
	4. Franchise building	Region Manager Report	Weekly	V-P Sales
		Area Manager Call Report	Weekly	
Effectiveness—Region plans	1. Progress reports on region plans	Special	Monthly	V-P Sales
Effectiveness—Company personnel	1. Personnel development	Performance Review	Annually	V-P Sales, President, Personnel
	2. Expenses	Expense Report	Weekly	V-P Sales, Sales Service, Director Finance, Management Finance
	3. Activities field sales	Daily Report	Weekly	V-P Sales, Sales Service, Sales & Promotion
	4. Personnel problems	Region Manager Report	Weekly	V-P Sales
		Special	As needed	
	5. Itineraries	Itinerary Report	Weekly	V-P Sales, Sales Service

Specific data on competitors' sales activities (new product tests, special promotions, package changes, point-of-sales promotions, and the like) was obtained from the field sales reports (Figure 7–1) and data on competitor advertising came from Enright's advertising agencies.

In addition to the above data, the normal internal financial data on sales (factory shipments) and expenses was available from central data processing files for preparing marketing information reports on financial results. These reports were prepared by central data processing and were used mostly for control, rather than current planning, since it was considered after-the-fact information and was not as currently available for decision making as other data.

Current Marketing Management Information Reports

All the data gathered from the various external and internal sources was reviewed by Dr. Hagen's department. In this sense, the department was the marketing management information administration center and clearing house—sometimes using external data collection and report preparation, sometimes utilizing internal sources, and sometimes preparing the analyses and reports themselves.

The department prepared on a monthly basis a list of all available reports (regular and one-time), as shown in part in Figure 7–2. Managers could request to receive reports on a regular or occasional basis. The department also handled requests for special study reports and analyses.

Changes Being Considered

Dr. Hagen felt that it was possible to provide marketing management with more relevant and useful information support and to better integrate marketing information systems. He was especially interested in studying ways to improve profitability reporting.

In current financial reports for marketing, the sales figures used were based on factory shipments to stores, not on actual consumer purchases. Such reports were thus affected by random store buying patterns, which made it difficult to project sales and to determine the significance of weekly and monthly variations in sales. In addition, no effort was made to allocate certain period expenses, such as advertising, to the sales which they generated. For example, September advertising expenses would be included in the September statement, even though the sales produced by those ads might be made over the following months.

Dr. Hagen thus began working on constructing a profit analysis report more appropriate to Enright's marketing operation. For example, a market

FIGURE 7–2

Marketing Management Information Reports
Enright Company Present Product Information

Product A National Market Data

Factory Sales

A-AAA-ABBA	03/09/74	Product A's factory sales history . . . 1972 through Feb., 1974*
A-AAA-ABFA	03/09/74	Product A's factory sales vs. forecast . . . year-to-date, 1974
A-AAA-ABJA	03/26/74	Sales by channels of distribution . . . all forms, year-to-date
A-AAA-ABJZ	03/31/74	Contributions of size and form . . . total sales, food and drug
A-AAA-ABOB	03/09/74	Percent of sales by flavor . . . powder, liquid, wafers, soups
A-AAA-ABOF	03/16/74	Factory sales of Product A 8 oz. liquid, 1973–1974
A-AAA-ABPA	06/06/73	Quarterly factory sales vs. consumer sales, factory dollars

Consumer Sales

A-AAA-ACAE	02/06/74	Consumer purchases . . . similar health food products
A-AAA-ACAF	02/06/74	Consumer purchases of Product A 8 oz. liquid, 1972–1974
A-AAA-ACGA	03/31/74	Contributions of size and form . . . consumer sales, food stores
A-AAA-ACHA	03/31/74	Contributions of size and form . . . consumer sales, drug stores
A-AAA-ACKA	03/31/74	Contributions of flavor, 8 oz. liquid consumer sales
A-AAA-ACKF	11/18/73	Trends in consumer purchases of competing products
A-AAA-ACKH	03/31/74	Contributions of flavor . . . wafer consumer sales, food and drug
A-AAA-ACKI	03/31/74	Contributions of flavor . . . soup consumer sales, food and drug
A-AAA-ACLA	01/29/74	Contributions of food and drug, total consumer sales
A-AAA-ACMA	02/06/74	Consumer sales history . . . consumer prices, 1971–1973
A-AAA-ACMB	09/06/73	Consumer sales, volume, and share . . . 1971–1973 by quarters
A-AAA-ACNA	02/06/74	Consumer dollar sales history . . . factory prices, 1971–present
A-AAA-ACOI	06/25/73	Seasonal variations in regular soup sales and expectations
A-AAA-AFBA	02/06/74	Consumer sales history . . . total dietary market, 1971–1973
A-AAA-AGAA	02/24/74	Advance release . . . dietary for weight control market, N.–D.–J.
A-AAA-AGAB	03/26/74	Advance release on weight control products, drug, J.–F.
A-AAA-AHBA	03/04/74	Product A's market share . . . food, Dec.–Jan., 1973–1974
A-AAA-AIAA	03/04/74	Major competing product's market share . . . food, Dec.–Jan., 1973–1974
A-AAA-BCGA	11/15/73	Product A situation analysis in selected cities
A-AAA-BIBA	10/04/73	Product A and major competing product store audits, metro Shreveport and St. Louis
A-AAA-BTAA	01/10/74	100-store panel audit report, Nov.–Dec., final report

Regional Comparisons, Product A

A-AAA-CHAA	03/26/74	Product A's regional market share comparisons . . . N.–D.–J., 1973
A-AAA-CIAA	03/26/74	Competitor's regional market share comparisons . . . N.–D.–J., 1973
A-AAA-DHAA	03/26/74	Product A's share of market, sales analysis districts
A-AAA-DHBA	03/06/74	Product A's market share . . . district, single-serving liquids
A-AAA-DIAA	03/26/74	Competitor's share of market, sales analysis districts
A-AAA-DIAB	03/06/74	Competitor's market share . . . district, single-serving liquids
A-AAA-DNJA	11/22/73	
A-AAA-EHBA	02/28/74	Product A's and competitor's market share area comparisons . . . D.–J., 1973–1974
A-AAA-EHBB	03/06/74	Product A's market share . . . area, single-serving liquids
A-AAA-EIAB	03/06/74	Competitor's market share . . . area, single-serving liquids

Eastern Region

A-AAB-AHBA	03/03/74	Market movement and share trends . . . by areas, food stores
A-AAB-ARBA	12/12/73	All-commodity distribution . . . by districts, food stores

(Similar information reports were available on the other three regions.)

---

* . . . Denotes that words or phrases have been omitted to preserve confidential information.

FIGURE 7–2 (*Continued*)

Product Evaluation, Product A

A-ABZ-ZIBA	08/29/73	Product A vs. competitor's product in sensory acceptance ratings
A-ABZ-ZPAA	09/11/73	Product A vs. competitor's product . . . visibility testing
A-ABZ-ZXAB	01/03/74	Lab reports . . . liquid evaluations and product improvement
A-ABZ-ZXAJ	11/13/73	Sens. evaluation . . . Product A
A-ABZ-ZXAN	11/18/73	Product A chocolate liquid
A-ABZ-ZXAD	10/08/73	Product A vanilla liquid

Marketing Activities, Product A

A-ACA-ANIA	11/21/73	Advertising costs per consumer dollar. . .
A-ACA-BMAA	07/24/73	Key city promotion reports
A-ACA-BNGA	04/04/73	Not important claim, Product A
A-ACA-BNHA	11/06/73	Product A media mix . . . preliminary report
A-ACA-BQCA	01/28)73	Product A rack display tests
A-ACA-BOCB	05/21/73	Product A rack display tests comparisons
A-ACA-BQAA	05/03/73	Evaluation of couponing
A-ACA-ONIA	09/01/73	Advertising expenditures by districts through September
A-ACZ-ZNCA	05/02/73	Copy tests . . . this man, the women, man in park, grand central
A-ACZ-ZNCB	12/21/73	Product A Nielsen multi-network area ratings
A-ACZ-ZNHA	05/29/73	Woman at the beach ad . . . visual communication test
A-ACZ-ZNHB	08/08/73	Product A candid photo ad . . . visual communication test
A-ACZ-ZQAB	03/14/73	Demographic characteristics of coupon redeemers

Consumer Information, Product A

A-ADA-ASDA	09/16/73	The importance of . . . , summary
A-ADA-BSDA	11/15/73	Dietary flavor preferences
A-ADA-BSFN	10/31/73	Preliminary results . . . dietary flavor preference study
A-ADO-ASCA	01/02/74	Trends in brand use
A-ADO-ASDA	01/02/74	Brand loyalty and brand switching in dietary market
A-ADO-ASDB	01/06/74	Consumer attitudes toward, beliefs about brands of dietaries
A-ADO-ASDC	01/10/74	Target market segments for . . .
A-ADO-ASDE	01/09/74	Source of customers for new products by makers of Product A
A-ADZ-ZNHA	07/30/73	Importance of ... , for Product A
A-ADZ-ZSBB	07/31/73	Reasons for discontinuing use of dietaries
A-ADZ-ZSCC	07/19/73	Weekly meal replacement by dietary for weight control users
A-ADZ-ZSCD	08/08/73	Differences in dietary product usage patterns . . . by sex

Miscellaneous Information, Product A

A-AZA-ACKZ	09/12/73	Increasing importance of single meal packages, dietary market

(Similar information reports were available for the company's three other products.)

Other headings in the Marketing Intelligence Catalogue covered Dalton Marketing reports and analyses and published information (articles, public reports, etc.) under the following headings. (The case writer has selected a sample item under each heading.):

Consumer Information, General

Special Purpose Nutritionals (12 items listed)

B-BVA-CAA	07/15/73	Demographic characteristics of dieters

Potential Products Information

Non-Prescription Remedies (40 items listed)

C-ABE-AAB	07/12/73	Marketing opportunities . . . liniments

Specialty Foods Market (20 items listed)

C-BBC-JIA	01/15/74	The market for infant foods

Special Purpose Nutritionals (16 items listed)

C-CBB-FAA	07/12/73	Sugarless soft drink market . . . consumer attitudes

Cosmetics (13 items listed)

Competitive Materials Information (12 items listed)

Reprints, Articles, and Notes Received

Marketing Techniques

FIGURE 7–2 (*Continued*)

Advertising (16 items listed)
F-ZAB-AAA   06/17/73   Relation, adv. pressure and consumer purchases, R. J. Williams
  Selling (3 items listed)
F-ZAC-AAB   01/01/69   How many salesmen do you need? *Harvard Business Review*
  Merchandising and Promotion (5 items listed)
F-ZAD-AAA   06/01/73   The Super Drugstore In-Store Displays, POPAI Research
  Distribution (2 items listed)
  Management (14 items listed)
  Research (25 items listed)
  New Products (14 items listed)
F-ZAI-AAA   08/01/73   New Product Failure Rate . . . A Marketing Disgrace, J. Merriman
  Nutritional Topics
  Weight Dieting (6 items listed)
F-ZBB-AAA   09/07/73   Nutritional Studies with 900-Calorie Diets, Lab
  Cholesterol (5 items listed)
F-ZBC-AAA   09/19/72   AMA Council statement, Fatty Foods and Cholesterol
  Medical Articles of General Interest (6 items listed)
F-ACA-AAF   08/04/72   The Regulation of Dietary Fat, Council on Foods and Nutrition
  Marketing Media Reports (20 items listed)
  Professional (10 items listed)
F-ZDC-AAA   06/01/71   Simmons Thoroughness of Advertising Readership Study
  Weight Statistics (6 items listed)
F-ZEB-AAA   03/71/72   Mortality Rates among Overweight Men, Metropolitan Ins.
  Stanford Research Studies (16 items listed)
F-ZFZ-AAA   12/01/72   Teenage Wave, Eating Habits of Teenagers
  Miscellaneous Articles of Interest (7 items listed)
F-ZZZ-AAA   12/01/72   How Consumers React to Out-of-stock, Chain Store Age
  Economic and Legal Information (15 items listed)
C-ZAA-AAL   06/03/72   Business Plans for New Plants and Equipment to 1975

survey revealed that the purchases generated by an advertisement produced the following pattern of sales: twenty percent within the first four weeks, sixty percent within nine weeks, and 90 percent within thirteen weeks. Data on consumer purchases at the retail store level was developed for each product line from the Nielson survey and other market research sources. Using these relationships and the survey data, his department developed profit and loss reports by product (and by special promotion) for product managers. These reports differed considerably from the monthly financial reports generated by the central data processing department in that they were based on retail sales and, in the special reports, period expenses were charged against the sales they generated.

Using such profit and loss statements, it was possible each month for product managers to more quickly, easily, and accurately identify significant variations from budget (and the market conditions causing them), since store ordering patterns and other distortions were removed.

Since sales managers were responsible for sales and distribution to brokers and wholesalers, reports on variations in sales to these outlets were more useful for sales management purposes. Dr. Hagen was, therefore, also working on preparing a different series of comparative profit reports designed specifically to meet the needs of this management group.

In addition, Dr. Hagen was working on ways to help marketing managers in other decision-making areas. For example, he believed, based on his studies of retail sales and store buying patterns, that it was possible to more accurately predict seasonal sales patterns at both the factory and retail sales levels. By refining and extending his market research surveys, he also believed he could more accurately measure the potential responsiveness of different segments of the market (age and interest groups, income brackets, male/female, etc.). These and other areas of possible improvement grew out of Dr. Hagen's continuing studies of the business factors which affected marketing management decision making and the variables marketing managers manipulated in making their decisions.

Sales Forecasting: A Telephone Company and a Consumer Products Company

Company sales forecasts are developed in different ways, depending on the nature and size of the company. The following are simplified examples of how two companies successfully used different methods to develop their sales forecasts.

A Telephone Company

In forecasting new telephone demand in one geographic area for a major telephone company, it was first necessary to examine the market factors that affected station or telephone demand. Two factors were initially examined: live births and marriage licenses issued. These factors were selected because marriages create households, which are potential new telephone users, and those marriages can be shown to be the result of births twenty-two years earlier. The lead time of twenty-two years was determined through a computer program. The problem was then to forecast marriages, using births as the controlling independent variable.

Once a projection of the marriages expected in any given year was made, then information was developed on the housing that would be available to accommodate these potential telephone users. Since, in the area being studied, it usually took one full year from the issuance of the permit to the completion of a building, data from the F. W. Dodge Corporation regarding building permits issued and building contracts awarded was analyzed. The data was then projected one year to provide meaningful forecast information. This information was then compared with the projections of marriages and with new telephone demand over the years, in order to determine the degree of correlation, if any, that had existed among the three variables (marriages, telephone demand, and new homes) in the past.

A computer program was used to perform the analysis of these three variables. The program showed that the index of determination was 0.998776, indicating that movements in the three variables was consistently very closely related. Since one could forecast marriages and new homes for the coming year, then, one could also forecast new telephone demand, by projecting the past relationship (or correlation) into the future.

The forecasts proved to be very accurate (the situation under study was a suburban community). For example, for 1974 the company had previously forecast 58,000 installations. In contrast, the new forecasting method predicted 55,000. The actual figure proved to be 54,000.

The above example illustrates how external market factors are studied and forecasting techniques can be used to arrive at an estimate of the potential market for a product. Since the telephone company in this case was the only one serving the market, the company proceeded to develop plans to produce and service the new telephones expected to be needed.

In most situations, however, additional steps would be required; for, normally, more than one company competes in a market. If the market had been served by more than one telephone company, for example, additional market studies would have been needed to determine the expected share of the market for each company before a company sales forecast could be made.

A Consumer Products Company

The company under study manufactures nondurable household supplies and small household equipment products in six manufacturing plants. The company's managers report to the Vice-President of Production.[2] Sales are about $50 million annually. Principal sales channels, each with its own field sales organizations, are grocery stores and hardware-household department stores. Sales managers report to the Vice-President of Sales, as does the Sales Administration Office which has staff specialists on customer relations, forecasting, sales quotas, and the like. Other organization components of the company have the usual functions except for the Vice-President—Secretary, who supervises a planning operation with a statistician responsible for sales forecasting work.

The company's fiscal year runs from October 1 to September 30. Short-term (annual) and long-term (five-year) sales forecasts are prepared.

---

2. Adapted from Vernon G. Lippitt, *Statistical Sales Forecasting* (New York: Financial Executive's Research Foundation, 1969), pp. 255-262.

Statistical Approach to Annual Sales Forecasting. In June, the statistician in the Secretary's Office and the forecaster in Sales Administration prepare independent preliminary sales forecasts for the 100 individual products or product categories sold by the company. Since there are no accepted industry statistics for most of the products sold by the company, the sales forecasting process does not use an industry and share-of-market approach, but forecasts company sales directly.

For established products, unit sales are expressed on a per household basis and the trend of this ratio is projected. Multiplication by a projected number of households then yields a forecast of unit sales. Alternatively, the trend of the raw data may be determined by plotting annual sales on semi-log graph paper. An attempt is then made to determine the causes for all peaks and valleys in the past sales curve (for example, periodic use of national TV advertising), and sales are projected on the basis of judgment. For new products, forecasts are based more on market research studies of the potential growth of the products.

The statistician and the forecasting specialist reconcile their estimates and check the reasonableness of the predictions by comparing them with the trend of the Nielson retail store audit data for individual products. They then prepare a report on their statistical forecasts for each product and send it to members of the Forecasting Committee. In this report, each product chart is preceded by a one-page commentary on recent market trends and on expectations for the year ahead for the product charted.

Forecasting Committee and the Official Sales Budget. The Forecasting Committee is composed of the President, the Vice Presidents for Sales, Advertising, and Finance, the Controller, department heads who may be affected, the sales forecasting specialist, and the statistician from the Secretary's Office. After receiving the statistical forecast report issued in late June, the Committee meets for a week-long sales budgeting conference the second week in July. At this conference, plans for marketing strategy, advertising, new product or new package size introduction campaigns, and other sales efforts planned are reviewed, as are expected competitive developments. The sales forecasts are used in deciding on marketing plans, and are revised in light of the marketing plans adopted at the meeting to reach the budgeted profit goal—an increase in earnings per share of about ten percent per year. All 100 products are reviewed during the week, and official annual sales forecasts are agreed upon for unit sales of all products.

The Sales Administration office next breaks sales down by plant area, and by sales regions, divisions, and districts, as well as by the two main channels of distribution. The official unit sales forecast or budget, including text and charts for each product, is then issued to each company executive and to users of the forecast in Production, Sales, Advertising, Purchasing, Traffic, and the Controller's and Treasurer's offices. For users who need finer detail, the statistician allocates total year sales for each product by months, in accordance with normal seasonal fluctuations, planned promotions, and the like.

Uses and Revisions of Sales Forecasts. The official unit sales budgets, broken down by product, by month, and by plant, are used by plant managers and production schedulers and by the purchasing and traffic departments for planning and scheduling their operations. These budgets are also used for setting sales objectives—by product for each of four regions and their divisions and districts in the two sales channels. These detailed geographical breakdowns of the monthly sales forecast are worked out by computer, using buying-power indexes which express the sales potential for geographical areas as a percent of the national total. The buying-power indexes, calculated from *Sales Management* county data cards, are weighted averages of indexes for population, retail sales of food stores, and effective income in the geographical areas. The official sales budgets also give some guidelines in setting advertising and promotion budgets and in checking on and improving the performance of distributors.

The Controller's office (with the help of sales personnel) estimates product prices for the year ahead, and uses these to convert the official unit sales forecast to revenue estimates. These estimates are combined with cost figures for company components to develop detailed budgets for central staff administrative departments and for individual plants. The detailed budgets are consolidated by the Controller, along with additional cost data, into a projected company profit and loss budget.

The President, Vice-President of Finance, and the Controller review the initial financial budget projections. Adjustments are made for expected increases in labor or materials prices, revenue trends by categories of products are rechecked, and consolidated results are checked against goals for growth in sales and profits set by the President. Through this review, an adjusted financial budget is arrived at, though any implied changes in product sales are not changed in the previously adopted official unit sales forecast.

The adjusted financial budget is sent to the Board of Directors for review and approval before the beginning of the fiscal year. When the fiscal year budget has been adopted, the Controller develops projected profit and loss statements and the Treasurer uses them to prepare monthly cash flow estimates.

Actual sales are compared to forecast levels monthly during the year and adjustments are then made in production forecasts and product sales forecasts. If the revised sales forecasts indicate that original budgets will probably not be met, then consideration is given to making changes in marketing plans. At year end, a report is prepared comparing forecasted and actual sales for the year and recording the percent change from the prior year.

Longer-Term Sales Forecasts. Long-term (five-year) forecasts are used for planning plant capacity and distribution facilities, for checking on the availability of raw materials, for developing future financial plans and maintaining lines of credit, and for checking on the prospective achievement of the company's goal of 10 percent per year growth in earnings per share.

Five-year sales forecasts are prepared annually. The statistician in the Secretary's office prepares long-term forecasts of unit sales on a product-by-product basis. For established products, the historical trends in their annual usage per household is projected ahead. Then, a forecast of households is prepared, or Census Bureau projections are used. Number of households multiplied by the projected usage per household yields forecasts of unit sales. For new products, marketing research projections are used.

In addition, the Vice-President of Finance makes projections of operations on an overall basis, not by detailed product lines. These long-term projections are compared to the long-term sales forecasts and to the company's goals for growth. Any inconsistencies indicate a need to take action to realize company objectives. Growth in sales of present products may be stimulated, new products may be developed, foreign markets may be expanded, or acquisitions of other companies may be sought.

Profitability Analysis for Marketing: Gizmo Novelty Company

The Gizmo Novelty Company is a manufacturer of inexpensive novelty gift items which are distributed mostly through wholesalers to gift shops, cigar stores, and variety stores.[3] One of the firm's executives has developed a new product, an inexpensive plastic seat belt for sports stadium seats, which top management feels has great potential.

Originally, the company had planned to market the product as a novelty, but after an intensive market research study of sports fans and the number of injuries which occur when fans fall out of bleachers, the company decided to attempt to market the product to manufacturers of stadium equipment or to variety or department stores. Management, therefore, had to select one of the following alternatives:

---

3. Adapted from James H. Donnelly Jr., and John M. Ivancevick, *Analysis for Marketing Decisions* (Homewood, Illinois: Richard D. Irwin, Inc., 1970), pp. 203-208.

Plan 1: Market the product as an industrial product through whole-salers to manufacturers of stadium equipment on a national scale.

Plan 2: Market the product as a consumer item through wholesalers to various retail outlets such as variety stores and depart-ment stores.

The market analyst at Gizmo Novelty Company first collected the follow-ing data for each of the alternative plans:

Plan 1		Plan 2	
Production costs (fixed)	$15,000	Production costs (fixed)	$15,000
Production costs (per unit variable)	.09	Production costs (per unit variable)	.09
Marketing costs (fixed)	25,000	Marketing costs (fixed)	135,000
(per unit variable)	.01	(per unit variable)	.01
Price to wholesaler (charged by Gizmo)	.30	Manufacturer's selling price	.40
Selling price	.50	Wholesale price	.50
		Retail price	.75

Next, he did a breakeven analysis of the two alternatives in order to determine which alternative would give the faster pay-back of investment. He used the following formulas in doing this analysis:

$$BE \text{ (in units)} = \frac{TFC}{P - V}$$

and

$$BE \text{ (in dollars)} = \frac{TFC}{1 - V/P}$$

BE — breakeven point
P — selling price per unit
TFC — total fixed costs
V — variable cost per unit

Applying these formulas to each of the alternatives in the problem gives the following results:

Plan 1

$$BE \text{ (in units)} = \frac{\$40,000}{.30 - .10} = 200,000 \text{ units}$$

$$BE \text{ (in dollars)} = \frac{\$40,000}{1 - .10/.30} = \$60,000$$

$$\text{Plan 2}$$
$$BE \text{ (in units)} = \frac{\$150,000}{.40 - .10} = 500,000 \text{ units}$$
$$BE \text{ (in dollars)} = \frac{\$150,000}{1 - .10/.40} = \$200,000$$

While breakeven points in units and dollars for each plan are useful, they do not provide a complete picture of the impact of changes in sales and costs on profits. To determine these varying relationships, the analyst next constructed breakeven graphs and charts for both alternatives, as shown in Figures 7–3 and 7–4.

FIGURE 7–3

Breakeven Graph for Plan 1

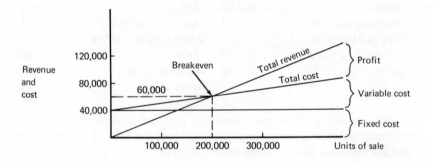

FIGURE 7–4

Breakeven Graph for Plan 2

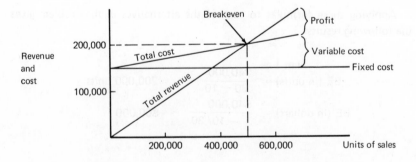

From the breakeven charts, the analyst determined the profit potentials at various levels of sales for both plans, as shown in Tables 7–1 and 7–2.

The figures up to this point showed first that the profit potential is much greater with Plan 2, but the risks are considerably higher, because a much greater investment is required in marketing costs and there is a considerably higher sales breakeven point. This risk is a significant factor, since the item under study is a novelty and, as such, is highly unpredictable.

The market analyst, therefore, went a step further and obtained estimates from marketing management of the probability of achieving the different levels of projected sales, based on their experience with similar products and their knowledge of the market for the new belt. Using these probability estimates, the analyst then estimated the expected value of each plan. His analysis is shown in Tables 7–3 and 7–4.

Based on the probability estimates, the probability of gain was greater under Plan 2, marketing the seat belts through wholesalers to variety stores and novelty stores. However, management would chose this alternative only if they were confident of the probability estimates, had sufficient risk funds to make the additional $110,000 investment in marketing costs, and were otherwise confident that they had a good chance of at least reaching and surpassing the high breakeven point. In this situation, as in other profitability analysis situations discussed in this book, then, the figures must be weighed

TABLE 7–1

Profit Levels of Plan 1

Level of output in units	Sales	Total costs	Profit or loss
100,000	$ 30,000	$50,000	$–20,000
200,000	60,000	60,000	-0-
300,000	90,000	70,000	20,000
400,000	120,000	80,000	40,000

TABLE 7–2

Profit Levels of Plan 2

Level of output in units	Sales	Total costs	Profit or loss
400,000	$160,000	$190,000	$–30,000
500,000	200,000	$200,000	-0-
600,000	240,000	210,000	30,000
700,000	280,000	220,000	60,000
800,000	320,000	230,000	90,000

TABLE 7-3

Expected Values of Plan 1

Level of output in units	Profit or loss	Assigned weight	Weighted profit or loss
100,000	$-20,000	.15	$-3,000
200,000	-0-	.30	-0-
300,000	20,000	.35	7,000
400,000	40,000	.20	8,000
			$12,000

in light of the assumptions on which they are based and in relation to other business factors affecting the outcomes.

Sales Management: Correspondence Schools Unlimited

Developing sales management information systems was discussed in the *Domby Publishing Company* study in Chapter Two (study exercise). In dealing with that situation, the sales management job was first defined: selling advertising space in controlled circulation publications to industrial companies through company-employed salesmen who worked on a salary plus commission basis. Carrying out the sales management job required researching the market to determine potential customers (especially how to get additional advertisers), soliciting old and new potential advertisers (which required knowing why they might be interested in using a Domby publication), and obtaining statements of intent and firm orders (which required information on intent orders).

The existing information system provided information on results of sales efforts (that is, reports were issued on intended and actual sales). The system

TABLE 7-4

Expected Values of Plan 2

Level of output in units	Profit or loss	Assigned weight	Weighted profit or loss
400,000	$-30,000	.20	$-6,000
500,000	-0-	.25	-0-
600,000	30,000	.35	10,500
700,000	60,000	.15	9,000
800,000	90,000	.05	4,500
			$18,000

provided no information on the many months of sales activities required to produce these sales results. The information system was, therefore, expanded to include the following: a report on total customers (advertisers) available for each publication, rated by degree of interest in the publication (intense, moderate, marginal); reports on salesmen activities in calling on potential new advertisers as well as on old customers; and a comparative report on statements of intent from new and old advertisers monthly for the next twelve issues and the preceding twelve issues. In other words, the new system reported on sales activities, as well as on the financial results of these activities, so that decision information would now be given to sales management at a time when action could be taken to affect results during the current result period.

Under the new system, the data file had to be expanded to include names of all potential and present advertisers. That file was updated by salesmen, based on their reading of industry publications and conversations with industry executives. The file (which was a master card index file) included information on the reasons why each advertiser might want to advertise in Domby publications and which Domby publication might fulfill their needs. A rating of the degree of interest was also established and notation was made of past use of Domby publications by each advertiser.

This master planning file was screened and updated periodically (at least quarterly) and, from it, lists of old and potential customers were prepared for use by salesmen. The information reports prepared on sales calls made to names on this list by each salesman were used by the sales manager to monitor each salesman's work in developing new customers and increasing business from old customers. The first phase of order solicitation, getting indications of intent, was also reported on well in advance of issue date and compared with the previous year's results for the same time period, in order to give sales management time to take corrective action where needed.

The *Little Publishing Company* study in Chapter One (study exercise) also involved developing information systems for sales management. In that study, only one aspect of sales management information system development was touched on, using existing computerized data files in accounting for sales analysis. The study involved defining management decision requirements and developing a coding pattern for each customer account file which would enable different kinds of customer and sales analysis reports to be produced.

A recent correspondence school study provides another example of developing information systems for sales management. The company, Correspondence Schools Unlimited, developed and sold three correspondence courses. The courses cost $700, took two to three years to complete (students mailed in their assignments which were corrected and returned by mail), and were generally paid for over a two-year period. The courses were sold through 800 company salesmen throughout the country, who worked on a straight commission basis.

The field sales staff was organized around products, with each product having its own salesmen and districts, regional and national sales managers. The three national sales managers (one for each product) reported to the company's overall sales vice president at the company's home office. Product A had 400 salesmen, product B was assigned 250 and product C used 150.

A sales promotion manager and market research manager serviced all three sales divisions. A separate advertising department (not under the sales vice president) provided salesmen with the names of prospects who had expressed interest in the product as a result of national ads in such publications as *Reader's Digest, TV Guide,* and *Ladies' Home Journal.*

Each salesman was assigned a different territory, based on a minimum population count. Salesmen called on the prospects who had written for information. Sales presentations were made in the prospect's home.

Prospect names (called "leads") cost the company about $7 each in advertising expense, so that the percentage of sales made to these prospects (called the "conversion rate") by each salesman had a major impact on sales costs and profits. For example, a 5 percent conversion rate gave a $140 advertising cost per enrollment; a 7 percent conversion rate gave a $100 cost: a $40 difference (or just about the profit normally made on each enrollment). Salesmen were paid $70 commission per enrollment, with the commission being paid out of payments received from the customer. District and regional managers also received a small "override" commission on each sale.

Because of the unique characteristics of this business, sales management needed information on the sales of each salesman in each sales management district in total and *as a percentage of the leads issued to each salesman.* A report (see Figure 7–5) was, therefore, issued weekly which showed sales by salesman and by district for that week and cumulative sales to date, along with commissions paid. The report also showed leads issued, leads returned as unusable (bad addresses, etc.), leads called on and not sold, the inventory of leads held by the salesmen, and the percentage of leads sold (exclusive of those leads held by the salesmen). New leads were issued as old ones were returned, once a salesman had a basic inventory of at least thirty leads. The report also showed the number of leads held at the home office for each salesman's territory. Supplemental summary reports of this information by district, region, and product were also prepared for all levels of sales management, as well as for advertising management (to know where leads were needed; copies of the detail reports on each salesman were also kept at regional offices and home office). These result reports were prepared by the company's central data processing department.

In addition to these result reports, reports on projected sales for the coming twelve months by month for each sales district were revised and

FIGURE 7–5

Weekly Sales Report
Course A
District 4, Region 1
Date

Name	Sales for week	Sales for year	Prior year's sales	Lead inventory Jan. 1	Leads issued to date	Leads returned unusable	Leads returned unsalable	Lead inventory current	Leads to be issued	Conv'n % this year	Conv'n % last year	Lead bank	Coms'ns earned this year
Bill Jones	3	28	211	38	496	45	426	35	14	6.2%	6.7%	175	$1,485
Sam Petry		etc.											
etc.													

Note: Salesmen airmailed orders and used leads for the week to the home office each Friday.
Orders were processed on Monday and reports prepared and issued the following Friday.
New leads were mailed to salesmen each Monday in the amount indicated in the "leads to be issued" column.

issued quarterly to enable district managers to make hiring plans. The information on planned or budgeted increases in sales per district was also sent to the advertising department to enable them to make plans to provide additional leads for expected increases in sales. These budget reports, unlike the sales result reports, were prepared manually by the national sales managers' personnel, working in conjunction with district and regional managers and top management.

Reports comparing these budgets with actual sales by management level (district, region, and national by product) were also prepared manually by the sales department at the national office. These summary reports were used by the national sales managers to evaluate the performance of their district and regional managers, and summaries by product group were used by top management to evaluate national sales managers' performance.

At the time a salesman was hired, personnel data was collected by district managers for each salesman, forwarded to the home office, and stored in the salesman's file there. When a salesman was fired, the reason for firing was recorded and sent to home office, along with notification of the termination. The file also carried information on how the salesman originally heard of the company and so applied for work. Quarterly, the sales promotion manager screened the salesman file to determine how effective his mailings and ads soliciting enquiries from potential salesmen were.

Many years work had gone into the development of this reporting system. Originally, district managers had received only a sales report (from the accounting department), which drew data from the sales ledger. The accounting department subsequently began providing cumulative reports on the commissions earned by each salesman. Reports on conversion rates and lead inventories were supplied in separate reports by the lead processing and filing section, which was not under the accounting department.

At the time new computer equipment was purchased, a centralized processing department was established which maintained basic lead, sales, accounts receivable, commissions, and other business files. Once this step had been taken, work began on different ways to coordinate management reporting. Several different combinations of sales management reports were tried over the years before the present reporting systems was finally developed.

Advertising: Bedrock Products Company

Bedrock Products Company manufactures bonded abrasive products, grinding wheels, sharpening stones, and a wide range of similar products.[4] Buyers of

---

4. Adapted from Harry Hansen, *Marketing Techniques and Cases* (Homewood, Illinois: Richard D. Irwin, Inc., 1967), pp. 709-728.

the company's products included metal trades companies, farm implement manufacturers, steel mills, stone trades companies, and glass manufacturers. Bedrock had sales of over $10,000,000 annually, a gross profit of 25 percent, and a net profit on sales of 8 percent.

About forty firms competed with Bedrock, who ranked third in industry sales. About 60 percent of industry sales came from two competitors, Mendel Company and Rabinol Products Company, both of whom had a product line directly competitive with Bedrock's. Many smaller competitors specialized in just abrasives, while others (both large and small) produced them along with other items.

Bedrock's advertising program was designed to make buyers more aware of the company's products and so "pave the way" for the firm's forty salesmen and 140 distributors. The company's ads stressed the fact that Bedrock had better products. The major advertising media used was regularly scheduled advertisements in major metalworking magazines and direct mail sent to tool room foremen, superintendents, purchasing agents, and others. Supplemental sales promotion material included two short motion pictures, stereoscopic slides, product catalogues and technical literature, sales manuals, souvenirs, and other sales aids, and classified telephone advertisements for distributors.

In his budget for the coming year, Bedrock's advertising manager asked for an increase of 22 percent over this year's spending, based on Bedrock's plans for expanded production and Rabinol's substantially increased advertising. Recent spot surveys had also shown that buyers favored Mendel and Rabinol products by a wide margin.

As part of the new advertising program, Bedrock retained the Burns advertising agency to evaluate the company's present advertising program and recommend changes. The agency collected background information for their evaluation in several ways: first, they interviewed Bedrock executives and salesmen, and publication, customer, and industry association executives to determine how the opinion of outsiders compared with Bedrock's view of its products and industry position; second, a mail questionnaire was sent to all Bedrock distributors to determine why users bought Bedrock products and to identify the strengths and weaknesses of Bedrock's products (this survey and the next also served as a check on the answers to the interview survey); third, questionnaires were sent to users of bonded abrasive products (about one-third were sent to firms which did not now buy from Bedrock) to determine buyer motivation and reaction to Bedrock's products and advertising.

In summarizing the results of these surveys, Burns agency prepared twenty summary tables, two of which are given in Figures 7–6 and 7–7. The survey results indicated that while users believed that Bedrock produced a complete line of quality products and was a leader in new and improved products, Bedrock's name was not as well-recognized or accepted as its competitors'

FIGURE 7–6

Distributor Ratings

Please *rate* and discuss the outstanding factors in making sales to important users of grinding wheels, such as those named below. (Indicate the most important one, in your judgment, by the number "1," and so on down the line.)

(a)   General reputation of Bedrock
(b)   Performance of trial wheels
(c)   Good relations of salesman with plant operating personnel
(d)   Technical assistance of Bedrock's abrasive specialist to the user
(e)   Bedrock advertising
(f)   Price
(g)   Past experience of user with Bedrock wheels
(h)   Effect of friendly relations of your company with purchasing agent
(i)   Prompt delivery

	(a)	(b)	(c)	(d)	(e)	(f)	(g)	(h)	(i)
1st	7	20	26	5	0	2	2	6	3
2nd	2	12	15	15	1	2	4	11	2
3rd	9	11	9	7	0	1	3	12	5
4th	8	10	6	10	3	1	5	7	10
5th	9	5	2	7	9	0	7	10	6
6th	10	2	2	3	7	1	10	6	11
7th	6	—	—	7	11	5	7	3	6
8th	3	1	—	5	15	8	10	1	3
9th	1	—	—	1	7	21	3	—	1
10th	—	—	—	—	1	8	1	—	1
	55	61	60	60	54	49	52	56	48
Median rating	5th	2nd	1st	4th	8th	9th	7th	3rd	6th

among purchasing agents, plant executives, or foremen and supervisors, all of whom influence purchasing decisions. In addition, weaknesses in service and delivery were evident.

In an effort to develop an advertising program which would help overcome these apparent weaknesses, the agency obtained a publication readership breakdown by job classification, as shown in Figure 7–8. This information was used in conjunction with the survey results to select media for a new magazine advertising campaign (see Figure 7–9). In selecting publications and determining the amount to spend in each, emphasis was given to reaching key decision makers not now convinced of Bedrock's quality leadership.

FIGURE 7-7

Recall of Magazine Advertising by Function and by Manufacturer
(Percent of Total Mentioning Brand Who Also Answered Question on Magazine Advertising)

Manufacturer		Purchasing Agents	Administrative and Executive	Tool Engineering	Tool Room Supervisors	Grinding Room and Machine
Rabinol	Respondents (100%)	69	36	69	70	37
	% advertising recall	92.8	97.2	89.9	91.4	97.3
Mendel	Respondents (100%)	61	35	63	60	35
	% advertising recall	78.7	88.6	81.0	81.7	65.7
Bedrock	Respondents (100%)	36	16	44	40	23
	% advertising recall	55.6	56.3	61.4	50.0	60.9
Simonds Abrasive	Respondents (100%)	13	9	19	23	7
	% advertising recall	61.5	88.9	47.4	69.6	57.1
Sterling	Respondents (100%)	13	6	14	16	6
	% advertising recall	61.5	33.3	50.0	56.3	66.7
Macklin	Respondents (100%)	13	4	9	13	5
	% advertising recall	53.8	75.0	55.6	46.2	—
Precision	Respondents (100%)	9	7	9	7	6
	% advertising recall	—	14.3	44.4	57.1	16.7
National	Respondents (100%)	3	3	6	6	5
	% advertising recall	33.3	25.0	33.3	—	—
A. P. DeSanno	Respondents (100%)	6	4	4	12	1
	% advertising recall	33.3	25.0	—	41.7	—
Peninsular	Respondents (100%)	5	2	5	2	6
	% advertising recall	40.0	50.0	80.0	—	16.7
Cortland	Respondents (100%)	7	4	2	2	6
	% advertising recall	14.3	25.0	—	—	16.7
Other companies	Respondents (100%)	31	25	32	33	24
	% advertising recall	25.8	40.0	53.1	15.2	33.3

The same survey information was also used to design new magazine advertisements, which emphasized not only Bedrock's strengths (complete line, new product leadership, and quality), but also those areas in which the company was believed weak (sales and engineering services). The direct mail program was completely revised to provide more useful information to users and to emphasize the availability of products for customer testing and the offer of technical assistance for solving specific user problems. For example, both the new magazine advertising and direct mail gave specific examples of how Bedrock's technical specialists helped solve a tough user problem, and mailings were made which included useful articles on problems of interest to customer plant managers and supervisors.

In line with the survey information, steps were also taken in other marketing areas: engineering services were improved, checks were made of distributor delivery performance and several distributors were replaced with

FIGURE 7–8

Percent of Individuals by Job Classifications Who Reported Regular Readership of Various Business Publications in Connection with Their Jobs

Publications (over 3 mentions)	Purchasing agents (86 out of 97 answered)	Adminis- trative and Executive personnel (47 out of 50 answered)	Tool En- gineers, methods of standard engineers (65 out of 72 answered)	Tool room foremen and supervisors (72 out of 87 answered)	Grinding room foremen and machinists (38 out of 44 answered)
American Foundryman	—	8.5%	—	—	—
American Machinist	—	21.3	41.5%	37.5%	31.6%
American Metal Market	4.7%	—	—	—	—
Business Week	16.3	8.5	—	8.3	—
Design News	—	—	6.2	—	—
Factory	4.7	23.4	21.5	9.7	13.2
Foundry	5.8	17.0	—	—	—
Grits and Grinds (Norton)	—	—	7.7	11.1	31.6
Industrial Equipment News	—	—	6.2	—	—
Iron Age	51.2	46.8	23.1	18.1	21.1
Machine & Tool Blue Book	7.0	—	23.1	37.5	10.5
Machine Design	—	—	12.3	5.6	—
Machinery	4.7	31.9	40.0	36.1	13.2
Materials and Methods	—	—	7.7	—	—
Metals Working	—	—	10.8	6.9	—
Mill and Factory	33.7	21.3	24.6	26.4	13.2
Modern Industry	—	8.5	—	—	—
Modern Machine Shop	4.7	10.6	16.9	29.2	10.5
New Equipment Digest	—	—	7.7	6.9	—
Product Engineering	—	8.5	10.8	—	—
Production Engineering and Management	—	—	7.7	5.6	—
Purchasing	55.8	—	—	—	—
Purchasing News	10.5	—	—	—	—
Steel	53.5	34.0	21.5	11.1	13.2
Steel Processing	—	8.5	—	—	—
Tool Engineer	—	10.6	30.8	11.1	—
Tooling and Production	—	—	23.1	31.9	—
Other publications	55.8	87.2	44.6	31.9	—

new ones, and Bedrock's salesmen were directed to spend more time than they had in the past calling on user company purchasing agents and executives. Sales promotion literature was also revised to complement the advertising material.

Customer Service: H. R. Watson Company

H. R. Watson Company, a family-owned retail company with an annual sales volume of $3,000,000, was established in 1908, in Brewster, New York. In

FIGURE 7-9

Advertising Agency's Proposed Budget for Bedrock Abrasives
Business Paper Space
A. Magazine Advertising
(All Two-Color unless Otherwise Noted)

Metalworking
American Machinst—13 pages	$ 7,098.00
The Iron Age—13 pages	6,688.50
Machine Tool Blue Book—12 pages	3,465.00
Machinery—12 pages	5,355.00
Modern Machine Shop—12 pages	3,717.00
Steel—13 pages	6,688.50
Foundry—12 pages	5,292.00

Purchasing
Purchasing—12 pages	5,670.00

Distributors
Industrial Distribution—12 pages	4,599.00

Specialties
Industry & Welding—12 pages	5,166.00

Automotive
Automotive Industries—12 pages	3,843.00

Executive
Mill & Factory—12 pages	8,114.40
Factory—12 pages	10,332.00
Total space	$76,028.40

NOTE: Bleed pages, if used, are approximately 10% over above figures.

B. Advertisement Production

Estimated $15,000.00

1950, as a result of growth in the area, a second outlet was established in Pawling, New York. Prior to 1950, the product line was principally appliance items that would be used by general consumers in a town of 20,000 people. With the increased population the demand for products also increased, and new products were added to the line somewhat haphazardly as demand warranted it. The philosophy of the company was, "If you can't find it, ask us for it; if we don't have it, we'll get it."

A study of the company's product mix in 1973 showed that 60 percent of the company's sales were now in consumer-oriented appliances and 40 percent in commercial/industrial-oriented appliances. The results were something of a surprise to management. It was due in part to the 1973 report, in part to increasing business costs, and in part to the threat of new competition that the company president decided to reorganize operations at his two stores. As part of this reorganization, Mr. John Perkins, Assistant Sales Director, was asked to recommend any changes he felt were needed in the customer service operation.

The Existing Customer Service Operation

Customer services presently offered included merchandise exchange, repairs and service calls (warranty and non-warranty), delivery, and installation. All items are fully guaranteed for thirty days after delivery. Beyond this point, specific guidelines are established for each product category. However, warranty policies are loosely interpreted and, wherever possible, customer demands are met.

There were no formal summary reports used to monitor overall customer service activities. Each sales department maintained a customer complaint "roster" and the two service departments (consisting of a supervisor and four service/repair men at each store location) maintain a service requested/completed log book to aid in manpower scheduling. At the end of each operating period, customer service costs were allocated to each sales department, based on the distribution of service among the various product categories, and included in the sales department's operating statements.

Mr. Perkins' Analysis of the Present Customer Service Operation

The present accounting system made it difficult to determine the exact cost impact of the present customer service policies. Mr. Perkins realized, therefore, that his first task was to determine the actual costs and revenues associated with the customer service operation.

He first developed a Product Service Requirement Report (Figure 7–10) and requested the service managers to prepare one each month for each sales

FIGURE 7–10

H. R. Watson & Co. Product SVC Req. Summary				
Department _____ Week ending _____				
Item Category	Problem Categories			
freezer # 18387 G.E.	Mfg. defect	Svc/delivery damage	Action req	Parts req
	Temp. dial broken	*Bottom white panel bent*	*replace dial replace panel*	*dial # 8356 panel # 0387*
Total				

FIGURE 7–11

H. R. Watson & Co. Customer Complaint Summary				
Department _Radio - TV_		Month ending _12-30-7-_		
Total customer complaints ___101___		Total sales _____		
Nature of complaint	Corrective Action Taken			
	Phone call	Letter	Visit	Other
Faulty product ___39___	10	9	20	0
Poor service ___49___	20	20	9	0
Other ___13___	3	0	10	0
Total ___101___	33	29	39	0

department (by product) from their log books during the coming three-month period. He also asked each sales department to send him copies of their customer complaint rosters at the end of each month for the coming three months. These complaint rosters showed the number and nature of complaints, and the types of corrective action taken. Based on this information, summary reports, such as the one shown in Figure 7–11, were prepared.

In order to gather accurate cost data, he revised the existing Work Order/Call Report to show figures, as shown in Figure 7–12, and he had service/repairmen use them for a period of three months. During this period,

FIGURE 7–12

H. R. Watson & Co. Work Order/Customer Call Report			
Item description __Stereo__	Date of purchase _12-29-7-_		
Code number __S-1369__	Check box if first purchase ☐		
Warranty number __122986__	Date of delivery requested _1-3-7-_		
Customer name/address	Action to be taken:		
J. Jones	_Supervise installation_		
	Assigned service personnel:		
	7. Smith / S-38		

Action Taken			
		Charges	
Description	Classification	Warranty	Non-warranty
Supervise installation	_Service_	15.00	
Date and time of service _1-3-73_ ³:³⁰		Employee signature _7. Smith_	

FIGURE 7-13

H. R. Watson & Co. Product Service Cost Summary					
Department _Radio -TV_ Week ending _12-29-7-_					
Item categories	Tot sales	Tot svc cost	Warranty	N-warranty	NW Inc.
T.V. Color	$ 8,000	$ 690	$ 490	$ 200	$ 300
T.V. B.+W.	6,000	510	400	110	160
T.V. Console	4,500	400	300	100	150
T.V. Portable	9,500	800	590	210	315
Parts	400	—			
Total	14,300	$11200	890	310	860

he had the accounting department prepare a report on income from service calls and parts sales. At the end of the three-month period, he accumulated all of this data and prepared a Product Service Cost Summary, as shown in Figure 7-13.

Further Changes Instituted by Mr. Perkins

The analysis of these reports showed that for many products the present warranty policies were too costly and that service income generated from parts sales and non-warranty service calls was extremely low. Specific guidelines and time limits for warranty service were reevaluated in light of these cost figures and warranty policies were revised. Prices for non-warranty services were also reevaluated and raised where necessary to cover actual expenses incurred.

Mr. Perkins next examined the problem of monitoring service personnel. He decided that a review of the Work Order/Call Reports, if done by a qualified person, would be a good means of monitoring personnel performance. These Work Order/Call Reports would also serve, he felt, along with the Product Activity Summaries, as the basis for scheduling service personnel, as well as for determining service personnel requirements. After the evaluation, which was done by an outside consultant from the local university, Mr. Perkins decided that the present service departments were overstaffed and that with improved scheduling the number of servicemen at each location could be reduced by one.

In addition, a system of spot checks by the service department managers was instituted and a performance checklist/report was developed (Figure 7-14). Mr. Perkins felt that a continuing evaluation of the Work Orders, coupled with the spot check reports, would insure effective control of servicemen's activities.

FIGURE 7–14

H. R. Watson & Co. Service Personnel Inspection Summary

Service person in assigned location?_____
Service person in command of situation with knowledge of problem and required corrective action? _____
Service person conveying the image of the company in an appropriate manner?_____
All parts and services are charged for and recorded? _____

Customer is satisfied with service provided?
Explanation: All no answers are to be discussed in detail below and
               initialed by serviceman in question.

Serviceman signature _____
Supervisor signature _____ Date of check _____

In order to obtain feedback from customers, Mr. Perkins developed a Customer Opinion Survey. The survey covered such areas as: frequency of use of Watson's service facilities; date, description, and amount of last purchase; general level of satisfaction with services; and recommendations for improvements. Since the other information reports were primarily quantitative, the survey provided the needed qualitative data. It would serve not only as another measure of past performance, but also as an aid in determining future customer needs.

As a last step, Mr. Perkins made the reports he had prepared during his situation analysis (Figures 7–10 through 7–13) a permanent part of the customer service operation information system.

Summary
Conclusion

As seen from the discussions in this chapter, information needs vary from marketing situation to marketing situation. These requirements cover, depending on the marketing area under study:

1. The objective of the systems development effort.
2. Overall company objectives, plans, and organization.

3. Marketing objectives and plans.
4. The work situation.
5. Management decisions and tasks, and the information required to make these decisions and carry out these tasks.
6. Existing information systems.
7. Organizational and personnel factors which will affect developing, implementing and using systems.

The kinds of systems developed in each marketing area varied considerably, from overall marketing plans, to profitability analysis reports, to a wide range of activity and financial reports in each marketing area.

A variety of marketing situations were presented in order to give the reader an idea of how information is developed in different areas of marketing and the kinds of management information systems used in these areas. The study exercises which follow provide practice in diagnosing marketing management information needs and developing systems appropriate to each management area using the techniques described in Chapter Six and in this chapter.

Case Study Exercises

Photom Corporation

The Photom Corporation is a producer of photographic equipment, including cameras, film, and accessories such as lenses and filters. Currently, the marketing vice president is attempting to appraise the sales performance of the new Model X-20 camera line at the retail level. The Model X-20 line had been introduced in June 1972 and was so advanced in design that all production was now being devoted to the new line.

Shipments to retailers during January and February of 1973 had not been satisfactory. However, estimates of dealer inventories derived from a survey of the company's "Dealer Panel" indicated that retail sales during these months were considerably higher than shipments to dealers. If these panel estimates were accurate, then retail sales of the Model X-20 compared favorably to previous forecasts and no changes in marketing plans were needed. The question of the validity of the figures arrived at by using dealer panel estimates was, therefore, important.

Distribution and Selling

Photom cameras and film were sold primarily through two main channels. Sales to retail dealers, including department stores, discount stores, photo supply stores, and drug and jewelry stores (about 8,000 outlets in total) accounted for about 85 percent of Photom's camera sales in 1972. Sales to wholesalers in drug, jewelry, and other miscellaneous areas accounted for the remainder of camera sales.

Photom's thirty-seven salesmen were responsible for calling on dealers periodically to set up displays, train retail personnel, and assist in advertising planning. Since salesmen's territories covered both big city and rural areas, some dealers who did not sell a significant volume and were located in rural areas were called on only a few times a year, while large-volume big city stores might be called on ten or twelve times a year.

Shipments and Retail Sales

Photom used an IBM 370-65 computer system for processing and storing shipment data, and each salesman was sent periodic reports of the shipments made to dealers and wholesalers in his territory. Although shipments to dealers were easily measured, there was little information available to marketing management on the actual sales to consumers by the dealers. Information was needed on these sales for several reasons:

1. To evaluate consumer acceptance of new products quickly.
2. To enable better forecasting for marketing planning and production scheduling.
3. To control inventories at the six company warehouses located around the country.

Prior to 1972, estimates of retail sales were obtained by asking each salesman to select twenty-five outlets in his territory with purchases of $20,000 or more annually and get an inventory count from them every six months. Volume of retail sales was then computed by adding the beginning inventory for the six months to shipments during the period, and subtracting the ending inventory. These sales figures were then projected to all dealers, under the assumption that the relationships between shipments and sales for the sample dealers were the same for all dealers in the territory.

The New Estimating System: A "Dealer Panel" Survey

Because of the need for more frequent and more accurate estimates of retail sales and inventories, a new "Dealer Panel" system was designed in the fall of 1972 for measuring retail sales. The method of selecting dealers for the panel was as follows:

1. All regular dealer outlets were arrayed in descending order of 1972 camera shipments (to date).

2. These dealers were categorized as follows: I–250 largest accounts; II–500 next largest; III–next 1,000; IV–remainder. The distribution of dealers and sales was:

Category	Dealers	% of total sales
I	250	25%
II	500	15
III	1,000	15
IV	6,250	30

3. The lists were divided up into salesmen's territories, and salesmen were asked to pick from each category the most reliable and dependable dealers, who sell primarily to general consumers, who can be surveyed by telephone, and who can be counted on to actually count their inventory. Where dealers have several branches, inventory counts had to be by stores.

FIGURE 7–15

Shipments to Dealers and Estimated Dealer Sales
October 1972 to February 1973
(index numbers: October 1973 = 100)

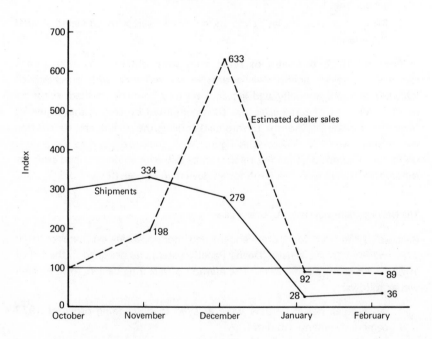

4. The dealer names chosen were submitted by the salesmen to the marketing research department, who selected the most representative dealer outlets in each category in each territory (three from category I, two from II and III, and one from IV).

The salesmen were then instructed on how to make telephone calls to the dealers on the panel each month. Starting in October 1972, calls were made by salesmen to dealers on the fifth working day each month and inventory counts were submitted to the marketing research department within three days. Projections were made on the basis of the percentage of shipments to panel dealers in 1972 as related to total shipments and were computed separately for each category. The panel dealers represented 35 percent of all shipments in category I, 18 percent in category II, 5 percent in category III, and 1.5 percent in category IV. The results of the early March 1973 survey, shown in Figure 7–15, showed that if survey figures were used, sales in January and February of 1973 were quite satisfactory; whereas, if shipment figures were used, there would seem to be a severe sales problem with the Model X-20.

Several marketing managers were reluctant to accept the survey projections, since in early 1973 panel dealer shipments had increased from 20 to 23 percent of total shipments. In addition, several panel dealers had changed categories, due to increased sales:

Category	Number of panel dealers in category	
	1972	1973
I	84	85
II	90	99
III	48	67
IV	85	56
Total	307	307

The marketing vice president was wondering whether he should base his decisions on the panel survey projections or on actual shipment figures.

Assignment

1. Evaluate the methods used for selecting the dealer panel and for estimating retail sales of dealers. What business factors are critical to your evaluation? What technical factors?
2. What is your estimate of the value of the projections, based on your answer to question 1? Explain the reasons for your estimate.
3. What action would you take as marketing vice president? Explain in detail the reasoning behind your answer.

The Austin Company

The Austin Company began operations in 1942, with the development of a special paste solder which had the advantage that it could be applied before a joint was assembled.[5] It was first used as a product in wartime construction and maintained a steady post-war market. Located in Austin, Minnesota, the company by the early 1970s had 135 distributors in seventeen states for its complete line of solid and liquid solders. A salesman was maintained in each district (major city) to work with the distributors and solicit business directly from large users.

Data was developed from industry publications on the total market for solder. This data was compared with Austin's own sales and it was found that the company's sales pattern differed markedly from the industry's as regards end-use of the product, as is seen in Table 7–5.

Company sales were made on average 56 percent through distributors and 44 percent direct to users. Additional sales analyses (Table 7–6) revealed that 81 percent of the total tonnage of solder sold direct by Austin in 1973 was to

TABLE 7–5

Total Industry and Austin Sales of Solder by End Use: 1973
(millions of pounds)

End use	Total industry sales	Austin sales	Austin percent of market
Manufacturing industry:	354	31.9	9.0
Electrical equipment and machinery	42	7.2	17.2
Fabricated metal products	58	8.4	14.6
Machinery (except electrical)	96	7.6	8.0
Primary metals	11	0.7	6.3
Transportation equipment	103	6.3	6.1
All other	44	1.7	3.9
Nonmanufacturing industry:	157	10.6	6.8
Construction	39	3.7	9.5
Utilities	22	0.6	6.6
Metal working shops	49	1.2	2.4
Transportation	25	0.3	1.1
All other	22	4.8	21.8
Total market	511	42.5	8.3

5. Adapted from Harper W. Boyd and Ralph Westfall, *Marketing Research: Text and Cases* (Homewood, Illinois: Richard D. Irwin, Inc., 1964), pp. 748-755.

TABLE 7–6

Austin Shipments Direct and to Distributors by Size of Account: 1973

Direct Sales

	Accounts		Shipments	
	No.	Percent	Millions of lbs.	Percent
Under 1,000 lbs.	302	44	.056	0.3
1,000– 4,999 lbs.	129	19	.374	2
5,000– 9,999 lbs.	44	6	.374	2
10,000–19,999 lbs.	48	7	.561	3
20,000–49,999 lbs.	68	10	2.151	11.5
50,000–99,999 lbs.	42	6	2.618	14
Over 100,000 lbs.	47	7	12.529	67

Sales to Distributors

	Accounts		Shipments	
	No.	Percent	Millions of lbs.	Percent
Under 20,000 lbs.	122	52	.714	3
20,000– 49,999 lbs.	42	18	1.666	7
50,000– 99,999 lbs.	22	9	1.904	8
100,000–249,999 lbs.	24	10	4.403	18.5
250,000–499,999 lbs.	17	7	7.616	32
Over 500,000 lbs.	8	3.4	7.378	31

89 accounts that represented only 13 percent of the total number of direct accounts. The same pattern existed in sales to distributors, where 82 percent of the company's shipments went to 21 percent of the distributors, all of whom purchased 100,000 pounds or more annually.

Data on the sales of solder to different types of firms of different sizes was obtained from trade publications and from the company's own sales records. From this data, estimates were made of the potential sales of solder to different types of firms according to their sales volumes. With these estimates and with data on the distribution of manufacturers in the United States from the Census of Manufacturers, the forecasting staff established forecasts by district for both direct and distributor sales. All firms with annual potential of 50,000 pounds or more were classified in the direct sales group. The total was adjusted to make the total potential approximately equal to the present industry's total sales volume, as shown in Table 7–7.

The forecasting staff felt that the company should establish a goal of total tonnage of solder Austin should sell in the coming year. Austin's present share of the total market was 8.3 percent. The goal would be 10 percent and would be distributed among the sales districts in proportion to potential: for

TABLE 7–7

Number of Direct Sales Prospects and Potentials for Direct Sales and Distributor Sales by Sales District
(millions of pounds)

Sales district	Number of direct sales prospects	Direct Sales			Distributor Sales		
		Est. potential	Austin	Austin percent of potential	Est. potential	Austin	Austin percent of potential
New York	127	16.3	0.4	2.4%	18.8	0.4	2.1%
Boston	195	18.9	1.1	5.8	21.8	1.6	7.3
Los Angeles	211	16.8	2.2	13.1	19.5	0.5	2.6
Detroit	271	40.5	2.3	5.7	46.9	3.9	8.3
Pittsburgh	297	34.1	2.6	7.6	39.4	1.3	3.3
Chicago	150	29.6	1.2	4.1	34.4	1.4	4.1
Minneapolis	86	8.1	1.9	23.5	9.4	1.1	11.7
Dallas	25	3.2	0.2	6.2	3.8	0.6	15.8
San Francisco	36	6.3	2.4	38.1	7.4	0.5	6.8
Seattle	19	7.9	0.1	12.7	9.2	1.2	13.0
St. Louis	33	8.5	1.6	18.8	9.9	0.5	5.1
Philadelphia	85	12.1	1.6	13.2	13.9	3.5	25.2
Milwaukee	28	9.4	0.4	4.2	10.9	3.1	28.4
Washington, D.C.	9	3.2	0.3	9.4	3.7	0.2	5.4
Norfolk	12	4.6	0.2	4.3	5.3	1.7	32.1
Denver	25	5.0	0.3	6.0	5.8	0.4	6.9
Kansas City	33	11.5	—	—	13.3	1.8	13.5
Total U.S.	1,665	236.0	18.8	8.0%	273.4	23.7	8.7%

example, if a district had 8.7 percent of the total industry potential, it would be assigned 8.7 percent of the Austin sales goal.

The goal for each district would be divided into a goal for direct sales and a goal for distributor sales, using the overall ratio of these sales (44 percent direct, 56 percent distributors). Both of these markets were to be developed equally. In many outlying areas, large accounts were held by distributors. It was recommended that a policy be established for direct solicitation of all prospective customers whose total solder purchases exceeded 50,000 pounds, and that smaller accounts be left exclusively to distributors.

Many of the districts would be unable to attain their goals immediately, so quotas would be set each year that would permit them to move at a reasonable rate toward their goals. Some districts were already over the 10 percent goal and would require quotas higher than their goals. An analysis of each district would be necessary in setting the quota to determine the district potential, the areas within the district which needed further development, and manpower requirements. The Chicago sales district was analyzed as an example, as shown in Table 7–8.

It was recommended that each area be further analyzed by class of user, so that the company could tell more precisely the industries from which additional business should come. The company could provide each district with a

TABLE 7–8

Example of Breakdown of Sales Goals in Chicago District
(millions of pounds)

		Direct Sales			Distributor Sales		
	Industry total	Industry	Austin goal	Austin 1973 ship-ments	Industry	Austin goal	Austin 1973 ship-ments
Total district	63.9	29.3	2.93	1.2	34.6	3.46	1.36
Chicago	41.9	19.2	1.90	1.1	22.7	2.27	.83
Gary	7.2	3.3	.30	.1	3.9	.39	.41
Hammond	3.3	1.5	.15	—	1.8	.18	—
Waukegan	3.2	1.5	.15	—	1.7	.17	—
Rockford	2.7	1.2	.12	—	1.5	.15	.01
Aurora	2.0	.9	.01	—	1.1	.11	—
Peoria	1.4	.7	.07	—	.7	.07	.05
Springfield	.8	.4	.04	—	.4	.04	.01
Elgin	.7	.3	.03	—	.4	.04	.04
Other areas	.7	.3	.03	—	.4	.04	.01

detailed list of accounts which should be solicited. The forecasting staff further recommended that in the future a refinement of the market analysis could be worked out on the basis of type of solder used.

The forecasting staff further recommended that the company consider methods of realigning sales districts so that they were all approximately equal. They felt it was desirable to divide the sales districts so that each had a sales goal between two and three million pounds annually.

The forecast staff concluded that in the long run the demand for solder would remain fairly constant with possibly a slight downward trend due to the introduction of new materials such as plastic pipe and new methods such as printed circuits in the electrical industry. This was not expected to significantly affect short term demand, however, since the demand for solder was tied closely to the demand for durable goods which was expected to have a continuing upward trend.

Assignment

1. What key factors will affect Austin's future growth? What areas represent the greatest potential?
2. Describe the sources of information you would examine in making short-term and long-term sales forecasts for Austin.
3. In light of your answers to questions 1 and 2, evaluate the sales goals and sales quotas set by the forecasting staff. Recommend alternative methods you would use in setting these goals.
4. Evaluate the forecasting staff's recommendations for improving sales and sales forecasting.

The Francine Candy Company

The Francine Candy Company manufactured packaged chocolates that sold for $1.30 per pound, as well as hard candies and bulk chocolates selling at lower prices per pound. Sales were made through about 2,000 retailers who generally took a 33-1/3 percent markup. Company sales amounted to about 300,000 pounds of candy, of which around one third was packaged chocolates. Although the company's packaged candy represented excellent quality for the price, the company sales had been declining due to the heavy advertising and lower prices of the packaged chocolates sold by larger competing companies. Since many retailers already carried a $.60 box of packaged chocolates, Francine's president was considering reducing the retail price of his boxed chocolates to $.50.

If the company continued its present pricing policy, the president expected the loss for the year would be $31,000, as shown in Table 7—9. He

TABLE 7–9

Cost and Income Estimates—Packaged Chocolates

Costs:

Boxes (2½ cents/lb.)	$ 2,500
Packing (1½ cents/lb.)	1,500
Selling (4 cents/lb.)	4,000
Material, labor, and production (30 cents/lb.)	30,000
Express (2½ cents/lb.)	2,500
Display (2 cents/lb.)	2,000
Bad debts and loss from returns (1½ cents/lb.)	1,500
Overhead	65,000
Total costs	$109,000
Sales (100,000 lbs.)	98,000
Loss	$ 11,000
Loss on items other than packaged chocolates	20,000
Total loss	$ 31,000

believed that a drastic reduction to a $.50 retail price for packaged chocolate was necessary because of the price of competing products and since a sales test with a $1 retail price the preceding year had produced disappointing results. In order to get dealer support, he intended to stamp the dealer's name on the box with a rubber stamp. The cost of printing the dealer's name on the box would be prohibitive.

Variable costs could not be appreciably lowered until an annual volume of about 750,000 pounds was obtained. The president, therefore, summarized the costs for a volume of 750,000 or more pounds, as shown in Table 7–10. The savings were substantial: for example, material, labor, and production

TABLE 7–10

Summary of Costs at Volume about 750,000 Pounds a Year

Item	Estimated cost per lb.
Box	1½ cents
Packing	Slightly less than 1 cent
Selling	Less than 2-2/3 cents
Material, labor, and production	20 cents
Express	Approximately 1½ cents
Display	1 cent
Bad debts and returns	Approximately 0 cents
Overhead	Total cost, approximately $90,000

costs would be cut by one third, from $.30 to $.20, due to bulk purchases and trimming the quality of the product and packaging somewhat.

In order to test demand, the company introduced trial packages of the $.50 packaged candy in parts of the company's market. At the end of three weeks, 300 stores, of which about half were new accounts, had purchased 30,000 pounds. Although the test was conducted in November, an important candy sales month, the president was nonetheless encouraged by the results. He estimated that, on an annual basis, these stores would sell 150,000 pounds. With the old price, he believed these stores would not sell more than 30,000 pounds.

Assignment

1. Determine the breakeven volume at a price of $.50 and $1.30, and develop breakeven charts for each price.
2. What sales do you feel the company might reasonably expect to get, based on the facts in the case, if the retail price was lowered to $.50? Explain the reasons for your answer.
3. Would it be reasonable to consider a $.55 price?
4. Are the results of the test in November usable within certain limits? Specify the limits. How would you go about doing further tests, assuming you had the time? Give specifics about the tests (for example, size of sample and length of test) and explain the reasons for your recommendations.
5. Assuming the decision on retail price had to be made now, recommend a price based on your analyses in answering questions 1 and 2. State the reasons for your recommendation.

National Petroleum Company

You have recently been appointed systems development manager of National Petroleum Company. The General Sales Manager for some time has been quite concerned whether National was actually getting maximum performance from its field sales force. He has asked you for assistance. The remainder of this text is based on his remarks.

Present Competitive Climate

The market for petroleum products is maturing rapidly. The increasing number of retail (that is, service station) outlets has made it more difficult for our company to find and develop prime locations for new stations; many areas already have more service station outlets than the market can support. Prices are softening, while at the same time rising labor and material costs have increased. Under these conditions, our field sales personnel must perform their marketing tasks more expertly than their competitors if the company is to continue to be profitable. And we must have better control over that performance if we are to compete profitably.

National's Sales Operations

As you know, this company was founded shortly after 1900 and has grown steadily until it is today one of the major competitors in many areas of the country. The company is completely integrated with its own producing, refining, distribution, and sales facilities. I am responsible for sales.

The field sales organization, my major concern here, breaks down as follows: 10 divisions, 40 districts, and 240 dealer salesmen. The basic unit on the "firing line" is the district. Here is a chart that shows the key people reporting to the District Manager and their major responsibilities (Figure 7–16). As you will note, some of these district functions are very specialized (Managers for Operations, Industrial-Commercial Sales, and Wholesale Sales), and we need not be concerned with them at present. Instead, I want to focus on two managerial positions and the salesmen reporting to them:

1. *Manager-Distribution Development.* This man is in charge of finding new service station locations and carrying out the necessary steps to acquire and build on new property. In carrying out this responsibility, he is assisted by Dealer Salesmen who report primarily to the Manager-Retail Sales.

2. *Manager-Retail Sales.* This man is in charge of all our sales through service station outlets in one district. In carrying out this responsibility he is assisted by about six Dealer Salesmen, whose duties I will describe in a minute.

The Sales Department assumes responsibility for product distribution upon delivery of the product at a sales department terminal point. Resale products pass through bulk plants to service station outlets. In our company, these stations are so-called "Third-Party" stations in which the dealer leases the building and pays us a rental fee based on the number of gallons of gas that he sells. There are more than 5,000 of these outlets. In addition, there are many more independent dealers who are connected with wholesalers and hence are not handled by our own company salesmen.

Although a wide variety of products are sold in each district to industrial accounts, the majority of our business is in the products sold to service

FIGURE 7-16

District Organization Plan National Petroleum Company

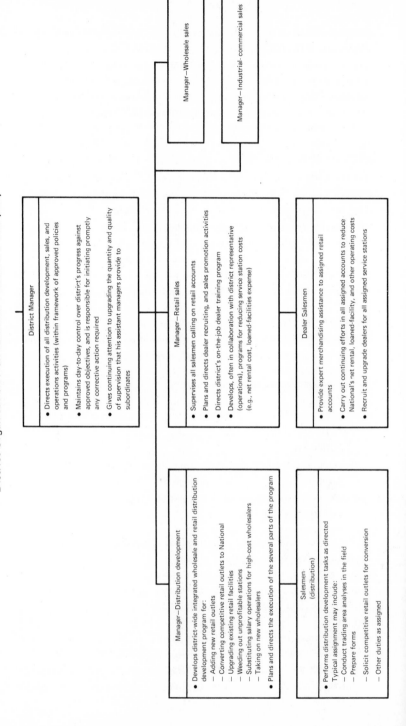

District Manager

- Directs execution of all distribution development, sales, and operations activities (within framework of approved policies and programs)
- Maintains day-to-day control over district's progress against approved objectives, and is responsible for initiating promptly any corrective action required
- Gives continuing attention to upgrading the quantity and quality of supervision that his assistant managers provide to subordinates

Manager—Wholesale sales

Manager—Industrial- commercial- sales

Manager—Retail sales

- Supervises all salesmen calling on retail accounts
- Plans and directs dealer recruiting, and sales promotion activities
- Directs district's on-the-job dealer training program
- Develops, often in collaboration with district representative (operations), programs for reducing service station costs (e.g., net rental cost, loaned-facilities expense)

Dealer Salesmen

- Provide expert merchandising assistance to assigned retail accounts
- Carry out continuing efforts in all assigned accounts to reduce National's net rental, loaned-facility, and other operating costs
- Recruit and upgrade dealers for all assigned service stations

Manager—Distribution development

- Develops district-wide integrated wholesale and retail distribution development program for:
  - Adding new retail outlets
  - Converting competitive retail outlets to National
  - Upgrading existing retail facilities
  - Weeding out unprofitable stations
  - Substituting salary operations for high-cost wholesalers
  - Taking on new wholesalers
- Plans and directs the execution of the several parts of the program

Salesmen (distribution)

- Performs distribution development tasks as directed. Typical assignment may include:
  - Conduct trading area analyses in the field
  - Prepare forms
  - Solicit competitive retail outlets for conversion
  - Other duties as assigned

244

stations. These are: regular gasoline; premium gasoline; motor oil; greases; antifreeze; and tires, batteries, and accessories (TBA).

Each salesman has about twenty-five service station outlets. In each station his job is to achieve these five goals: increase sales of our refined products; increase TBA sales; improve the profitability of our dealer; control station operating expenses; and maximize recovery of rental costs from our dealers.

To achieve these goals, there are many things that a salesman does at each station location. In the first place, he interviews candidates for the dealer's job, installs the new dealer in the station, and teaches him how to set up his books properly. Once the station is open, there are many other things the salesman must make sure are done. Here is a list of them (Figure 7—17). In addition, he must reserve part of his time—we estimate two hours per day—for activities involved in finding new service station locations. He is, in short, a very busy man.

FIGURE 7—17

Major Examples of Problems Solved by Dealer Salesmen

Financial management is inadequate:
  a. Inadequate records.
  b. Inadequate capital (for inventory or equipment.
  c. Poor control over cash, personal credit, or inventory.

Gasoline prices are not competitive.

Hours of operation are too short.

Station, rest rooms, or grounds are not clean and neat; displays and lighting are poor.

Dealer himself gives poor service to customers.

Dealer lacks enough employees to service customers adequately.

Management of employees is poor:
  a. Inadequate supervision.
  b. Continual changes of employees.
  c. Employees not clean, well-trained, or properly dressed.

There is too little tune-up and other minor repair work.

Advertising and special promotions are not used as much as is desirable:
  a. Company promotions.
  b. Self-developed promotions.

Dealer does not do enough credit-card business.

Dealer lacks backlog of steady customers for lubrication and oil changes.

Sales of tires, batteries, and/or accessories are low in relation to gasoline gallonage.

Major Control Limitations

First, the salesman must *work with* the dealer; but he cannot give orders; since the dealer is an independent businessman, not a company employee. This means that the salesman can only assist, help, suggest, and show the dealer. Because good dealers are extremely difficult to find, our salesmen must have an ample measure of tact and diplomacy or the dealer may quit.

Second, there are no direct measures of profit performance for either the station or the salesman. This is because there are different volume and cost alternatives in finding crude oil, drilling wells, shipping crude to refineries, refining it into various combinations of products, transporting it to local markets, and selling it through a variety of outlets such as stations, distributors and the like. Of course, we can figure out the profit made on the overall system—but this lack of any direct profitability measure for salesmen alone makes control of their performance difficult.

Controlling Field Sales Activities

Let me review briefly the control reports that we now use.

1. *Figure 7–18.* This is a form that the salesman submits to his manager to show how he plans to spend his day and what he intends to accomplish at each station. For example, the first copy of this form is submitted on Monday for Tuesday's working day; and the second copy, with the third column filled in, is submitted on the Wednesday after Tuesday's calls. This form is only used by district personnel—it does not come in to headquarters.

2. *Figure 7–19.* This a running record that shows each station's volume and cost performance by year. This form is filled in by the salesman and is reviewed by the Manager-Retail Sales and by the District Manager. It may also be reviewed from time to time by the Division Manager on his trips to the district. However, these forms are too numerous to be submitted to headquarters.

3. *Figure 7–20.* This is a summary form that lists the results by product for each station. Each salesman gets this summary for his stations, and copies also go to the Manager-Retail Sales, District Manager, and Division Manager. Salesmen take the information from this form and post it on the form in Figure 7–19.

4. *Figure 7–21.* This is actually two forms in one. In the first place, it summarizes the results for each district, and is reviewed by the District Manager and the Division Manager. In the second instance, it summarizes the results for each division. I get copies of both the district and division versions, but usually only look at the latter.

FIGURE 7–18

Number __12__   Daily Call Report

Name __Doe, John__   Location __Major City, U.S.A.__ Date __Mar. 6__

Scheduled Calls	Purpose of Call	Results of Call
Joe's S.S.	Clean up Station	
6th + Main	Set up new TBA display	
7th + Olive	Arrange spring promotion	
Art's Super	Improve records + bookkeeping	
Three D Truck	Sell 12 cases of antifreeze	

Number __12__   Daily Call Report

Name __Doe, John__   Location __Major City, U.S.A.__ Date __Mar. 6__

Scheduled Calls	Purpose of Call	Results of Call
Joe's S.S	Clean up station	Done
6th + Main	Set up new TBA display	Dealer will order $500; shelves clean; rearranged
7th + Olive	Arrange spring promotion	Dealer won't sign; will call again
Art's Super	Improve records + bookkeeping	Set up National's Dealer Accounting System
Three D Truck	Sell 12 cases of antifreeze	Sold 6

5. *Figure 7–22.* This form is my primary control. It is prepared here at headquarters and sent to me, as well as to Division Managers. This is the most helpful piece of paper I receive because it shows the results for the whole system.

FIGURE 7-19

Record of Individual Service Station Results

Index No. _____
City & State _____
Bulk station number _____   S.S. no. _____
Street _____
Date originally opened _____
District no. _____
Salesman no. _____
Expiration of current lease _____
Location no. _____
Type of operation _____
Number of bays _____

Average Monthly Gallonage Since Last Calculation

Year	Gasoline Goal	Gasoline Actual	Lube Oils Goal	Lube Oils Actual	Other Gallonage Products Goal	Other Gallonage Products Actual	Total Goal	Total Actual	TBA Goal	TBA Actual
1974 Jan.–June										
July–Dec.										
Total										
1979 Jan.–June										
July–Dec.										
Total										

Actual Average Monthly Costs

Gross Rental	Rental Recovery	Net Rental	Other Costs	Sales Commission TBA	Net Total Cost Amount	Net Total Cost Per Gallon

Dollar Investment in Company Property

As of:	Land	Improvement	Other	As of:	Land	Improvement	Other

Company Fixed Rental Obligations

As of:	Dollars Per Year

Company Lease Conditions

Lease Dated:	Term (In Years):

248

FIGURE 7–20

Statement of Deliveries to Customers

Month of _____				Station no. _____				District no. _____		
				Quantity—Current year		Revenue—Current month	Quantity—Previous year		Percent increase or decrease	
Customer number	Salesman number	Product class	Product brand	Month	Since January 1		Month	Since January 1	Month	Since January 1

FIGURE 7-21

Sales, Earnings and Expenses

District_____

Division_____

Product	Consigned commission rate	Normal refinery Supply point	Freight rate per gal.
Premium			
Regular			
Kerosene			
Lube oils			

Month	Gasolines Aviation gallons	Premium	Other gallons	Total gallons	Kerosene gallons	Furnace oils gallons	Tractor and diesel fuels gallons	Aviation turbine fuels gallons	Total auto oils gallons	Total industrial oils gallons	Anti-freeze gallons	Total gallonage products	Greases pounds	Waxes pounds
Jan.														
Feb.														
Mar.														
Apr.														
May														
June														
July														
Aug.														
Sept.														
Oct.														

Month	Asphalt tons	Surfacing materials barrels	Residual fuel oils barrels	Gas oils barrels	TBA sales (dollars)	Net revenue from sales (inc. packages)	Net cost of products (inc. packages)	Product handling losses and temp. adj'ts	Other station earnings	Gross earnings (before expenses)	Station operating expenses	Station oper. expense per gal.
Nov.												
Dec.												
Total												
Jan.												
Feb.												
Mar.												
Apr.												
May												
June												
July												
Aug.												
Sept.												
Oct.												
Nov.												
Dec.												
Total												

Annual summary

Description	Amount
Gross earnings	
Station expense	
Loaned facilities expense	
District expense	
Advertising and sales promotion expense	
Division, region dept. and general expense	
Total all expenses	
Net earnings	

FIGURE 7–22

Comparison of Sales Results						
Division _____			Month of _____			
	Net quantities		Increase or (decrease) over previous year			
			Month		Since January 1	
Product Group/ organizational responsibility	Month	Since January 1	Quantity	Percent	Quantity	Percent
Gasoline (gals.)						
District no. 1						
District no. 2						
District no. 3						
District no. 4						
Total division						
Middle distillates (gals.)						
District no. 1						
District no. 2						
District no. 3						
District no. 4						
Total division						
Automotive oils (gals.)						
District no. 1						
District no. 2						
District no. 3						
District no. 4						
Total division						
Industrial oils (gals.)						
District no. 1						
District no. 2						
District no. 3						
District no. 4						
Total division						
Greases (lbs.)						
District no. 1						
District no. 2						
District no. 3						
District no. 4						
Total division						

Of course, we have many other miscellaneous forms for controlling district operations, such as truck reports, maintenance and repair reports, etc. However, these are not particularly significant here.

General Sales Manager's Evaluation

Here are some of the problems I see with our control information system:

1. How does the District Manager or anyone up the line know that a salesman is actually spending his time in the stations where it might do the most good? In this system, we *assume* that the salesman knows where the greatest potential volume is. However, it may well be that they are spending their time with the dealers that squawk the loudest.

2. How do we know that the salesman actually accomplishes what he sets out to do in each station and that this is really what he should be doing in that station? As you can see from the call reports, he does write down the purpose of the call and the results, but is this really enough? For example, a salesman might write down that he went to the station to make sure the rest rooms were clean and he might report that they are now clean. However, it may well be that this effort is not nearly so important as getting better visual identification for the station, increasing its hours of operation, or teaching the dealer to do a better selling job.

3. How do we compare the job that salesmen do in one district with that of other salesmen in other districts? It is true that we do have reports on volume for each district, but that may not tell the whole story. For example, one area may be suffering from depressed economic conditions and that automatically means lower volume; whereas salesmen in a booming growth area should do far better.

4. Does our report structure meet the needs of various levels of management? Does each get the information that he needs to know in order to adequately control his operations?

5. Do we do enough planning, particularly at the salesman's level, before trying to control results? Maybe this is the key to the whole thing.

Of course, I am sure that other problems come to your mind, and I would like your thinking on them. We can discuss it again when you've had a chance to review this material and develop recommendations.

Assignment

1. Evaluate the present report structure. What are its major strengths and weaknesses (if any)?

2. List the key types of information the company needs to know in order to maintain adequate control over its salesmen. In doing so, it might be helpful to distinguish among the types of information needed at each level—salesman, district manager, and division manager.

3. Identify the major changes that you would recommend in order to

strengthen the present control report system. This should be based on your evaluation of the types of information that you want and should include an explanation of how to obtain this information.

4. Lay out a simple control structure that meets the needs of each level of management. In drawing examples of recommended reports, you need not be artistic; simply write clearly and lay out each report in a rough fashion. Give at least five and no more than ten reports.

5. Identify the major limitations of the system that you have laid out, placing stress on the basic fundamentals of the system rather than the details of the reports themselves.

6. Give the steps that you would take, once you have prepared your reporting system, to test its practical use in the sales operation.

7. Identify the information system principles from this case that would apply to any problem concerning planning and controlling field sales activities.

Wolman Carpet Company

Wolman Carpet Company's growth has been steadily upward since its founding in 1950; sales hit a high of $98,000,000 last year, with a net profit of 4.5 percent of sales.[6] Profit margins have increased moderately, but the company's share of market has declined sharply, in recent years.

The company uses various types of fibers, styles, and construction to manufacture several different kinds of carpeting. Basic constructions include tufted, velvet, wilton, and axminster. Fibers used include nylon, acrylics, rayon, wool, and cotton. Using these materials enables the company to produce pile, twist, and looped carpeting in plain, textured, sculptured, and figured styles. Each type of carpet comes in a variety of grades, colors, and widths. The company's sixty carpet models ranged in price from $6 to $18 per square yard, with the largest number in the $6 to $12 range.

A sales force of 120 men sell directly to 4,000 retail outlets throughout the United States. Carpet specialty stores account for 40 percent of the company's consumer sales, followed by furniture stores with 35 percent, department stores with 15 percent, and 10 percent from all other stores. Commercial and institutional sales are handled by the salesmen of fifteen distributors.

Last year, Wolman spent $975,000 (almost one percent of sales) on promotional activities; this was considerably higher than the industry average.

---

6. Adapted from Roger Blackwell, James Engel, and David Kollat, *Cases in Consumer Behavior* (New York: Holt, Rinehart and Winston, Inc., 1969), pp. 196-209.

Wolman used radio and television for advertising, which differed from the usual industry practice of advertising in general and Sunday magazines. Wolman's ads stressed the carpet's durability, appearance, and economy.

Because of Wolman's declining market share, the company's president has asked the advertising manager to thoroughly research changes occurring in the consumer carpet market and use the results to design a new advertising program.

The market research team was made up of members of Wolman's advertising and research department and personnel from their advertising agency. Their first step was to conduct (through an outside research firm) a cross-sectional personal-interview survey using a national probability sample of 5,000 households that had purchased carpeting within the last six months. The object of the survey was to determine how consumers evaluate carpeting, what influences consumer buying decisions, and how Wolman compares with its major competitors.

Respondents were first asked what features they sought when buying carpeting. Wolman purchasers most often mentioned color and pattern, quality, washability, and price in that order. Purchasers of other brands mentioned quality, color and pattern, washability, fabric, and durability in that order. Respondents were then asked to rate each major brand of carpeting according to several features. As seen from the summary of answers to this question in Figure 7–23, Wolman ranked below competitors in every feature.

Questions on price (price ranges were $6–$8, $8–$10, etc.) indicated that purchasers of other brands often considered two or three price ranges (57 percent), while Wolman purchasers most often (58 percent) considered only one price range. When questioned about fabrics, Wolman purchasers also considered a fewer number of fabrics than purchasers of other brands. Similarly, purchasers of other brands considered a greater number of colors and patterns than did Wolman buyers. In addition, they also considered several brands and visited several stores before purchasing, whereas the majority of Wolman carpet buyers considered only one brand and visited only one store (Figures 7–24 and 7–25).

The study also covered the role of information sources in making carpet-buying decisions. The survey showed that buyers of all brands were exposed most often to salesmen, personal contacts, and magazine advertising in that order. The information most often discussed with personal contacts was brand recommendations, dealer recommendations, and carpet cleanability; though the emphasis varied somewhat between Wolman buyers and buyers of other brands. Surprisingly, the impact of personal recommendations on Wolman buyers was considerably less then on other buyers, as seen from

FIGURE 7–23

Evaluations of Selected Features of Carpeting by Brand*

| Feature | Brand of carpeting | |
	Wolman	Average for other Brands
Reasonableness of price	2.6	3.8
Price ranges available	3.2	3.3
Quality	2.7	4.1
Color-pattern selection	2.9	3.7
Fabric selection	2.8	3.4
Durability	2.2	4.3
Washability	2.4	4.2
Dependability of delivery	1.9	3.1
Helpfulness of salesmen	1.7	3.3

* Respondents were asked to rate each brand of carpeting on each of the above features on the following scale:

Unacceptable 1	Below average 2	Average 3	Above average 4	Excellent 5

Figures in the table are mean scores.

FIGURE 7–24

Number of Brands Considered

| Number of brands considered | Brand purchased | |
	Wolman (percent of respondents)	Average for other brands (percent of respondents)
One	67	43
Two	21	28
Three	10	21
More than three	2	8
Total	100	100

Figure 7–26. In addition, of the 40 percent of other brand buyers who switched, very few bought Wolman carpets.

After reviewing the findings, Wolman's advertising manager was wondering:

1. How much confidence he should place in the research study results.

2. What further information he might like to have before making any decisions.

FIGURE 7–25

Number of Stores Visited

Number of stores visited	Brand purchased	
	Wolman (percent of respondents)	Average for other brands (percent of respondents)
None	12	13
One	63	42
Two	22	28
Three	2	14
More than three	1	3
Total	100	100

FIGURE 7–26

Relationship between Brand Recommended through Personal Contacts
and Brand Purchased

Brand recommended   Purchasing behavior

Wolman

{ 35 percent purchased the brand recommended

65 percent purchased a different brand

Average for all other brands

{ 60 percent purchased the brand recommended

40 percent purchased a different brand

3. What conclusions he should draw from the study.
4. What action should be taken (in advertising or some other area) based on the study findings.

Assignment

Answer the advertising manager's questions. Explain in detail the reasons for your answers.

Chase Department Store

In order to determine the cause and impact of the growing number of customer complaints, Mr. John Lloyd, in charge of customer relations activities at Chase Department Store, reviewed three reports: the weekly store-side Profit and Loss Statements (Figure 7–27), the weekly Customer Complaint Summary (Figure 7–28), and the Product Service Requirement Summary by department (Figure 7–29). Based on the information obtained from these reports, Mr. Lloyd concluded that the problems stemmed from poor product performance and that the problem was serious.

FIGURE 7–27

Chase Department Store Appliance Dept Profit & Loss Statement Week ending _____				
	Current week		Past week	
	Budget	Actual	Budget	Actual
Total sales	115,400.00	117,000.00	130,000.00	131,000.00
Returns	1,000.00	2,200.00	1,000.00	3,000.00
Net sales	114,400.00	115,800.00	129,000.00	128,000.00
Cost of goods sold	55,000.00	56,800.00	62,000.00	63,500.00
Gross profit	59,000.00	59,000.00	67,000.00	64,500.00
Expenses				
Payroll	18,000.00	19,300.00	21,800.00	21,500.00
Fixed	7,750.00	7,750.00	7,750.00	7,750.00
Variable (other)	16,000.00	18,500.00	17,000.00	19,000.00
Net profit	17,250.00	13,450.00	21,250.00	16,350.00

FIGURE 7–28

Chase Department Store Customer Complaint Summary				
Department _Appliance Dept._ Week ending _12-29-7-_ Total customer complaints _108_ Total sales _117,000.00_				
Nature of complaint	Corrective action taken (method)			
	Phone call	Letter	Visit	Other
Poor service _48_	36	2	10	0
Faulty product _50_	30	10	10	0
Other _10_	10	0	0	0
*Total _108_	76	12	20	0

FIGURE 7-29

Chase Department Store Product Service Req Summary				
Coverage Period _11-30-72_ through _12-30-72_				
Item/number	Problem categories			
	Mfg. defect	Delivery damage	Action required	Parts req.
air cond. West #1P36	doesn't cool		check cooling units	freon
T.V. Color Famirtle #842	poor color		check TV + antenna	tube # P-8783
T.V. B+W # 387	✓ no sound		check T.V.	tube # 3645
Darnard turntable #8006		✓ item dropped	service check	needle # P336
Total	38	20		

Concurrently, warranty policies were also evaluated. It was found that one of the chief causes of customer complaints was minor product failures (for example, burned out light bulbs, loose hinges, etc.), which the customer often fixed himself. The Work Order/Customer Call Report shown in Figure 7–30) and the Customer Complaint Summary shown in Figure 7–28 were the major sources of this information.

To minimize the problem over the short run, Mr. Lloyd took two steps: he contacted the purchasing department to inform them of the large number of product deficiencies and he revised warranty policies to indicate clearly that they guaranteed full coverage of all defects of any kind reported within thirty days after delivery. While realizing the potential costliness of this action, Mr. Lloyd felt that it was necessary, especially in light of ever-increasing competition from other outlets.

FIGURE 7-30

Chase Department Store Work Order/Customer Call Report
Item description _T.V._   Date of purchase _1/28/7-_
Code number _#842_   Check box if first purchase ☐
Warranty number _SC-8624_   Date of delivery requested _N/A_
Customer name/address,   Action to be taken:
Frank Smith   SAMPLE   poor color reception
Kent, Conn.   Employee assigned:
Description of action taken: J. Jones CS-46
Serviced above set and replaced tube # P-8783
Date and time of service _11-30-7-_   Employee signature _J. Jones_

The immediate effect of Mr. Lloyd's action was a reduction in the number of customer complaints. However, the number of service calls increased substantially. Mr. Lloyd once again contacted the purchasing department to question whether his previous recommendations concerning product deficiencies had been acted on. He was assured that they had and that necessary changes were in the process of being made and in many instances had already been made.

Mr. Richard Johnson, the Vice President of Sales, became increasingly concerned over the rising operating cost problem and discussed the matter with Mr. Lloyd. After reviewing Mr. Lloyd's actions to date, Mr. Johnson indicated that he was not fully satisfied and that he was concerned over the depth and accuracy of Mr. Lloyd's analysis of the problem and the initial steps he took to solve the problem. Mr. Johnson was particularly concerned over the lack of cost information relevant to the situation.

Mr. Johnson also indicated that, in solving this particular problem, he also wanted a reevaluation of the existing reporting and information systems with recommendations for improvements, to be sure that the existing information system provided the necessary feedback to insure effective management of the customer service operation.

Mr. Lloyd returned to his office to reevaluate the problem, the initial actions he took to correct them, and, in general, all the events that had transpired in connection with the current problem. Having been disappointed by the results of his initial action, he decided to start at the beginning and reanalyze the entire situation before trying to develop a new solution.

Assignment

1. What are the key factors relevant to the customer service problem at Chase Department Store?

2. Describe the present customer service operation at Chase Department Store and the customer service information system.

3. Did Mr. Lloyd use the existing information system effectively in making his decisions? Was the problem in the existing system or in its use, or in both?

4. Is the existing information system adequate to meet the needs of customer service management? Identify any problems you find with it.

5. What changes should be made in the customer service operation and in its supporting management information system, both to solve the current problems and in general to improve the effectiveness of customer service management? Explain the reasons for your recommendations.

Information Systems for Operations Management

OPERATIONS MANAGEMENT REFERS TO MANAGEMENT OF THE OPERA-
tions required to produce the products or services which are marketed by
a company. In those companies which manufacture products, operations
management is production management and in such situations either term can
be used. Operations management is, however, a broader concept than production management, since it also includes management of service-type operations, such as air transport.

This chapter concerns information systems for operations management.
The discussion covers the nature of operations management, decisions to be
made and information needed in managing operations, and basic operations
management information systems. Examples of how information systems are
developed and used in typical operations management situations are given in
the following chapter.

Operations Management

The term "operations," as used in this chapter, refers to the use of resources
(men, materials, machines, capital, or any other company resource) to pro-

duce a company's products or services within specific quantity, quality, schedule, and cost limitations. The objective of operations management is to manage the operating processes which transform inputs into outputs of market value to the company. Managing operations involves many jobs, from scheduling and procurement to maintenance and quality control.

Operations management may involve products or services. In air transport companies, for example, operations management involves managing the use of airplanes, terminals, and personnel to provide travel services to passengers. In manufacturing companies, in contrast, it involves managing the production of products for sale to customers. As with marketing management, therefore, specific operations management tasks will vary from company to company, depending on the nature of the company's business. Because of the wide variety of operations management situations, the following is a general discussion, covering only the principal tasks commonly performed in operations management situations. These tasks range from short-term scheduling of day-to-day production to long-term planning of major facilities design and acquisition.

Production planning and control involves managing the movement of products through the entire manufacturing cycle. The job includes overall planning of production, as well as such operational tasks as production

263

scheduling and control. Overall planning responsibilities include developing long-term production programs in light of existing and anticipated company resources and sales demand. Scheduling responsibilities include determining what specific products to produce (and the quantity and timing of the production of each of them), machine loading, manpower allocation, and sequencing. Production control responsibilities include analysis of actual and scheduled activities, and rescheduling production where required.

Since inventory control very often generates orders for production, inventory management is closely related to the scheduling job. Inventory management involves insuring the availability of stocks of raw materials, work in process, finished goods, and supplies adequate for production needs without excessive investment in these inventory assets. Specific management tasks include overall inventory planning and policy development, forecasting demand or checking the accuracy of demand forecasts, setting inventory levels, establishing reorder points and quantities, administering inventory movement, safeguarding inventories, controlling inventory storage costs, and generally coordinating inventory activities with other business activities.

Materials management involves the economical procurement and storage of materials needed in the production process and their timely delivery to locations where they are needed. The materials management job thus involves planning and administering procurement of materials according to user specifications, as needed by production, by inventory control, or by other users, and can cover standard production items, non-productive goods, tools, maintenance equipment, and other material used in all phases of company operations. In addition, the job involves administering receipt of goods (including inspection, price and condition verification, etc.) and shipping (packaging and labeling of materials as required), as well as monitoring materials operations (both performance and price) and advising operating departments on availability and price of desired materials. The job sometimes also includes storage and delivery of finished goods to where they are needed by marketing.

Product design and development is another concern of operations management. This job involves the engineering of new products and processes, as well as the improvement of existing products and processes. Product engineering is responsible for developing the specifications for products.

Industrial engineering involves designing systematic manufacturing processes. The responsibilities of industrial engineering include (depending upon the type of company and its product or service): developing manufacturing flow plans, developing systems for cost and schedule control, providing detailed man-hour requirements and performance trends to develop a factual basis for bid estimating and methods improvement, and budget analysis by department.

Operations management also involves maintaining product specifications throughout the production process, that is, quality control. Quality control management is responsible for assuring that newly acquired material, as well as manufactured products and services rendered customers, meet specific quality standards. Managing quality control activities involves such overall planning activities as developing general quality control policies, defining the responsibilities for the quality control operation, and developing specific quality standards based on materials, product design, and process specifications. The job also involves development of quality control programs and procedures for inspecting and maintaining product or service quality throughout the production process, as well as the monitoring of quality control operations to insure that quality standards are maintained within specified cost restraints. In addition, quality control management initiates action to correct quality deficiencies that may be found and recommends improvements in the product or production process.

Maintenance, another responsibility of operations management, involves maintaining the entire production system, including buildings and equipment, at top mechanical efficiency. Maintenance management responsibilities include planning maintenance facilities and scheduling economical maintenance programs that maximize equipment availability and minimize equipment wear and deterioration with minimum disruptions in production, selecting and training qualified maintenance personnel, maintaining adequate maintenance supplies, and monitoring maintenance programs and their costs.

Facilities management involves overall planning for current and future programs to provide adequate facilities for the manufacture of a company's products, as well as planning and directing selection of locations and sites for new facilities, development of detailed designs and layouts for production processes and selection of machinery, designing new buildings and planning for their construction, and monitoring facilities construction and the move to new facilities. Where the situation warrants it, facilities management also involves developing and implementing revised plant layouts to improve the efficiency of existing facilities and personnel.

Since operations management is also responsible for producing a company's products or services at the right price, operations management also involves cost control. Cost control extends into all areas within an operations manager's scope of responsibility, and relies heavily on the cost accounting techniques described in Chapters Four and Five.

In addition to the operations management areas covered above—production planning and control, inventory management, materials management, product design and development, industrial engineering, quality control, maintenance management, facility management, and cost control—there are other tasks involved in operations management, such as manpower management. And, as in marketing management, operations management decisions range from long-term strategic planning decisions (such as whether or not to maintain company-owned manufacturing facilities or contract to have an outside company manufacture the products sold) to short-term planning and control decisions (such as those involved in day-to-day production scheduling).

The following sections discuss management decision making and information systems development in several of these key areas. Not all areas are covered, since the intent here is not to cover the entire field of operations management, but only to illustrate how information systems are developed in a variety of management areas.

Supporting
Information Systems

Since a high degree of control is possible (and needed) in operations management, since control requires extensive result information, and since result reports are the easiest kind of information reports to generate systematically, information systems for operations management have always received considerable emphasis in systems development work.

For example, cost accounting systems, which measure product costs for inventory valuation and which are discussed in Chapters Four and Five, were in existence in all manufacturing companies studied and had been for quite a while. And there are examples in the paper, oil, and chemical industries of fully integrated, computerized data processing and management information systems which have been in use in the production area for over a decade.

Because of the wide range of existing operations management information and data processing systems currently found in business, the following discussion of operations management information systems is selective, covering the highlights of management information systems found in such major operations areas as production planning and control, inventory management, materials management, quality control, maintenance management, and facilities management.

Production Planning
and Control

In overall planning for production, decisions are made about the kinds and amounts of production facilities, resources, and manpower which will be needed by the company. Information needed to make these decisions includes data on expected sales or demand over the long-run, product plans, technological developments expected over the near- and long-term, and the status of existing and planned production facilities. The information systems used in obtaining this information are discussed in detail in the last section of this chapter on facilities management.

In short-term production scheduling, a scheduler not only determines production requirements, but also routes operations and assigns the workload to available men and machines in a way that balances the production or assembly line process. In scheduling production, then, management not only needs to know (from marketing, product design, or production and inventory control) what the anticipated demand is *for each product* and what to expect in the timing of the delivery requirements; it also needs detailed specifications for the product to be made (including shop drawings, lists of materials required, and lists of operations broken down in a sequential manner), machine loading schedules, work-force schedules, information on the operating status of each production section, and data on priority requirements.

Sales or demand forecasts are needed in considerable detail for production scheduling, since production decisions are made on a product-by-product and production cycle-by-production cycle basis. As overall sales projections are developed in greater detail, they are converted into forecasts of overall production requirements, as for example in Figure 8–1. Since production scheduling decisions are made on a product-by-product and day-by-day (or week-by-week) basis, these overall production requirements forecasts are subsequently translated into even more specific production requirements. For

FIGURE 8–1

Forecast of Production Requirements for a Seasonal Product

Month	Expected production requirements	Cumulative requirements	Required buffer stocks	Production days	Cumulative days
Jan.	700	700	300	22	22
Feb.	900	1,600	340	18	40
Mar.	1,100	2,700	375	22	62
Apr.	900	•	340	21	83
May	650	•	290	22	•
June	600	•	275	21	•
July	550	•	265	21	•
Aug.	400	•	230	13	•
Sept.	400	•	230	20	•
Oct.	300	•	195	23	•
Nov.	300	•	195	21	•
Dec.	400	7,200	230	20	244

example, Figure 8–2 shows one company's weekly production requirements report. Using this report, which gives estimates of the number of production hours needed for each product program each week, a production scheduler would be able to schedule production on a department-by-department basis.

In preparing such detailed production schedules, a manager needs the following information:

> *Engineering specifications.* This might include drawings suited for shop use with specifications and tolerances, chemical formulation and processing requirements, etc.
>
> *Bill of materials.* An accurate and complete statement of the items used in manufacture is needed. Where these are stock components or parts, this should be indicated and component number or reference should be shown. Where materials, components or parts are needed from outside suppliers, the items to be purchased should be indicated.
>
> *Routing and list of operations sheet.* This should show the detailed routing of the order from selection of items to be processed through each processing stage to completion. The specific type of processing equipment or machine needed at each stage should be shown, together with any special equipment or tooling required. For example, see Figure 8–3. This report also shows the reasonable time estimate to complete each specific operation. These estimates may be based on standard times—if these are available—they may be set by special time studies or methods analysis; or they may be arrived at based on experience or the judgment of an experienced estimator.

The actual production schedule will vary considerably from situation to situation. For example, Figure 8–4 shows in summary form a master schedule

FIGURE 8–2

Weekly Production Program by Models

Model no. ROF/2   Week ending: 6-7-72

Product program	Hours		Equivalent units		% Completion	
	Schedule	Actual	Schedule	Actual	Schedule	Actual
Machining	15		10			
Head assy.	25		5			
Take up	31		6			
Frame	22		8			
Knit down	16		9			
Total regular	109		38			
Rework	10		12			
Grand total	119		50			

Note: This could also be used for control purposes by filling in the actual columns.

FIGURE 8-3

Routing and Operations Sheet

Model	Dia.	Feed	Group	Part name cylinder	Part no.	Quantity
ROF/2	24"		O	block	110219	

Type	Shape open end	Size	Made from	To be finished on

Routing Dept.	M/C	Op. No.	Description	Tooling & gages	SPD	FD	STD minutes Set-up	Cyc	Total
		61	Draw part from stock	Floor Arbor Press			1	0.50	1.50

form used by a manufacturer of knitting machines which have relatively long lead times. Another kind of master schedule used at Hughes Aircraft for large orders covers due dates and requirements for the following:

1. Proposal to management for approval.
2. Proposal to the customer for approval.
3. A contract—initially a letter contract followed by a firm contract.
4. Advance bills of materials—this is a listing of purchased items requiring a long lead time.

FIGURE 8-4

Holman Company Master Schedule

Month: Dec. '72		Scheduled data:		Date issued:				
Item	Machine no.	Customer	D	F	CYL #	SM #	YS #	Set-up
1	31803	STD Knit	28	20	203020	B/M 707	540 B/M1Y	
2	31658	Royal	24	54	208012	B/M 712	884 B/M	

Nomenclature: D   — diameter   SM — stopmotion
                F   — feed   YS — yarnstand
                CYL — cylinder

5. Schematic drawings and specifications.
6. Outline and mounting drawings.
7. Release of production drawings—engineering data received prior to this has been for information, for prototype construction, or for advance planning.
8. Manufacturing planning—this includes fabrication and assembly planning.
9. Procurement.
10. Tool design and fabrication.
11. Production fabrication—this includes the fabrication of detailed parts and sub-assemblies, such as sheet metal assemblies.
12. Assembly.
13. Completion of the first production unit.

Many techniques are used in translating these master schedules into specific machine and manpower schedules. One familiar scheduling tool used in smaller job-shops is the Gantt chart. A Gantt chart consists of a series of light horizontal bars, each of which represents a given amount of planned performance over a specific period of time. Below each bar is a contrasting heavy bar representing actual accomplishment, as of a certain date. The chart in Figure 8–5 was last posted on Tuesday evening, as indicated by the small "V" mark at the top. The order on machine number one, which was started on Monday noon and is to be completed on Wednesday evening, is ahead of schedule since the heavy line extends beyond the present time. The order on machine two is behind schedule as indicated by the bar, and the order on machine number three has not been started yet.

Machine load ledgers are often used in planning and control for scheduling, for they enable management to compare the available capacity with actual load conditions as far in advance as manufacturing orders are issued and, thus, provide management with advance knowledge of possible excesses or shortages of capacity. With this information, corrective action can be taken in time to remedy the situation. Machine load ledgers are most often maintained in a central planning office. The loads generated by new manufacturing orders are added to the ledgers as the orders are issued. As each operation is completed, the corresponding load is deleted from the ledgers, in much the same way a Gantt chart is posted periodically. Figure 8–6 gives an example of a machine load ledger.

Computer simulation is also used in production scheduling. For example, Hazeltine Corporation has made use of computer simulation for its complex job-shop scheduling. A "simulated" model of the job shop was first programmed for the computer, incorporating priority rules for dispatching orders.

FIGURE 8–5

A Simplified Gantt Chart

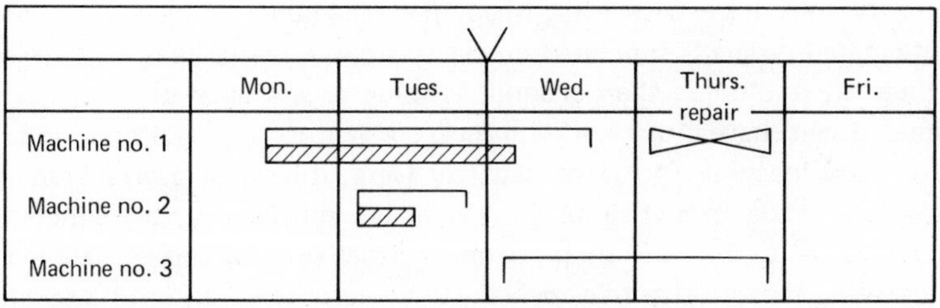

	Mon.	Tues.	Wed.	Thurs. repair	Fri.
Machine no. 1					
Machine no. 2					
Machine no. 3					

Key to symbols:

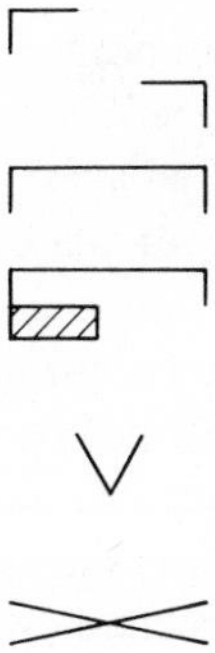

⌐ The start of an activity.

¬ The end of an activity.

⌐———¬ A light line connecting the two inverted "L's" shows a proposed activity.

⌐▨——¬ The heavy line shows the actual progress of an activity.

∨ A caret at the top of a column shows the instant the charting is stopped. Charts being dynamic, this indicates when the activities are frozen.

✕ Time set aside for other than productive activities, as for maintenance.

FIGURE 8–6

Machine Load Ledger

Machine Load Ledger   Machine group _____   Date _____

Machines available _____   Machines   Shift 1   Hrs./shift 1___
                                  operated   Shift 2   2___
                                             Shift 3   3___

Weekly capacity _____

Week starting	Overdue		10/18		10/25		11/1		11/8		11/15	
	+	−	+	−	+	−	+	−	+	−	+	−
Total load: 10/18 10/25 11/1												

A large number of different factors were taken into account in calculating priorities, including estimated processing time, order due data, amount of work remaining after current operation, and the value of the order. Once such priority rules have been established, the scheduling of orders on hand and anticipated orders is simulated on the computer, using the priority rules. The simulated results are then examined: some orders have been completed on time, others have not; work-in-process inventory has averaged some given level; and machine and labor capacity were utilized at a given rate. If the decisions made in the simulated model are satisfactory, the simulated job sequence is used in the shop. If not, corrective steps can be taken, such as modifying the priority rules or adjusting overtime work, until a satisfactory schedule is developed.

Other information tools are also used in production scheduling. In designing a balanced line, for example, the scheduler needs information on sequence restrictions, performance times for the smallest possible whole units of activity, and diagrammatic representations of the sequence requirements and groupings of elements. Figure 8–7 shows a line balance design for the mass production of cylinder assemblies. In this case, the line was to be balanced for a ten-second cycle—a completed unit would be produced by the line each ten seconds. To meet this output requirement, no station could be assigned to more than ten seconds worth of the elements shown. The total of all element times is 45.8 seconds; so that, with a ten-second cycle, five stations would be the minimum possible.

In order to control the flow of orders or products through the plant, management needs information on the actual load and the performance status (or progress status) of orders at critical stages of the manufacturing cycle (by machine group or work section) to compare with the schedules. Comparative information is also needed on production costs in relation to budget, both by product and by production section.

Gantt charts, for example, are used for control, since they show the actual performance compared to the planned performance. Machine load ledgers can also be used for control purposes, since they can be used to compare the available capacity with actual load conditions. Examples of comparative cost reports are shown in Chapter Four, and an example of a comparative output report is shown in Figure 8–8.

As is seen from the examples above and in the following chapter, a considerable number of additional information documents may have to be prepared in production scheduling and control, including:

1. Job tickets, showing the data pertaining to each operation individually, for use by foremen in assigning work, in unit costing by accounting, and in the timely scheduling of work from operation to operation.

FIGURE 8-7

A Solution to a Line Balancing Problem Which Requires
No More than 10 Seconds per Station and Does Not
Violate Sequence Requirements

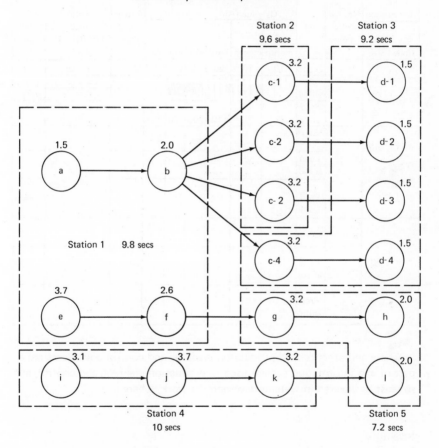

2. Material requisitions, to authorize removal of parts components, or materials from stock.
3. Tool or equipment requisitions.
4. Move tickets, for use in controlling the movement of an order from one department or center to another.
5. Purchase requisitions, to authorize the purchasing agent to procure special purchase items.
6. Instructions to make or buy materials.

FIGURE 8-8

Production Load and Performance Report

Month: Code: Date issued:

Description	Normal			Overdue (A)			Current schedule (B)			Future sched.	Total load	No. of weeks
Name Code size	del'y. time	Ref	Beyond 1 month	1 month	1 Total	Mar	Apr	May	(Total) (C)	(A) + (B) + (C) (T)	loaded
25		Sched	10	10	20	200	125			A 20	
		Load ahead								B 325	
										C –	7.72
		Prod auth	2%	9%	11%	200	200	250		T 345	
37½		Sched									
		Load ahead									
		Prod auth									
50		Sched									
		Load ahead									
		Prod auth									

These and other related production planning and control documents are all part of the information system used in production planning and control, and so must be covered in systems development work, where needed.

Inventory Management

Key decisions in inventory management involve questions not only about overall inventory plans and policies, but also about how much inventory to carry (the level of inventories), and when to reorder (the reorder point), and how much to order each time. These decisions require information not only about overall company marketing and production plans, but also about the amount marketing expects to sell and when (forecasts), and about the range of possible deviations from those estimates. In addition, inventory management needs information on production set-up costs and inventory ordering costs, product or production costs, inventory carrying costs, space availability, past inventory usage and expected usage in the future, spoilage rates, and the estimated cost of not filling orders and resulting loss of customer good will. Information needed for controlling inventory activities includes data on the movement of inventories, inventory storage costs, and inventory losses.

Overall inventory policies are developed in conjunction with overall production plans, held within established cost restraints and dictated by production requirements. New product plans, quality control plans, and production process needs are among the key overall production planning factors considered in developing general inventory policies.

As in production scheduling, sales information (both forecast and actual) by item is needed in making short-term inventory management decisions. For example, in many inventory situations, sales projections (with possible ranges of variations) are used to estimate the minimum inventory which should be kept on hand for each item, considering the time required to get materials or products (or manufacture them) and the most economical amount of inventory to reorder each time (economic order quantity or production lot).

The minimum inventory level, which is called the reorder point, is the inventory level at which a new manufacturing or supplier order should be placed. This order point is determined by calculating the manufacturing or purchasing lead time in weeks and multiplying this by the average weekly usage; this figure is then added to the minimum stock quantity (or safety stock) needed to be kept on hand to allow for variations in sales or manufacture or delivery. Reordering when the order point is reached assures the delivery of a new lot into inventory before the supply on hand is exhausted under normal operating conditions.

The quantity to order, or reorder quantity, can be determined through use of economic lot or order quantity formulas. The economic lot size is the quantity that must be ordered at any one time to yield the lowest possible cost; this requires balancing two opposing kinds of costs:

1. Those costs which increase or multiply over a period of time as the lot size decreases. Set-up costs, paper work costs, and ordering costs are in this category.
2. Those costs which increase as the lot size increases. Inventory carrying charges, obsolence, shortages, and spoilage are in this category.

The following formula has been developed for determining the most economical lot size:

$$EOQ = \sqrt{\frac{2RS}{KC}}$$

Q = Economic lot size or
economic order quantity

R = Annual requirements

S = Set up cost

C = Unit cost

K = Inventory carrying charge

To solve this equation and determine the economic lot size, a manager substitutes the actual values for R, S, C, and K. A convenient graph, called a nomograph, has been developed for solving such equations quickly. An example of a nomograph is shown in Figure 8–9.

Reorder points and reorder quantities are used in inventory management information systems to maintain and control inventory levels. Figure 8–10 shows one type of inventory record-keeping system used in inventory management. Such stock records may be maintained either manually or by computer.

A more comprehensive stock record file report is shown in Figure 8–11. Like the report in Figure 8–10, this one shows the reorder quantity and reorder point (but not the safety stock or average daily usage). The report in Figure 8–11 goes further, however, in showing order and cost information, as well as allocations of items. The footnote to Figure 8–11 gives a detailed explanation of the data processing (or manipulation) required to maintain this inventory file and so generate such reports.

Such systems generate orders not only for materials, but also for finished goods to be produced by a company's production department. These reports on products needed for inventory and how they are used in production planning were discussed in the preceding section.

Several other kinds of reports may be used in inventory control. For example, inventory status reports are needed to check on damaged goods and shortages, and so on any possible thefts. In addition, reports may also be required on usage of inventory space during any given control period.

Computerized inventory management information systems are in common use today. For example, computers can be used to calculate economic order quantities, maintain inventory stock records, generate information needed for ordering (when minimum inventory levels are reached), and report to management on inventory status and activities. An example of such a computerized inventory system is described in Chapter Nine.

FIGURE 8–9

A Nomograph for Determining Economic Order Quantities

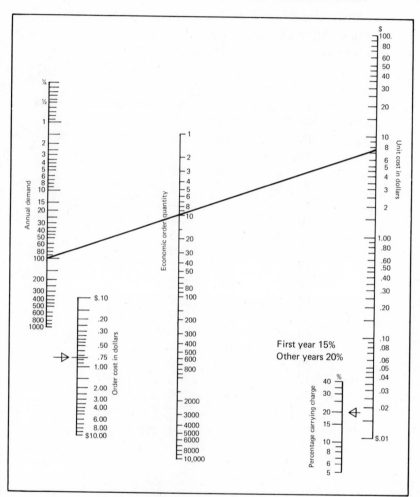

Note to Figure 8–9: To use this nomograph, suppose that the ordering cost is $0.75, that carrying cost is 20 percent of the cost of the item, that the cost of the particular item for which we are determining the E O Q is $7.50 and its annual usage or demand rate is 100 units. Draw a straight line connecting the annual usage of 100 on the left scale with the unit cost of $7.50 on the right scale. The place where it intersects the center scale—10 units—is the E O Q.

FIGURE 8-10

A Stock Record Card

Stock Record Card in the Two-Bin System (an example)

Item: ROTA spindles   Order quantity: 1,200
Spec. no.: 0375B6   Reorder point: 800
                         Safety stock: 300

Date		In	Out	Balance	On order
May	31	1,200		1,200	0
June	7		100	1,100	0
	10		250	850	0
	20		100	750	1,200
July	1		150	600	1,200
	6		225	375	1,200
	10	1,200		1,575	0
	16		320	1,255	0
	26		300	955	0
Aug.	8		55	900	0
	10		350	550	1,200
	15		100	450	1,200
	20		150	300	1,200
Sept.	5		100	200	1,200
	10	1,200		1,400	0
	22		150	1,250	0
	30		250	1,000	0
Oct.	10		325	675	1,200
	18		125	550	1,200

Average demand in the first period, $\frac{825 \text{ units}}{40 \text{ days}} \simeq 21/\text{day}$.
Average demand in the second period $\simeq 23/\text{day}$.

Materials Management

Materials management involves first answering the questions "What kind of material is needed, at what time, and in what quantities?" Information required to answer these questions comes from the production schedule or forecasted schedules, inventory control, or user requests, as well as from the list of materials (and material specifications) required to make the product. In deciding how best to obtain or procure the materials needed, information is needed on available suppliers, the materials available from these suppliers, internal production capabilities and inventories, prices charged or costs involved, and the ability of suppliers to meet delivery requirements and quality standards. Decisions relevant to receiving, storing, and issuing materials require information on available storage facilities, date of receipt, condition of material on receipt, actual charges, etc. Control is also important in materials management, so that detailed follow-up information on the delays in meeting delivery dates, variations between quoted and actual prices, delivered items differing from specifications, inventory withdrawals for use in production, and the like is needed on a continuing basis.

Inventory requirements are one of the major information sources used in materials management. For example, using stock records such as the ones shown in Figure 8–11, materials management would order materials when each item reached its reorder point or quantity. In other situations, such as a job-shop operation, the materials manager might order items based on production schedules or orders. The Hughes Aircraft master production schedule discussed earlier, for example, would be the basis for materials ordering. At other times, action might be initiated by user departments needing the material.

In determining how much and when to order—either to replenish stock used in production or to meet specific user needs—materials management needs a purchase requisition or order of some sort. If the material is for replenishment of stock, the requisition might be prepared by the purchasing clerk or stock room clerk. If it is for new stock, the form might be prepared by a member of the engineering or factory staff or someone from another requisitioner's department.

In planning to meet user requirements, materials management needs information on product or production specifications in order to know what to order. For standard items, a materials manager might maintain his own file of product specifications. Specifications for new materials or changes in materials needed will be supplied by the user, based on his needs, government or customer specifications, production requirements, etc., and may involve consultations with the materials manager. An example of a product specification is shown in Figure 8–12.

As the purchasing department explores various ways to obtain the item (make it "in-house," buy it from an outside supplier, or draw it from excess inventories of some other department), available inventories or lists of supplies used by other departments would be checked, information on costs and available machine time may be requested from production, or bids may be requested from different qualified suppliers. Inventory files are thus needed, as are files on suppliers and their qualifications.

Such supplier files range from simple three-by-five card files givir _ basic supplier data to extensive looseleaf files giving various information on prices,

FIGURE 8–11

A More Comprehensive Stores Record Card

STORES RECORD

Name *Bushing, Bronze*
Description *1" i.d. × 1¾" o.d. × 2" long*
Specification *no. 2,240*
Minimum economic order quantity *6,000*

Symbol *SBBB 1 × 1¾ × 2*
Unit *Each*
Dwg. no. *C-14750*   Part no. *W-16842*
Location in stores *AC3F4*
Requisition when available shows *1,500*

Date	Order no. (shop or purchase order)	1-Ordered (but not delivered) Req. no	Quantity	Total	Received	2-On hand (in the storeroom) Issued	Balance	Unit price	Total value	3-Allocated (not yet issued) Quantity	Total	4-Available (for new orders) Quantity
Jan. 3					Inv'y		3,000	$.09	$270.00			3,000
4	S.O. 115					300	2,700	.09	243.00			2,700
5	S.O. 131									+200	200	2,500
7	S.O. 156									+700	900	1,800
10	S.O. 131					200	2,500	.09	225.00	−200	700	
11	S.O. 210									+400	1,100	1,400
11		Req. 230	6,000									
14	S.O. 115				(credit)	+50	2,550	.09	229.50			
15	S.O. 156					700	1,850	.09	166.50	−700	400	1,450
18	P.O. 471		+6,000	6,000								
19	S.O. 275									+300	700	
21	S.O. 210					400	1,450	.09	130.50	−400	300	
27	P.O. 471		−6,000	0,000	6,000		6,000	.10	600.00			7,450
							7,450	.0980	730.50			
28	S.O. 131				(Repl.)	20	7,430	.0980	731.96			7,150
31	S.O. 275					300	7,130	.0980	702.56	−300	000	7,130

An Explanation of Entries in Figure 8-11

Entry Date	Kind of Entry	Procedure in Making Entry	Entry Date	Kind of Entry	Procedure in Making Entry
Jan. 3	Inventory	Assume that sheet is started from physical inventory (Equation: 0 + 3,000 = 0 + 3,000).	Jan. 18	Purchase	Standard order placed. Ordered (= 6,000) is considered to be bought to arrive before stock falls below cushion or reserve, therefore to be available for planning future manufacturing (= 7,450). Some authorities do not count purchases as available until actually received.
4	Issue	System just started so this order was not preapportioned.			
5	Apportion	Balance on hand (2,700) unchanged but quantity available reduced (= 2,500).	19	Apportion	Add to apportioned (= 700), subtract from available (= 7,150).
7	Apportion	Add to total apportioned (= 900), subtract from available (= 1,800).	21	Issue	Subtract from balance (= 1,450) and from apportioned (= 300).
10	Issue	Subtract from balance (= 2,500) and from apportioned (= 700).	27	Receipt	Subtract from ordered (= zero), post to received, insert in balance column, put unit price and total value of new order in their respective columns.
11	Apportion	Add to total apportioned (= 1,100), subtract from available (= 1,400).			
11	Requisition	Available (= 1,400) is now below 1,500, the re-order point. Standard purchase amount is requisitioned for ordering by purchasing department (if a purchased item).	28	Calculation	Add old balance and new receipt (= 7,450), add old and new values (= $730.50). Divide: $730.50 ÷ 7,450 = .0980, new unit price under average method.
14	Credit	Received back from previously issued shop order. Add to balance (= 2,550) and to available (= 1,450).	28	Replacement	Spoilage or shortage on shop order. Subtract from balance (= 7,430), price valuation of balance at new unit rate, subtract from available (= 7,130).
15	Issue	Subtract from balance (= 1,850) and from apportioned (= 400).	31	Issue	Subtract from balance (= 7,130) and from apportioned (= zero).

The total value is recalculated whenever the balance is increased by receipts or reduced by issues, and at the unit price of that date. The equation, Ordered (total) + On hand (balance) = Apportioned (total) + Available (quantity), can be checked at any point by taking the last entry in each of these columns and inserting it in the equation. If the equation does not balance, an error has been made in posting.

FIGURE 8–12

Information on Materials Specifications

Purchasing Specification

2010024
Page 1 of 1

SUBJECT   Spring Steel Strip, Blued   Commodity Code 3211

1. *Scope*—This specification applies to hardened and blue tempered spring steel strip for use in the manufacture of high quality steel springs.

2. *Composition*—The material shall conform to the following requirements as to chemical composition:

Element	Percent
Carbon	0.89 to 1.04
Manganese	.30 to .50
Silicon	.10 to .20
Sulfur	.050 maximum
Phosphorus	.040 maximum
Iron	Remainder

3. *Temper*—The material shall conform to the following requirements as to temper.

3.1 *Over .020 Inch Thick*—Material over 0.020 inch in thickness shall be tested for hardness only. The hardness shall be 66 to 70, inclusive, Rockwell 30N Scale.

3.2. *Up to .020 Inch Thick*—Material 0.020 inch and under in thickness shall be tested for bending properties only. Strip of any width shall be bent 180 degrees between the jaws of a vise or testing machine, around pins of the diameters specified in Table I, in accordance with Figure 1. The center line of the pin shall be approximately one inch from the outside of the bend.

The material shall either fracture transversely or remain intact in accordance with Table I. When a break occurs, it shall approximate a straight line perpendicular to the longitudinal axis of the test strip.

4. *RCA Part Numbers*—RCA part numbers for some thicknesses are given below. In former issues of this specification, material was identified as "PS-24" and the thickness was separately specified.

Assignment of an RCA part number does not necessarily indicate ready availability in any quantity. See RCA standards for guidance in selection of thickness.

5. *Dimensions*—Dimensions shall be as specified in accordance with the tolerance listed below:

Nominal Thickness, Inch	Tolerance Plus or Minus
Up to .020, incl.	.0005
Over .020 to .040, incl.	.001
Over .040	.002
Width	Plus or minus .005 inch

Strips shall be free from transverse bow, and the lateral bow or camber shall not exceed .38 inch in eight feet.

6. *Form and Finish*—Unless otherwise specified, material shall be supplied in coils of approximately equal length, in accordance with the usual commercial practice. The finish shall be the polished and blued grade.

The steel shall be uniform, clean, blue and smooth. It shall be free from rust, dirt, pits, stains, spots, cracks, slivers and other imperfections, in accordance with good commercial practice.

Edges shall be free from burrs, unless the order specifies that slit edges are acceptable.

7. *Packing and Marking*—Material shall be packed in such manner as to protect it from damage during transit or storage.

Each bundle or shipping unit shall be suitably marked or tagged with the RCA part number; the width, length and net weight of material; the Purchase Order number and the name of the supplier.

Similar Specifications

Aeronautical Material Specification	5122B
American Iron and Steel Institute	C1035 (Chemical Composition)

Nominal Thickness In.	RCA Part Number	Nominal Thickness In.	RCA Part Number
.001	2010024-1	.018	2010024-18
.002	2010024-2	.020	2010024-20
.003	2010024-3	.024	2010024-24
.004	2010024-4	.025	2010024-25
.005	2010024-5	.030	2010024-30
.006	2010024-6	.032	2010024-32
.007	2010024-7	.036	2010024-36
.008	2010024-8	.040	2010024-40
.009	2010024-9	.042	2010024-42
.010	2010024-10	.043	2010024-43
.012	2010024-12	.050	2010024-50
.014	2010024-14	.060	2010024-60
.016	2010024-16		

TABLE I—Bead Test Requirements

Thickness, Inch	Diameter of Pin (D), Inch	
	Without Fracture	With Fracture
Up to .0015	.062	.010
Over .0015 to .003 incl.	.033	.035
Over .003 to .006 incl.	.156	.062
Over .006 to .009 incl.	.218	.093
Over .009 to .012 incl.	.312	.140
Over .012 to .015 incl.	.375	.187
Over .015 to .020 incl.	.488	.218

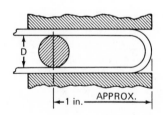

D

1 in.   APPROX.

supplier qualifications, and product specification (at times along with pictures or samples of products), past experiences with suppliers, lead times, capacities, and ratings for each supplier. Such files are useful not only in determining which suppliers to use, but also in answering user department questions about available products or in completing specifications detail where a requisition is vague. Where "in-house" production, standard priced items, or reorders of items against open purchase orders are not involved, a purchasing manager may make use of a bid request form.

Where the item is to be purchased from an outside supplier and bids solicited, a supplier is selected on the basis of his price quotations and his ability to meet purchase order specifications, and a purchase order is issued authorizing the supplier to ship goods in accordance with the specifications and quantities ordered, prices and terms agreed upon, and at the time and place requested. At times the mode of transportation will be specified, as in the sample purchase order shown in Figure 8–13. A similar form may be used for recording information verifying receipt of the item as ordered and in good condition, as shown in Figure 8–14. It is important to note that the forms shown in Figures 8–13 and 8–14 are part of an integrated carbon-copy series, a type of system used by many companies to reduce document preparation, since with these forms the basic information must be filled in only once. Additional copies may be included in the series for the originator of the order, for an order expeditor, for verification of order receipt by the supplier, for inspection, for accounting, or for any other purpose dictated by individual company needs. Some companies have as many as eighteen copies in the series.

Many types of data files, processing systems, and information reports are thus used in materials management, depending on the type of business involved and the size of the company. For example, a large brewery had an elaborate system for reporting on truck trailer arrivals and unloading, since bottles were stored on the trailers in the yard until actually used in production. Other situations require extensive materials "tagging" systems and inventory withdrawal information reporting, in order to make certain that inventory records are accurate and unneeded material is not purchased.

Computers can be used in materials management information systems. For instance, computer data processing systems can be used to produce requisitions (from inventory requirements review), write purchase orders, initiate follow-up orders, and prepare payment vouchers and checks. Computer systems can also be used to prepare management information reports on the status of open orders, amounts of expenditures, supplier performance, and the like. An example of such a computerized materials data processing and management information system is given in Chapter Nine.

FIGURE 8–13

A Purchase Order

PRINTED BY THE STANDARD REGISTER COMPANY U.S.A. ZIPSET ®

PURCH. REQ.	ACCT. NUMBER	REQUISITIONED BY	DEPT.	SPECIAL ORDER NO.	CUSTOMER

DALE Electronics Corporation

7 Friendship Court · Dayton, Ohio · 293 - 8128

"*Corp. Dale*" — **standing guard in space.**

VENDOR

PURCHASE ORDER NO. ➡ MP 3825

OHIO STATE SALES TAX		MANUFACTURER'S EXCISE TAX		CONFIRMING DO NOT DUPLICATE
EXEMPT	TAXABLE	EXEMPT	TAXABLE	

P.O. DATE	VENDOR NO.	TERMS	SHIP VIA	F.O.B. POINT
TO ARRIVE	DALE RFQ.	BUYER	TELEPHONE & EXT.	SHIPPING POINT

VENDOR QUOTE	CONTRACT NO.	REL. NO.	DALE INSPECTION	GOV'T. INSPECTION	GOVERNMENT CONTRACT NUMBER

ITEM	DESCRIPTION	QUANTITY	UNIT PRICE	AMOUNT

FORM 4003

PLEASE FILL OUT, SIGN AND RETURN THE ATTACHED ACCEPTANCE OF THIS ORDER AT ONCE.
SUBSTITUTION OF YOUR ACKNOWLEDGMENT WILL NOT SUFFICE. THANK YOU.

SELLER NOTE: By accepting this purchase order, Seller agrees to perform subject to and in accordance with the terms set forth on both sides of this purchase order, and with any additional terms attached hereto and made a part hereof.

1. P.O. Number must appear on all invoices, correspondence, shipping papers and packages.
2. Invoices must be supplied in duplicate.
3. No Invoice is to apply to more than one purchase order.
4. Packing slip must accompany each shipment.
5. Buyer's count will be accepted as conclusive on all shipments not accompanied by a packing slip.
6. If our part numbers appear on this order, they must be stamped, printed, or tagged on all items and must also show on all invoices, correspondence, shipping papers and packages.
7. No charges will be allowed for transportation, boxing, crating, or other packaging unless agreed upon herein.
8. Supply & ship the above material in exact accordance with specifications and the terms and conditions on reverse side hereof.

DALE Electronics Corporation

By ____________________
DIRECTOR OF PURCHASES

VENDOR COPY

FIGURE 8–14

A Receiving Report

Quality Control
Management

In determining overall quality control policies, information is needed on company goals, operating characteristics of the products, the environment in which the products are used, field installation and maintenance requirements, customer specifications, potential end uses of the product, selling prices of the company's products or services, competitive products and services, manufacturing and engineering requirements and costs, production processes, costs, and capabilities, and testing and inspection costs in general. Based on an examination of this information, statements of quality control policies, such as those shown in Figure 8–15, can be developed. Based on the above analyses, management decisions are also made during this phase on the scope of the quality control program (should it cover new design, incoming materials, product manufacture, or all of these?) and on the reporting relationships of the quality control manager.

In developing specific product, process, or material standards, information is needed on customer or engineering design specifications, production department capabilities and restraints, marketing requirements, purchasing requirements, and cost data. Based on an analysis of this information, and working in conjunction with production engineering, quality control management will develop specific standards for *measurable characteristics* of the product (such as weight, strength, or dimension) and communicate them to concerned departments using forms such as the raw materials report shown in Figure 8–16, which is used for vendor certification and selection, purchasing, and inspection or testing of incoming raw materials.

Planning and developing quality control programs and procedures requires answering such questions as: what types of measuring methods and measuring and control equipment should be used; where should the product be sampled, tested or inspected (for example, centralized or decentralized along the production line), and how much of this monitoring should be done (for example, 100 percent inspection or sampling); and what statistical controls should be used (if any), and what constitutes an acceptable deviation from standard before a product is rejected?

Information needed to make these decisions and develop a quality control program comes from production and production engineering, which supplies: product diagrams, lists of component parts, and specifications; production line diagrams; data on where in-process measurements can be taken; and the like. In addition, information is needed on availability and costs of testing equipment and quality control personnel; the costs of testing time; and alternative cost analyses of different measurement methods, testing and inspection locations, sampling methods, and statistical controls. In these

FIGURE 8-15

XYZ Electronics Company
Product Quality Policy

Need for Policy

To enhance the Company reputation, competitive position, and profitability, it is necessary to produce products of good quality. Meeting this objective requires a properly directed approach by all functions to the elements which concern product quality.

Statement of Policy

It is the policy of the XYZ Electronics Company to market only products of a quality that will merit and earn customer satisfaction by performing expected functions reliably and effectively in accordance with customer expectations, and which are discernibly better than competitive offerings. In support of this objective, the XYZ Electronics Company continuously strives to lead its product field in research and development, design, manufacture, and marketing of work related to its area of business responsibility.

Courses of Action

1. Selection of Business Opportunities
   This Company will not accept business which will compromise its product quality reputation. In this regard the customer's specifications will be reviewed to determine that they serve the common interests of the customer and the Company and to ensure that minimum quality standards can be met. When these conditions are not met, the Company will not submit a proposal. A comprehensive contract review will be carried out by all functional areas before a contract is signed in accordance with Company instructions.

2. Product Development and Design
   1) Only approved components and processes shall be used. In cases where new components and processes are needed to meet product requirements, adequate qualification tests or process capability measurements will be carried out prior to their use. Department instructions shall specify procedures for obtaining component and process approval.

Source: From *Total Quality Control* by A. V. Feigenbaum, copyright © 1961. Used with permission of McGraw-Hill Book Company.

analyses, costs are weighed against benefits realized from alternative quality control programs.

Once initial quality control programs are developed, additional information is obtained from a pilot run of the product manufactured or from actual operation of the quality control program. This actual experience provides

FIGURE 8–16

Detailed Raw Material Requirements
Raw-Material Purchase
Physical Requirements

Test Spec. no.	Req. test	Spot test	Requirement description	Std. avg. X	Min. X	Max. X	Std. range R	Max. X	Unit of meas.	Smp. per test
			Weight							
			Count—warp							
			Count—filling							
			Dry strength—warp							
			Dry strength—filing							
			Wet strength—warp							
			Wet strength—filing							
			Thickness							
			Mesh count							
			Yarn slippage							
			Stretch							
			Yarn shift							
			Yarn size—warp							
			Yarn size—filling							
			Seam efficiency							
			Dimension restorability							
			Micro—fiber analysis							
			Micro—fiber analysis							
			Shrinkage							
			Chemical Requirements							
			Launderability—soap							
			Launderability—deter.							
			Fiber content							
			Fiber content							
			Hydrogen potential (pH)							
			Bleach permanence							
			Flammability							
			Crease resistance							
			(CF) dry pressing							
			(CF) wet pressing							
			(CF) dry cleaning							
			(CF) wet cleaning							

FIGURE 8–16 (*Continued*)

			(CF) fresh water							
			(CF) salt water							
			(CF) perspiration							
			(CF) atmospheric							
			(CF) chlorine							
			(CF) sunlight							
			(CF) crocking							
			(CF) bleeding							
			Finish—dry cleaning							
			Finish—wet cleaning							
			Finish—water repel.							

Source: J. Juran, *Quality Control Handbook* (New York: McGraw-Hill Book Company, 1961),   p. 601.

information useful in refining all aspects of the quality control program, including: whether standards need to be modified, whether measuring, inspection, sampling, and testing methods need to be changed, or whether personnel, equipment, and space allocations should be revised.

Out of this program development phase will come instructions, procedures, and manuals of operation to be used by testers, inspectors, and supervisors in the quality control program. An example of such instructions is shown in Figure 8–17. These information documents will contain information on how to use control charts, tests, and the like to perform quality checks, quality limits, and rejection procedures.

Several statistical methods are used in monitoring product quality; the control reports using these methods show the variances or deviations from predetermined standards for certain measurable characteristics, such as dimension, hardness, and chemical content. The four statistical methods commonly used are frequency distributions, control charts, sampling tables, and various special methods.

A *frequency distribution* is a tabulation or tally providing information on the number of times a given measurable characteristic occurs within the samples of product being checked. Figure 8–18 shows a frequency distribution plot of a measurable characteristic, voltage: if a product lot being tested exceeds a normal or acceptable distribution pattern (for example, too many high or low voltage readings), it is rejected. A *control chart* provides a chronological (hour-by-hour, day-by-day) graphical comparison of actual product-quality characteristics. When the curve approaches or exceeds the

FIGURE 8-17

Quality Control Testing Instructions

Q.C. Instruction No. 5.04

Subject: Product Control Tests—Class 7321-7322 Sub-assembly Treating.

Purpose: 1. To detect unsatisfactory sub-assembly characteristics caused by faulty operation of the sub-assembly treating system.

2. To detect such characteristics as soon after treat as possible, before the doubtful sub-assemblies become mixed with previously treated sub-assemblies.

General: These instructions apply to all Class 7321-7322 sub-assemblies treated with any of the treating materials and in any of the treating processes covered by Laboratory and Engineering Instructions.

Procedure: Each day, three sub-assemblies, all of the same catalog number, shall be taken from each treating tank unloaded between 8:00 AM and 5:00 PM. These sub-assemblies shall be selected after the baskets are turned over for unloading, where baskets are loaded on their sides, but shall be taken before actual unloading begins. Sub-assemblies shall be taken from the center of one of the top baskets.

Over a period of days, all catalog numbers of Class 7321 and 7322 sub-assemblies being built in quantity shall be sampled.

The samples selected shall be immediately sealed, degreased, and placed in a forced circulation oven operating at $70°C$, with a minimum of elapsed time between selection of samples and placing them in the oven. Sub-assemblies shall remain in the oven long enough to bring their dielectric temperatures within the range of $65°-75°C$ after which they shall be measured for power factor and capacity at either rated 60-cycle volts, or at a 60-cycle voltage in accordance with the following table if sub-assemblies are rated for DC voltage.

D.C. Rated Volts	60-cycle Test Volts	DC Rated Volts	60-cycle Test Volts
400	220	1500	680
600	330	2000	880
1000	440	Over 2000	35% of DC rating

In the event the desired test voltage exceeds the maximum rated voltage of the bridge, measurements may be taken at the maximum voltage available.

If the power factors obtained exceed those given in the tabulation given below for the applicable case style, voltage rating and treating material, the tank load of sub-assemblies represented by the sample shall be removed from the production flow and an additional sample shall be taken and measured. Results of tests on both samples shall be referred to the Engineering Department for decision as to disposition of the tank load in question.

If elevated temperature power factors are satisfactory, the samples shall be cooled to a dielectric temperature of $20°-30°C$ and the power factor and capacity measurements repeated at the same voltage as was used for the previous measurements.

$65°-75°C$ Power-factor limits

		Max % P.F.		
Case style and size	*Rated AC volts	1476	1436	Oil
All round cans	660 and below	.50	.50	.30
All round cans	Above 660	.40	.40	.25
2 in. X 2½ in. oval	660 and below	.50	.50	.30
1¾ in. X 2½ in. oval	Above 660	.40	.40	.25
All other oval	All	.40	.40	.25
All rectangular	660 and below	.50	.50	.30
All rectangular	Above 660	.40	.40	.25
Bathtubs	All	.60	.60	.30
AVDG	All	.60	.60	.30

* For DC sub-assemblies—consider 1500 V DC equivalent to 660 V AC.

Records: A permanent record of all measurements shall be kept in the office of the Quality Control Manager. Each week the over-all Quality Performance report for Class 7321-7322 sub-assemblies shall include a record of the number of tanks sampled and the number of tanks whose samples had high power factors.

A. R. JONES
Eng. Department

APPROVED
B. F. SMITH Mfg. Superintendent
T. D. GREEN Mgr. - Q.C.
R. M. BROWN Eng. Department

Source: From *Total Quality Control* by A. V. Feigenbaum, copyright © 1961. Used with permission of McGraw-Hill Book Company.

FIGURE 8–18
Frequency Distribution Plot

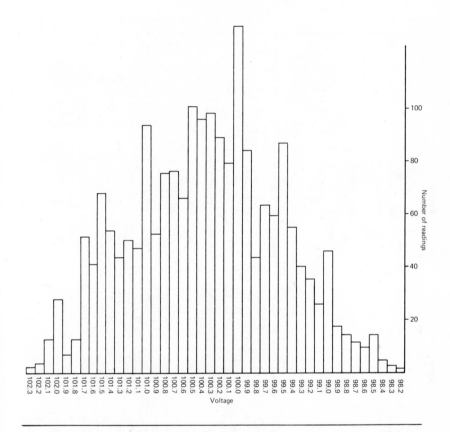

Source: From *Total Quality Control* by A. V. Feigenbaum, copyright © 1961. Used with permission of McGraw-Hill Book Company.

limits, the specification tolerances have been exceeded and the product or product lot is rejected and, in some instances, the production process is adjusted. These charts provide quality control information based on partial samples (Figure 8–19) or entire lots (Figure 8–20). *Sampling tables* provide a schedule of the probable quality relationships of an entire lot to the samples selected from that lot; when sampled lots exceed the schedule, the entire lot is rejected. *Additional methods* which are used to provide information for quality control include analyses of tolerances, correlation analyses, and variance analyses.

FIGURE 8-19

Control Chart with Sampling Limits

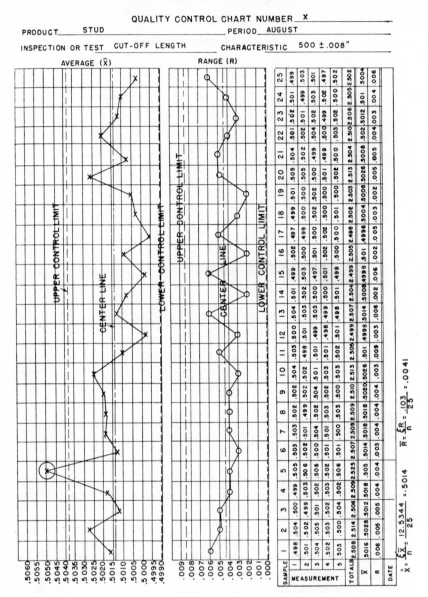

FIGURE 8-20

Control Chart—100 Percent Inspection

STATISTICAL TECHNOLOGY OF QUALITY CONTROL

QUALITY CONTROL CHART NUMBER _____

PRODUCT MOTOR END SHIELD   MONTH AUGUST

INSPECTION FINAL   CHARACTERISTIC ____ All DEFECTS

2.9   7.1

PERCENT DEFECTIVE

DAY	INSP.	DEF.	%
1	1005	40	4.0
2	1000	45	4.5
3	1015	90	8.9
HOLIDAY			
HOLIDAY			
4	995	70	7.0
5	1000	30	3.0
6	985	20	2.0
7	990	40	4.0
8	1010	50	5.0
HOLIDAY			
HOLIDAY			
9	1000	40	4.0
10	1005	75	7.5
11	990	80	8.1
12	995	25	2.5
13	1010	40	4.0
HOLIDAY			
HOLIDAY			
14	1000	30	3.0
15	1000	20	2.0
16	1005	75	7.5
17	1000	55	5.5
18	995	60	6.0
HOLIDAY			
HOLIDAY			
19	990	70	7.1
20	1010	45	4.5
21	1000	70	7.0
22	1005	45	4.5
23	1015	60	5.9
HOLIDAY			
HOLIDAY			
24	990	35	3.5
25	990	40	4.0

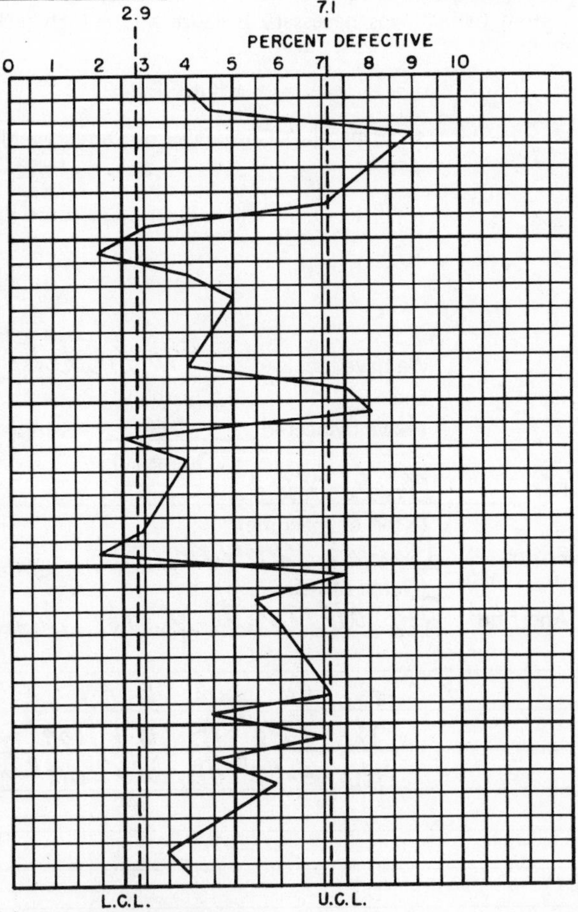

L.C.L.   U.C.L.

	INSP	DEF	%
1 WK.	3020	175	5.8
2 WK.	4980	210	4.2
3 WK.	5000	260	5.2
4 WK.	5000	240	4.8
5 WK.	5020	290	5.7
6 WK.	1980	75	3.8
MO	25000	1250	5.0

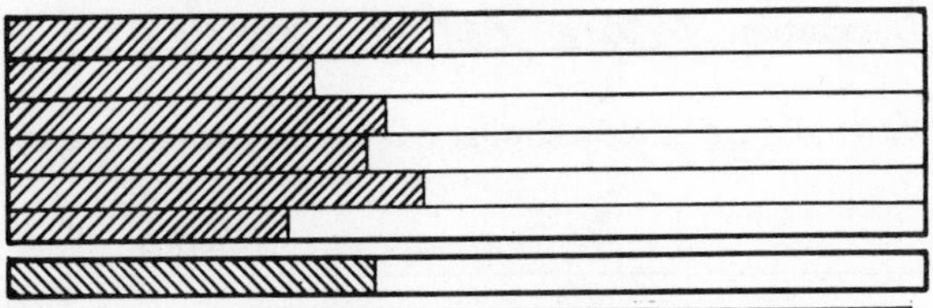

Source: From *Total Quality Control* by A. V. Feigenbaum, copyright © 1961. Used with permission of McGraw-Hill Book Company.

Many other kinds of control reports are used in monitoring product, process, and material quality. For example, some operations make use of simple inspection reports, such as the one shown in Figure 8–21. A detailed description of the control reports and reporting system used by one company which had developed a complex computerized quality control information system (which was necessary because of the high technical standards of the

FIGURE 8–21

Inspector's Complaint on Defective Material

Date _8/4/60_

Pat. no. _____   Dr. No. _761832_

We have received _570 Gaskets_

and   (Quantity)   (Name of article)

I have inspected _____50_____ Sample _Gaskets_

(Quantity)   (Name of article)

For _____Brake XR32_____

(Kind of machine)   (Kind of material)

From _____Brown Company_____   Req'n _Z-32181_

(Name of mfr.)

And find _For all Units in the Sample (50)_

the 1/16" Dim. is O.K.
The 6-7/8" ID is +.009" over tolerance
the 4-1/4" OD is +.010" over tolerance

Disposition _Return lot to vendor_

When did we make a similar complaint against this vendor? _6/24/60_

Signed _J. R. White_

Source: From *Total Quality Control* by A. V. Feigenbaum, copyright © 1961. Used with permission of McGraw-Hill Book Company.

products and the massive amount of control data collected) is described in Chapter Nine.

Maintenance Management

In overall planning for the maintenance operation, a maintenance manager first needs to know what equipment and buildings are to be maintained (a kind of facilities' inventory report) and what changes are planned for the future (the company's long-range facilities' plans). Next, he needs information on what kinds of maintenance services may be needed (including design and operating specifications of equipment and production processes involved) and which of these are his responsibility, since some maintenance may be performed by machine operators.

Maintenance work can be divided into two categories, routine (preventive) and non-routine. Routine maintenance work involves repetitive jobs done at planned frequencies, such as inspecting or lubricating equipment or replacing light bulbs. Non-routine maintenance work is repair work performed because of breakdowns, failures, damages, or defects in equipment or facilities.

In determining which units should be included in a preventive maintenance program, information is needed on the relative importance of the unit (for example, would the unit's breakdown seriously disrupt production?), the frequency and types of breakdowns, the relation of preventive maintenance costs to breakdown repair costs and down-time costs, and the availability of manpower and supplies.

In developing a preventive maintenance program, it is not necessary to have a planned maintenance program for every piece of machinery or facility, nor is it possible to eliminate all breakdowns: a manager can only hope to minimize excessive and preventable interruptions caused by equipment breakdowns. This goal is achieved by concentrating on "critical" units. A unit qualifies as critical, for example, if its failure would endanger the health or safety of operating personnel, affect product quality, or interrupt production.

Initially, when new equipment or facilities are purchased, preventive maintenance may be scheduled and routine inspection reports prepared (Figure 8–22) based on manufacturer's recommendations. These preventive maintenance schedules for critical equipment or facilities would subsequently be adjusted based on analyses of actual experience. Several kinds of information reports and records are used in performing these analyses.

In planning all types of maintenance programs, records are needed on each major piece of equipment or facility to show the history of breakdowns, emergency repairs, and regularly scheduled maintenance. Figure 8–23 gives an example of such an "Equipment History Record."

FIGURE 8-22

Inspection Order

JAN	FEB	MAR	APR	MAY	JUN	JUL	AUG	SEP	OCT	NOV	DEC		Unit no.

Equipment _____ Container Loader

Manufacturer _____

Date purchased _____

Dept. _____

Building _____ Floor _____

Inspection Procedure	Insp.	G	F	P	G	F	P	G	F	P	G	F	P	G	F	P	G	F	P	G	F	P
Machine cleanliness																						
Condition of finish or paint																						
Main drive assembly																						
Drive motor—temperature, vibration, and/or unusual noise.																						
Reducer—temperature, vibration and/or unusual noise and leaks. Drain and flush annually.																						
V-Belts—check for wear, tension and alignment.																						
Sprockets—check for wear and alignment.																						
Chains—check for wear, tension and alignment.																						

296

Clutches—check dog, springs, and cleanliness (oil spring).																					
Cam—check for wear.																					
Solenoids (if applicable)																					
Check for operating action and connections.																					
Safety features																					
General condition of machine																					
Check entire unit for proper lubrication																					
Date inspected																					
Inspected by																					

G — Good —Requires no repair

F — Fair — Requires careful inspection next period

P — Poor — Requires immediate repair — write job sheet

Source: Reprinted by permission of the publisher from AMA Management Report No. 77, *Modern Maintenance Management* © 1963 by the American Management Association, Inc.

FIGURE 8-23

Equipment History Record

| JAN | FEB | MAR | APR | MAY | JUN | JUL | AUG | SEP | OCT | NOV | DEC | Unit no. |

Equipment————

Manufacturer————

Date purchased————

Review at Dept.

Repair cost $

Breakdown Per

Building Floor

Date	B/P	Work performed	Material	Labor	Cumulative total

Source: Reprinted by permission of the publisher from AMA Management Report No. 77, *Modern Maintenance Management* © 1963 by the American Management Association, Inc.

In this record, control points are established (the "Review At" box), which when exceeded trigger action to either change the preventive maintenance schedule or type of work done, or include the piece of equipment in the preventive maintenance program.

A second key information document is the report on breakdown repairs (Figure 8–24). This report provides information on the cause of the breakdown and so enables management to determine the kind of maintenance

FIGURE 8–24

Job Sheet

Ordered by _J. L. K._ Job no. _2531_

Approved by _L. Q. Q._ Date _March 15_

Charge _____

Repair ☐ P.M. ☐ Charge ☐ Breakdown ☐   Work Group(s) ■ ☐ ☐ ☐

| Machinery unit no. _3412_ | Location _2nd Floor Package_ |
| When Available _Now_ | When wanted _Soon as Possible_ |

Description of work to be done _Repair broken Duck Bill actuating assembly on #1, F, & F Scale_

Breakdown Report

Description of work done _Replaced actuating casting and button block linkage on this F + F scale_

Corrective maintenance report (what needs to be done to assure that this breakdown will not occur again) _Proper dimension on the actuator linkage installed last week would have eliminated this breakdown._

Hours lost _4¼_ Production lost _1,000 bales_

Add breakdown to preventative maintenance list   Yes ☐ No ☒

Repair work checked by production department: OK ☒ Unsatisfactory ☐

Remarks: _A new part of proper design has been ordered. When it arrives this scale will be scheduled out of production for parts replacement._

Source: Reprinted by permission of the publisher from AMA Management Report No. 77, *Modern Maintenance Management* © 1963 by the American Management Association, Inc.

action needed to assure that the breakdowns will not become repetitive. At some companies these reports are supplemented by monthly analyses of breakdowns by department.

Two information documents commonly used in scheduling and carrying out actual routine and non-routine maintenance work are: a maintenance schedule by work area (Figure 8–25) and a work order (Figure 8–26). The maintenance schedule shows the schedule of maintenance work planned for the coming day or week. In developing this schedule, the scheduler considers the availability of craftsmen, materials and equipment, the best sequence of work operations, and the best mix of crafts required to accomplish those operations. The work order authorizes maintenance work, based on preventive maintenance schedules and on requests for repairs from operating departments; in addition, it serves as a control tool, since it shows labor and material costs for all work completed.

FIGURE 8–25
Maintenance Work Order Form

Charge	Bldg-floor		Shutdown	Priority	Work order no.
					59586

Date	Wanted by	Units	Earned hours	Actual hours		Job code

Work Required

List job irregularities

Elec.	Mach.	Tool maker	Plumb.	Yard	Out. mech.	Lube	Weld	Carp.	F.T.	Inst.

Approved by originator

Source: Reprinted by permission of the publisher from AMA Management Report No. 77, *Modern Maintenance Management* © 1963 by the American Management Association, Inc.

FIGURE 8–26

Maintenance Area Schedule				Area no.					Week ending		
				M	T	W	T	F	SS	Total	Remarks
Total no. of man-hrs. Overhead—vacation —other Fixed assignments Available for scheduling											
Work order	Eqpt. no.	Craft code	Description	Weekly assign- ment	Carry over	Sch. act.					

Source: E. T. Newbrough, *Effective Maintenance Management* (New York: McGraw-Hill Book Company, 1967), p. 143.

Completed work orders are thus the source of information on the costs of repair work and preventive maintenance work. Analyses of this cost information, combined with information on the frequency of breakdowns (Figure 8–23), the nature of the problem causing the breakdown (Figure 8–24), and the costs of lost production time caused by the breakdown, are used by management to determine whether regularly scheduled preventive maintenance is required or if changes are required in the preventive maintenance work now done.

The work orders are also a means of monitoring performance of the maintenance staff. In many situations, where the maintenance work is largely routine or somewhat repetitive, standards can be established for the time required to complete repair or inspection jobs. These standard times can then be compared to actual time spent on inspection or repair work to measure the efficiency of maintenance personnel. At the same time, foremen need to monitor the quality of the work performed by their personnel—through personal inspections, feedback from user departments, or reviews of subsequent breakdowns of repaired equipment.

Controls are also needed for inventories of maintenance supplies. These would be similar to, but on a much smaller scale than those described in the earlier section on inventory management information systems.

As in other operations management areas, the maintenance activities will normally have a cost budget. And, during the year, periodic (monthly or quarterly) reports will be issued comparing actual to budgeted costs. These reports may be broken down by type of maintenance performed, by department for which the maintenance was performed, or by some other category appropriate to the operational or management needs of the situation. In addition, some companies are experimenting with periodic reports on trends in overall breakdowns, lost production time due to breakdowns, and the like in an effort to measure the efficiency of the maintenance operation.

Facilities Management

In making long-term facilities planning decisions, overall company planning information is neeeded on long-range sales forecasts, anticipated product diversification, changing markets, changing sources of raw materials, and other relevant company planning factors. Within the framework of these definitions of overall facilities requirements, a series of decisions would then be made about each new facility needed.

In determining new plant location, decisions must be made about what region or community to locate the plant in, as well as about the exact site of the plant. Information needed in making plant location decisions includes proximity of transportation, supply of labor, nearness to product markets, nearness to raw material supplies, water supply, power supply, etc. This external information is obtained from local government (city and state) agencies and business association and special research studies, either by the facilities planning manager and his staff or through outside consulting firms that specialize in location studies.

Rarely is the decision on facility location a simple, clear-cut one: for example, one location may have a better labor supply, another may be closer to raw materials supplies, and another closer to the customer markets. In attempting to weigh the impact of these different factors, two kinds of analytical reports are used: rating plans and cost analyses.

1. *Rating Plan.* In the rating plan, weights are assigned to each of the factors that should be considered. The factor deemed most important is given the highest weight (Figure 8–27), and each of the other factors a lesser amount. For example, a nearness to raw materials might be weighed at 400 points, nearness to market at 300, the labor supply at 275, and the other factors at lesser amounts. The total number of points for each of the alternative locations could then be determined and used to assist in making a decision. In most cases, the rating should be supplemented with a cost analysis.

2. *Cost Analysis.* As an aid in evaluating alternative plant locations, estimates should be made for all costs entering into the operation of the

FIGURE 8–27

Rating Chart for Three Alternative Locations

Factor	Maximum Possible Points	City A	City B	City C
Nearness to raw materials	400	300	250	150
Nearness to market	300	140	200	250
Labor supply	275	150	275	275
Transportation	125	150	225	125
Water supply	200	120	150	175
Power	200	150	190	120
Waste disposal	100	50	75	95
Land & construction costs	70	60	50	50
Climate	50	35	60	35
Taxes & laws	40	35	25	70
Locale site	40	40	80	35
Total	1800	1265	1580	1380

plant in each of the locations. This estimate should cover the initial cost of raw materials, the cost of manufacture, and the cost of distribution (Figure 8–28). After the determination of each of these costs, the unit cost for manufacturing the products in each of the locations can be reckoned and may be used to aid in deciding on the optimum location.

Similar analytical studies would also be done of alternative sites within the location or region selected. Information needed for this decision would include that used in the location study, as well as detailed data on local conditions affecting plant construction and operation, such as local tax and zoning regulations, access roads leading to the site, location of rail sidings or spurs or other transportation facilities, etc.

Using these analytical studies, company management would weigh the comparative cost data with longer-term planning considerations, such as trends in the consumer market, possible technological developments, competitor moves, and available company resources, in making a final location and site decision.

In selecting machinery and in making plant design and layout decisions, information is needed on manufacturing process and materials handling requirements, process, equipment and material availability, initial costs, and operating costs. For example, the following is a partial list of information

FIGURE 8–28

Cost Comparison Chart

Costs	Location		
	City A	City B	City C
Operating Costs			
Transportation costs:			
Incoming materials	$ 110,000	$ 90,200	$ 85,500
Outgoing materials	160,000	165,000	175,000
Labor	250,000	225,140	257,000
Utilities:			
Power	60,000	65,000	65,000
Water	30,000	29,000	35,000
Fuel	65,000	70,500	65,000
Plant overhead:			
Rent or carrying costs	60,000	55,000	66,500
Taxes	10,000	12,000	14,000
Insurance	3,550	5,550	5,550
Miscellaneous	5,000	8,100	8,510
Total	$ 753,550	$ 725,490	$ 777,060
Construction Costs			
Land	$ 211,000	$ 61,140	$ 75,000
Building	1,521,000	1,350,000	1,600,000
Special requirements	45,500	––	––
Total	$2,531,050	$2,136,630	$2,452,060

requirements used by one company during this phase in a situation involving construction of a new plant:

1. *Engineering Design and Construction.*

   a. Prepare preliminary flow sheets showing various possibilities of handling the different products.

   b. Present flow sheets for discussion.

   c. Obtain approval of flow sheets noting all processes and equipment to be evaluated and developed.

   d. Evaluate and develop all processes and equipment.

   e. Present revised flow sheets for discussion indicating state of evaluation.

   f. Revise flow sheets and present for final approval and signature.

   g. Investigate airveying of sugar and handling of one grade of sugar.

   h. Prepare detailed list of new and old equipment.

   i. Obtain detailed information on old equipment.

   j. Obtain data on new equipment.

   k. Prepare preliminary equipment layout for discussion purposes—layouts to be based on flow sheets and minimum manpower requirements.

   l. Use data obtained in discussions to revise layouts for final approval.

   m. Make an analysis of typical building construction for sanitation and cost.

   n. Develop building sections.

   o. Develop finished schedules.

   p. Size buildings based on equipment layouts.

   q. Prepare model showing entire plant with its equipment.

2. *Industrial Engineering.*

   a. Make economic analyses of major equipment costs where the choice of two or more systems exists.

   b. Analyze the basic materials flow requirements, assist with the layout analysis, and make recommendations.

   c. Define the preliminary stores items inventory level, storage space and equipment requirements, layout and labor requirements.

Etc.

Once the building design and process layout have been completed, based on these engineering studies, the construction phase would begin. Project management planning and control techniques are used during this phase to plan and monitor both the costs and the timing of the construction of the new facility and the move to the new facility. Project management information tools used in facilities management are discussed in Chapter Ten.

TEXT DISCUSSION QUESTIONS

1. Describe the operations management job and the principal tasks involved in managing operations.

2. Describe the kinds of information needed for short-term production planning or scheduling. Discuss the ways in which such information needs differ with various sizes and types of business operations.

3. Describe the key decisions made in inventory management and the information sources used in making these decisions.

4. As with other operations areas, materials management (purchasing) job responsibilities can differ considerably from industry to industry and

company to company. Describe two business or company situations with which you are familiar and describe the ways in which the different job situations will affect the materials management information systems needed.

5. Discuss the types of overall information reports the Vice President of Operations might need to insure control of materials (purchasing) or inventory operations in an industrial motors manufacturing company.

6. Describe the ways in which the job responsibilities of the maintenance manager dictate the kind of information he needs. Discuss ways in which a change in these responsibilities in a specific business situation can lead to changes in the maintenance manager's information requirements.

7. Define the four or five critical factors affecting (or decisions involved in) quality control management. Discuss the ways in which these critical factors (or decisions) will affect the structure and content of information systems developed in this area.

8. Discuss the ways in which facilities planning and development can be considered to be one of the key overall operations management jobs.

Developing Systems for Operations Management

THIS CHAPTER COVERS A VARIETY OF SITUATIONS IN WHICH INFORMA-
tion systems were developed for operations management. The concluding
section contains case study exercises.

Production Planning and Control:
Hughes Aircraft Company

The following is a description of the production planning and control system
developed at Hughes Aircraft Company, a large aerospace firm which designs,
develops, and manufactures complex electronic systems.[1]

The plant under study produces a diverse product mix of machine and
sheet metal parts, machine assemblies, waveguides, and etched circuit boards.
There are 2,000 to 3,000 orders being processed at any one time, with an
average of seven operations per order. The average operation requires 2½
hours of processing time and the average order cycle time is between three
and four weeks. The shop consists of approximately 1,000 machines and/or

---

1. M. H. Bulkin, J. L. Colley, and H. W. Steinhoff, "Load Forecasting, Priority
Sequencing, and Simulation in a Job Shop Control System," *Management Science*,
October 1966, pp. 29-51.

9

workplaces, which are grouped into 120 functional machine and work centers. The work centers are manned by 400 direct workers. The demand for Hughes' products is fluctuating and the market is moderately competitive. Orders are obtained throughout the year.

Reporting to the manufacturing vice-president are all the plant managers, including the manager of the plant under study. Reporting to the plant manager are the production planning and control manager and the works manager. The shop foremen, who supervise day-to-day production, report to the works manager.

The production planning and control manager is responsible for preparing projections of overall yearly production requirements broken down by month. Sales forecasts by products or product groups are the primary source documents used in preparing this overall plan for production requirements. This plan shows the kinds and amounts of various products to be produced and overall machine and man-hour requirements by month for the coming year.

The works manager and the shop foremen are responsible for short-term scheduling and control. To prepare the *master schedule,* they use the overall annual plan for production requirements by month, along with the engineering specifications, bills of materials, routing, and lists of operations for each product. The master schedule lists delivery dates for all product lots or orders and gives such details as contract identification, bill of materials, schematic drawings and specifications, fabrication and tooling requirements, and so on for each product. Such a complex schedule was necessary because there were at least eight levels of assemblies, each containing numerous parts, purchased or manufactured. Data from the master schedule (and from operations) was then used to prepare the following reports:

1. *Weekly Shop Load Forecast.* Projects the anticipated load for each machine group and work center for ten weeks in advance. The projected work load in standard hours is divided into total active load and preshop load (not yet released to the shop) and further subdivided into orders which are on schedule, behind schedule, or held due to lack of production plan, material, tooling etc. Figure 9–1 shows a portion of the actual forecast used by the company.

2. *Daily Order Schedule Report.* Indicates the daily sequencing of operations on orders at each machine group in the shop. This information report helps the foremen to plan the work for the shift. Figure 9–2 shows a portion of this report.

3. *Hot Order Visibility Report.* Segregates all orders that are in rush classification. This was introduced a couple of years ago when it was found that a significant number of orders were being assigned unantici-

FIGURE 9–1
Weekly Shop Load Forecast

M-Day 605 Calendar Day 01-06-65 Machine Group Load											
Dept. MG 71-43 Mills 6 M/CS Std. Hours											
Week of Performance											
	1	2	3	4	5	6	7	8	9	10	710	Total
Total load	208	175	227	204	126	116	42	52	28	23	53	1254
On schedule	138											
Behind schedule	70											
Held	37											
Total active load	123	115	102	64	46	53	21	6	15	23	53	621
On schedule	85											
Behind schedule	38											
Held	11											
In M/C group	96											
Total Pre-shop load	85	60	125	140	80	63	21	46	13			633
On schedule	53											
Behind schedule	32											
Held	26											

FIGURE 9–2
Order Schedule Report

Report No. 3699-04		M-Day 517	Date 10-28-64	Page 1						Machine Group 71-91		
Effort	Priority	Part number				Work order			Proc. code	Proj. code	Prev. loc.	Arr. time	Order quantity	Estimated actual hours/ oper.	Ops. left	Estimated run time left	Date prom- ised

Effort	Priority	Eng.	Pre	Basic	Dash	Pre	Basic	Split	Proc. code	Proj. code	Prev. loc.	Arr. time	Order quantity	Estimated actual hours/oper.	Ops. left	Estimated run time left	Date promised
				Orders in station													
1	5.4			443209		21-487403			11	03	71-15	Insta	4322	7.3	03	15.2	5-10
				Incoming orders													
	1.6																

311

pated rush classifications, thus disrupting the regular production program.

A computer system is used to prepare these three reports. Data from the master schedule needed for scheduling purposes is first entered into the Fabrication Open-Order Master File, which is maintained on magnetic tape. This file, which is updated daily, contains the critical information on every open order. A segment of the file is shown in Figure 9–3. The header section of the file holds fixed identification data, plus current data on the status of the order (shown at the right of the header section). In addition, "open operations" data is given for each open fabrication operation necessary to complete the order. The trailer of the file contains summary information. At the end of each day, a paper tape containing all order moves carried out during the day is used to update current order locations and to code completed operations in the file.

The Weekly Shop Load Forecast (Figure 9–1) is prepared by the computer from data in the Fabrication Open-Order Master File for each machine group.

The Daily Order Schedule Report and Hot Order Visibility Report are developed using a computerized job-shop simulation model. The priority dispatching decision rule used in the simulation model is the dynamic slack time per operation. Dynamic slack time is the number of days remaining to the due date less the remaining number of days of processing time. The priority index is then computed by dividing the dynamic slack by the number of remaining operations.

The simulation scheduling model contains a table of machine group capacities and manpower capacities. Manpower is divided into labor classes which can be assigned to one or more machine groups, and this capacity table is updated as changes occur. The simulation program makes an initial assignment of each order in the open file to the machine group indicated by its current location in its header record (see Figure 9–3). The orders are then ranked in priority sequence according to the priority index and are assigned sequentially until either all available machines or men have been accounted for. An event clock is used to record operation completions at the machine groups based on the estimated run times. On the completion of an operation in the simulation run, a new priority index is computed for the order, and it is moved to its new operation location and placed in the proper queue. This continues for one shift and all activities taking place during the simulation are recorded and the daily operating reports printed.

The Daily Order Schedule Report shows the orders in the machine group at the beginning of the shift and the orders expected to arrive (incoming orders) during the shift. Within these two categories, the orders were sequenced in terms of a pre-established priority sequencing rule. The report

FIGURE 9-3
Fabrication Open-Order Master File

Header:

Work Order #	Part #	Project code	Procurement code	Bill of mat'l.	Cost acct.	Make span	Due date	Order quantity	Cur. Location			Prev. location		Held code	Level of effort
									Dept.	Mach. group	Oper. no.	Date	Mach. group.		

← Fixed → Updated daily →

Open operation: Fabrication requirements

Work order #	Operation #	Make location		Set-up std. hours	Run-time std. hours	Setback	Completion code
		Dept.	Mach. group				

Trailer:

Work order #	Part number	Number moves remaining	Days in current location

also indicates which orders are hot orders (with a number 1 in column 1, Figure 9–2).

The Daily Hot Order Visibility Report reported on all orders within a department which were "rush" orders and was used by the production expediter.

The works manager and the shop foremen analyze the Weekly Shop Load Forecast to determine what orders are behind schedule and how efficiently machines and manpower are being utilized. Depending on the situation, the foremen or the works manager would modify the original schedules—for example, by redefining the priorities or adjusting overtime work, in order to meet scheduled requirements or improve operating efficiency.

The Daily Order Schedule Report and Hot Order Visibility Report are used by the shop foremen in the daily sequencing of orders in the machine groups in the shop and assigning work loads to the various men and machines in their groups. If the decisions made by the simulation model are not satisfactory, corrective steps can be taken, such as modifying order priorities, until a satisfactory daily schedule is developed by the foreman.

A Monthly Load and Performance Summary Report, also produced by the computer system, gives information on actual performance of each machine group or work center in relation to schedule. Corrective action would be taken by the foremen or works manager as needed. For example, if the backlog of work for a given machine group indicated a continuing bottleneck problem, developing alternative routing might be considered to relieve the problem over the short-run, or hiring more men and buying more machines might be an alternative, if the problem appeared to be a longer-term one. This latter decision was usually made by the production planning and control manager.

Inventory Management:
The Handpower Company

The Handpower Company produces and sells a line of 1,000 power tools and accessories for the home workshop, as well as a line of 6,000 replacement parts, through four regional warehouses and fifty distributors and through direct contact with customers. Due to recurring production problems in the past, company management decided to develop a new inventory control system, which would be integrated with the production scheduling system.

Requirements of the System

Management wanted a system that would be able to:

1. Maintain inventory records.

2. Convert product schedules (supplied by production schedulers) into component part requirements by manufacturing cycle (five-day) time periods.

3. Measure requirements against on-hand, on-order, and reorder points for each inventory item to determine when manufacturing shop orders and purchase orders must be prepared to replenish inventory stocks.

4. Generate manufacturing shop orders and purchase requisitions in economical size lots by time period, indicating standard costs for all components.

5. Cancel and/or reschedule unreleased manufacturing or purchase orders.

6. Generate periodic management information reports on the status of inventories and orders for replenishing inventories.

7. Give immediate answers to questions about any item in inventory.

8. Revise economical order quantities and reorder points by constant evaluation of the factors involved in their calculation.

After analyzing available computer equipment and its ability to meet the management requirements listed above, a medium-size computer system with expandable random-access storage and on-line, real-time capabilities was ordered. The final processing system developed, which is described below, was dictated not only by management requirements, but also by the large number of company products, the homogeneity of production processes, the relatively short production cycle, and the relative stability of the product line.

Material Transactions and Inventory Records

Thirty-five types of material transactions are processed. These are generally classified as receipts, adjustments and issues, or shipments. These transactions are input into the system through punch cards.

For each of the 15,000 items (1,000 end products, 9,000 manufactured parts, and 5,000 purchased parts or raw materials), there are five 100-character records (Figure 9–4) on magnetic tape. The first two records store inventory data. As each material punched card is read, the inventory record for that item is selected and the on-hand, usage to date, or last activity is updated. The third record is the requirements record, which indicates the quantity required for each of twenty five-day manufacturing periods to replenish inventory stocks. The fourth record stores commitments (that is, the quantity to be ordered to cover requirements) by time period; since these commitments are for economical lot quantities, they will differ from requirement amounts. The fifth record is either a bill of material—that is, a list of component parts or subassemblies for end products (if the product is manufactured)—or released orders to a vendor (if the item is purchased).

FIGURE 9-4   Basic Records

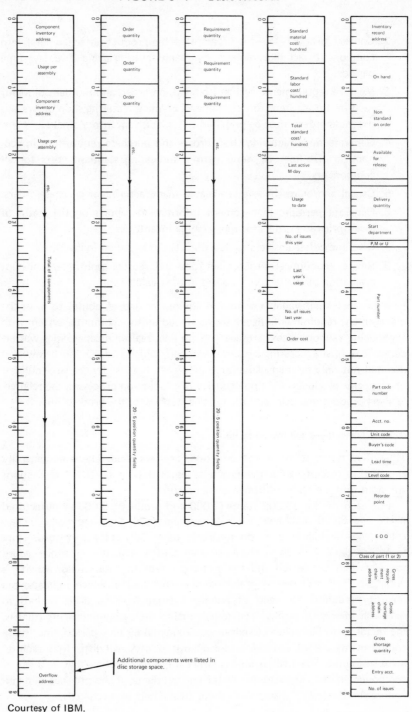

Courtesy of IBM.

Computer Processing

Sales forecasts are prepared by the sales department. The sales and production control departments working together determine the overall production schedule or schedule revisions (increases or decreases) by time period and by product (end product and replacement part). This schedule data is then entered into the computer periodically through punched cards.

As each schedule card is read by the computer, the computer finds the inventory record for the item and checks the on-hand and on-order (commitment) portion to determine whether there is enough stock to satisfy the schedule. If there is not, the computer determines the lead time needed to replenish stock and stores the quantity in the requirements record for release at the proper time. If the product has component parts, the computer examines the bill of material record to determine what component parts (and their quantity) are required to make the item. The computer then posts the quantity required of each component part or subassembly to the requirements record of the component part or subassembly by time period, taking into account the manufacturing lead time.

The computer system next determines the quantities that need to be ordered (commitments). The computer examines each item having changes in requirements to determine whether these items have sufficient inventory on hand or on order. If there is not sufficient inventory, an order is created in the economical lot quantity by the correct time period and stored in the order file. The same is done for the component parts or subassemblies of end products. As a by-product of this routine, various types of punched cards are created: for example, rush shop-order cards, when an item should have been started in production before the current manufacturing cycle (these cards are sent immediately to the production control department), and exception cards, when data is missing from the file.

The system is now prepared to issue manufacturing orders to the shop or purchase order requisitions for the coming five-day manufacturing cycle. When requested by the computer operator at five-day intervals, the computer examines the order (commitment) files of all items for the time period under study and does the following:

1. If the part is to be manufactured, a complete material requisition or a manufacturing shop order is printed indicating the part and quantity to be made, its components, parts and quantities, standard costs, and the start and finish manufacturing days. A commitment card is punched for each shop order and is placed in an off-line, open-order file. On completion of manufacturing it is reintroduced into the record to reduce the quantity on order and update inventory. Shortage cards are

punched for any component parts which are not in stock at the present time.

2. If the part is to be purchased, purchase requisition cards are punched and sent to the purchasing department. The computer also updates the "Released to Vendor" order record.

Management Information Reports

The data files described above are used to produce periodic management information reports on the status of inventory (Figure 9–5) and manufacturing shop orders. In addition, managers are able to make inquiries at any time about the status of any inventory item through the use of a computer terminal which is connected on-line to the random-access inventory file.

Materials Management: Bantom Pharmaceuticals Company

Bantom Pharmaceuticals Company manufactured and distributed over 500 different products, including drug extracts, vitamins, insect sprays, inorganic fertilizers, antibiotics, measles virus vaccines, and birth control drugs.[2] Consolidated sales last year were $172.5 million and net earnings $29.9 million. The company employed 13,000 persons in twenty-two domestic and foreign manufacturing facilities.

The Purchasing Department

The company's purchasing department was organized in four sections: purchasing of production materials (commodity chemicals, hormones, oils, acids, gases, etc.); purchasing of non-production materials (hardware supplies, graphic arts, animal cages, etc.); consolidated contract purchases; purchasing services. In all there were fourteen buyers, five managers, and thirty-two clerks and secretaries in the department. Annual purchases were $34.2 million for production materials and $14.1 million for non-production materials. A total of fifteen kinds of chemicals and other raw materials accounted for approximately 40 percent of dollar procurement volume. Over 99 percent of items received met purchasing's quality standards, and about 75 percent of deliveries were on time.

---

2. Adapted from Wilbur B. England, *Modern Procurement Management,* 5th ed. (Homewood, Illinois: Richard D. Irwin, Inc., 1970), pp. 218-244.

FIGURE 9-5

Inventory Stock Status Summary—
Requirements By Time Period

								Date			
								Period				
Part number	Part description	SCE	On hand	Transaction	1	2	3	4	5	6	Balance total
27057	Condenser	2	1200	Balance							1200
				required	400	410	420	450	410	420	2510—
				ordered					600		1200
				avail.	800	390	570	120	310	110—	110—
27058	Condenser	2	1500	Balance							1500
				required	450	480	500	500	510	520	2960—
				ordered			2000				2000
				avail.	1050	570	2070	1570	1060	540	540
27069	Plate	1	15000	Balance							15000
				required	310	350	400	300	350	300	2010—
				ordered				5000			5000
				avail.	14690	14340	13940	18640	18290	17990	17990

Courtesy of IBM.

The Purchasing System

Requisitions, which originated either from user departments or from inventory control (and so could be either manually prepared or computer printed), were first checked against inventories and then sent to buyers for review. Once the requisitions were approved and buying arrangements made, the requisitions were forwarded to the department's machine room, where IBM 632 electronic typing calculators were used to prepare most purchase orders. (Orders with lengthy specifications or unusual conditions were prepared manually; and orders against open purchase orders for non-production materials were prepared by computer, as described below.) After review and approval by the buyer, the completed purchase order was released and distributed as shown in Figure 9–6.

In addition to purchase orders, the IBM 632 also produced punched cards containing the data in the purchase order. These cards were sent to the central data processing division, where an open-order file was set up. When items were received, the receiving department forwarded one of its copies of the purchase order to data processing, where a receipt card was punched and matched against the open order file. If the order was incomplete, a new open-order file entry card for the balance was punched; if the order was complete, the receipt card and the original order card were stored for use in preparing the weekly purchasing follow-up report. The receipt copy of the purchase order was returned to the buyer, where it was matched against the buyer's open-order file of original purchase orders.

Management Information Reports

Every Wednesday, a comprehensive *Purchasing Follow-Up Report* was prepared for each buyer, which showed all on-order items for which data processing had not gotten a receiving report as of the preceding Friday. Since these reports were not current (receiving often took two days to forward their forms to data processing, so that the follow-up report could be as much as a week behind), they were updated manually by the buyer, based on information he received directly from the vendor. In addition, in many instances buyers got receipt information directly from the receiving department on important items. This updated report was then used by the buyer to follow-up on open orders.

Quarterly, data processing issued a *Vendor Performance Report,* which showed, for each vendor, summaries of purchase order activity, dollar commitments, and delivery performance for the year to date. Since these reports were used to evaluate a vendor's delivery performance, buyers made correc-

FIGURE 9–6

Purchasing Data Processing System—IBM 632 Procedure

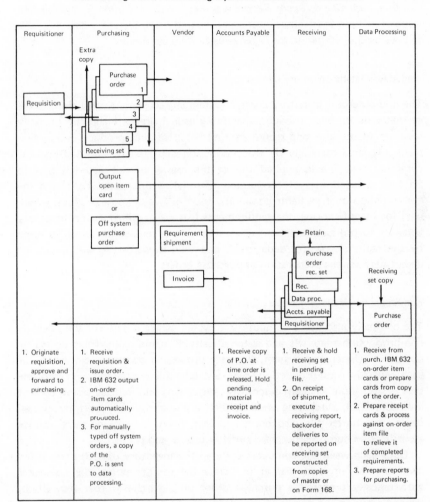

Requisitioner	Purchasing	Vendor	Accounts Payable	Receiving	Data Processing
1. Originate requisition, approve and forward to purchasing.	1. Receive requisition & issue order. 2. IBM 632 output on-order item cards automatically produced. 3. For manually typed off system orders, a copy of the P.O. is sent to data processing.		1. Receive copy of P.O. at time order is released. Hold pending material receipt and invoice.	1. Receive & hold receiving set in pending file. 2. On receipt of shipment, execute receiving report, backorder deliveries to be reported on receiving set constructed from copies of master or on Form 168.	1. Receive from purch. IBM 632 on-order item cards or prepare cards from copy of the order. 2. Prepare receipt cards & process against on-order item file to relieve it of completed requirements. 3. Prepare reports for purchasing.

tions on them where products were shipped on time and the delay was caused by in-transit problems. A *Buyer Performance Report* was issued monthly to purchasing managers, which showed the item, order, and dollar activity handled by each buyer and delivery performance for the items; this report was used for balancing work loads and evaluating buyer effectiveness in getting on-time delivery. A quarterly *Commodity Report* which showed the amount of each commodity purchased, distribution among vendors, and number of orders in relation to total volume, was used to study areas of greatest potential savings on volume purchases and bunching orders. A monthly *Cash Commitment Report* was used by the Treasurer in making cash forecasts. These four reports were all prepared using the same data files and sources used in preparing the *Purchasing Follow-Up Report.*

Production Material Inventory Control

The computerized inventory control system stored, among other things, bills of materials for each product, specifying each ingredient and the quantity required to produce one manufacturing batch of that product. Production plans, prepared manually by the production department, were fed into the computer system and applied against the master bills-of-materials tape to produce detailed lists of production material requirements. Following the consolidation of ingredients commonly used in two or more products scheduled for manufacturing, the requirements lists were applied against inventory balances to produce material requisitions. These requisitions were reviewed by the materials control department and then forwarded to the purchasing department for the preparation of purchase orders.

Non-Production Material Inventory Control

The company also had a computerized system which monitored the stores of non-production materials and automatically prepared replenishing orders by computer. Under this system, the data processing division maintained, for each repetitive non-production item, a master file containing such information as stock number, item description, dispensing unit, reorder point, current inventory level, purchasing unit, and delivery quantity. For most, but not all items, the master file also contained lead times in working days, vendor identification numbers, purchase order numbers, and prices.

Once each week the computer updated the inventory of each item. If the inventory of an item was at or below the reorder point, the computer automatically prepared a purchase order or a purchase order requisition, depending upon the degree of completeness of information in the master file. For items covered by blanket purchase orders, the computer prepared a purchase release order. Computer-printed purchase orders were sent out to vendors once a week, after being reviewed by buyers. If the information contained in the master file for an item to be ordered was incomplete, for example a missing vendor identification or missing price, the document generated by the computer served as a purchase requisition rather than a purchase order, and was handled like other purchase requisitions.

Areas of Possible Improvement

The purchasing manager felt that with the introduction of on-line computers and less expensive random-access computer storage, improvements in his information system were possible, especially in purchasing follow-up reporting. For example, a computer terminal could be set up in the receiving department where receipt information could be entered directly into the open-order file, which could be converted to random-access disc or drum storage. In this way, the weekly follow-up reports would be more current. In addition, inquiries could be made continually by buyers through a computer terminal placed in the purchasing department and hooked up on-line to the file.

He also felt it was possible to computerize the preparation of some of the purchase orders for production items (as had been done with the nonproduction items), though he realized that because of the size and complexity of the orders there were limitations on just how much computerization was possible in this area beyond requisition preparation. He had read that, in general, computer preparation of purchase orders was confined to large volume, low-priced items.

Plans also called for integrating the inventory and open-order files, once a new computerized open-order file had been established.

Quality Control:
General Dynamics Corporation

When the F-111 fighter program began in 1964, a quality control system for reporting and correcting product discrepancies was installed.[3] By the fall of 1968, it was evident from the problems being encountered that the initial quality control system was not effective.

To overcome the problems, a project was undertaken in October 1968 to modernize and upgrade quality assurance data collection and processing through adaptation of the latest electronic data processing facilities. The project was assigned to a task force of quality assurance and business data center personnel. After examining the weaknesses in the existing system and studying various alternatives, the team evolved a concept called PAAC (Product Assurance Action Center), that would consist of (1) a centralized staff of product-oriented, problem-solving quality control specialists operating from

---

3. J. Y. McClure, "General Dynamics PAAC Program: A Coalition of Minds and Machines for Quality," *Quality Progress* (Milwaukee, Wisconsin: The Quality Control Society), Feb. 1970, pp. 17-28.

a modern communications and display center, and (2) a decentralized on-line computer system for use of specialists, management and others who needed access to quality assurance information.

Figure 9–7 shows PAAC as conceived and visualized by the task force. The detailed plan for implementing PAAC was approved by Frank W. Davis, president of the Fort Worth Division, in December 1968. The steps in the time-phased plan were: redesign quality assurance forms; revise and coordinate operating procedures; determine equipment needs and place orders; activate the communications center; program the computer for input, update, and output; convert the old data bank to the new format; train some 1,500 employees in new procedures and techniques; hire and train thirty-three terminal operators; reassign and train quality assurance factory liason personnel; and obtain corporation and customer approvals.

Under the new system, remote computer terminals were located at selected points throughout the company's facilities. These terminals enabled the immediate processing of quality control data. The source of this data was a newly designed battery of quality control documents (forms) consisting of

FIGURE 9–7

Total PAAC Network

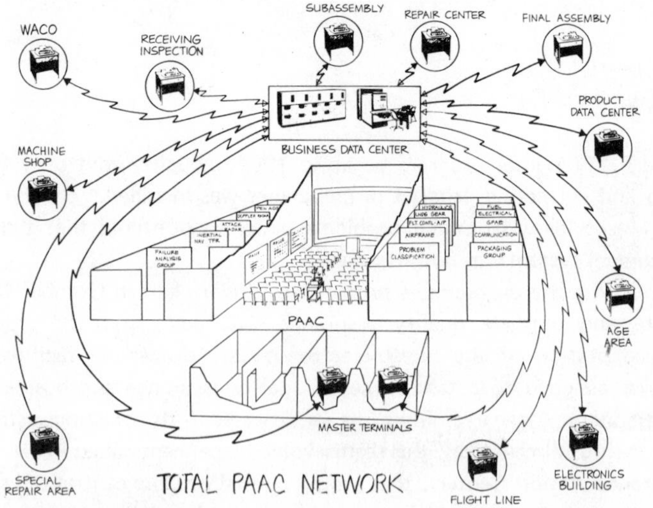

PAAC is the bringing together of many things: a problem-solving function, an advanced display center, an on-line computer system.

Reprinted by permission of the American Society for Quality Control, Inc., and J. Y. McClure, General Dynamics Corporation.

inspection completion orders, standard repair authorizations, quality assurance data reports, and discrepancy reports. Customer field complaints were also entered into the system by converting the complaints to parts failure and service difficulties reports. Examples of these input documents are shown in Figure 9–8

A PAAC liaison man was assigned to each remote terminal to monitor the data input, approve inquiries, and provide guidance in filling out documents. Under the new system, within minutes data is transmitted from the remote terminals, computer-edited upon input, and transferred to disc storage.

Inquiries for information are made through use of the Quality Inquiry Document (QID), which is shown in Figures 9–8 and 9–9. This document, which was a major innovation of PAAC, allows anyone with a basic knowledge of the quality control system and the production operation to construct questions in a format the computer will recognize and answer. An inquirer simply circles a few preprinted blocks on the QID, enters a data element or two, and presents the form to the terminal station specialist for input.

Four types of management information responses are provided by the new computer system: immediate, delayed, periodic, and automatic.

FIGURE 9–8

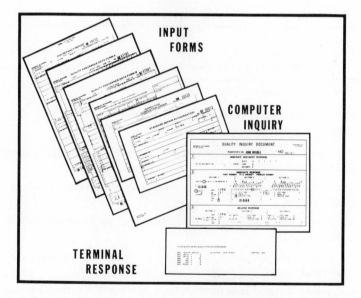

Reprinted by permission of the American Society for Quality Control, Inc., and J. Y. McClure, General Dynamics Corporation.

FIGURE 9–9

Quality Inquiry Document

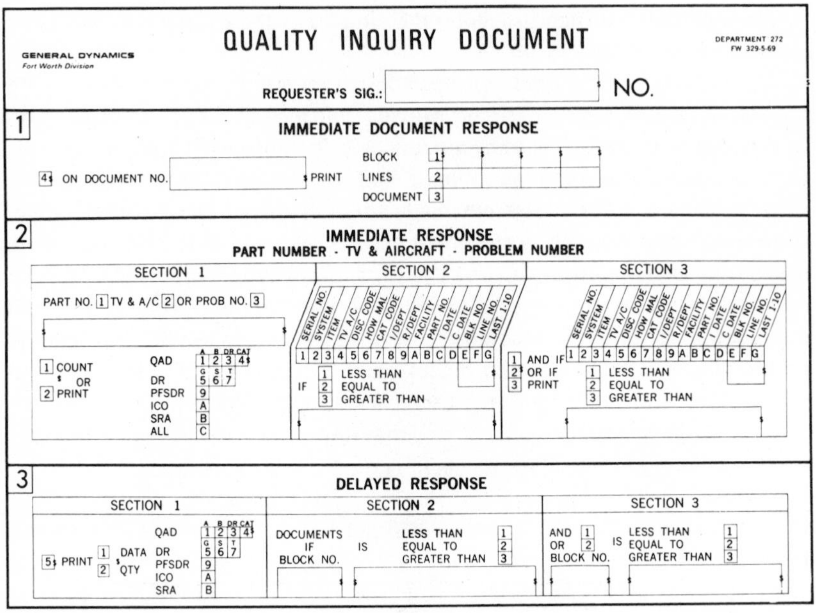

GENERAL DYNAMICS
Fort Worth Division

QUALITY INQUIRY DOCUMENT

DEPARTMENT 272
FW 329-5-69

REQUESTER'S SIG.: NO.

1 IMMEDIATE DOCUMENT RESPONSE

4 ON DOCUMENT NO. PRINT BLOCK 1 LINES 2 DOCUMENT 3

2 IMMEDIATE RESPONSE
PART NUMBER - TV & AIRCRAFT - PROBLEM NUMBER

SECTION 1: PART NO. 1 TV & A/C 2 OR PROB NO. 3
1 COUNT OR 2 PRINT
QAD 1 2 3 4 (A B DR CAT)
DR 5 6 7 (G S T)
PFSDR 9
ICO A
SRA B
ALL C

SECTION 2: SERIAL NO., SYSTEM, ITEM, TV A/C, DISC CODE, HOW MAL, CAT CODE, I/DEPT, R/DEPT, FACILITY, PART NO., I DATE, C DATE, BLK NO., LINE NO., LAST 1-10
1 2 3 4 5 6 7 8 9 A B C D E F G
IF 1 LESS THAN 2 EQUAL TO 3 GREATER THAN

SECTION 3: 1 AND IF 2 OR IF 3 PRINT
SERIAL NO., SYSTEM, ITEM, TV A/C, DISC CODE, HOW MAL, CAT CODE, I/DEPT, R/DEPT, FACILITY, PART NO., I DATE, C DATE, BLK NO., LINE NO., LAST 1-10
1 2 3 4 5 6 7 8 9 A B C D E F G
1 LESS THAN 2 EQUAL TO 3 GREATER THAN

3 DELAYED RESPONSE

SECTION 1: 5 PRINT 1 DATA 2 QTY
QAD 1 2 3 4 (A B DR CAT)
DR 5 6 7 (G S T)
PFSDR 9
ICO A
SRA B

SECTION 2: DOCUMENTS IF BLOCK NO. IS LESS THAN 1 EQUAL TO 2 GREATER THAN 3

SECTION 3: AND 1 OR 2 BLOCK NO. IS LESS THAN 1 EQUAL TO 2 GREATER THAN 3

Reprinted by permission of the American Society for Quality Control, Inc., and J. Y. McClure, General Dynamics Corporation.

Immediate responses, which make the computer system seem conversational, answer such frequently asked questions as:

—How many rejections are open against airplane XXX? Identify them and print their status.

—What is the name of the inspector who accepted standard repair number XXX?

—Have there been customer complaints against part number XXX in the last sixty days?

—How many rejections were charged to my department Friday? What are the accrued rework and scrap costs on the rejections?

—What repair method was used on part number XXX that was rejected about three months ago?

As for delayed responses, the computer is programmed to handle complex and non-routine questions overnight. Inquiries are made by filling out Section

3 of the QID (Figure 9–9). Answers to these queries usually involve considerable printing time and, therefore, are serviced overnight at the computer center on a highspeed printer.

The computer is also programmed to issue periodic reports. Microfilm indexes, supplier quality ratings, departmental and division quality performance reports, and aircraft malfunction summaries are examples of the routine reports printed by the computer. Figure 9–10 gives an example of a weekly report on recurring conditions produced by the system.

In addition, the computer is programmed to provide automatic, or bell ringer responses. This printout is received in PAAC headquarters on an unattended terminal. The computer continuously compiles and scans information on part numbers and discrepancies. When two like discrepancies are recorded on a part number within thirty days, preselected data on the discrepancy is printed out. When the discrepancy falls within prescribed parameters, rejection data for all defects reported during the prior thirty days for the part is included in the printout. High cost rejections also are selected for automatic printout.

This data alerts the PAAC problem specialists to a recurring problem and investigation is initiated to determine what action is necessary. Management is thus kept constantly alert to problems or potential problems as they develop through these automatic responses.

Maintenance Management: Port Authority of New York

The Port of New York Authority runs a combined transportation system for New York, New Jersey, and Connecticut.[4] Its areas of responsibilities cover: piers and warehouses for shipping; flight operations for the airports— including control towers, rescue units, access roads, runways, fuel facilities, restaurants, and security operations; rail facilities—including trains, stations, and road beds; and highway facilities—including bridges and tunnels.

Since so many commuters depend on the reliable operation of these systems, the maintenance department of the Port Authority is a key operation. The following is a brief description of the information system used in planning and controlling the Port Authority's maintenance activities.

The maintenance department is organized into four separate sections, one for each method of transportation: water, air, rail, and highway. The maintenance sections are located at various maintenance depots (called maintenance units) throughout the metropolitan area. Within each maintenance unit,

---

4. E. J. Miller and J. W. Blood, *Modern Maintenance Management* (New York: American Management Association, 1963), pp. 109-121.

FIGURE 9–10

Weekly Computer Report on Recurring Conditions

Recurring Conditions Report

Week ending XXX

Department Resp.	Orig.	Part No.	Disc code H/M code	Cause op. stp.	Operation number	P/A status	Doc. no.	Initiation date	Problem number
030	030	12A14501-101	HLELG	020		9	DG90123	30 08 69	
030	033	12A12501-101	HLELG	020		9	DG31129	25 08 69	
030	078	12A12501-101	HLELG	025		0	DF80981	27 08 69	
150	150	12L560-1	CNINR	045	2610	0	DF50126	29 08 69	3500-006
150	156	12L560-1	CNINR	045	2610	0	DF49988	02 08 69	3500-006
150	156	12L560-1	CNINR	055	2610	9	DF50012	15 08 69	
VEND	175	342665	290			—	BC60006	30 08 69	
VEND	175	342665	290			—	BC59680	24 08 69	
VEND	175	342665	290			—	BC58995	17 08 69	
VEND	175	342665	290			—	BC58601	15 08 6	
VEND	178	342665	290			—			
VEND	178	342665	290						
VEND	178	342							

① ② ③ ④ ⑤ ⑥

SORT SEQUENCES

Purpose

This comprehensive tabulation report is compiled weekly against all recurring conditions during the past 90 days as a "fail safe" double check against daily bell ringers occurring in PAAC.

328

operations are subdivided into craft or specialty groups (electrical, mechanical, and the like). A supervisor is in charge of each depot and each craft group has a foreman.

The basic document used in planning maintenance work is the *Roster of Routine Maintenance Jobs,* a segment of which is shown in Figure 9–11. This roster is prepared quarterly by the data processing department, based on a master file of routine jobs they maintain and update continually. These rosters list all jobs of a routine nature which are performed within the shop, building, or facility. Copies of those sections of the quarterly roster applicable to each craft group are distributed to the responsible foremen. These rosters enable foremen to make manpower, parts, and equipment plans for their operations.

The master file of routine jobs to be performed is also used to prepare a *Daily Schedule of Maintenance Work,* a segment of which is shown in Figure 9–12, and routine job work orders. These schedules and work orders are produced by the data processing department for a week at a time and sent to each craft foreman in advance so that he can plan his work for the coming week. The daily schedule is used as a guide by the foreman for assigning his men. At times, however, the routine work must be delayed until completion of an emergency work order.

Non-routine maintenance work is handled through a non-routine work order (Figure 9–13). The non-routine maintenance work order (a four-part, snap-out form) is a combination request for work and a work order control mechanism. When non-routine maintenance work is required, the requesting department completes the form and describes the work required. The last copy is retained by the department requesting the work and the other three copies are sent to the supervisor in charge of the maintenance depot for that area. The supervisor reviews the requests and designates the craft group required to complete the work. A copy is sent to the craft foreman, and the other two copies are retained by the supervisor's clerical office. The foreman estimates labor hours and material costs for the job and returns his copy to the clerical office. If the supervisor approves the estimate, copies of the work order are returned to the foreman and forwarded to the data processing department with the estimates included.

A timekeeping system is used to provide feedback of performance data. A maintenance time card (Figure 9–14) is prepared for each employee for each day of the year. At the end of each day, each employee returns to the maintenance unit to complete his time card. He enters the work order numbers, the time spent on each job, and the status of the completion of each. All work orders, whether completed or not, are returned with the time cards to the supervisor's clerical section. The clerical office examines all time cards and completed work orders received from the employees to determine

FIGURE 9-11
Roster of Routine Maintenance Jobs

Date	Routine job no.	Description	Equip. record no.	Area and location	Accounting code	Craft	No. men	Month(s)	Freq. code	Freq.	Man hours per Week	Man hours per Month	Man hours per Year	Weather	F/P
10/–	3001	Check toll sheets and service equipment.	-	N.J. plaza	35-208	Elec I	1	All	(1) W-7	2	14		730	Any	7
8/–	3002	1. Check "Parcoa" gates for proper operation—report any repairs necessary. 2. Check batteries and charger in switch houses #1 and #2.	-	Various	35-774.132	Elecl	1	All	(1) W-7	4	28		1460	Good	7
5/–	3003	Check circuits on public address system; check "mikes" for operation and damage.	102	Main lobby bldg 10	35-611	Elec I	1	All	(2) M-24	3		6	72	Good	2
10/–	3004	Group Relamp 11 single fixture light poles beside and behind Bldg. 10.	-	Service roads bldg. 10	35-314	T.H.E. / Elec I	2 / 1	1	(8) 2Y-E	8 / 4		8 / 4	8 / 4	Good	1
10/–	3005	Group relamp 10 street lamps along back entrance to storage area.	-	Service roads bldg 84	35-317	T.H.E. / Elec I	2 / 1	1	(9) 2Y-0	8 / 4		8 / 4	8 / 4	Good	1
6/–	3006	Wipe clean and spot relamp all flight board panels. (Bring a box of #24-E and a box of 7.5W, 110W).	-	Main bldg.	7-235	T.H.E. / Elec I	1 / 1	1,4,7, 10	(2) Y-4	4 / 4		4 / 4	16 / 16	Any	1
6/–	3007	Overhead doors—check operation, clean and lubricate control unit.	149 / 150	Ground floor bldg. 30 P.E.G.	35-634	T.H.E. / Elec I	3	All	(1) W-7	3 / 1	21 / 7		1095 / 365	Good	7

330

FIGURE 9–12

Daily Schedule of Maintenance Work

Day _____
Date _____

Group _____

Shift	Order no.	Description of work	Location	Craftsmen assigned	Use vehicle no.	Approx. starting time	Est. hrs.	For foreman's use			Reason for delay
								Status-end of shift			
								Run	Compl.		
1	4000	Check toll sheets and service equipment	N.J. plaza	E II (1) <u>Pico</u>	—	8:00 A.M.			✓		
1	4007	Service & lubricate C O recorders	N.J. vent bldg.	E II (1) <u>Brown</u> T.H.E. (2) Able, Baker	—	8:00 A.M.			✓		
1	4008	Spot relamp public stairways	Main lobby building 63	E II (1) <u>Pico</u> E.1 (1) Smith	718	10:00 A.M.			✓		
		Service all overheight		Smith		12:30 P.M.					*supersded by* 1-830190
1	4001	Indicators	Bldg. #10	Baker, Able	—	12:30 P.M.					
1	4010	Inspect emergency generator #201	Bldg. #10	~~Brown~~ <u>Knott</u>	—	12:30 P.M.			✓		*Brown re-assigned to* 1-820360
1	2-819660	Clean and repair contacts in square "D" aux. circuit breaker	Bldg. #12	<u>Smith</u>	—	8:00 A.M.		✓			

FIGURE 9–12 (Continued)

1	1-820020	Replace armature in aux. motor #514	Bldg. #12 Room 401	Jones Knott	710	8:00 A.M.			✓
1	1-820360	Repair railroad gate	Service road "B"	~~Pico~~ Brown ~~Jones~~ Able	710	12:30 P.M.			✓
1	1-819630	Replace defective switch	Control office bldg. #63	Brown Knott	—	2:00 P.M.			superseded by 1-830160
	1-830160	REPAIR DEFECTIVE HEATER	BOOTH #10	PICO JONES		12:30 P.M.		✓	
	1-830190	TRAFFIC SIGNALS DO NOT RESET	SECTION N-3 NORTH TUBE	SMITH BAKER	—	12:30 P.M.			✓
		R.D.O. English, Foote							

Reprinted by permission of the publisher from AMA Management Report No. 77, *Modern Maintenance Management.* © 1963 by the American Management Association, Inc.

FIGURE 9–13

Maintenance Work Order—Nonroutine

Craft group
code no. |3|1| No. /123456

1. Location of job _shell station on conduit_	2. Requested by date _1-15-62_ M. McMahon	Pro. _A3_	Orgn. _3,4_	Act. _23_	Area and/or job. no. _332_

3. Description of job _CLEAN AREA OF DEBRIS- INSIDE & OUTSIDE OF FENCE AREA. FIRE HAZARD & BOULDERS IN WAY OF CUTTING EQUIPMENT._

Was this job started prior to the preparation of the request? _No_ If this work was previously requested indicate w.o. no. _No_

Foreman's comments and material requirements

|C|L|E|A|N| |A|R|E|A| |O|F| |D|E|B|R|I|S| |V|I|C|I|N|I|T|Y|
|S|H|F|I|L|L| |S|T|A|T|I|O|N| |F|I|R|E| |H|A|Z|A|R|D|

4. Urgency*	Starting date	Names of men assigned	Craft title	Class spec no.	For office use	
					Est.	Actual hours
			GARD.	2020	56	
			T.H.(GARD)	2005	56	
			T. LAB.	2000	112	

Aviation Dept. T&B Dept.
Mar. Term Dept. ☐ Emergency
Terminals Dept. ☐ Contingency
☐ Emergency ☐ Complete
☐ Rush by _/ /_
☑ Non-rush ☐ No Priority

6. Equip. no.	Copy no.	Estimated by	No. approved
	2	_EwS_	

Work order no.

5. Type work**
☐ Tenant Property
/ 123456 ☐ 30 service ☐ 31 damage ☑ Other _36_

123456

Originator—complete items 1 to 6. Retain copy #4 and forward remaining copies to Maintenance Scheduler.
* Emergency jobs are repairs of major importance involving grave hazards to life and property.
** Type Work—if work required is not "tenant service" or "property damage," select the appropriate classification from the following list and insert the code number after "other."
32. Repair thru Insp.; 33. Breakdown; 34. Alteration; 36. Rehabilitation; 37. Support to other department; 36. Support to contractor;
39. V.I.P. or special event; 40. Other

Reprinted by permission of the publisher from AMA Management Report No. 77, *Modern Maintenance Management.* © 1963 by the American Management Association, Inc.

FIGURE 9–14

Maintenance Time Card

Name	Class Code	Org.	Employee No.	Hrly. Rate	Status
G. Davy	2160	204	3013		1

Time	Date	Time	Date
8:00 ☑AM ☐PM	9/20/73	☐AM ☑PM 6:30	9/20/73

0 Admin. ☐ 1 Elec. ☑ 2 Mech. ☐ 3 Struct. ☐ 4 C.H. & R.P. ☐
5 Gen'l ☐ 6 Oper. ☐ ☐ ☐

Description	Work Order Number
Authorized absence (use last digit)*	
Personal (Non-essential) excused time	500001
Essential excused time	500002
Death in family	500003
Sick	500004
Injured on duty	500005
Vacation	500006
Short term military leave	500007
Jury duty	500008
Meetings, lectures, seminars, etc.	540000
Medical	550000
Examinations, interviews, etc.	560000

Work Order Number	Hours	Fin	Open	Work Order Number	Hours	Fin	Open
3.007	1	✓		Comp. time off 521000		X	X
2-560111	3	✓		Authorized absence* 50000		X	X
1-155036	3		✓	RDO 610000		X	X
1-157830	3	✓		Holiday 610001		X	X
				Total hours	10	X	X
				Overtime hours 51001	2	X	X
				Holiday work 510002		X	X
				Holiday excess 510003		X	X
				Comp. time earned 522000		X	X

Signed G. Davy
Employee

Approved MR
Foreman

Reprinted by permission of the publisher from AMA Management Report No. 77, *Modern Maintenance Management*. © 1963 whether all pertinent data has been entered. On the following day, the time cards are batched by craft groups and along with completed work orders are sent to the data processing department for processing.

The data on the time cards and work orders is used in conjunction with schedule data to prepare a routine maintenance job analysis report. The data in this monthly report is grouped by maintenance unit, and by craft group within each maintenance unit. The report lists each routine job and compares actual performance to planned performance (both man hours and material costs); comparative summaries are also given. This report is used by the section supervisors and craft foremen both to determine if adjustments are needed in the preventive maintenance program schedule and to evaluate the performance of maintenance sections and craft groups.

Two reports on non-routine work orders (one on completed work and one on non-completed work) are prepared by the data processing department monthly and distributed to the maintenance manager, supervisors, and foremen. The *Completed Non-Routine Work Order Report* (by maintenance unit and craft group) compares estimated hours (foremen make these estimates) to actual hours, as well as estimated material costs to actual material costs. This report enables supervisors to evaluate both the performance of craft personnel and the ability of foremen to estimate jobs accurately. The *Schedule of Non-Completed Non-Routine Work Orders* lists all non-completed jobs, the date of request, the foreman, the maintenance unit, and a job description. Using this report, the supervisor examines specific jobs and verifies their need, eliminates duplicate requests for work, and (where possible) shifts manpower with specific skills between craft groups and assigns them to areas which have accumulated a comparatively high backlog. When trends show that the work load is building up in an area requiring specialized skills, management may also decide to hire additional personnel or contract the work out to reduce the backlog.

Facilities Management:
Condor Foods Corporation

Condor Foods Corporation, one of the nation's largest producers of packaged convenience foods, was formed by a series of consolidations and acquisitions dating back to 1925.[5] The company now has sales in excess of $1 billion, 30,000 employees, and sixty plants located throughout the world. Its Joy Division is one of the company's largest United States operating divisions.

All of the Joy division's five plants had been built prior to 1920 and although extensive improvements and alterations had been made to the

---

5. Adapted from Edmund S. Whitman and W. James Schmidt, *Plant Relocation* (New York: American Management Association, 1966).

plants, they were still old and outmoded; and none of them was at a location chosen by Condor management. Thus, the Joy division was faced with the problem of accommodating a growing dynamic business, which over the years had been crowded bit by bit into existing plants.

In early 1960, a task force was set up to study the possibility of new plant construction for the Joy division. It was composed of one man from each of Joy division's major operating areas, one from the division's controller's office, and one from the corporate manufacturing and engineering area. All were under the supervision of the Director, Facilities Planning. The first job of the task force was to formulate overall objectives, the most significant of which was a recommendation to consolidate as many as possible of Joy's production operations in a single new and enlarged facility.

The task force study of how to achieve this objective was conducted in six phases: analyses of transportation costs; general estimates of construction costs for new facilities; estimates of overhead staffing of new facilities; comparisons of direct costs at new facilities and existing ones; estimates of shutdown, employee termination and start-up costs; and projections of profits and losses under the various alternatives explored. Based on these analyses, which were done for a wide range of alternative plant combinations and locations, it was determined that four of Joy's five plants (excluding Chicago) should be consolidated into a single East Coast facility.

Condor's management agreed with the conclusions of this preliminary study, and a program was outlined for carrying the work forward through construction of the new plant, shutdown of the old plants, and startup of the consolidated facility:

Phase I. Savings and cost verification. Doing only that work necessary to justify or reject a recommendation for building a new Eastern plant consolidating the Hoboken, Dorchester, LeRoy, and Orange operations and, if indicated, obtaining board approval of required funds for preliminary engineering.

Phase II. Preliminary engineering. Doing all engineering work necessary to finalize costs and savings, identify and institute new equipment developments, undertake site selection, and obtain approval for final engineering.

Phase III. Final engineering and appropriation request. Doing all engineering work for the complete facility and preparing an appropriation request.

Phase IV. Construction. Building the facility according to developed specifications and within approved time and budget and developing the final scheduling required for facility startup.

Phase V. Shutdown and startup. Transferring production from existing lines to a new facility with a minimum of lost efficiency and according to developed schedules so that no out-of-stock situations occur.

The following steps were taken as part of Phase I:

1. Develop preliminary general plant layout on the basis of using only proven equipment (new equipment developments would be taken into consideration in Phase II).
2. Develop manning tables and an administrative organization plan to establish overhead savings.
3. Re-estimate construction costs.
4. Determine what improvements could be made at existing locations.
5. Compare costs and savings of new facility with the best that could be done at existing facilities and calculate payback.
6. Develop time schedules.

The corporate engineering department prepared these studies. Additional financial analyses were also prepared for the task force, based on these engineering studies. Six months were required to complete Phase I. The task force then submitted the information reports developed for Phase I to Joy division's operating manager who, with the general manager, reported the findings to Condor's operating policy committee. After studying these reports, Condor management authorized funds for preliminary engineering and site selection studies, Phase II of the program.

The site selection study was done by an outside consulting firm. They considered such factors as freight costs, raw materials supplies, availability of transportation, wage and salary levels, availability of manpower, living conditions in the area, local taxes, land and construction costs, and the like. The consulting firm concluded that a location in the Mid-Atlantic area would be best, and recommended a site in Granger, Delaware as the best one. A consulting firm specializing in survey research was then hired to study both the attitudes of the community residents in the Granger area and the availability of skilled labor. This firm's report was also favorable, and Condor's management decided on the Granger site.

During this period, work was also started on preliminary engineering studies for the plant itself. Flow sheets were prepared for all the processing and packaging lines in the four old plants. Plant managers were asked to supply detailed lists of all old equipment, as well as suggested new equipment. However, the basic objective remained to move as much as possible of the existing equipment from the old plants to the new one. Preliminary equipment layouts were prepared based upon the flow sheets and minimum manpower requirements established. From these the shape and size of the various sections of the building were determined.

A partial list of the kinds of studies and reports conducted and prepared during this phase and Phase III was given in the final section of Chapter Eight.

They ranged from equipment and process layouts to scale models showing the entire plant and its equipment. An outside engineering firm was hired to assist the corporate engineering department during Phases II and III.

Several presentations were made to Condor management during this period, some showing models of alternative new plants and some covering cost projections and comparisons. One of these presentations involved increased costs, which management approved. After nine months of design and engineering study, Condor management approved the final new plant design and layout. The building was to be a single-story structure, with few columns and servicing equipment installed in overhead trusses; such a design permitted uniform illumination, greater flexibility—since expansion was possible by simply moving a wall—more efficient handling and routing of materials, and easier supervision.

Construction of the plant was then begun. Bids were solicited at the beginning of Phase IV and reviewed, and a contractor selected with the approval of corporate management. Since Joy's business was a dynamic one, many changes were made during both the planning and construction phases to accommodate changes in business conditions and so to have the most up-to-date facilities possible.

In planning and controlling Phases IV and V, management relied on network planning tools and control reports on both activities and costs. A detailed description of these kinds of information systems is given in Chapter Four.

While not all of the information systems used in planning and completing the new plant at Condor Foods have been covered, the description does give some idea of the enormous amount of information needed at both the corporate management and operating management levels in facilities management situations. Although such information systems differ markedly from those found in other operations areas, such as inventory management, they are developed in much the same way as other operations management information systems. Management information needs are first defined by identifying key situation factors; specific information requirements and reporting systems are then outlined in detail, and the information gathered systematically from the appropriate sources. In this sense, then, information systems such as the one described at Condor Foods Corporation can be considered another operations management information system.

Summary
Conclusion

As in the marketing and financial areas, the resolution of the management information systems problems presented in this chapter followed the basic systems approach presented in Chapter Two:

1. Defining the objective of the development effort.
2. Identifying such key factors as:
   a. Nature of the company's business and overall company plans.
   b. Nature and organization of the operations function under study.
   c. Management decisions and tasks, and the information needed to make these decisions and carry out these tasks.
   d. Existing information and data processing systems, and strengths and weaknesses.
   e. Organizational and personnel factors affecting system development, implementation and use.
3. System development.
4. Implementation and use of the system developed.

The different examples described in the text illustrate the variety of ways in which the overall systems approach is used in the many operations areas found in business today. The examples also showed how some of the systems tools described in Chapter Eight are used in actual work situations.

The case study exercises which follow are designed to give the reader practice in putting these tools and the systems approach to work in the different operations areas covered in this chapter and in Chapter Eight.

Case Study Exercises

Supreme Gear Manufacturing Company

Supreme Gear Manufacturing Company is a medium-size manufacturer of high-quality gears ranging in size from less than one inch to about four feet in diameter. Most of the gears are made from forgings purchased from outside suppliers or provided by customers, and only a small percent are made from bar stock.

Depending on the gear and its complexity, between seven and fifty operations may be required on different machines. These operations include cleaning, sizing and shaping, heat-treating the raw materials, cutting and grinding gear teeth, final heat-treatment, and drilling and finishing to obtain the desired characteristics. Each of these operations is organized in a different work center headed by a foreman. For example, the drill shop foreman is responsible for all drilling operations on all products and orders. Orders vary from one to 5,000 pieces, with a large number of orders in the 50- to 300-piece range.

The company has a relatively large number of customers and a shifting mix of orders. Technical quality and on-time delivery are important factors in making a sale. The company has been experiencing severe competition for the last couple of years and lost approximately 2 percent of its share of the market last year. The plant now operates three shifts a day, seven days a week.

The plant manager, David Coffee, reports to the manufacturing vice president. The works manager, Norman Peabody, who is responsible for production scheduling and control, and a staff analyst, Bob Davidson, who is responsible for installing or upgrading production systems, both report to the plant manager. The shop foremen report to the works manager and are responsible for day-to-day scheduling and control of the operations within their work centers.

Based on the company's sales estimates for the coming year, each fall the plant manager (in conjunction with the works manager) prepares a forecast of production requirements for the coming year, a portion of which is shown in Figure 9–15. Once the forecast is approved by the manufacturing vice president, it is the works manager's responsibility to see that the production requirements forecast are met. Each quarter the works manager prepares a detailed master schedule by product order for each of the next three months. Each week, the shop foremen submit detailed forecasts for the coming week for their respective work areas based on the master schedule (adjusted for changes that occurred). The works manager helps the foremen work out the

FIGURE 9–15

Production Requirements Forecast

Month	Forecasted units	Forecasted annualized cost—$	Production days	Cumulative days
Jan.	325	157,000	22	22
Feb.	440	212,000	18	40
Mar.	580	278,000	22	62
Apr.	450	223,000	21	83
May	.	.	.	.
Jun.	.	.	.	.
Jul.	.	.	.	.
Aug.	.	.	.	.
Sep.				
Oct.				
Nov.				
Dec.				

sequencing of orders in each shop and coordinates the movement of orders between the work centers.

The shop foremen use Gantt charts to translate the detailed weekly forecasts into specific weekly machine and operator load schedules; a portion of one of them is shown in Figure 9–16. The foremen also maintain order backlog records on each machine in their shop. Whenever bottleneck problems develop, the shop foreman uses his own judgment to develop alternative routing or sequencing to relieve the immediate problem. Under the present scheduling system, promised delivery dates are often missed.

After receiving several complaints from the sales vice president and losing a good customer because of late deliveries, David Coffee, the plant manager, asked Bob Davidson, the staff analyst, to check out the latest delivery complaint from Lawrence Manufacturing Company to determine the cause of

FIGURE 9–16

Gantt Chart for Loading

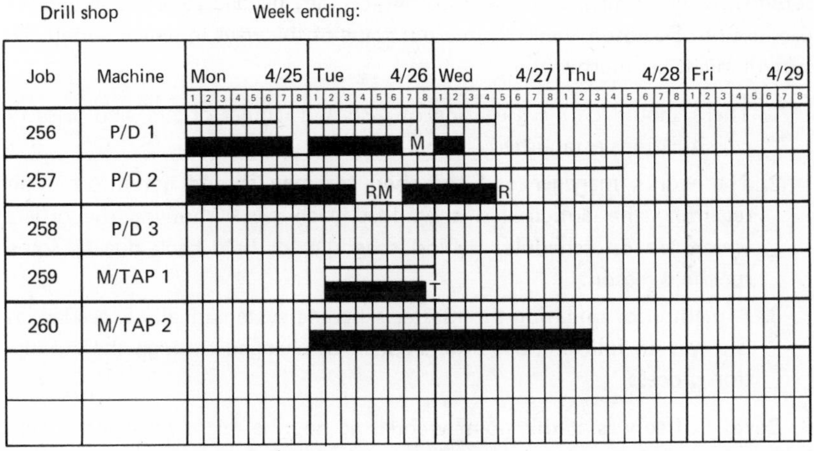

Drill shop   Week ending:

Job	Machine	Mon 4/25	Tue 4/26	Wed 4/27	Thu 4/28	Fri 4/29
256	P/D 1		M			
257	P/D 2	RM	R			
258	P/D 3					
259	M/TAP 1		T			
260	M/TAP 2					

Denotes time when work is supposed to begin.

Denotes time when work is supposed to end.

Indicates planned work.
Indicates actual work.

Following abbreviations used in case of discrepancies between actual and planned work:

A — Operator absent
I — Instruction lacking   R — Machine or tool in need of repairs
L — Slow operator   T — Tools inadequate
M — Hold up due to lack of materials   V — Holidays

it and suggest ways to improve the situation. The following is a summary of the results of Davidson's investigation:

> When I found the parts for Lawrence in the finished goods storeroom, I also discovered that there were only 6,000 of them, even though the master schedule showed that there should be 8,000. They were being held until the remaining 2,000 pieces were finished. Norman phoned Ralph Bergstrom, the finishing department foreman, who didn't know where the unfinished order was. They finally discovered that the drillers had drilled only 6,000 of the order; the other 2,000 milled castings were found in the milling center waiting for somebody to pick them up for delivery to the drilling center. When asked for an explanation, Tom Sullivan, the drill shop foreman, said that he had to leave the job incomplete because he received orders from Norman to start drilling on another job which had been given a rush classification by Jim Nichols, the sales manager.

While discussing his report with David Coffee, Davidson pointed out that the basic problem was in the production scheduling and control system. Under the present system, according to Davidson, neither Norman nor the foremen received all the critical information they needed to plan and control production. Davidson then pointed out some of the ways in which he felt the system might be improved:

1. There should be a segregation of rush and regular orders, and priority classifications established.
2. The works manager and the shop foremen should get information regarding the anticipated shop load each week showing the orders which are on schedule, behind schedule, or held back due to some specified reason.
3. A method of updating the master schedule systematically is needed, as is a way to follow those orders added or changed through the production process.

David Coffee was at this point wondering how he might most effectively follow up on Bob Davidson's suggestions.

Assignment

1. Describe the work situation and identify the factors which are relevant to production scheduling and control in this company.
2. Draw an organization chart for the production area. Describe the responsibilities of and decisions made by the works manager and the shop foremen. What kinds of information do they need to make these decisions?
3. Comment on the present production scheduling and control system in light of the information needs defined in your answer to question 2.

4. In light of your analysis of the existing situation and information needs, what kind of production scheduling and control information system would best provide management with the information they need for planning and controlling production? Comment on Bob Davidson's suggestions in making your recommendations.

Meany Motors, Inc.

Over the years the auto repair business at Meany Motors (a new car dealer) had increased substantially; last year, repair billings amount to 22 percent of total sales. The garage crew consisted of a foreman and fifteen mechanics (at this time, additional part-time mechanics were employed).

Mr. Meany, the owner, personally managed used car sales and the repair service, and had a policy of giving customers the best service in town. As part of his cost control program for the coming year, Mr. Meany was currently studying what might be done to reduce his spare parts inventory without reducing customer service performance standards.

At the suggestion of a friend, Mr. Meany (with the help of his friend) experimented with economic order quantity (EOQ) purchasing techniques, using an adaptation of the EOQ formula described in the text of Chapter Eight:

$$EOQ = \sqrt{\frac{2UO}{IC}}$$

In this formula, U stands for annual unit usage, O for the ordering costs, I for inventory carrying costs, and C for unit cost. The formula, he learned, would give the minimum total inventory costs. Mr. Meany also learned that a resonably accurate estimate (not precise figures) was all that was required.

Mr. Meany started with the largest single inventory item, Part P—1, of which there was now $9,500 in inventory (total spare parts inventory was $200,000, which, as his friend indicated, was about 50 percent higher than seemed to be needed for the repair business done by Meany). It took Mr. Meany considerable time to estimate ordering costs and inventory carrying costs, since many parts were ordered in one purchase order, so that their costs, as well as such general expenses as light, heat, taxes and salaries, had to be allocated to Part P—1. He arrived at $5.00 average order cost and $.20 inventory carrying cost. The cost of the part, $25, he took from the latest invoices, and his parts manager estimated that 200 units would be used in the coming year, based on last year's usage and expected increases in business this year. He then calculated the EOQ for Part P—1:

$$\sqrt{\frac{2 \times 200 \times \$5}{\$.20 \times \$25}} = \sqrt{\frac{2000}{5}} = \sqrt{400} = 20$$

Since orders were filled within one week by the supplier, Mr. Meany figured that if he reordered Part P–1 every time the inventory dropped below twenty (about a five-week supply) he would never be out of stock, since usage was fairly steady over the year and orders were usually processed by his accountant once each week.

He had hoped to develop a simple inventory system, whereby an inventory card would be kept on each part. This card would carry an EOQ that would serve as a reorder point. Each time the parts manager gave out a part or received a parts order he would record it on the appropriate card. During the day, he would set aside the cards of those parts which fell below the reorder point when he posted usage. Each morning the accountant would make a list of parts needed for ordering and return the cards to the parts manager. While he saw this would be an effective system, Mr. Meany felt that the time involved in calculating the EOQ's and posting the cards would be excessive, since he carried over 1,000 items in inventory.

Mr. Meany was wondering what to do at this point.

Assignment

1. Analyze the inventory situation. For example, how long will the supply of Part P–1 last? In what condition is the inventory overall if Part P–1 is representative of all parts in inventory?

2. Is Mr. Meany's problem one of deciding on whether or not to use a somewhat sophisticated and time-consuming technique like EOQ? Or, is there a more basic inventory problem?

3. What key decisions are made in inventory management and what key information is needed at Meany Motors in making these decisions?

4. In light of your analysis of the inventory situation and the company organization, manpower and financial capabilities, what kind of system would best provide management with the information it needs for managing inventory?

Mickle Aircraft Company

The Mickle Aircraft Company was one of the foremost producers of components parts for jet aircraft engines.[6] Because of the complex technical nature of the work and close tolerances required, the engineering department (in-

---

6. Adapted from England, *Modern Procurement Management*, pp. 330-335.

cluding quality control) was highly influential in decisions made in all operating areas, including purchasing.

The Purchasing Department's Role

When a part was scheduled for production, the engineering department forwarded part drawings and specifications to the production control department, including definitions of what types of material must be used, how the material should be treated, what manufacturing processes should be used, and what inspection procedures should be followed. Production control and the purchasing department reviewed this data and determined whether each part should be manufactured by Mickle or purchased from outside suppliers. For those parts to be purchased, production control drew up a purchase requisition and designated the quantity and delivery dates required. The requisition, part drawings, and specifications were then forwarded to the purchasing department.

When a buyer received a requisition, he usually solicited bids from at least three suppliers. When the bids were returned, the buyer awarded the contract to the supplier that presented the best combination of price, delivery, and quality. The buyer was usually also responsible for insuring that the supplier met quality, performance, and delivery requirements.

In the past, contracts had been amended occasionally by the quality control department with more restrictive material or production process specifications after the order had been awarded. These revisions resulted from occasional mistakes by the engineers, weaknesses uncovered in investigating preproduction samples, or the desire of quality control for more restrictive specifications than those designated by the design engineers.

Increasing Problems

Recently, the number of such changes had increased substantially. Upon investigation, Mr. Elmo, the purchasing manager, discovered that over 40 percent of the purchase orders were being amended on an average of five times per order by the quality control department. He also found that 70 percent of the revisions had produced a request from the supplier for a higher unit price because the change required more expensive material or a closer control of tolerances. The buyers felt that they were not able to keep the cost of a revision to a minimum, because a buyer lost most of his negotiating power after the supplier received the order; in addition, a buyer did not have the authority to question aggressively the relative merits of a quality control revision. Mr. Elmo concluded that the quality control department was significantly limiting the purchasing department's ability to control the costs of purchased material.

Mr. Elmo recognized that some revisions will always occur. Many of the ones he studied, however, had included such things as marking instructions and surface finish standards which Mr. Elmo believed should have been included in the original specifications or were not worth the cost.

Early in June, the quality control department recommended that they be given authority to disqualify suppliers, based on a periodic survey of the supplier's plant by the quality control department. Mr. Elmo felt that quality control should have the right to disqualify suppliers, but based only on a review of the products received—because this is the major criteria of acceptability and because such inspections might jeopardize purchasing's relations with suppliers.

A New System Proposal

The time seemed ripe to Mr. Elmo to present a plan for solving what he felt was the major problem, too frequent changes in specifications by quality control. He, therefore, developed the following plan and submitted it to the Vice President of Production (see Figure 9–17). In his opinion, the plan

FIGURE 9–17

Organization Chart

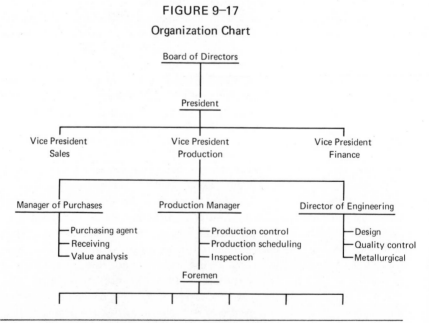

Reproduced with permission from England, *Modern Procurement Management* (Homewood, III.: Richard D. Irwin, Inc. 1970 c.), p. 332.

would lead to more carefully prepared specifications and provide a more equitable means of evaluating the worth of proposed changes:

1. The engineering department would supply the production control department with part drawings and specifications.

2. The production control department would then originate a purchase order requisition for the parts which were to be manufactured by outside suppliers, indicating the quantity to buy and the required delivery schedule. The requisition, drawings, and specifications would then be sent to the quality control department.

3. The quality control department would check the quality specifications that should apply to the part being requisitioned, using a checklist similar to that shown in Figure 9–18. The information would then be returned to production control. Mr. Elmo did not believe that his suggested quality checklist would cover every possible specification. He felt, however, that if the quality control engineers filled out the list carefully, they would be forced to consider material specifications, production requirements, and methods to assure the supplier's compliance with the specifications. Any additions or corrections to the specifications desired by quality control would be made at that point and would become part of the original requisition.

4. When the purchasing department received from production control the requisition, drawings, specifications, and a signed quality checklist (see Figure 9–18), it would then initiate quotation requests to the suppliers.

Once the purchase order had been awarded to a supplier, Mr. Elmo recommended that any changes in specification desired by engineering should be made using a change request form which would be forwarded to the buyer. The buyer would then investigate any increased costs or delivery problems arising from the proposed change and forward the change request form with the results of his investigation to an engineering change board.

The board, according to Mr. Elmo's proposal, would be composed of representatives from purchasing, production control, quality control, and production. A majority vote by the board would determine whether the change request was approved, revised, or rejected. If the change was approved, the board would determine which department was initially responsible for requesting the revision. Subsequently, the accounting department would segregate the original cost of the part from the additional costs created by the revision, and the cost of the revision would be charged to the department originating the change. With this information, Mr. Elmo hoped to avoid numerous unnecessary and costly changes by demonstrating to the top management the effects of numerous purchase order changes by the engineering departments on material costs. Mr. Elmo also believed that his system

FIGURE 9-18

Specification Checklist—Quality Control

1. Vendor's affidavit of conformance required on each shipment.
   ___Yes. ___No.
   The affidavit should state the following:
   All parts, materials, and processes used in manufacture of parts supplied under this purchase order are in accordance with the requirements set forth in the applicable prints and specifications which are part of this purchase order. These records are on file and available for inspection at your convenience.

2. Vendor must submit____samples to Mickle Aircraft quality control department for written approval prior to start of production run.

3. Vendor must certify that following material quality standards have been complied with:
   AMS*   _____
   MIL†   _____
   MS‡   _____
   MS–104 (Alum. Allog. Cstg.)   _____
   MS–192 (Sintered Leaded Bronze)   _____
   MS–235 (Titanium Allog. Forging)   _____

4. Vendor must comply with following requirements but need not certify that he had done so:
   Functional test reports   _____
   Government source inspection required   _____
   Facility survey by Mickle required   _____
   Vendor marks part number on material   _____
   Vendor marks serial number on material _____

5. Vendor must certify that he had complied with the following process requirements:
   Anodizing–Type 1   _____
   Anodizing–Type 2   _____
   Brazing–low temp.   _____
   Brazing–high temp.   _____
   Heat treating:
     MIL–H–6088A   _____
     MIL–H–6875A   _____
   Stress relieve   _____
   Magnetic inspection:
     MIL–H–6868A   _____
     AMS–2640   _____
     PS–99   _____
   Pickling   _____
   Plating   _____
   Soldering   _____
   Welding   _____
   X-ray inspection   _____
   Fluorescent inspection   _____

6. Remarks

                                    Signed_____

                                    Quality Control Department

* Material standards suggested by the American Standard Association.
† Material specifications used by government procurement agencies.
† Material and process specifications designated on Mickle's part drawings.

Reproduced with permission from England, *Modern Procurement Management* (Homewood, Ill.: Richard D. Irwin, Inc. 1970 c.), p. 333.

would provide a better method of evaluating the individual buyers performance.

Assignment

1. Identify the four or five critical factors which you think will affect systems development.
2. Evaluate Mr. Elmo's proposal and recommend changes where you think they are appropriate, in light of key factors.

Barton Company

The Barton Company produced testing and measuring devices using a combination of optical and electronic systems. These high precision products were used in hospitals for diagnosis and in manufacturing companies for inspection and testing. The company was seven years old and had grown rapidly. Management attributed this rapid growth to the unique design features of their products and to the care given to parts production and product assembly. Every instrument produced was given elaborate tests, and users of the product rarely found it necessary to have the instruments repaired, adjusted, or recalibrated.

The company employed approximately 350 production personnel, 25 supervisors and foremen, 63 quality control inspectors, and 6 final product testers. Most of the workers in the parts producing section were skilled workers in the electronic and mechanical fields (optical components were purchased from companies specializing in the field). In the assembly department, the workers were highly skilled and were given special training when first employed. Quality control inspectors had varying skills: inspectors of mechanical parts required no more than a couple of months training and experience to become proficient, but final instrument inspectors required extensive training and experience in their specialized fields. The manager of the quality control department and his two assistants were graduate engineers.

Parts Production and Inspection

Most parts were produced in small lots (fifty pieces was a common lot size). A few of the parts, such as fasteners which were common to several products, were made in longer runs for stock. When a worker completed an operation on a parts lot, he notified his foreman who then had the lot taken to the central inspection area. There each part was inspected, and any parts that did not meet specifications for that operation were rejected; there were few rejections and no attempt was made to rework rejects. The batch of inspected parts was then moved to the operator assigned to perform the next operation on the part. Upon completion of each operation, the part was moved to the central inspection department where *the operation last performed* was checked by the inspector. Parts that passed the final operation inspection were moved to the finished parts' stock room. An average of six operations were required to finish a part.

Centralized Inspection

Prior to the time the central inspection department was established four years ago, a force of roving inspectors had checked each lot of parts in the production department after each operation. As volume increased, it had become difficult to schedule and control the activities of the roving inspectors and frequent problems were encountered. Conflicts between an inspector and the worker who had performed the operation were common, for example. The movement of parts to a central inspection location had overcome these difficulties.

Assembly and Inspection and Testing

Instruments were assembled in lots of ten to fifty instruments. Parts withdrawn from the finished parts stock room were first made up into sub-assemblies. There were three to eight sub-assemblies in each instrument. Upon completion of a sub-assembly lot, the lot was moved to the central inspection department where each sub-assembly was subjected to a test designed to establish the satisfactory performance of its function in the finished instrument. Sub-assemblies then went to the final assembly department where they were combined with additional parts to make up finished instruments.

A crew of skilled test technicians in the final assembly department gave each finished instrument rigorous tests. Few assembled instruments would meet the test specifications until after the test inspectors had made additional adjustments or calibrations. Testers were trained in this work, and such final adjustments was considered to be a normal part of the test procedure. Upon completion of the final test, the inspector prepared in duplicate a detailed record of the instrument's technical performance. One copy of this report was attached to the instrument for the use of the customer, and the other was retained in the company files.

Problems Arising with Growth and Change

During the last six months Barton Company sales had doubled. In the factory, this was a difficult period. Rapid expansion of the work force and the development of new products resulted in problems throughout the organization. Many new quality control inspectors were added to the inspection and test forces, and the quality control department found it difficult to handle the increased work load. For the first time, the quality control department was plagued with complaints from the sub-assembly and final assembly departments about defective parts.

To overcome this problem, the quality control manager added a final parts inspection. Before parts were placed in the finished parts stock, a group of six inspectors now gave each part a final inspection *covering all operations.* The new inspectors found it necessary to reject many parts because they did not meet specifications. Upon checking, it was discovered that earlier inspections had been done efficiently, but that the parts had been mishandled after the inspection, in subsequent operations. This happened because there were so many new production workers and because of the pressures to increase production output. Since sales were continuing to increase at a rapid rate, little headway was made in solving the problems, and scrap costs continued to be excessive, with production costs high and quality control costs way out of line.

In the third quarter of the current year, Barton Company had its first loss. Following a meeting of the board of directors, the president held a meeting with the production manager and the quality control manager. Both of these men reported to the president. The president told them "you simply have to keep costs down." He pointed out that competition was increasing and that he considered the company's reputation for dependable products of the utmost quality the company's most valuable asset. He stated, however, that at the same time both departments had to show some improvement in lowering costs by the end of the year.

Assignment

1. Draw a flow diagram of the parts production operation, showing the flows to and from the central inspection department.
2. Assuming that the production manager can make some headway in upgrading the performance of the parts production workers, what changes would you recommend in the quality control inspection program to reduce costs, keeping in mind the importance of maintaining the high quality of the company's products?
3. Describe the kinds of reporting and record-keeping systems you feel would be needed if no changes were made in the parts inspection program. Explain how these reports would highlight critical aspects of the production operation for management.
4. Describe the kinds of reporting and record-keeping systems you feel would be needed if the quality control inspection were changed along the lines

you suggested in your answer to question 2. Explain how these reports would highlight critical aspects of the production operation for management.

American Manufacturing Company

Since 1960, when the company started producing automobile spare parts, American Manufacturing Company has grown to be a major producer of new parts and supplies for a large automobile manufacturer. Their products include radios, transmissions, auto clocks, generators, and other similar products.

During this period of growth and change, the company's production facilities have increased substantially. Since most of the production facilities are relatively new, the company has not encountered any major equipment breakdowns. The plant is presently working two shifts, five days a week. Production is running at about 90 percent capacity, which provides just enough slack time to handle occasional machine failures. Approximately 40 percent of the production involves assembly line work, while the remainder involves manufacturing parts on standard punch-out, single-unit, all-purpose machines (these parts are subsequently used in assembly).

Mr. John Mills, chief engineer of the plant, had recommended to the vice president of operations, Mr. Larry Bowles, that the company install a new preventive maintenance program. Mr. George Weber, assistant plant engineer, was in charge of the maintenance operation. His staff consisted of a secretary, four watch engineers for the boilers, three electricians, two plumbers, four mechanical men, and six handymen. The electricians and mechanical men were used mainly for production line equipment—to perform routine maintenance recommended by the equipment manufacturers and to handle emergency repairs. The other men were used to maintain the plant facilities, and performed both routine and non-routine maintenance work. A new preventive maintenance program would require hiring at least three more maintenance personnel.

Since Mr. Bowles was initially against the idea, Mr. Mills sent him some background material including an article from *Factory Management,* a publication for plant engineers, which described how the introduction of a preventive maintenance program in an automobile manufacturer's sixteen assembly plants resulted in a decrease in assembly-line downtime from an annual total of 300 hours to 25 hours (downtime costs $1,000 per minute). The article's recommendation was that "no well-managed company can afford not to develop a preventive maintenance program." After reading the article and other material, Mr. Bowles was impressed enough to ask Mr. Mills to submit a preliminary plan for establishing a preventive maintenance program for American Manufacturing. He also requested that a reporting system be installed to monitor maintenance operations. He specifically wanted to know how the maintenance staff spent their time, so as to be able to evaluate the need for additional personnel.

Mr. Mills immediately began to work on developing preliminary plans for a preventive maintenance program. Since his time was limited, Mr. Mills decided to turn the maintenance reporting project over to his assistant, Mr. Weber, whose first step was to outline the existing system. Under the present system, all requests for non-routine maintenance work were made through work orders (a two-part, snap-out form) prepared by the requesting department. The requesting department retained the duplicate copy and sent the original to the maintenance department. Mr. Weber (or his secretary) would record the request in a log book and would then give the request form to the maintenance man best able to handle the job. When the job was finished, the order form would be returned and the completion noted in the log book. Emergency calls were handled by telephone: Mr. Weber's secretary would record the request in the log book, fill out a work order, and either contact Mr. Weber or a maintenance man to take care of the emergency. Routine maintenance was assigned to different maintenance men by Mr. Weber according to schedules he kept. All maintenance employees used time cards, which they punched in and out at the factory each morning and evening.

Mr. Weber next hired an accountant part-time to help him develop a new reporting system, which would tell how efficiently maintenance personnel were being used. They decided to use a new three-part work order form. Under the new system a work order would be filled out for all jobs, either by the requesting department (for non-routine jobs) or by Mr. Weber's secretary (for emergency and routine jobs). All work orders would be assigned a work order number and entered into the maintenance log book. When the job was completed, the maintenance man would note his employee number on the work order and the time spent on the job, along with the cost of materials.

After the secretary noted completion of the job in the log book, she would forward a copy of the completed work order to the accountant. Since the accountant had records of the hourly rate paid each employee, he would be able to calculate the labor costs, as well as the material costs, for each job. In addition to summary totals showing the monthly costs of each type of maintenance job, the report also showed total monthly costs for maintenance labor and maintenance materials, based on the total of all jobs performed.

The new system was installed and the accountant's reports were accumulated for three months, and then reviewed by Mr. Mills and Mr. Bowles. During this review, Mr. Bowles noted that a discrepancy of 25 percent existed between the maintenance labor dollars reported on the firm's financial report and the total labor costs for maintenance work actually performed shown in the new monthly department reports. Mr. Bowles concluded that the maintenance department personnel worked only 75 percent of the time, so the department would not need any additional men to staff a new preventive maintenance program.

While Mr. Mills was sure that maintenance personnel were not idle 25 percent of the time, he was at a loss to explain the difference between the financial payroll figures and maintenance department report figures. He, therefore, asked Mr. Bowles to meet with him again in a week, after he had had time to recheck the figures and reexamine the maintenance operation.

Assignment

1. Describe the major kinds of maintenance work which is now (and will be in the future) performed by the maintenance department at American.

2. Describe the organization of the existing maintenance operation at American and the responsibilities of the different people involved, including the maintenance manager.

3. What kinds of information does the maintenance manager need to effectively run his operation?

4. Examine the new information system installed by Mr. Weber and identify its weaknesses in meeting maintenance management needs. Explain some of the factors which may account for the difference in labor costs noted by Mr. Bowles in the two reports.

5. Recommend changes in the information reporting system, both for the existing maintenance operation and for an expanded operation, including a new preventive maintenance program. Where appropriate, include rough sketches of the work order forms and reports to be used. Be sure to explain how this system will better meet both maintenance management and corporate management's information needs.

Information Systems for Project Management

M ANY MANAGEMENT SITUATIONS INVOLVE PROJECTS RATHER THAN continuing operations. For example, building a new factory and introducing a new product are both projects; that is, they are one-shot affairs in the sense that each involves a specific task that is in some ways unique and non-repetitive.

Information is needed for managing projects, but the information systems which provide this information differ from those discussed earlier because of the special characteristics of project situations. This chapter discusses project management situations and the ways in which their requirements affect the development of management information systems.

Project Management

Project management situations in business can involve a wide range of tasks. For example, a manufacturer may decide to switch from plain paper labels on his bottles to a new foil type; a marketing manager may want to create a market for an entirely new type of food product; the purchasing manager may decide to institute an entirely new buying procedure; or top manage-

10

ment may decide to move their business to a new location. All of these projects involve the planning, coordination, administration, and control of a variety of sub-activities.

Projects are not limited to private business. The construction of Interstate 80 from the George Washington Bridge in New York City to the Ohio Turnpike in Warren, Ohio, a distance of over 450 miles, was a project of enormous scope. The Apollo moon-shot program was one of the largest projects ever undertaken by man.

The factors emphasized in different projects may vary. In some projects, time is important—as, for example, in a weapons development program such as the rebuilding of the U.S. Navy after Pearl Harbor was destroyed. In other situations, cost is important—as when an operations manager is trying to relieve the congestion at one of his processing points for the least possible cost. And, there are many situations where time and cost are equally important—when, for example, a marketing manager is trying to penetrate a new market by a specific date at a cost which will yield a reasonable profit.

In projects where management has little or no previous experience, planning can be difficult. Planning a research and development (R & D) project is an example of this type of problem, since many R & D projects involve areas of research that are new to management. In these situations, management cannot draw upon past experience in planning and estimating project activity times and costs.

The larger a project gets, the more difficult becomes the coordination of activities. For example, thousands of key activities were involved in the Apollo program over many years; the same was true in building Interstate 80. Coordination of activities was an extremely demanding and complex task in these projects. On the other hand, a program to introduce a new bottling label may require only a dozen key activities and so would demand very little coordination.

The possibility of trade-offs exists in many projects. On the one hand, it may be possible to complete an activity at a slower rate to decrease overall project costs. For example, in developing a new product, the development manager may decide to use no overtime work in building the product prototype, thus decreasing the overall labor cost but increasing the time required for completion. Or, a manager may consider speeding up completion of the project, at increased cost. For example, in constructing a building, activities may be speeded by using more overtime in order to meet a completion deadline and avoid penalty costs. A project manager always searches for the optimum balance between time and cost, in light of the relative importance of each to project objectives and total costs.

In addition to developing objectives and plans, project management requires control of project activities to determine if they are being performed within the planned times and costs. This control will be continuing throughout a project and preferably focus on the key activities.

Questions to be Answered, Decisions to be Made, and Information Needed

The first question asked in project management is "What is to be accomplished?"—that is, "What are the objectives of the project?" The objective of a project may be to enlarge the capacity of a particular processing center in order to eliminate dependence on outside suppliers for components, with the proviso that the company's enlarged processing center can produce the components at a cost below that charged by the outside supplier. A road construction project may have as its objective the creation of a high-speed link between two major population centers within the restraints of the government's subsidized highway program.

Another question raised is "Who will be planning and administering the project?" In simple projects one person might perform both functions. For example, a project designed to reduce the number of delivery trucks required by a firm and to reroute the remaining trucks might be handled by one man, the distribution manager. On the other hand, a project whose objective is to design and manufacture a new gas turbine may require several people to plan and manage its many different activities.

Early in the project planning, the planner defines the activities required to achieve the project objectives. For example, a company plans to introduce a new training program. There are four basic activities involved in this project: developing a syllabus, training teachers, preparing facilities, and recruiting students. The development and manufacture of a new hinge, on the other hand, involves these basic activities: designing the hinge, testing the design by constructing a model, acquiring needed materials for mass production of the hinge, retooling as required, and manufacturing the redesigned hinge. Subsequently, the basic activities in each project would be broken down into greater detail, until every key activity affecting the successful completion of the project was identified. For example, in the new training program example above the basic activity, "training teachers," can be broken down into a number of sub-activities: recruiting teachers, scheduling classes, instructing teachers, and the like.

Once a manager has defined the required activities (and this can be a complex, demanding job in large projects), he should define the required sequence of these activities. In the example of the new training program, the activity of "formulating the syllabus" has to proceed the activity "training teachers." However, the activities "preparing facilities" and "recruiting students" can take place simultaneously, as long as they are completed no later than the completion of the "teacher training" activity.

After the activities and their sequences have been defined, the question is raised "What is the cost of each activity and the time required to complete it?" The answer to this question will also provide the answer to the question of the completion time and cost of the entire project. In the new training program example, the times and costs for each basic activity can be summarized as follows:

Activity	Time	Cost
Formulate syllabus	3 weeks	$1,000
Train teachers	2 weeks	700
Prepare facilities	4 weeks	1,200
Recruit students	3 weeks	650
Total project cost		$3,550

As seen from the preceding summary, the total project cost is $3,550, the sum of the four activity costs. The time needed to complete the project, however, is not the sum of all the activity times, since certain activities will be occurring at the same time. A planner needs to know the length of time required by the most "critical" activities—that is, the longest sequence of activity times required to complete the project. This is called the "critical path." In the training program example, the critical path involves two activities, "formulating the syllabus" and "training teachers," because these activities must be done in sequence and together they require five weeks to complete, the longest time. Since "preparing facilities" and "recruiting students" can both be done simultaneously with the first two activities and since they both take less than five weeks, they do not affect the completion time.

Depending on the requirements of the project, it may be necessary to study how to reduce activity times (if time is an important restraint) at the least additional cost. In other situations, a planner may study ways to decrease costs. During this phase, a manager studies the estimated activity and project times and costs in relation to project objectives and reconciles any inconsistencies.

Once the final plan is completed, organizations are set up to carry it out, resources are allocated, and the project is begun. While the project is in progress, management will want to know whether the project is progressing according to plan; if it is on schedule, they will want to assess what the actual costs are compared to plan, and where there might be possible delays in the future. For example, in a road construction project, the manager will want to know the progress of key activities at certain critical points in time. He will also need information on costs that have actually been incurred to check against budgeted costs.

Project Management
Information Systems

The type of information system needed by a project manager will depend on the specific situation. For example, in small projects, a manager might need only a simple time schedule, which he refers to each time he receives progress reports.

A schedule board is another technique used by project managers in smaller-scale projects. A schedule board is a large board with the planned schedule of activities on the top and with room just below the schedule for posting the results periodically. Such a board gives management ready visual reference for checking the present status of the project.

A variation of the Gantt bar chart (see Chapters Eight and Nine) is a useful management tool for projects with ten or fewer activities. Using such a chart, connecting lines are drawn between activity starts and completion dates to indicate which activities cannot start before others are completed. These charts are called "connected" Gantt charts and give a picture of the dependency among activities and of the extra time available for activities.

All of these simple information techniques have similar characteristics or requirements: an initial plan, a simple control mechanism for summarizing the plan, and a systematic means of collecting data on actual results and comparing it against initial plans. While the same basic characteristics are found in all project management systems, more sophisticated information systems techniques are needed in projects where many activities must be monitored and coordinated. Network techniques are among the most familiar and useful information tools in more complex project management situations.

A network is a visual representation of the activities and events that take place in completing a project. To construct a network, a planner needs first to define the major activities required and their time relationships. For example, in the training program problem described in the preceding section, the activities and times were given in chart form.

These activities and their relationships could then be pictured in a network (or arrow) diagram. If the training program example also included such activities as "registering students" and "purchasing textbooks," then the network for this project could be pictured as shown in the network diagram in Figure 10–1. In this network, the starting and ending points of the activities are called "events" and are shown as circles (circles 0 through 4). The activities are shown as arrows between the event points (or nodes). Events are points in time, whereas activities have a length of time associated with them.

Many variations on the network technique have been developed over the years, starting with the work of Mort Walker and James Kelly at Dupont using CPM and with the Navy Special Projects Office using PERT in the late 1950s. These variations include:

FIGURE 10–1

Network Diagram

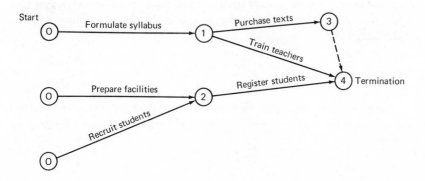

PERT—Program Evaluation Research Task (now called Program Evaluation and Review Technique)

CPM—Critial Path Method

PRISM—Program Reliability Information System for Management

PEP—Program Evaluation Procedure

IMPACT—Integrated Management Planning and Control Technique

SCANS—Scheduling and Control by Automatic Network Systems.

All of these techniques require developing network diagrams and identifying the critical path, and are used for management planning and control of projects. The most familiar of these techniques, PERT/Time, PERT/Cost, and CPM, are discussed in the following sections.

Pert/Time requires:

1. Developing the network.
2. Estimating the time requirements of each event or activity.
3. Developing critical path and calculating slack.
4. Transferring resources from slack areas to critical areas in order to meet scheduling requirements.
5. Monitoring progress and comparing it to the planned schedule.

PERT/Time was designed as an aid to planning and controlling research and development projects. Since R & D projects are notorious for the difficulty of making time estimates, PERT/Time makes use of three time estimates: an optimistic time, a most likely time, and a pessimistic time. As explained below, these time estimates are combined in order to develop expected activity times.

The first step in using PERT/Time is the construction of the network. Figure 10–2 shows a simple network.

The next step is to calculate the expected time for each activity or event (t_e). The expected time is equal to the optimistic time estimate (t_o), plus four times the most likely time estimate (t_m), plus the pessimistic time estimate (t_p), divided by six:

$$t_e = \frac{t_o + 4t_m + t_p}{6}$$

These times are shown in parentheses in Figure 10–2. Calculation of the earliest expected time and the latest allowable time for each event is now possible.

FIGURE 10–2

Network Diagram

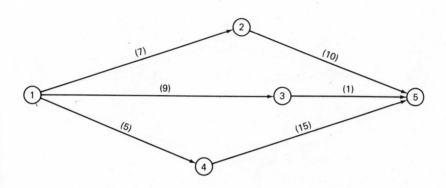

The earliest expected time for any one event (t_e) is calculated by adding up the expected times for each preceeding step in the network. These times are shown in the boxes in Figure 10–3.

The latest allowable time (t_L) is calculated by starting from the end of the project and working backwards, subtracting the expected time of each preceding activity. In the case of an event that preceeds two or more other activities, the earliest of these times is used, as with activity 0-1 in Figure 10–3. Figure 10–4 shows the latest allowable times in the circles that have been added to Figure 10–3.

FIGURE 10–3

Network Diagram: Earliest Expected Times

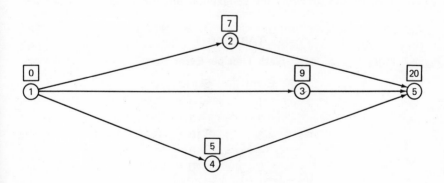

FIGURE 10–4

Network Diagram; Latest Allowable Times

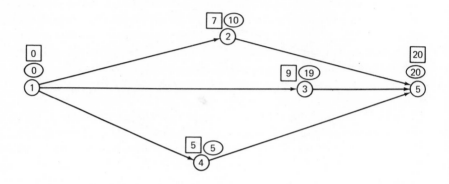

It is now possible to calculate the slack of an event. The slack is the latest allowable time (t_L) less the earliest expected time (t_E). In other words, if you are allowed nineteen weeks to complete a task and you can actually complete it in nine weeks, you have a ten-week grace period. In PERT/Time this grace period is called "slack."

The value of slack can be positive or zero, depending on the relationship between t_L and t_E. Positive slack is an indication of an ahead-of-schedule condition, or excess resources. Zero slack indicates an on-schedule condition, or adequate resources. Table 10–1 shows the slack times for this network.

As seen from the table, events 1, 4, and 5 have zero slack time. Any delay in the activities between them could cause a corresponding delay in completion of the project. The activities connecting these events, 1–4 and 4–5, are thus critical. Since events 2 and 3 have three and ten-weeks slack respectively, the activities connecting either of these two events could be delayed by the slack time without affecting the completion time of the project. The slack

TABLE 10–1

Slack Time per Event

Event	Slack
1	0
2	3
3	·10
4	0
5	0

table shows that the resources of activities 1–2 and 1–3 can be shifted to aid activities 1–4 and 4–5.

In most projects there are many paths which lead from the initial event to the terminal point. One or more of these paths will be critical—that is, any delay in the activities along the path will affect completion time of the project. In Figure 10–4, the critical path is 1–4–5, the path of the events with zero slack. Analysis of the critical paths and slack values for the events shows where more resources are needed and where there are excess resources and enables transferring resources from one activity to another to complete the project faster.

The last step, monitoring progress and comparing it to a schedule or plan, is accomplished through the use of progress reports. The project manager can determine where he is behind or ahead of schedule, and transfer resources as needed.

PERT/Time is most useful in projects in which management has had little previous experience. Research and development projects are prime examples of this, but use of PERT/Time is not limited to them, as is seen in the later sections of this chapter.

PERT/Cost

PERT/Cost was developed in 1962 as an extension of PERT/Time. It integrates time data with cost data into the network, so that trade-offs of time and cost can be evaluated.

In developing cost data in PERT/Cost, two time and cost estimates are required for each activity, a normal estimate and a crash estimate. The normal time estimate is similar to the expected time estimate, and normal cost is the cost associated with finishing an activity in the normal time. The crash estimate of time is the time required to complete an activity if no costs are spared to reduce project time. Crash cost is the cost associated with doing the job on a crash basis in order to minimize completion time.

PERT/Time, then, provides information that can help in determining the shortest completion time at the least possible cost. Since PERT/Cost is similar in concept to CPM which is discussed at length in the next section, and since a detailed example of PERT/Cost's use in a project management situation is given later in the chapter, the details of how PERT/Cost works are not discussed here.

CPM

The Critical Path Method network (or arrow) diagram, like the PERT network, gives a graphical representation of the interrelationships among jobs for each project. For CPM purposes, the duration of the activities is assumed to be under some control of management, or deterministic. This is one of the main differences between CPM and PERT/Time, since PERT/Time assumes that the duration of a job is uncertain and thus uses three times estimates. Another significant difference between CPM and PERT/Time is that CPM (as well as PERT/Cost) considers costs while PERT/Time does not.

The steps in the use of the critical path method vary slightly from PERT/Time:

1. Developing the network.
2. Calculating cost slopes.
3. Identifying all paths, including the critical path.
4. Reducing time to complete the project (if needed) at the least possible cost.

Figure 10–5 shows a simple CPM network diagram with eight activities. Associated time and cost estimates, both crash and normal (similar to the estimates explained in the PERT/Cost discussion), are given in Table 10–2. The table also includes a value for the cost slope of each activity. The cost slope of an activity is that cost associated with the reduction of one day in the completion time of the activity. It is calculated as follows:

$$\text{cost slope} = \frac{\text{crash cost} - \text{normal cost}}{\text{normal time} - \text{crash time}}$$

Once the diagram is prepared, a list can be made of all the activity paths. Each path is identified by the combined letters of the activities interrelated to form the path. The following are the paths within the CPM arrow diagram in Figure 10–5:

Path	Normal time
A,E,G	5 + 2 + 2 = 9
A,C,D,F,G	5 + 4 + 6 + 3 + 2 = 20
A,C,D,H	5 + 4 + 6 + 6 = 21
B,D,F,G	3 + 6 + 3 + 2 = 14
B,D,H	3 + 6 + 6 = 15

Path A,C,D,H is the critical path under normal conditions, since it takes the longest time, twenty-one days. The cost of this path is calculated by adding up the cost of the four activities (A = $140, C = $180, D = $110, H = $120) shown in Table 10–2.

FIGURE 10–5

A CPM Network Diagram

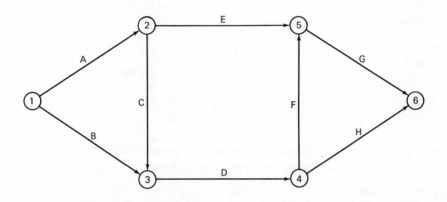

If the manager wants to complete the project in less than twenty-one days, activities along the critical path must be performed under crash conditions. For example, if the manager wants to complete the project in twenty days, one of the activities along the critical path must be reduced by one day. The cost slope tells which of the activities along the critical path can be reduced at the least cost, since the cost slope gives the cost of one day saved for each activity. Activity C has the lowest cost slope of $60: so, for an additional $60, the project can be completed in twenty days. A simple rule for choosing which activity to shorten can thus be established: reduce the activity along

TABLE 10–2

Time and Cost Estimates

Activity	Normal time	Normal cost	Crash time	Crash cost	Cost slope
A	5 days	$140	3 days	$450	$155
B	3	85	3	85	—
C	4	180	2	320	60
D	6	110	3	430	107
E	2	60	1	100	20
F	3	90	2	270	180
G	2	120	1	300	180
H	6	120	3	390	90
		$905			

the critical path that has the lowest cost slope, since this will give the least
additional cost.

Now, suppose the manager wanted to complete the project in eighteen
days. He would first reduce the time of Activity C, at a cost of $60, and
revise his list of paths as follows:

$$
\begin{array}{ll}
\text{A,E,G} & 5 + 2 + 2 = 9 \\
\text{A,C,D,F,G} & 5 + 3 + 6 + 3 + 2 = 19 \\
\text{A,C,D,H} & 5 + 3 + 6 + 6 = 20 \\
\text{B}^*\text{,D,F,G} & 3 + 6 + 3 + 2 = 14 \\
\text{B}^*\text{,D,H} & 3 + 6 + 6 = 15
\end{array}
$$

(An asterisk indicates an activity
being completed in its crash time.)

Following the same procedure as above, Activity C would be reduced
again. The critical path is now nineteen days long at a total project cost of
$1,025 ($905 + $60 + $60) as shown in the following revised list:

$$
\begin{array}{ll}
\text{A,E,G} & 5 + 2 + 2 = 9 \\
\text{A,C}^*\text{,D,F,G} & 5 + 2 + 6 + 3 + 2 = 18 \\
\text{A,C}^*\text{,D,H} & 5 + 2 + 6 + 6 = 19 \\
\text{B}^*\text{,D,F,G} & 3 + 6 + 3 + 2 = 14 \\
\text{B}^*\text{,D,H} & 3 + 6 + 6 = 15
\end{array}
$$

One step remains, to reduce path A,C,D,H from nineteen to eighteen.
However, it is no longer possible to reduce Activity C, since the minimum
time required to complete it is two days. Of the remaining activities, H has
the lowest cost slope, so H is reduced next. The new cost of the project is
$1,115 (1,025 + 90) and it will be completed in eighteen days. The final
paths are:

$$
\begin{array}{ll}
\text{A,E,G} & 5 + 2 + 2 = 9 \\
\text{A,C}^*\text{,D,F,G} & 5 + 2 + 6 + 3 + 2 = 18 \\
\text{A,C}^*\text{,D,H}^* & 5 + 2 + 6 + 5 = 18 \\
\text{B}^*\text{,D,F,G} & 3 + 6 + 3 + 2 = 14 \\
\text{B}^*\text{,D,H} & 3 + 6 + 6 = 15
\end{array}
$$

If the manager wanted to reduce the project to the minimum possible
time, the final revised paths would be:

$$A^*,E,G^* \qquad\qquad 3 + 2 + 1 = 6$$
$$A^*,C^*,D^*,F^*,G^* \quad 3 + 2 + 3 + 2 + 1 = 11$$
$$A^*,C^*,D^*,H^* \qquad 3 + 2 + 3 + 3 = 11$$
$$B^*,D^*,F^*,G^* \qquad 3 + 3 + 2 + 1 = 9$$
$$B^*,D^*,H^* \qquad\qquad 3 + 3 + 3 = 9$$

The cost for completion of the project in eleven days, the minimum time, is $2,286. Note that Activity E is not being completed in its crash time, since it is not part of a critical path.

The above example illustrates a very simple CPM project. Another kind of CPM network is shown in Figure 10–6. This figure shows the use of "dummy activities," activities J and K in the diagram. These activities do not require any time to complete but are essential coordinating activities required to finish the project. For example, paths D,E,K and G,H must be completed before Activity I can begin. The subsequent analysis of this arrow diagram would proceed as in the previous example, depending on the management requirements in the situation.

The CPM and PERT methods described above work well with small projects, but become cumbersome for larger ones. Computer program packages exist that can handle larger networks, but very large projects (such as major road construction) exceed even the capabilities of the computer. Different approaches are needed in such situations.

One approach is to reduce the size of the network to one that can be handled by the computer, by combining activities and treating each group of

FIGURE 10–6

Network Diagram

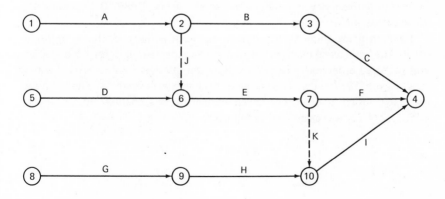

activities as though the group were only one activity. Another method is to divide the total network into segments, and handle each segment as though it were a separate network. The computer outputs for each segment become the inputs for another program, which determines a practical (but not necessarily optimal) solution to the whole arrow diagram.

Developing
Specific Systems

Network techniques can be used in many business management areas: marketing (for example, advertising and market research); operations (product design, process control, and the like); finance; or, in fact, almost any business area where projects must be managed. The following are two examples illustrating the development of network techniques for project management.

A Marketing Management Project: The Omega Company

The Omega Company's main products were men's dress shirts and slacks. Recent sales had been only fair, so that management felt that now was the time to introduce a new and more aggressive sales program. Consequently, they set a sales goal of a 20 percent increase in sales for the coming year. As part of the overall marketing program, advertising management developed a program of expanded advertising on radio and in newspapers designed to reach the company's three major outlets. The advertising manager wanted to determine the timing of the impact of his new program (to coordinate it with sales programs), anticipate any possible trouble spots, and have continuing control of key activities affecting successful completion of the program. PERT/Time seemed ideally suited to his needs.

He first identified the different activities required to carry out the program. He defined eleven activities and seven events. Table 10–3 summarizes these events and activities.

He then made three time estimates for each activity, as shown in Table 10–4. The advertising manager calculated the expected times for the activities and prepared a network diagram to show the interrelationships of the activities. Figure 10–7 shows this network and the associated t_es. The t_es were calculated using the formula given earlier in this chapter: for example, activity 2–4's t_e was calculated as follows:

$$t_e = \frac{6 + (4)7 + 7}{6} = 7$$

TABLE 10–3

Table of Events and Activities

Number of event	Description
1	Start of advertising program.
2	Radio advertisements prepared and placed.
3	Newspaper advertisements prepared and placed.
4	Response from Outlet 1 begins.
5	Response from Outlet 2 begins.
6	Response from Outlet 3 begins.
7	End of program.

Number of activity	Description
1–2	Prepare radio advertisement.
1–3	Prepare newspaper advertisement.
2–4	Radio reaches outlet 1.
2–5	Radio reaches outlet 2.
2–6	Radio reaches outlet 3.
3–4	Newspaper reaches outlet 1.
3–5	Newspaper reaches outlet 2.
3–6	Newspaper reaches outlet 3.
4–7	Response by outlet 1.
5–7	Response by outlet 2.
6–7	Response by outlet 3.

TABLE 10–4

Project Activities and Time Estimates

Activity	Optimistic time	Most likely time	Pesimistic time
1–2	14 weeks	21 weeks	28 weeks
1–3	7	14	21
2–4	6	7	8
2–5	4	5	6
2–6	3	4	5
3–4	3	4	5
3–5	2	3	4
3–6	1	2	3
4–7	6	7	8
5–7	6	7	8
6–7	5	6	7

FIGURE 10-7

Network Diagram with Expected Times

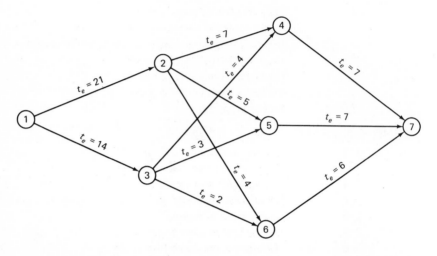

The advertising manager then calculated the earliest expected times (t_E) and the latest allowable time (t_L) for each event, as shown in Figure 10-8.

The advertising manager analyzed the data to determine which activities were critical and which activities could be delayed without affecting the completion time of the project. The advertising manager calculated the slack times for the events and isolated reasons why these slack times existed. Table 10-5 shows the slack values and proposed reasons for the particular values.

From Figure 10-8 and Table 10-5, the advertising manager was able to determine that path 1-2-4-7 was the critical path, since the critical path is the path of zero slack. He therefore knew that any lag in the completion of the activities along this path would delay completion of the project.

Three weeks after the start of the project the manager was faced with a possible problem of a two-week delay in the completion of activity 1-2. Since this activity was on the critical path, the completion time of the whole project would be delayed if no action was taken. The advertising manager referred to the slack table he had compiled at the beginning of the project and noted that the start of Activity 1-3 could be delayed by as much as ten weeks. He decided to use some of the resources used in Activity 1-3 (creative personnel) to get Activity 1-2 back on schedule. By asking for continuing periodic reports on the progress of each activity, the manager was able to uncover similar delays as he went along and make shifts in personnel where

FIGURE 10–8

Network Diagram with Earliest Expected and Latest Allowable Times

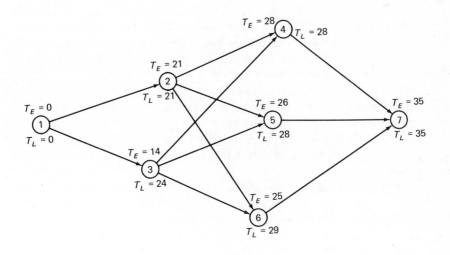

TABLE 10–5

Slack Values and Causes

Event	Slack in weeks	Possible reasons for slack
1	0	$t_L = t_E$
2	0	This event is on the critical path and must be completed on time.
3	10	Quicker preparation of newspaper ads as compared to radio ads.
4	0	This event is on critical path and must be completed on time.
5	2	Response from outlet 2 is faster than from outlet 1.
6	4	Response from outlet 3 is faster than from outlets 1 & 2.
7	0	$t_L = t_E$ (Events that start and terminate a project must begin and end on time.)

these delays were critical and would affect the completion of the project on time.

A Production Management Project: Standard Aircraft Company

The management of Standard Aircraft Company was planning the manufacture of a new component for use in the manufacture of a new army fighter. The component was critical to government defense plans and the government indicated that the component would be needed in twenty-five weeks. However, government agents stated that the component might have to be available sooner, possibly within twenty-one weeks, depending on the international situation. The project manager was given the job of determining the length of time required to complete production of the component in normal time, as well as developing crash program information for completion of the project in less than twenty-five weeks (to a minimum completion time of twenty-one weeks, if possible).

The project manager considered using several project management tools, such as linear programming, simulation, and PERT/Cost. He eliminated linear programming because, while providing information on the optimal solution in terms of costs, it would not provide the information needed for evaluating alternative courses of action in relation to time. Simulation, although an excellent method of determining results given a specific situation, was eliminated, because it was again not able to provide adequate data for evaluating alternative costs *and* times. The project manager chose PERT/Cost, since it would provide information on completion time of projects (where time estimates are uncertain) and associated costs, and also would give data on costs associated with reducing the completion time of activities.

FIGURE 10–9

Network Diagram for New Component Development

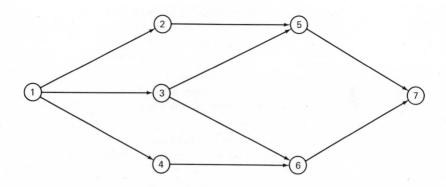

TABLE 10-6

Estimated Activity Times (in weeks)

Activity	Description	Optimistic time	Most likely time	Pessimistic time
1-2	Special component study	3.0	3.5	4.5
1-3	Layouts	4.0	5.0	6.0
1-4	Subsystem design	3.5	4.5	6.0
2-5	Vendor evaluation	2.0	2.2	3.5
3-5	Subcontract specifications	3.0	3.5	4.5
4-6	Subsystem tests	8.0	9.0	12.5
5-7	Subcontract work	7.5	8.5	11.5
3-6	Final drawings	6.0	7.5	12.0
6-7	Fabrication	7.5	9.0	12.5

The first step taken by the project manager was to isolate all the activities that had to occur to complete the project and to show their interrelationships in an arrow diagram. Figure 10-9 shows in summary form the arrow diagram he developed.

The next question the project manager answered was "How long will the project take?" Table 10-6 shows the information on activity times that he compiled.

Using information furnished by accounting and finance personnel, the project manager prepared a table of normal and crash costs and calculated the "incremental cost" ("cost slope" in CPM terminology) of each activity. Table 10-7 shows this data, along with the crash time for each activity.

TABLE 10-7

Normal and Crash Costs for New Component Project

Activity	Normal cost	Crash cost	Crash time	Incremental cost
1-2	$ 8,000	$10,000	2.6	$ 2,000
1-3	15,000	20,000	3.0	2,500
1-4	25,000	32,000	3.6	7,000
2-5	4,000	6,000	1.4	2,000
3-5	6,000	7,500	2.6	1,500
4-6	45,000	60,000	8.4	15,000
5-7	35,000	50,000	6.8	7,500
3-6	30,000	40,000	6.0	5,000
6-7	35,000	42,500	7.33	3,750

FIGURE 10–10

Network Diagram with Relevant Times

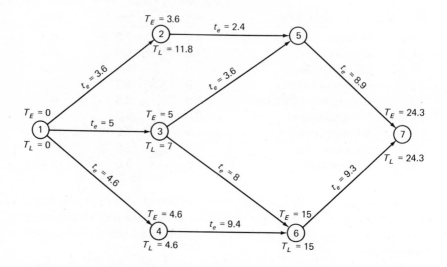

The expected times for each activity (t_e) were calculated next, using the formula $t_e = \dfrac{a + 4b + c}{6}$. T_Es and T_Ls (earliest expected and latest allowable event times) were also calculated and are shown in Figure 10–10.

The last step in preparing the PERT/Cost information system was the calculation of slack values. The project manager's calculations are shown in Table 10–8.

The project manager was now ready to study the critical areas of the project. He first determined the critical path or the path with zero slack, path 1–4–6–7. Under existing conditions the project would take 24.3 weeks to

TABLE 10–8

Slack Times

Event	Slack
1	0
2	8.2
3	2.0
4	0
5	6.8
6	0
7	0

TABLE 10–9

Project Times and Costs

Time to project completion	Critical path	Total cost
24.3	1–4–6–7	$203,000
23.3	1–4–6–7	206,750
22.3	1–4–6–7	210,500
21.3	1–4–6–7	217,500
20.3	1–4–6–7	232,500
	1–3–6–7	

complete at a cost of $203,000 (see Table 10–9). He then calculated the costs of reducing the time of completion by one, to 23.3 weeks. To do this, he reduced the time of activity 6–7 by one week for a new total cost of $206,750 ($203,000 + $3,750, as shown in Table 10–9). He continued to reduce the completion times, one week at a time until he reached the lowest crash time limits. The results of his work are shown in Table 10–9.

As is seen from Table 10–10, when the project time was reduced to 20.3 weeks in length there were two critical paths. Project time could not be reduced further, because path 1–4–6–7 was being completed in crash time. The project manager was able to conclude from his study that no effort should be made to accelerate any activities except those along path 1–4–6–7, since no further reduction in the total time required to complete the project could be made by accelerating any of the other activities.

The use of PERT/Cost in this situation provided management with needed information. It prevented spending funds on crash activities that would not decrease the completion time of the project, and showed management how much money would have to be spent if the government wanted the component in less than twenty-five weeks. Management could now tell the government that under no circumstances could the component be supplied in less than 20.3 weeks. It also provided a control mechanism that could be used in conjunction with feedback information to follow progress and take corrective

TABLE 10–10

Crash Time of Activity Paths at 20.3 Weeks

Path	Time
1*–4*–6*–7	20.3 weeks
1–3–6*–7	20.3
1–3–5–7	17.5
1–2–5–7	14.9

action if and when such action was needed. In this way, PERT/Cost was used in this situation as both a planning tool (to create a schedule and plan expenditures) and a control tool (to keep track of progress and indicate possible courses of action if necessary).

Summary
Conclusion

The information requirements for project management situations differ somewhat from those found in other situations described in Part Two:

1. Project objectives.
2. The persons responsible for planning and administering the project.
3. Project activities.
4. Sequence and interrelationships of activities.
5. Cost and time required for activities.

With this information in hand, a manager can make use of a wide variety of network techniques, such as those described in this chapter.

Network techniques provide management with an excellent source of information for planning and controlling projects. The situations described in this chapter are intended to convey only a basic understanding of how these techniques are developed for and used in project management. The examples described were intentionally kept simple. In actual business situations, the complexities of a project can be staggering. For instance, in the construction of the World Trade Center in New York, a separate PERT analysis was developed for each of over 100 floors in the two buildings. While the situation was more complex, however, the basic principles at work were the same.

TEXT DISCUSSION QUESTIONS

1. Describe the nature of project management and its distinctive characteristics which affect development of project management information systems.
2. Discuss the similarities in and differences between the planning and controlling tasks in project management.
3. Describe the basic decisions made in managing projects, and outline the information needed to make these decisions.

4. What is a network or arrow diagram? Discuss the ways in which it is useful in project management.

5. Describe PERT/time, and its distinctive characteristics. Give some examples of management situations in which it might be a useful information tool, and explain how it might be applied.

6. Define critical path, slack time, event, activity, expected activity time, and earliest expected and latest allowable event or activity time.

7. Describe CPM and its distinctive characteristics. Give some examples of management situations in which it might be a useful information tool, and explain how it might be applied.

8. Discuss the differences and similarities between the basic steps involved in using CPM and in PERT/Time.

9. Discuss some of the problems involved in using PERT and CPM in large complex projects, and how these problems might be overcome.

Case Study Exercises

Beelow Merchandising Company

Network Diagramming Exercise

The marketing manager at Beelow Merchandising Company was working on a problem in developing a network for preparing and conducting a market survey. He had gathered the following information. The project will begin with the planning of the survey (three weeks). After the plan is complete, data collection personnel may be hired (five weeks), and the survey questionnaire designed (ten weeks). After the data collection personnel are hired and the questionnaire designed, the personnel may be trained in the use of the questionnaire (seven weeks). Once the questionnaire has been designed, the design staff can also select the households to be surveyed (four weeks). At this stage, the questionnaire may also be printed in volume for use in the survey (five weeks). After the households have been selected, the personnel trained, and the questionnaire printed, the survey may begin (fifteen weeks). When the survey is completed, the results may be analyzed (five weeks).

Assignment

Develop an arrow diagram for the marketing manager at Beelow and select the critical path.

Robernal Company

Critical Path Exercise

The project manager has been given estimates for the various activities required to research and develop a new product. These activities and their respective normal and crash times are listed in Table 10–11.

Activity A must precede all others, and Activity E must follow all others. All other activities can run concurrently.

TABLE 10–11

Activity	Normal Weeks	Dollars	Crash Weeks	Dollars
A	5	$30,000	4	$40,000
B	6	$12,000	2	$20,000
C	4	$10,000	3	$18,000
D	5	$12,000	3	$20,000
E	3	$16,000	3	$16,000

Assignment

1. Draw a network diagram for the project manager showing all activities at normal time.

2. Reduce the total project duration as much as possible without unnecessary additional costs. Indicate the new critical path or paths. Show how much slack time remains in the non-critical paths. Show the total project costs for each week reduction in total project duration.

3. What effect on total project time and costs would a reduction in Activity B from six weeks to two weeks have?

Kerner Company

PERT/Time Exercise

The personnel manager at Kerner Company has decided to institute a management development program in his organization. Not having any experience in this area, he has solicited time estimates for the various key activities and developed a network arrow diagram for the project.

The optimistic, most likely, and pessimistic time estimates he received, plus the network diagram he developed are shown in Table 10–12 and Figure 10–11.

FIGURE 10–11

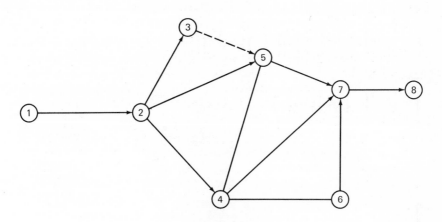

TABLE 10–12

Activity	t_o	t_m	t_p
1–2	0.5	1	1.5
2–3	3	4	11
2–4	1	2	9
2–5	2	4	6
4–5	1	2	3
4–6	4	5	6
4–7	2	10	12
5–7	2	3	10
6–7	1	2	3
7–8	1	1	7

His problem involves estimating the time for each activity and calculating the slack time, given the above network diagram and optimistic, most likely, and pessimistic time estimates.

The personnel manager has selected the PERT/Time technique as an aid to planning his project, because PERT/Time makes use of various time estimates to develop the expected activity times.

Assignment

1. Using PERT/Time, estimate the time required for each activity.
2. Develop the critical path.
3. Calculate the slack for each activity using the earliest expected time (t_e) and the latest allowable time (t_L) for each event.

Simulating Management Decisions

N MAKING DECISIONS, STRATEGIC AND OPERATIONAL, MANAGERS ASK many "What if. . . ?" questions. For example, an office-services manager may be faced with the problem of determining the layout of new executive offices. Each office is ten feet by twelve feet and will contain a desk, table, bookcase, four chairs, and a file cabinet. His objective is to provide maximum working efficiency for the executive when working either alone or with subordinates.

One tool he might use is a floor plan drawn to scale on a piece of paper on which he could lay out paper cutouts of the furniture also drawn to scale. Using the scale drawings (or models), he would then try out (or simulate) different office arrangements until a *satisfactory* arrangement was found.

As this example shows, then, simulation for business decision making involves developing some kind of model of a situation and subsequently manipulating that model to study the impact of different decisions on situation elements and on outcomes or results (that is, on the achievement of decision objectives). Through simulation, different decisions (or courses of action) can be evaluated and potential problems can be identified. In this sense, a simulated system is another information system which provides managers with useful information for decision making.

11

As suggested by the office layout example above, simulation does not generally provide an optimal or best solution, though at times it can—if, for instance, a manager tries out *all possible* alternatives. Rather, it normally only enables examining the outcomes of different decisions, often over an extended period of time in the future, to determine which course of action is *the best of those examined.*

The kind of simulation which should be most familiar to readers involves the use of physical models—for example, when a model of a new airplane is constructed and then tested under simulated wind, weather, and other flight conditions. The scaled floor plan and paper cutouts of office furniture described earlier in the chapter are examples of two dimensional physical models used to simulate a business decision. Physical simulation models are used infrequently in management decision making, though very often in product design and development.

Another kind of simulation model used in business decision making is the network diagram for project management described in Chapter Ten. In developing networks, a project manager first analyzes situation factors and management objectives, and then constructs a diagrammatic model of the interrelationships of project activities and costs (where required). He next uses the model to study the impact of different decisions (for example, shortening completion time) on different project activities (and sometimes costs) and on his objective (for example, simulating the conditions under which a project could be completed at a specified time at the least cost).

In addition to physical and diagrammatic simulation models, many mathematical or quantitative models are used in simulating business decision situations. A financial budget, for example, can be used as a simulation model. Using a budget format, with its established mathematical relationships among costs, sales, and profits, a manager might calculate expected profits (that is, he might simulate what would happen to profits) at different levels of sales at different time periods in the future.

Besides financial budgets, other kinds of mathematical simulation models can be developed for almost any area or aspect of business activity. Because of the complexity of the computations involved in using many of these models, they are often programmed for a computer. The basic mathematical techniques employed in this kind of simulation are, however, relatively simple for the most part, so that they can be understood and used by the average business manager.

This chapter describes several basic simulation techniques used in different kinds of management decision-making situations. Additional uses of simulation in management decision making are discussed in Chapter Twelve. In reading these discussions, the reader should keep in mind that the use of computerized simulation models is still somewhat limited in business today.[1]

Operational Planning Under Conditions of Certainty: The Richman Company

The first kind of situations to be discussed involve decisions under conditions of certainty—that is, situations in which all key elements and outcomes are known or can be determined. This class of decisions is called *deterministic* decisions. For example, in many production situations, labor and material costs, production time, demand, and other situation factors are known (or can be predicted fairly accurately) by management. Since the relationships of these factors to total output, production costs, idle time, or some other outcome under study are also known, the impact of different management decisions affecting the outcome under study can be calculated.

The following is an illustration of how mathematical simulation might be used in making management decisions where key situation factors are known or certain.

---

1. Jerome Marullo and James J. Cribben, "Whatever Happened to Management Simulation?", *Management Review*, May 1972, pp. 12-18.

The Richman Company is a small distributor of men's and women's accessories. On July 1, Mr. Richman, the sole proprietor, was reviewing the least profitable line to determine what could be done to increase its profitability. During his review, Mr. Richman gathered the following information on one of the items in the line.

Current inventory on July 1 was 150 items. An order for restocking inventory was sent out the last day of each month. The method which Mr. Richman is considering for use during the coming year to determine the number of items reordered is to multiply sales during that month by 2½ and then subtract the amount of inventory on hand. Delivery of goods always occurred five weeks after the order was sent. An order sent on May 31 would thus be delivered on July 6.

Marketing expenses for the item for the coming year will be $5,000 in September and will decrease for six months at the rate of $500 a month to $2,500 in February. In March, marketing expenses will rise again to a high of $5,000 and then decrease at the rate of $500 a month through August. The variable cost of the product is $10 each. Fixed costs are $5,500 a month.

Demand is stimulated by two factors: marketing expense and selling price. Historical data shows that by increasing marketing expense $100 sales are increased an extra twenty units within the present range of sales. The historical relationship of unit price to sales is represented by the formula 5,000 divided by the unit price, again within the present range of sales. Demand is the sum of the impact of these two factors (marketing expense and selling price). Marketing expenses for July are $3,000 and those in the previous month, June, were $3,500. The selling price is currently $20.

Actual sales are approximated by the demand for the month as calculated in the preceding paragraph, except when demand exceeds the total inventory on hand that month. In that case, actual sales are equal to beginning inventory plus deliveries received during the month.

Inventory at the end of the month is equal to the beginning monthly inventory plus deliveries received, minus units sold and loss allowance. Loss allowance is currently zero and expected to remain at that level during the coming year. Inventory orders were made on May 31 for July 6, for 700 units, and on June 30 for August 5, for 1,000 units.

Mr. Richman was interested in developing a way to study the impact on profits of his new inventory policy. Since he had recently taken a course in mathematical simulation at the local university, he decided to apply the technique to his problem. Before constructing his mathematical simulation model, Mr. Richman made a list of the notations or symbols he would use (it should be noted that in mathematical simulation any notation you can recognize and remember can be used):

t   = starting data (July 1, for example)

1   = one month

I(t) = inventory at starting point, time t

OR(t, t + 1)* = order shipments received during month

D(t, t + 1) = demand during month

US(t, t + 1) = sales in units during month

&S(t, t + 1) = sales in dollars during month

SP(t, t + 1) = price per unit during month

MC(t, t + 1) = marketing costs for month

VC(t, t + 1) = variable costs for month

FC(t, t + 1) = fixed costs during month

TC(t, t + 1) = total costs during month

O(t, t + 1) = orders placed at end of month

E(t, t + 1) = earnings during month

---

*The symbol (t, t + 1) means from the first of one month to the first of the next month, or for a one-month period.

Mr. Richman's next step was to develop mathematical equations (using these notations) to represent the relationships of the factors, identified above, affecting the item's profitability.

Since unit sales are equal to demand, if demand is *less than or equal to* (the symbol for this operation is $\leq$) inventory at the beginning of the month plus orders received during the month, then the following equation can be formulated for calculating sales:

(1)   US(t, t + 1) = D(t, t + 1),
   if $D(t, t + 1) \leq I(t) + OR(t, t + 1)$.
   Otherwise, US(t, t + 1) = I(t) + OR(t, t + 1).

In order to solve this equation, demand must be calculated. Demand can also be expressed as a mathematical formula, since it is equal to 5,000 divided by price plus one-fifth of a unit for each dollar of marketing costs:

(2) $D(t, \; t + 1) = .20MC(t, \; t + 1) + \dfrac{5,000}{SP(t, t + 1)}$

Substituting the marketing costs and price given for July, equation (2) can be solved for July:

$$D(t, \; t + 1) = .20(3000) + \frac{5,000}{20}$$

$$= 600 + 250 = 850$$

Since the inventory on hand in July of 850 (150 at the beginning of the month plus the receipt of an order of 700 on July 6) fulfills the demand of 850, then actual sales will equal demand in July, according to equation (1).

Equations representing other situation factors can be developed and solved in a similar manner. Since the order placed for the month equals 2½ times the sales made during the month less inventory on hand at the end of the month, the following equation can be formulated for inventory orders placed at the end of each month:

(3) $O(t, t + 1) = 2.5 \ US(t, t + 1) - I(t + 1)$

Substituting the known values for July, the July 31 inventory order can be calculated as follows:

$$O(t, t + 1) = 2.5(850) - 0$$
$$= 2,125$$

Since the price is given at $20, sales in dollars can be found by multiplying price times unit sales, as represented by equation (4):

(4) $\$S = SP(t, t + 1) \times US(t, t + 1)$

Substituting actual figures, unit sales for July can be calculated as follows:

$$\$S = 20 \times 850 = \$17,000$$

To determine earnings for any given month, costs must first be determined. Variable costs are $10 for each unit sold, which is expressed:

(5) $VC(t, t + 1) = \$10 \times US(t, t + 1)$

For July, then:

$$VC(t, t + 1) = \$10 \times 850 = \$8,500$$

Total costs are the sum of variable costs, plus fixed costs, and marketing expenses, or:

(6) $TC(t, t + 1) = VC(t, t + 1) + FC(t, t + 1) + MC(t, t + 1)$

Since for July fixed costs are $5,500 and marketing expenses $3,000, then:

$$TC(t, t + 1) = \$8,500 + \$5,500 + \$3,000$$
$$= \$17,000$$

Earnings can now be found by subtracting total costs from dollar sales, or:

(7) $E(t, t + 1) = \$S(t, t + 1) - TC(t, t + 1)$

Substituting the data for July, the earnings for July can be calculated as follows:

$$E(t, t + 1) = \$17,000 - \$17,000 = 0$$

Since beginning inventory at August 1 is equal to July beginning inventory, plus orders received minus units sold and loss allowance, the following equation for calculating new monthly inventory figures is used:

(8) $I(t, t + 1) = [I(t) + OR(t, t + 1)] - [US(t, t + 1) + \text{loss allowance}]$

Substituting the given values for July gives the August 1 inventory level:

$$I(t + 1) = [150 + 700] - [850 - 0] = 850 - 850 = 0$$

Mr. Richman now had a series of equations which expressed the significant relationships showing (within the present range of sales) the impact of his inventory ordering, pricing, and marketing expense decisions on profits. In addition, he had tested his formulas for the month of July to check the validity of these formulas.

Next, Mr. Richman took his equations to a friend at the university, who programmed them in the proper sequence for computer processing.

Using this program, with the price set at $20 for the coming year and marketing expense and inventory policies remaining the same, the computer simulated the following year's (twelve-month) results, as shown in Table 11–1. Checking the July figures against his manual calculations, he found that they were accurate, as were the fixed costs, marketing costs, and order quantities generated by the computer model.

Confident that the computer program (or simulation model) and the figures it generated were accurate, Mr. Richman examined the simulation run to see how his proposed inventory policy would affect profits. He noted that in April the demand was 1,150, but that he had only 650 items on hand and so lost $5,000 in operating income (500 units times $20 selling price less $10 variable cost). Instead of a loss of $3,500 in April, then, he would have had a profit of $1,500, if he had had sufficient inventory. He also noted that inventories were somewhat high in relation to sales in several other months.

Based on his examination of the sales pattern, he began trying out several different inventory policies (for example, setting the order level at 1½ instead of 2½ times current month sales; using last year's sales in the same month as the basis for calculations; varying the ordering pattern by season; and the like). After making appropriate minor adjustments in the computer model where each alternative dictated, he had a twelve-month simulation run done for each, until he developed what he felt was an adequate inventory policy.

The next decision problem which interested Mr. Richman was the impact of his pricing and marketing expense policies on profits. Following the model

TABLE 11–1
Twelve-Month Simulation Run

	I	OR	[I + OR]	D	US	P	$S	VC	FC	MC	TC	E	O
July	150	700	850	850	850	20	17000	8500	5500	3000	17000	-0-	2125
Aug.	0	1000	1000	750	750	20	15000	7500	5500	2500	15500	-500	1625
Sept.	250	2125	2375	1250	1250	20	25000	12500	5500	5000	23000	2000	2000
Oct.	1125	1625	2750	1150	1150	20	23000	11500	5500	4500	21500	1500	1275
Nov.	1600	2000	3600	1050	1050	20	21000	10500	5500	4000	20000	1000	75
Dec.	2550	1275	3825	950	950	20	19000	9500	5500	3500	18500	500	0
Jan.	2875	75	2950	850	850	20	17000	8500	5500	3000	17000	-0-	25
Feb.	2100	0	2100	750	750	20	15000	7500	5500	2500	15500	-500	525
March	1350	25	1375	1250	1250	20	25000	12500	5500	5000	23000	2000	3000
April	125	525	650	1150	650	20	13000	6500	5500	4500	16500	-3500	1625
May	0	3000	3000	1050	1050	20	21000	10500	5500	4000	20000	1000	675
June	1950	1625	3575	950	950	20	19000	9500	5500	3500	18500	500	0
	2675	675	3350			20			5500				

building approach described above, Mr. Richman first defined the range of sales within which any increases or decreases in marketing expenses or prices would affect sales according to the formulas developed for his first simulation model. After looking over historical records, he decided that sales would increase or decrease with price changes according to his original formula only within the range of $18 to $22. He, therefore, had simulation runs done with his original model at the $18, $19, $21, and $22 price levels. He developed a similar range for marketing expenses and had several simulation runs done at different marketing expense levels within this range. Based on these simulation runs (and what they showed about the impact on profits of different alternatives), he revised his pricing and marketing policies.

His university friend had told him a computer model could also be developed for other price and marketing expense levels, providing the relationships of sales to price and marketing expense increases and decreases could be defined accurately in mathematical terms. Mr. Richman consequently decided that during the coming year he would conduct some tests of exactly how these variables might affect sales beyond the ranges he had already studied. Based on these tests, Mr. Richmond hoped that he might be able to refine his model further next year and do additional simulations.

Mr. Richman's experience was in many ways typical of most management decision situations in which simulation models are used. First, the validity of the models and the information they generate depend on the validity of the initial assumptions about the interrelationships of factors affecting the outcome, here profits. For example, the results of Mr. Richman's runs were accurate only to the degree that the mathematical relationships between different levels of marketing expense and sales reflected what actually happened in his business. Second, simulation models can generate a lot of information, but only about those questions asked. Since a decision maker cannot always be certain that he has explored all possible alternatives, or all combinations of alternatives, he can never be certain he has found the best answer. Mr. Richman, for example, didn't have time to refine his model enough to enable him to simulate prices other than whole dollar amounts, such as $18.50, $18.51, and so forth. These limitations become increasingly significant in more complex (and so, more realistic) decision situations, such as those described in the following chapter. Simulation must always be used with these limitations in mind.

The Richman study, while admittedly overly simplified, does illustrate the basic concept of mathematical simulation. The mathematical notation used in simulation is merely a short-hand for expressing relationships, levels, and flows of resources in a business. This short-hand is necessary because:

1. It represents an easy means of expression and one that the computer can handle efficiently.

2. It represents a general situation that can easily be changed—for example, by changing a few parameters (such as the change in month in the Richman sample).

Although the Richman study was a very simple one, it represents exactly the type of mathematics used in even the most complex simulations. If, instead of using only one product, all of Richman's products had been simulated, there would have been an immediate increase in the size of the simulation. In general, more complex simulations differ from the one used by Mr. Richman in three ways:

1. There is a much larger number of factors included in the model.
2. The relations among the equations are more complex.
3. The decision rules are more complex.

Nevertheless, it is only size and complexity that increase; the mathematics would be identical and as easy to understand.

Operational Planning under Conditions of Risk or Uncertainty: The Power Company

Quite often, key variables cannot be predicted with certainty in management decision situations. For example, a manager normally does not have a precise estimate of what demand or sales will be. If, in these situations, a manager can estimate the likelihood or *probability* of different sales levels occurring, then a probabilistic simulation model can be developed and used.

The concept of probability is a familiar one. For example, if someone had a bag of tennis balls, all of which were white, and if he were to select one randomly, he could be certain that the one he picked would be white. If there were also yellow tennis balls in the bag, however, he could not be *certain* of the color (outcome) of the individual selection (sampling). If he knew there were nine white balls and one yellow one in the bag and he was asked to predict the color of the ball to be selected at random from the bag, he would undoubtedly predict the selection of a white one. The chances of his being right would be good—nine to one. Thus, a person is able to assign a numerical value (or probability) to the confidence of a prediction of the outcome of a sampling, if certain facts about the situation (such as the composition of the total universe being selected from—the number of balls of each color in the bag, in the above example) are known. Probability then allows a manager to assign weights to the various outcomes that will occur, and so enables him to predict a specific outcome with more confidence.

The following is an illustration of how a *probabilistic* simulation model is developed and used in management decision making.

The Power Company, a manufacturer of power tools is considering introducing a new power drill in order to fill out the company's line of power drills and to take advantage of idle production capacity. After a management study, two drills Model H (a home model) and Model I (an industrial model) were selected for further evaluation. Table 11–2 gives a breakdown of estimated costs and projected sales and prices for each model.

TABLE 11–2

	Model H	Model I
Selling price	$18	$38
Costs		
Production costs	5	12
Marketing costs	4	9
Fixed costs	3	6
Total costs	$12	$27
Profit per unit	$ 6	$11
Units produced and sold annually	22,500	10,000
Yearly profit for each drill	$135,000	$110,000

Realizing that it was impossible to predict sales, costs, prices, and profits with certainty, management thought that it would be more realistic to estimate a range of likely prices, costs, and sales which might occur. In addition, they estimated the probability of different levels of prices, costs, and sales within the ranges occurring, that is, the *frequency distribution* of each range.

The concept of a frequency distribution can be illustrated by using the tennis ball example above. If, in the example, there were eight white balls, two yellow ones, six blue ones, and six orange ones in the bag, the following would be the distribution of probabilities (or frequency distribution) for selecting any one color at random from the bag:

	Number	Probability or Frequency Distribution
White	8	.40
Yellow	2	.10
Blue	6	.30
Orange	4	.20
	20	1.00

In calculating the probabilities in this example, the probability of each color being selected is the percent the number of balls of each color is of the total balls in the bag. The total of the probabilities, then, will equal 100 percent or 1.00.

Table 11–4 shows management's estimates of the probability (or frequency) of the different costs, unit sales, and prices occurring.

Management was now faced with the problem of projecting the impact of all these possible variations in costs, prices, and unit sales on profits. They decided to use a simulation model.

In order to simulate the random occurrence of the different variations, random number tables are used, such as the one shown in Table 11–3. These tables are developed by selecting numbers randomly and printing the numbers in sequence. Since a random number table represents the chance occurrence of events in the real world, it can be used in conjunction with probability estimates of real world events occurring to simulate the random pattern of their occurrence.

In the power tool decision situation, for example, numbers from 00-99 were assigned to the probabilities for each price, cost, and unit sales volume. In doing this, a .01 probability is assigned one number. For instance, in Table 11–4 the .10 probability of the $16 price for Model H occurring was assigned the ten numbers 00-09, the $17 price twenty-five numbers (10-34), and so forth. This was done for each set of variables.

After the number assignment is complete, random numbers are selected from the *Table of Random Digits* (Table 11–3) to simulate the random occurrence of actual events. The table given in part in Table 11–3 is published by the Rand Corporation and is the most popular source for random numbers in hand-calculated simulations.

The selection from this table must be done in a systematic sequenced order. The starting point may be any position in the table. Movement from this point must be continued vertically or horizontally in the same column or line as the starting point. There are several ways to do this:

1. Method A involves starting in the upper left hand corner using the first two digits of the number 54,941 (see Table 11–3); continuing down the column from this point, the random numbers 54, 02, 98, 11, 96, 81, 56, and so forth, are generated.

2. Method B involves starting in the middle and continuing horizontally using the last two digits. The random numbers produced this way would be 59, 00, 43, 68, 53, 91, 65, 52, 17, 34, 49, and so forth, as indicated on the table.

3. Method C involves starting at the bottom and continuing up the column. Random numbers generated in this way would be 01, 93, 50, 67, 11, 78, 55, 81, and so forth.

TABLE 11-3

Table of Random Digits

54941	72711	39406	94620	27963	96478	21559	19246	88097	44026
02349	71389	45608	60947	60775	73181	43264	56895	04232	59604
98210	44546	27174	27499	53523	63110	57106	20865	91683	80688
11526	91326	29664	01603	23156	89223	43429	95353	44662	59433
96810	17100	35066	00815	01552	06392	31437	70385	45863	75971
81060	33449	68055	83844	90942	74857	52419	68723	47830	63010
56135	80647	51404	06626	10042	93629	37609.	57215	08409	81906
57361	65304	93258	56760	63348	24949	11839	29793	37457	59377
24548	56415	61927	64416	29934	00755	09418	14230	62887	92683
66504	02036	02922	63569	17906	38076	32135	19096	96970	75917
45068	05520	56321	22693	35089	07694	04252	23791	60249	83010
99717	01542	72990	43413	59744	44595	71326	91382	45114	20245
05394	61840	83089	09224	78530	33996	49965	04851	18280	14039
38155	42661	02363	67625	34683	95372	74733	63558	09665	22610
74319	04318	99387	86874	12549	38369	54952	91579	26023	81076
18134	90062	10761	54548	49505	52685	63903	13193	33905	66936
92012	42710	34650	73236	66167	21788	03581	40699	10396	81827
78101	44392	53767	15220	66319	72953	14071	59148	95154	72852
23469	42846	94810	16151	08029	50554	03891	38313	34016	18671
35342	56119	97190	43635	84249	61254 ·	80993	55431	90793	62603
55846	18076	12415	30193	42777	85611	57635	51362	79907	77364
22184	33998	87436	37430	45246	11400	20986	43996	73112	88474
83668	66236	79665	88312	93047	12088	86937	70794	01041	74867
50083	70696	13558	98995	58159	04700	90443	13168	31553	67891
97765	27552	49617	51734	20849	70198	67906	00880	82899	66065
49988	13176	94219	88698	41755	56216	66832	17748	04963	54859
78257	86249	46134	51865	09836	73966	65711	41699	11732	17173
30946	22210	79302	40300	08852	27528	84648	79589	95295	72895
19468	76358	69203	02760	28625	70476	76410	32988	10194	94917
30806	80857	84383	78450	26245	91763	73117	33047	03577	62599
42163	69332	98851	50252	56911	62693	73817	98693	18728	94741
39249	51463	95963	07929	66728	47761	81472	44806	15592	71357
88717	29289	77360	09030	39605	87507	85446	51257	89555	75520
16767	57345	42285	56670	88445	85799	76200	21795	38894	58070
77516	98648	51868	48140	13583	94911	13318	64741	64336	95103
87192	66483	55649	36764	86132	12463	28385	94242	32063	45233
74078	64120	04643	14351	71381	28133	68269	65145	28152	39087
94119	20108	78101	81276	00835	63835	87174	42446	08882	27067
62180	27453	18567	55524	86088	00069	59254	24654	77371	26409
56199	05993	71201	78852	65889	32719	13758	23937	90740	16866
04994	09879	70337	11861	69032	51915	23510	32050	52052	24004
21725	43827	78862	67699	01009	07050	73324	06732	27510	33761
24305	37661	18956	50064	39500	17450	18030	63124	48061	59412
14762	69734	89150	93126	17700	94400	76075	08317	27324	72723
28387	99781	52977	01657	92602	41043	05686	15650	29970	95877

Source: Extracted from "Table of 105,000 Random Decimal Digits," Statement No. 4914, File Nol 261-A-1 (Washington, D.C.: Interstate Commerce Commission, 1949).

TABLE 11-4

	Variable	Frequency	Random #'s	Variable	Frequency	Random #'s
Selling	$16	10	00-09	$36	8	00-07
price	17	25	10-34	37	21	08-28
	18	40	35-74	38	35	29-63
	19	20	75-94	39	24	64-87
	20	5	95-99	40	12	88-99
Production	5	50	00-49	12	65	00-64
cost	6	20	50-69	13	15	65-79
	7	20	70-89	14	10	80-89
	8	10	90-99	15	10	90-99
Marketing	4	65	00-64	9	70	00-69
costs	5	15	65-79	10	15	70-84
	6	15	80-94	11	10	85-94
	7	5	95-99	12	5	95-99
Fixed costs	3	55	00-54	6	60	00-59
	4	30	55-84	7	15	60-74
	5	10	85-94	8	15	75-89
	$ 6	5	95-99	$ 9	10	90-99
Units	20,000	5	00-04	8,000	10	00-90
	21,250	15	05-19	9,000	15	10-24
	22,500	50	20-69	10,000	60	25-84
	23,750	20	70-89	11,000	10	85-94
	25,000	10	90-99	12,000	5	95-99

Method A is used for the power drill simulation, which consisted of twenty simulations. Twenty random numbers are selected in sequence and each of the twenty random numbers selected is used to simulate an actual event, as shown in Table 11-5. In constructing this table, the first simulation involved selecting all the selling prices, costs, and unit sales figures for the first random number, 54. The next random number (02) was used for simulation 2, and so forth. (Note: statistically, it would be preferable to select a random number separately for each variable.)

The net profit for each model was then calculated for each simulation run, and the average of the net profits for each model for each run was determined.

Based on the twenty simulations shown in Table 11-5, the average profit for Model H is $67,375, while for Model I it is $85,150. The range of profits for Model H is from a loss of $25,000 to a profit of $135,000 and for Model I

TABLE 11-5

Simulation run	1	2	3	4	5	6	7	8	9	10	11	12	13	14	15	16	17	18	19	20
Drill "H"	54	02	98	11	96	81	56	57	24	66	45	99	05	38	74	18	92	78	23	35
Selling price	18	16	20	16	20	19	18	18	17	18	18	20	16	18	18	17	19	19	17	18
Production cost	6	5	8	5	8	7	6	6	5	6	5	8	5	5	7	5	8	7	5	5
Marketing cost	4	4	7	4	7	6	4	4	4	5	4	7	4	4	5	4	6	5	4	4
Fixed cost	3	3	6	3	6	4	4	4	3	4	3	6	3	3	4	3	5	4	3	3
Net profit	5	4	-1	4	-1	2	4	4	5	3	4	-1	4	6	2	5	0	3	5	4
No. of units	22.5	20	25	21.25	25	23.75	22.5	22.5	22.5	22.5	22.5	25	21.25	22.5	23.75	21.25	25	23.75	22.5	22.5
Net profit	112.5	80	-25	85.0	-25	47.5	90	90	112.5	67.5	90	-25	85	135	47.5	106.25	0	71.25	112.5	90

$$\frac{13{,}475.00}{20} = \$67{,}375$$

Drill "I"	1	2	3	4	5	6	7	8	9	10	11	12	13	14	15	16	17	18	19	20
Selling price	38	36	40	37	40	39	38	38	37	39	38	40	36	38	39	37	40	39	37	38
Production cost	12	12	15	12	15	14	12	12	12	13	12	15	12	12	13	12	15	13	12	12
Marketing cost	9	9	12	9	12	10	9	9	9	9	9	12	9	9	10	9	11	10	9	9
Fixed cost	6	6	9	6	9	8	6	6	6	7	6	9	6	6	7	6	9	8	6	6
Net profit	11	9	4	10	4	7	11	11	10	10	11	4	9	11	9	10	9	8	10	11
No. of units	10	8	12	8	12	10	10	10	9	10	10	12	8	10	10	9	11	10	9	10
Net profit	110	72	48	80	48	70	110	110	90	100	110	48	72	110	90	90	55	80	90	110

$$\frac{1703.00}{20} = \$85.15$$

from a profit of $48,000 to one of $110,000. In addition, Model H incurs a $25,000 loss in three of its simulations.

The original analysis shown in Table 11—2 had clearly indicated that Model H was the most profitable choice. Yet, after management estimated its chances of achieving the original estimates, as well as variations from those targets, and after the impact of these estimates on profitability were simulated, an entirely different profit projection emerges. On average, Model I seems more likely to produce a significantly higher profit than Model H. In addition, Model H seems to carry a greater risk of incurring heavy losses. If, after the original estimates were rechecked and additional simulation runs made, the same relationship prevails; then management would probably decide to manufacture Model I.

As can be seen from the above example, a massive amount of computations are needed to use such probabilistic simulation models, especially if management would like to see the results of many thousands of simulation runs in order to be more certain of the accuracy of the results. It is common, therefore, to computerize these models. In order to computerize these models, mathematical formulas representing the relationships of variables are developed; the logic steps in making the calculations and assignments are flowcharted; and the data, formulas, and a random number table are stored in the computer. The computer can then run as many simulations as are desired and feasible and calculate the average profit and range of profits for each alternative.

Once a computer simulation model is developed, a so-called "sensitivity analysis" can be done to determine the impact of different variables on the eventual profit outcome. For example, in the power drill simulation example, production costs might be varied to judge their effect on profits; this can be done by changing either the range of costs or the probabilities of their occurring (and so the random numbers assigned to them). By doing this, management can study how great an impact changes in each variable will have on profits and so perhaps study more closely the way these estimates were arrived at. At a later date, management may choose to pay closer attention to controlling such factors as production costs (or any other costs that have the most significant impact on profits) as a result of these analyses.

Sensitivity analyses are done both as an aid to management planning and control after the decision has been made, and as a means of defining and limiting the uncertainty of probability estimates in actual business situations. In reality, these estimates are only educated guesses, based on historical data and executive experience and judgment, and, as such, should be studied carefully.

One of the most critical and difficult jobs in probabilistic simulation models then is specifying a range of variance for each variable and the appropriate frequency distribution for each range of variables. Thus, while the technique of simulation is easy to apply, developing the assumptions underlying the model is not, and probabilistic simulation should be used with this limitation clearly in mind.

Summary
Conclusion

Several kinds of simulation models have been covered in this chapter: physical, diagrammatic, and quantitative or mathematical (including financial). The discussion concentrated on quantitative models, since diagrammatic models used in management decision simulation were discussed in Chapter Ten and physical models are used infrequently in management decision evaluation.

The discussion began with simple *deterministic* models, in order to introduce the basic concept of mathematical simulation. *Probabilistic* models were discussed next. These models are more complex, and their usefulness in management decision analysis and evaluation depends in large measure on the accuracy of initial management estimates of the risks involved. Whatever the degree of complexity, however, the basic steps are the same: defining the decision objectives and restraints, translating these into mathematical equations, establishing relationships between equations and programming them, and using these mathematical models to simulate the outcomes of alternative courses of action over some period of time in the future.

The management situations discussed in this chapter (in which these models are used) involve operational planning decisions. In those situations where deterministic models are used, such as the Richman Company application, the key variables are known or certain. More commonly, a manager encounters situations in which key variables cannot be predicted with certainty. The Power Company study illustrates the way a manager goes about defining key situation variables in these kinds of operational planning situations.

Simulation can also be used in more complex situations—for example, the longer-term strategic planning and overall corporate financial planning discussed in Chapter Twelve. In all these situations, the computer is used because of the complexities of the calculations involved.

Since simulation models generate information useful in management decision making, they can be considered another type of management information system—similar in concept to budgetary systems. They have much more limited use in business today, however, both because of the difficulties involved in constructing and programming complex simulation models and because of their limitations to making only one type of decision—like project management networks—and so are simply too costly in relation to what they may be used for. In contrast, most of the management information systems discussed in Part Two can be used on a continuing basis once they are set up.

As in developing other kinds of management information systems, management has a key role in developing simulation models—both in constructing the model itself and in deciding on the assumptions underlying the model. Without such participation, it is unlikely that management will have sufficient confidence in (or familiarity with) the simulation model developed to make effective use of it.

TEXT DISCUSSION QUESTIONS

1. Define simulation. Describe the ways in which it is useful in management decision making, as well as some of the limitations of its use.

2. Describe the three basic kinds of simulation models discussed in this chapter. Discuss some of the problems involved in developing these simulation models.

3. Based on your reading of Chapter Ten and this chapter, discuss the ways in which network diagrams are developed and used in simulating management decisions. In what kinds of situations are they useful?

4. Describe the ways in which budgets can be used to simulate management decisions and can provide information useful in evaluating alternative management decisions.

5. Describe what is involved in developing a simple deterministic mathematical simulation model. In what ways can it be used in management decision making? In what kinds of management decision situations are these models most useful?

6. Describe what is involved in developing probabilistic simulation models. In what ways can they be used in management decision making? In what kinds of management decision situations are these models most useful?

7. What are random numbers and how are they used in simulation?

8. What are the limitations of the usefulness of the information generated by probabilistic simulation models? What is the most difficult problem encountered in developing these models?

9. What is sensitivity analysis and how is it useful during and after the time management decisions are made?

10. Discuss the ways in which simulation and simulation models are similar to (and different from) other kinds of management information systems discussed in this book thus far.

Case Study Exercises

Cardone Brothers Company

The Cardone Brothers Company, which sells and installs garage doors at $120 apiece, is well established in its area. Since the garage door business peaks in the spring and summer and sales during the winter decline sharply, there are major problems with inventories and cash flow during the year.

The company's inventory control policy is to have enough doors on hand to satisfy one month of sales demand. The amount of each monthly order to replenish inventory is determined first by multiplying sales for the preceding month by 1.75 from August to January, and by 3.00 from February to July, and subtracting ending inventory. The doors cost Cardone $75 per door, which includes shipping expenses.

Inventory problems in the past have been caused by running out of stock, as well as by having too much inventory for the available storage space. Late in December, management began questioning the effectiveness of their present inventory policy and looking for ways to improve the inventory situation throughout the year. You have been asked to help.

Inventory on January 1 is estimated at fifty-five garage doors. Orders are placed at the end of each month and delivery takes place about five weeks later. Marketing expenses are $800, $900, $1,000, $1,000, $900, and $800 respectively each month from April through September, and $100 from October through March. The variable handling costs of each door are $5. Fixed costs are $1,000 a month. Sales figures are generated by price changes and marketing expenditures in the following relationship: 3,000 divided by the price, plus one unit of sale for each $10 in marketing expenditures. Actual sales during the month can never exceed beginning inventory plus orders received for the month. The order placed on November 30 for delivery in early January was thirty doors, and the order placed on December 30 for early February delivery was twenty doors. Sales demand for December was estimated at thirty doors.

Your first step is to develop a mathematical simulation model. The notations used and formulas developed are given below:

Notations

t = January 1
1 = one month
$I(t)$ = inventory at starting point; time t: January 1
$OR(t, t + 1)$ = orders received during month: January
$D(t, t + 1)$ = demand during month
$US(t, t + 1)$ = sales in unit during month
$\$S(t, t + 1)$ = dollar sales during month
$SP(t, t + 1)$ = selling price during month
$MC(t, t + 1)$ = marketing costs during month

VC(t, t + 1) = variable costs during month
FC(t, t + 1) = fixed costs during month
TC(t, t + 1) = total costs during month
O(t, t + 1)   = orders during month
E(t, t + 1)   = earning during month

Mathematical Relationships

(1) $O(t, t + 1) = 3.00 \, US(t, t + 1) - I(t + 1)$ (Feb.–July)
    $O(t, t + 1) = 1.75 \, US(t, t + 1) - I(t + 1)$ (Aug.–Jan.)

(2) $US(t, t + 1) = D(t, t + 1)$, if $D(t, t + 1) \leq I(t) + OR(t, t + 1)$
    Otherwise,
$$= I(t) + OR(t, t + 1)$$

(3) $D(t, t + 1) = \dfrac{MC(t, t + 1)}{10} + \dfrac{3000}{P}$

(4) $\$S(t, t + 1) = P(t, t + 1) \times US(t, t + 1)$

(5) $VC(t, t + 1) = 5 \times US(t, t + 1)$

(6) $TC(t, t + 1) = MC(t, t + 1) + VC(t, t + 1) + FC(t, t + 1)$

(7) $E(t, t + 1) = \$S(t, t + 1) - TC(t, t + 1)$

(8) $I(t, t + 1) = [I(t) + OR(t, t +1] - US(t, t + 1)$

Your simulations for the coming twelve months are given in Table 11–6.

As they review these simulation results with you in early January, the management of Cardone Brothers are concerned by the excess of inventory shown on hand during the fall months, and by the opportunity losses shown during April and May. They ask you to advise them on how the inventory control policy might best be revised to avoid excess inventories and opportunity losses. They also inform you that they have just been notified that the cost of each door has been increased to $85 (including shipping charges), and they have accordingly raised the price for each door to $125, the most they feel they can raise the price at this time. All other costs remain the same.

Assignment

1. Calculate an inventory order formula which will reduce inventory accumulation, but not cause any opportunity losses.

2. Do a twelve-month simulation to show how your formula works.

All-Purpose Tire Store Simulation *

The All-Purpose Tire Store is located in Kingswood, Vermont. A small store, all its tires are sold at a price of $16 apiece. It is solidly established in the

*Source: Reproduced with permission from Dearden and McFarland, *Management Information Systems* (Homewood, Illinois: Richard D. Irwin, Inc., 1966), pp. 107-113.

TABLE 11-6

	I	OR	I+OR	D	US	SP	$S	SC	VC	FC	MC	TC	E	O
Jan.	55	30	85	35	35	120	4200	2625	175	1000	100	3900	300	0
Feb.	50	20	70	35	35	120	4200	2625	175	1000	100	3900	300	70
Mar.	35	0	35	35	35	120	4200	2625	175	1000	100	3900	300	105
Apr.	0	70	70	105	70	120	8400	5250	350	1000	800	7400	1000	210
May	0	105	105	115	105	120	12600	7875	525	1000	900	10300	2300	315
June	0	210	210	125	125	120	15000	9375	625	1000	1000	12000	3000	290
July	85	315	400	125	125	120	15000	9375	625	1000	1000	12000	3000	100
Aug.	275	290	565	115	115	120	13800	8625	575	1000	900	11100	2700	0
Sept.	450	100	550	105	105	120	12600	7875	525	1000	800	10200	2400	0
Oct.	445	0	445	35	35	120	4200	2625	175	1000	100	3900	300	0
Nov.	410	0	410	35	35	120	4200	2625	175	1000	100	3900	300	0
Dec.	375	0	375	35	35	120	4200	2625	175	1000	100	3900	300	0
Jan.	340	0												
Feb.		0												

region and for a number of years has been getting 15 percent–20 percent of the region's tire business. The Vermont tire business is somewhat seasonal in nature with sales peaks in October and April. Sales decline sharply in January and July. These peaks and troughs are roughly 35 percent above and below the year's average tire sales. This has caused severe fluctuations in both the company's tire inventories and cash position during the year. The company's inventory policy has been to have enough tires on hand at all times to satisfy sales demand for two months. Two months' sales demand is determined by adding up the sales of the past 13 weeks and multiplying the figure by two-thirds. The number of tires to be ordered from the manufacturer is then determined by subtracting the actual number of tires in inventory from this figure. This is the amount ordered during the week. It always takes exactly six weeks for the tires to be delivered after the order has been placed. All deliveries are COD and cost $10 per tire. The manufacturer has always delivered promptly and it is expected that he will continue to do so. All other operating costs are fixed.

Management is concerned by the sharp rises and falls in the cash and inventory balances during the year. Inventory stockouts followed by problems of storing excess inventory were hampering the company's operations. Questions began to be raised by managment as to whether their inventory ordering rule was the best under the circumstances and whether changing to another manufacturer who could deliver tires two weeks after the order was sent would be a good idea. At this point it was decided to build a model of the company's operation for purposes of exploring the long-range effect of some of these decisions. The following sets of equations were developed to describe the company's operations:

The amount of cash generated through operations each week is given by the following equation:[2]

(1) $TSR\ (t-1/t) - CTP\ (t-1/t) - FC\ (t-1/t) = CC\ (t-1/t)$, where:

$TSR\ (t-1/t)$ = Tire sales revenue for the week
$CPT\ (t-1/t)$ = Cash paid for tire purchase by company during the week
$FC\ (t-1/t)$ = Company fixed costs during the week
$CC\ (t-1/t)$ = Increase or decrease in the company's cash position during the week.
$WSI\ (t) = WSI\ (t-1) + A$, when $D > TSR\ (t-2/t-1) > C$, and $WSI\ (t-1) > WSI\ (t-2)$, where:

---

2. Note that, in this example, "t" is the *end* of the week and the "1" represents a week.

WSI (t) = Amount by which this week's sales level is either above or below the annual level

WSI (t − 1) = Amount by which last week's sales level is either above or below the annual level

WSI (t − 2) = Amount by which two weeks' ago sales level is either above or below the annual level

TSR (t − 2/t − 1) = Tire sales revenue last week

A = The increment that either increases or decreases a week's sales level from that of the preceding week

D = Maximum weekly sales level attainable under present operations

C = Minimum weekly sales level attainable under present operations.

The following equations represent the values of the constants and the initial values of the variables for the last two equations:

(7) $ASL = 5{,}000$

(8) $D = 6{,}750$

(9) $C = 3{,}250$

(10) $A = 270$

(11) $WSI\ (t − 1) = 0$

(12) $WSI\ (t − 2) = − 270$

These equations may appear formidable, but they really are not. They are designed to increase the volume of sales by a fixed increment (A) each week until a maximum weekly sales volume (D) is reached. Then the sales are decreased by (A) each week until a minimum sales volume (C) is reached. Then, the sales volume begins to increase again and this pattern continues for as many weeks as the simulation is run. Incidentally, these equations demonstrate how involved putting even simple mathematics into equation form is when decision rules are involved.

The preceding sets of equations have defined the company's pattern of cash generation. Now a group of equations which will satisfactorily define the company's inventory and ordering cycle must be developed.

The following equation defines the company's tire inventory. (The figures represent the number of tires on hand rather than their dollar value.)

(13) $IT\ (t) = IT\ (t − 1) − TS\ (t − 1/t) + TRM\ (t − 1/t)$, where:

IT (t) = Tire inventory at end of week

IT (t − 1) = Tire inventory at end of previous week

TS (t − 1/t) = Total number of tires sold during the week

TRM (t − 1/t) = Tires received from the manufacturer during the week

The next two equations relate TS (t − 1/t) back to equation 1:

(14) $TS\ (t - 1/t) = \dfrac{TSR\ (t - 1/t)}{TP}$, where:

$TS\ (t - 1/t)$ = Number of tires sold during the week
$TSR\ (t - 1/t)$ = Tire sales revenue for the week
TP = Selling price of a tire

(15) $TP = 16$

(16) $IT\ (t - 1) = 2{,}000$

The company's desired level of inventory at the end of the week can be expressed by the following equation:

(17) $TID\ (t) = 2/3 \sum\limits_{a=1}^{13} TS\ (t - a)$, where:

$TID\ (t)$ = Tire inventory desired at the end of the week.

$\sum\limits_{a=1}^{13} TS\ (t - a)$ = Number of tires sold over the past 13 weeks

$TID\ (t) = 2{,}316$

The following equation defines the number of purchase orders that are sent out each week:

(18) $TPOR\ (t - 1/t) = TID\ (t) - I\ (t)$, where:

$TPOR\ (t - 1/t)$ = The number of tires ordered from the manufacturer during the week
$TID\ (t)$ = Tire inventory desired at the end of the week
$I\ (t)$ = Actual tire inventory on hand at the end of the week.

The next equation defines the number of tires being received each week:

(19) $TRM\ (t - 1/t) = TPOR\ (t - 7/t - 6)$, where:

$TRM\ (t - 1/t)$ = Tires received during week
$TPOR\ (t - 7/t - 6)$ = Tires ordered six weeks ago.

The next two equations relate the number of tires purchased back to the cost of tires item mentioned in equation (1):

(20) $CPT\ (t - 1/t) = TRM\ (t - 1/t) \times TC$, where:

$CPT\ (t - 1/t)$ = Cash paid for tires during the week
$TRM\ (t - 1/t)$ = Tires received during week
TC = Cost of an individual tire

(21) $TC = 10$

(22) $TPOR\ (t - 7/t - 6) = 300$
$TPOR\ (t - 6/t - 5) = 300$
$\qquad * \qquad\qquad\quad *$
$\qquad * \qquad\qquad\quad *$
$TPOR\ (t - 2/t - 1) = 300$

This completes construction of the model. Running through one week's operation will indicate how it can be used to generate useful information. (The technical term for this is hand simulation.) No attempt will be made to arrange the equations in their optimal order for computer solution. This solution will merely indicate one way of arranging the equations for a solution.

The first equation in the model to be solved is equation 6, which reveals how much the week's sales are above or below the year's average. Equation 11 indicates WSI $(t-1) = 0$ and equation 12 indicates WSI $(t-2) = -270$. Therefore, WSI $(t-1) > WSI$ $(t-2)$. Comparison of equations 8 and 9 with TSR $(t-2/t-1)$ indicates that $C < TSR$ $(t-2/t-1) < D$. Therefore the option of equation 6 which should be used is the one which says WSI $(t) = WSI$ $(t-1) + A$. Since equation 10 indicates that $A = 270$, it follows that WSI $(t) = 0 + 270 = 270$.

Taking the results of equation 6 and equation 7, equation 5 calculates total tire sales revenue as follows:

$$TSR \ (t-1/t) = 5,000 + 270 = \boxed{5,270}$$

The next equation to be presented for solution is equation 19, which indicates the number of tires to be received during the week. Equation 22 says $TPOR$ $(t-7/t-6) = 300$ so TRM $(t-1/t) = 300$. Then, since equation 21 indicates that $TC = 10$, equation 20 can be solved to show how much cash was paid for tires during the week:

$$CPT \ (t-1/t) = 300 \times 10 = \$3,000$$

Equation 17 is then solved to find the desired tire inventory:

$$TID \ (t) = 2,316$$

Attention is next directed to the solution of equation 13. Using the result of equation 5 (TSR $(t-1/t) = 5,270$) and equation 15 where $TP = 16$, equation 14 indicates that 330 tires were sold during the week. Using the results of equation 16 [IT $(t-1) = 2,000$], equation 14 [TS $(t-1/t) = 330$], and equation 19 [TRM $(t-1/t) = 300$], equation 13 indicates that tire inventory at the end of the week is 1,970 tires.

Using the result of equation 17 (TID $(t) = 2,316$) equation 18 indicates the number of tires ordered from the manufacturer at the end of the week would be 316.

Equation 1 can now be solved. The results of equation 20 [CPT $(t-1/t) = 3,000$], equation 3 [FC $(t-1/t) = 1,000$], and equation 5 [TSR $(t-1/t) = 5,270$] indicate that CC $(t-1/t) = +1,270$. Equation 2 can then be solved with the aid of equation 4 [CP $(t-1) = 100,000$] to give the result CP $(t) =$

$101,270. At this juncture the simulation model has completed one week's operation.

If this problem were being solved on a computer, the following changes would be made preparatory to beginning calculations for the second week:

(1) Amount in location CP (t) would be moved to location CP $(t - 1)$ (updating equation 4).

(2) Amount in location WSI (t) would be moved to location WSI $(t - 1)$ (updating equation 11).

(3) Amount in location WSI $(t - 1)$ is moved to location WSI $(t - 2)$ (updating equation 12).

(4) Amount in location IT (t) is moved to location IT $(t - 1)$ (updating equation 16).

(5) Amount in location TS $(t - 12)$ is moved to location TS $(t - 13)$, amount in location TS $(t - 11)$ is moved to location TS $(t - 12)$, etc. This allows equation 17 to be updated.

(6) Amount in $TPOR$ $(t - 6/t - 5)$ 15 is moved to location $TPOR$ $(t - 7/t - 6)$, amount in location $TPOR$ $(t - 5/t - 4)$ is moved to location $TPOR$ $(t - 6/t - 5)$, etc.

The model would then go through the same series of computations for the second week of operations. This process can be continued for as many weeks of operations as desired. The output figures concerning cash balances and inventory can either be listed tabularly or plotted graphically.

The All-Purpose Tire Store management must then decide whether this output appears realistic in terms of the company's actual experience. If it is satisfactory to them, the model can be accepted as having captured many of the essentials of the environment which the model is simulating. Otherwise, the equations must be modified and possibly some new ones added.

When it is complete, it can be used to analyze the effect of making certain alterations in the model. Some of the areas that management might want to test include:

(1) The effect of using an ordering rule which recognizes the seasonal nature of the company's business.

(2) The effect of responding more slowly (or more quickly) to changes in sales pattern as far as ordering more or less in inventory. A decision rule which would cause the company to make its ordering pattern respond more quickly to the changes in sales pattern would be the following rule. Desired inventory level at the end of a week should be 7 times as great as the week's sales. This could be accomplished by introducing the following change into the model:

Change equation 17 to:

$$TID\ (t) = 7\ TS\ (t - 1/t)$$

(3) The effect of reducing the time lag between the time the product is ordered and the time it is delivered. Reduction of this time lag from six to two weeks could be accomplished by introducing the following change into the model:

Change equation 19 to:

$$TRM\ (t - 1/t) = TPOR\ (t - 2/t - 1)$$

Korman Toy Company

The Korman Toy Company is in the process of considering which of two different types of football games—a mechanical model or an electrical model—to market. In the time remaining before Christmas, an effective advertising and distribution campaign can be conducted for only one product.

An estimate of the probable range of costs, prices, and unit sales was made by the marketing group to assist you in making a decision as to which model would be more profitable to market. The following table lists the ranges of variations for each variable for each model.

	Mechanical	Electric
Selling price	$11–15	$17–21
Production cost	$ 2–6	$ 3–7
Marketing costs	$ 2–4	$ 5–7
Fixed costs	$ 1–3	$ 2–4
Units (weekly)	400–600	300–500

Marketing plans call for introducing the product in retail stores on October 1, so that your projections of sales and profits will cover a twelve-week period ending at Christmas.

A marketing research study has been conducted using costs and prices from three companies who market similar products. For this study an estimate was made of the profit at the most likely level of sales, costs, and prices for each model (Table 11–7). Probabilities have also been assigned to the likelihood of different levels of sales, costs, and prices within the established ranges occurring, as shown in Table 11–8.

Assignment

1. Assign random numbers to variables in Table 11–8, using the probabilities given.

TABLE 11-7

	Mechanical	Electric
Selling price	$ 13	$ 19
Production cost	4	5
Marketing cost	3	6
Fixed cost	2	3
Total costs	$ 9	$ 14
Net profit per unit	$ 4	$ 5
Annual units produced	500	400
Total new profit	$2,000	$2,000

TABLE 11-8

	Mechanical			Electric		
	Variable	Frequency	Random #'s	Variable	Frequency	Random #'s
SP	$ 11	10		$ 17	10	
	12	25		18	20	
	13	40		19	40	
	14	20		20	20	
	15	5		21	10	
PC	2	20		3	05	
	3	20		4	10	
	4	50		5	30	
	5	5		6	30	
	6	5		7	25	
MC	2	20		5	15	
	3	50		6	75	
	4	30		7	10	
FC	1	25		2	25	
	2	60		3	50	
	$ 3	15		$ 4	25	
Units	400	15		300	20	
	500	75		400	60	
	600	10		500	20	

2. Do a twelve-week simulation, using the Table of Random Digits in the text.

3. Recommend which product to market, justifying your decision based on an analysis of your simulations.

Advanced Management Information Systems

THIS CHAPTER GIVES A BRIEF INTRODUCTION TO MORE COMPLEX AND more advanced information systems used in business management today. The discussion covers both more advanced decision-supporting systems, which make use of simulation and other operations research models, and larger-scale, computer-based data processing systems, which serve the data and information needs of a wide range of departments within a company.

Advanced Management
Decision-Supporting Systems

Essentially, advanced information systems are complex, computer-based data processing and information systems which make use of advanced computer technology, such as random-access retrieval, on-line direct-access transmission, and graphic output displays. Many of these systems also make use of *simulation* models (which can assist managers in evaluating alternative courses of action) and *analytical* operations research models (such as economic order quantity formulas which give the best answer). Three kinds of such decision-supporting systems are discussed in this section: operational planning, corporate financial planning, and longer-term strategic planning.

12

Operational Planning

Several advanced management decision-supporting systems have been briefly described in earlier chapters, for example: the job shop scheduling system used by Hazelton Corporation (Chapter Eight), the inventory management system which calculated economic order quantities by computer (Chapter Nine), computer-based PERT and CPM systems (Chapter Ten), and the mathematical simulation models covered in Chapter Eleven. The following sections describe additional examples of advanced decision-supporting systems used in such operational planning situations as planning airport facilities and airline scheduling, marketing planning and production scheduling, and manager training.[1]

Planning Airport Facilities and Airline Scheduling. Airline management has successfully used computerized simulation models extensively to determine

---

1. For a description of other computerized simulation models used in operational planning see: Morris Hamburg and Robert J. Atkins, "Computer Model for New Product Demand," *Harvard Business Review,* March—April 1967, pp. 107-120; John R. Russell, Robert B. Stobaugh, Jr. and Frederick W. Whitmeyer, "Simulation for Production," *Harvard Business Review,* September—October 1967, pp. 162-172; Philip Kotler, "Corporate Models: Better Marketing Plans," *Harvard Business Review,* July—August 1970, pp. 135-149, 168; Victor Cook, "Computer Pay-Off in Marketing," *Business Horizons,* April 1972, pp. 25-34.

the optimum number of arrival and departure gates needed at airport terminals and to schedule use of airline facilities and equipment.

Airline systems are complex operations today. United Airlines, for example, had twenty-seven gate positions handling hundreds of flights daily at O'Hare Airport in Chicago in 1973. Since each decision about a flight schedule or facility has an impact on many other parts of the airline system, a considerable amount of data manipulation is required to determine the consequences of each individual decision. Airline management thus needs an easy way to study the impact of changes in facility layouts and flight schedules on the total air-service system and its profitability. In making these decisions, management is trying not only to minimize delays, which are very aggravating to passengers, but also to maximize use of expensive airline equipment and facilities.

"Typical-day" computer simulation models have been developed to assist management in making these decisions. These computer models are specifically designed to allow managers to "try out" different combinations of gate facilities, and study the impact of these decisions on service and costs. The kinds of decisions such computer analysis can assist management in making include:

1. Determining the minimum number of gate positions required at a terminal facility.

2. Identifying the best mix of gate types to service the fleet schedule (ideally for maximum flexibility all gate positions would serve all types of aircraft; but this is not always economical, especially as larger aircraft, such as the Boeing 747 and Douglass DC-10, are introduced more widely).

3. Determining the number of back-up gate positions needed to prevent excessive aircraft delays due to periodic schedule bunching which may occur during bad weather or severe air-to-ground congestion.

4. Identifying flights which might be particularly vulnerable to delays under unusual local conditions.

5. Evaluating the impact of changes in flight schedules on facility and equipment usage, and on passenger delays and service.

The computer model is constructed in such a way that it can read raw input data, such as schedules, flight numbers, type of aircraft, available gate positions, and special features of a flight that may affect arrival and departure times, and then determine the sequence of events (actual arrival and departure times), depending on the initial flight schedules set up by the analyst and the type of facilities that the analyst determines are to be available (number and size of loading gates, for example). The model then permits the analyst to make changes in schedules or add and subtract gates (or change the types of gates) to determine what combination is likely to produce the least flight delays, customer waiting time, and idle equipment time.

Following programmed instructions, the computer reads in sequence each scheduled flight and decides whether it will be an "early" or "late" arrival. The arrival times are calculated by using a random number distribution table, which approximates the impact of weather conditions and the like on arrivals, to select positive (late) or negative (early) arrival increments. If the flight arrives later than the scheduled time, then a "late carryover time" is computed which will automatically be added to the departure time and to all subsquent scheduled times for this aircraft. The simulation program, using the probability of delay for passenger inspection and other reasons (from the table of random numbers described in the last chapter), also calculates new departure times. When delays occur, they are added to any late arrival carryover time.

Arrival and departure times are also affected by gates available. Certain types of aircraft cannot be serviced at specific gates (for example, Boeing 747s need larger gates than do Boeing 707s). Depending upon the restrictions, the program then proceeds to test the list of gates available which can accommodate the flight arrival being studied. The flight is assigned by the computer to the first available appropriate gate found for the plane. If no suitable gate is found, the time the next gate will be available is calculated and a delay record is noted and added to subsequent schedules.

The program proceeds to examine each scheduled flight in this manner until the typical day is completed, and the sequence is printed out, along with delay summaries. These printouts can then be examined to determine if any types of aircraft are more prone to delays than others, if some gate positions are underused, if some flights are more susceptible to delays than others, and other similar questions. The analyst then may change the number of gates, or mix of gates, or flight schedules, enter this information into the computer program at his terminal, rerun the "typical day" sequence, and restudy the results until he has a satisfactory solution.

These simulation models can also take into account additional factors affecting arrivals, departures, and ground service time. For example, the chance of mechanical failure can also be included in the program, as can time needed for movement of aircraft on the ground after they have landed.

Using a computer terminal connected to the model in the central computer processor, an analyst can test a wide range of gate position combinations when making a facility decision—at times, all of the possible combinations, under given flight schedule conditions. He can then vary the flight schedules and retest his alternative gate position combinations. With the computer simulation model, he can have his calculations of the impact of these alternatives in seconds. In decision situations where the gate positions are already in existence and the problem is developing economical and efficient flight schedules, the same model can be used to test a wide range of possible schedules and equipment assignments. While the computer simulation model does not provide the best answer, since the analyst probably will not think of all alternatives (nor have time to test them all), the model nonetheless does provide a useful information tool for studying the decision alternatives.

Marketing Planning and Production Scheduling. An example of how an even more complex computer simulation system was developed and used to assist in marketing planning and production scheduling is described by Michael S. Scott Morton in *Management Decision Systems: Computer-Based Support for Decision Making.*[2] In this situation, the decision process was fairly unstructured, so that the analyst's first step was to define the decision process and then subsequently to develop the simulation system. As happens in so many systems development situations, the actual management decision-making process changed and improved during the study.

The company involved was a large multi-product firm with sales in the billions of dollars. The company was decentralized by product group with some seventy divisions producing everything from large turbines to electric toothbrushes. The marketing organization for the consumer products groups was responsible for dollar profit for the groups. Within the marketing organization, responsibility for specific products, or groups of products, was assigned to individual *product or product group managers.* In addition, *marketing planning managers* were assigned to coordinate the work of product managers with *production management.*

Annual sales planning began with a computer-based sales forecast, which was developed by projecting overall market demand and then estimating the company's expected share of that market by product group. This forecast was then modified by the product manager, based on his judgment of what was a reasonable sales objective for the year in light of specific planned selling programs and competitive conditions. Similarly, the production plan started as a forecast of the production required to meet the initial sales demand forecast. This forecast was then modified by production management to reflect manufacturing capacity and cost restraints and changes in the marketing plan. These annual plans are reviewed and updated each month, when product managers received a revised sales demand forecast.

Marketing planning managers were responsible for setting specific monthly production targets for the various products. In setting these targets, a market-

2. Michael S. Scott Morton, *Management Decision Systems* (Boston, Mass.: Division of Research, Harvard Business School, 1971).

ing planning manager was pressured on one side by the product manager, who wanted to have ample supplies of all products everywhere, and on the other side by production management, which was responsible for keeping inventory and production costs as low as possible. The marketing planning manager's problem, then, was to balance the two sets of operating management requirements in a production schedule that was the best choice for the company as a whole.

The marketing planning manager had to consider several key variables in setting production targets: expected demand forecasts, marketing (or sales) plans, available inventory, and production availability and costs.

The expected demand was a forecast of potential possible sales in the marketplace, modified by the product manager's estimate of what portion of those possible sales the company could hope to get in light of sales plans and available product.

Sales program decisions were made by the product managers, since they were responsible for meeting the expense, sales, and profit targets set at the beginning of the year. The marketing planning manager's problem was to translate the product manager's sales plans into a concrete number of units sold by model; for example, a heavy advertising campaign in any section of the country for a particular product line had to be translated into a model-by-model expected sales figure. These model-by-model forecasts then had to be reconciled with overall sales forecasts.

As for current available inventory, computer printouts, broken down by model, were produced monthly and the accuracy of these reports was satisfactory for decision making. However, the problem was the vast amount of inventory data, since the printouts listed the status of all models and styles in all warehouse and production locations. Locating specific details of a product's color, size, model type, and the like was a time-consuming search problem.

The requirements of efficient and economical production also had to be considered. Probably the most difficult part of the marketing planning job was to reconcile the production schedules prepared based on the economics of production with the sales requirements given in the proposed sales plan.

The decision process through which these factors were considered by the marketing planning manager (MPM), working with the production manager (PM) and the product marketing manager (MM) is diagrammed in Figure 12–1. In all, the process spanned twenty working days. The fact that so many calculations were required and that these were done manually by clerks placed severe limitations on how the managers went about analyzing background data and developing and evaluating alternatives, and to some degree dictated the structure of the decision-making process. Problems were encountered, then, in all phases of decision making (the search for problems, the

FIGURE 12–1

Decision-Making Process Flowchart
Setting Monthly Production Targets

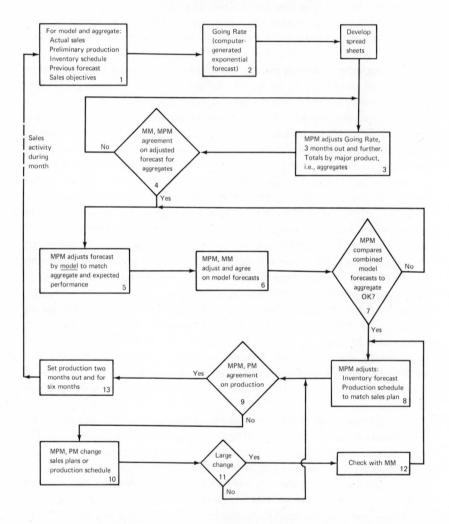

Source: All figures for this study by permission from Michael S. Scott Morton, *Management Decision Systems* (Boston, Mass.: Division of Research, Harvard Business School, 1971).

development of solutions, and the selection of courses of action): not only in generating basic data, but also in manipulating the data. Because of the data limitations, considerable intuitive judgment and negotiation was required among the three managers.

Management decided to develop a computer simulation system, in an effort both to save management time and to improve the accuracy of the forecasting and scheduling process.

Because of the nature of the decision situation, it was decided to use a large-screen, interactive, visual display computer terminal in the new simulation system. This would permit all three managers involved in the decisions (production, marketing planning, and product) to view data and calculations and to ask for additional data which could be displayed instantly. These visual display devices had full alpha-numeric capability—that is, they were similar to a television set which could display on the picture tube letters, numbers, and in some cases special symbols—and they were usually quicker than a typewriter output device, since they could display whole pages of information in seconds. In addition, they had the ability to draw and display vectors, circles, and any combination of the two, so that they could show trend graphs and graph comparative relationships where desired. The graphical capability was extremely useful, since it permitted the users faster assimilation of the information content of the display. These devices could be hooked up to telephones and so could be installed in any convenient location. A picture of the display unit used is given in Figure 12–2.

A crucial additional feature of this form of display was its interactive capability. Using a "light" pen, the user could point the light at the piece of information he wanted and this information would subsequently be printed on the screen.

Since random-access storage was used, the new system was able to display instanteously all the raw data used in the former decision process, make the calculations done before, graph trends, etc. The system was activated by typing a five-digit number. It would then print the data available for that designated subject—for example, information about a product line under study as shown in Figure 12–3. The decision maker would then ask for the next chart he wanted to see by pointing his light pen for example at GRAPH-CUMULATIVE, TUMBLERS, SEASONAL, JAN 1967, DEC 1967, and PROCEED in the chart, Figure 12–3. The chart shown in Figure 12–4 would then be flashed on the screen.

After examining Figure 12–4, perhaps the product manager does not like the working forecast (present sales plan) for the tumblers, presently set at 128,000 by December 31. Instead, he decides to expand advertising in the last half of the year and feels he can meet his objective of 138,000 by December 31. He wants to expand his sales rate, starting in JUL, in order to meet his objective by year end. The simulation for this act of specifications is elicited by hitting the following control points with the light from the pen:

FIGURE 12–2

Display System for the MDS

1. WORKING FORECAST and END-POINT PROJECT (to indicate which manipulation is to be carried out on which variable).
2. JUL (to indicate the starting month of the projection).
3. An ending value to the project—in this case, 138,000. This value is entered on the keyboard.
4. PROCEED (this results in the next picture, Figure 12–5).

The new display shown in Figure 12–5 shows that there is only .8 months supply of inventory on August 31 (small number at very top of graph). If the manager regarded this as unsatisfactory, he might change his production plan. In this example, the following control points were hit to generate the next picture:

1. PRODUCTION; CHANGE POINTS (to identify the variable and the manipulation).

FIGURE 12-3

Graph Specifications

DISPLAY FORMAT

GRAPH-CUMULATIVE

GRAPH-NON CUMULATIVE

RECONCILE

PROCEED

DATA

WASHERS
TUMBLERS
AGITATORS

T - 100
T - 200
T - 300
T - 500
T - 550

A - 100
A - 200
A - 300
A - 400
A - 500
A - 600
A - 700
A - 800
A - 900

AXIS

SEASONAL
NORMAL

TIME

JAN   1965
FEB   1966
MAR   1967
APR   1968
MAY   1969
JUN
JUL
AUG
SEP
OCT
NOV
DEC

JAN   1965
FEB   1966
MAR   1967
APR   1968
MAY   1969
JUN
JUL
AUG
SEP
OCT
NOV
DEC

419

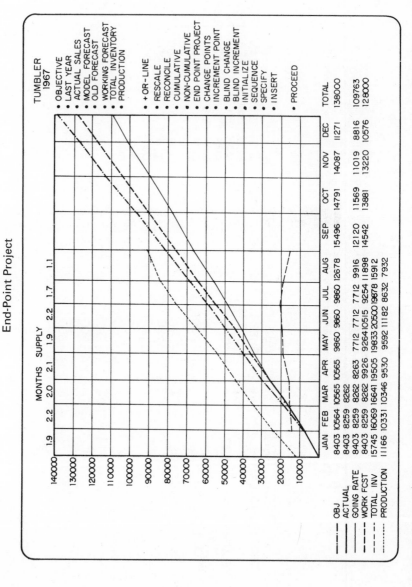

FIGURE 12-4

End-Point Project

FIGURE 12-5

Change Points

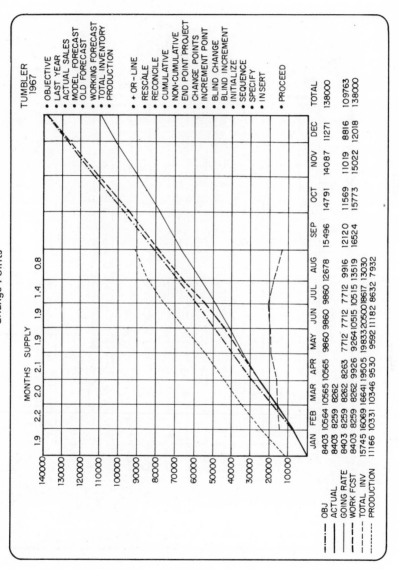

421

FIGURE 12-6

Reconcile

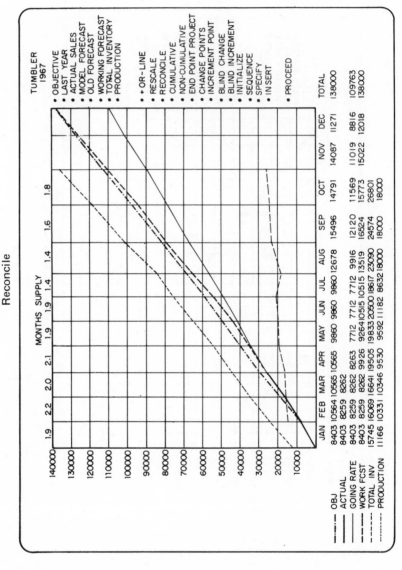

2. AUG (to identify month).

3. Type in the new value (for example, 18,000 in August).

4. PROCEED.

5. Repeat for September and October.

The new picture that is generated in Figure 12–6 has, obviously, a new production line. In addition, the month's supply has been recalculated and a new Total Inventory line plotted (bottom of screen). If the manager now wanted to check this with last year's sales, he could bring those data on the screen by hitting the following control points with his light:

1. Data-control point LAST YEAR.

2. Manipulation point or LINE.

3. PROCEED (picture not shown here).

After confirming that tumbler sales were now satisfactory, then the manager might want to see the relation of total tumbler sales to sales by models, which he may already have gone through model by model in a way similar to the way he went through aggregate tumbler sales. At this point, he would reconcile any difference between the aggregate sales forecast for all tumbler sales and the total of the sales forecasts for each individual model.

Naturally, there was considerably more to the system than described here. However, this description should give a good idea of the dynamics of the interaction among managers and the simulation model in sales forecasting and production scheduling.

Developing the new system took around twenty months: six months of observation, nine months for system development; and several more months for testing, debugging, modification, and user orientation. During the period of testing, many changes were made in both the way managers made decisions and in the system itself—as managers asked for additional information or systems changes.

In using the new system, there was a marked change in the overall decision-making process, in both its timing and structure. Instead of taking six working days over twenty elapsed working days, the entire process took half a working day. In addition, the managers were now able to take one model and study it all the way through; and, when all the models had been covered, could examine the aggregate forecast of all models to determine the aggregate solution to the problem. This was not possible under the old system, where aggregate sales (for example, tumblers as a group) were forecast, and then the individual models (for example, T-100, T-101, etc.) were examined; the sum of these model forecasts was then matched against the appropriate aggregated category and reconciled as best the managers could with the information they had. With the new system, the managers invariably worked with the model forecasting first and then developing their

FIGURE 12–7

New Process—Decision-Making Cycle*

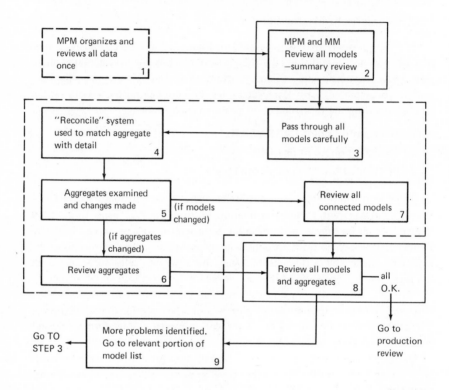

*See Notes for explanation.

Notes: (Comments are keyed to box)

1. This process was employed by the MPM in sessions 1 and 2 but not thereafter. The manager indicated (see Appendix D) after the third session that he would no longer do this. Box 2 now became the first step.

2. No models are changed. This is a once-over-lightly review to find potential problems.

3. Each of the models is taken in turn and examined.

4. When the last model is finished, all models are compared with the relevant aggregate. No changes are made until step 7 is finished.

5. Step 3 repeated for aggregate.

6. 7. Depending on results of steps 4 and 5 one or both of the aggregates and various models are changed.

8. Models are then reviewed as in step 2.

9. If any problems are seen from step 8, then the process is iterated from step 3.

aggregate forecasts; and in reconciling them they tended to attach more importance to the detailed model forecasts, since they now had immediate access to the detailed model data and could manipulate it easily. Since this system enabled greater control of the model by model forecasting, the aggregate forecasts were more accurate.

As it turned out the old decision process (shown in Figure 12–1) had been dictated by the way data was collected and calculations made. When managers were given flexibility to ask detailed questions about each model at the time the decisions were made about aggregate group forecasts, their decision process changed. This new decision process is shown in Figure 12–7.

Manager Training. Computer simulation models (called management games) have also been developed for management training purposes. The following is a description of one of the simpler management games in use today, which illustrates their interactive nature and their construction.[3]

The game involves an industry composed solely of the companies represented by the participating players or teams. A single product is made by the companies, and this product is sold in a single market. The companies (players) receive a balance sheet, profit and loss statement, statement of cash flow, and a summary of industry data each simulated period of play. The period of operations covered by the reports is usually assumed to be one quarter of a year. For each simulated period, the teams make decisions regarding price, marketing expenditures, production rate, plant and equipment purchases, and loan repayments. These decisions, together with a value of the economic index for the period, are given as input data to the computer program, which then calculates the results of play for the next quarter. The program prepares a new set of reports, which are returned to the players, and the cycle continues until the end of the game.

The program that provides the environment for the game and calculates results of team decisions is composed of seven major sections. These sections perform the following functions in the order stated:

1. Read in data regarding game environment, number of companies, characteristics of market, industry data for previous period, and previous period data for each company.

2. Read in economic index for current period and company decisions for each company for current period.

3. Edit company decisions for proper increments and check compatibility of production rate with plant capacity. (Decisions are rounded to even numbers of dollars and units and production rate decisions in excess of plant capacity are reduced to plant capacity.)

---

3. Robert C. Meier, William T. Newell and Harold L. Payer, *Simulation in Business and Economics* (Englewood Cliffs, N.J.: Prentice-Hall, Inc., 1969), pp. 182-188.

4. Compute size of total market and each company's sales in market.

5. Prepare data for company statements and revised industry data.

6. Print out results of play for period for each team.

7. Punch out data to be used as input in step 1 above in next cycle and terminate computer run.

As suggested by the outline of the program above, much of the work done by the program is simply reading and writing of data and elementary arithmetic operations. Preparation of the company statements, for example, involves only basic arithmetic operations; but a substantial amount of calculation is required, since the program essentially maintains a small accounting system for each company.

Several oversimplications are used to program the game. For example, the computer calculates step 4 first by using the formula:

$$B_t = T_{t-1} \left(\frac{I_t}{I_{t-1}} \right)$$

where B_t is the total base market available to the industry in any given period t, I is the economic index, and T_{t-1} the total market for the previous period. To this base market are added the effects (positive or negative) of changes in average marketing expenditures by the companies and the weighted average price charged by the industry (using tables such as those shown in Tables 12–1 and 12–2). These additions are represented by the formula:

$$T_t = B_t \text{ (total price effect and total marketing effect)}$$

Since the tables are arbitrary simplifications of market behavior, they do not necessarily represent realistic market behavior. However, based on tests of their use in actual games played, they seem to provide a semblance of reality and so are sufficient for gaming purposes.

Management games of much greater complexity have been created. For example, the Carnegie Tech Management Game allows the players to make over three hundred decisions each period and provides players with between one and two thousand items of information. And other games have been developed which allow the game administrator to enter economic data which makes the response of the economic environment more realistic. Computer simulation models developed for management games, then, can be among the most complex types of computer simulation models used by operating managers, although they are not used to actually assist in management decision making, as are the computer simulation models described earlier.

TABLE 12–1

Sample Price Effect Table Used
in Business Game[a]

Last Period Industry Weighted Average Price[b]	Percentage Increase or Decrease in Market
$10.00 (and above)	−42.0
9.50	−40.5
9.00	−38.0
8.50	−34.5
8.00	−30.5
7.50	−26.0
7.00	−20.5
6.50	−15.0
6.00	− 9.0
5.50	− 4.5
5.00	0.0
4.50	+ 3.5
4.00	+ 6.5
3.50	+ 8.5
3.00	+11.0
2.50	+12.5
2.00	+14.5
1.00 (and below)	+17.5

[a] The table is for a product with an initial selling price of $5.00 at the start of the game.

[b] Note that the use of last period average price causes changes in the market due to price changes to lag one period behind actual price changes.

Source: Tables 12-1 and 12-2 from Meier, Newell, and Pazer, *Simulation in Business and Economics* © 1969. Reprinted by permission of Prentice-Hall, Inc., Englewood Cliffs, New Jersey.

Corporate Financial Planning

Many companies have developed complex computerized financial planning models, similar in concept to the simulation models discussed in the preceding section which are used in management decision making. Typical of the "What if. . . ?" questions answered by using these simulation models are:

1. If product prices are changed, what will be the effect on cash flow? On profits?

2. If a proposed new item of equipment is purchased or leased, what will

TABLE 12–2

Sample Marketing Effect Table Used
in Business Game

Ratio of Last Period Industry Marketing Expenditures to Expenditures Two Periods Previous[a]	Percentage Increase or Decrease in Market
2.40 (and above)	+10.0
2.20	+ 9.5
2.00	+ 9.0
1.80	+ 8.5
1.60	+ 7.0
1.40	+ 5.0
1.20	+ 3.0
1.00	0.0
0.80	− 3.0
0.60	− 6.5
0.40	−10.5
0.20 (and below)	−14.5

[a] Note that the use of last period expenditures to the previous period causes changes in the market due to changes in marketing expenditures to lag one period behind actual changes in expenditures.

be the effects on profits and cash flow of alternative financing methods?

3. If a wage increase is granted, what will be the effect on production rates, use of overtime, risk of seasonal inventory, and so on, for a production program?

The cost of developing these programs has been reduced greatly by the development of general systems models, which can be adapted to any company's situation.[4] For example, Figure 12–8 shows the outline of such a model's logic. The business series data file and the corporate model logic are unique to the particular enterprise; the economic series data file and the general system program are common to all applications.

Stored in the business series data file are proprietary data of the particular company, including sales, costs, and other information. These company data, as well as the corporate model logic, are accessible only to authorized personnel. As for the economic series data file, it contains a wide variety of

4. James B. Boulden and Elwood S. Buffa, "Corporate Models: On-Line, Real-Time Systems," *Harvard Business Review,* July–August 1970, pp. 65-83.

national and industry economic series such as gross national product, indexes of industrial production, and housing starts. These data series are maintained and updated by the operators of the general system, very often an outside data processing service company.

The first step in using the system is to manipulate the raw data in the business and economic series files in meaningful ways so as to forecast future sales or other aspects of performance. The relationships are shown in a very general way in Figure 12–8, where it is seen that the result of the mathematical and statistical routines is a forecast which is fed into the report generation and simulation phase. Figure 12–9 shows more clearly the kinds of

FIGURE 12–8

Interrelationships of General System Program

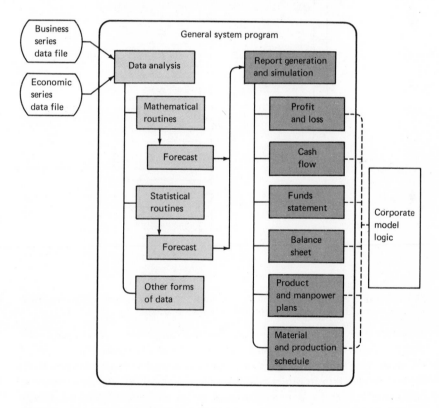

Source: James B. Boulden and Elwood S. Buffa, "Corporate Models: On-Line, Real-Time Systems," *Harvard Business Review,* July-August, 1970.

FIGURE 12–9

Data Analysis Phase

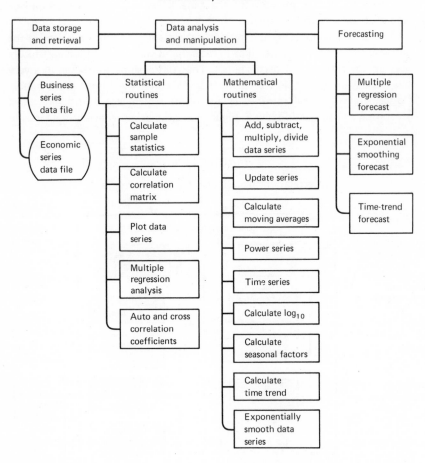

Source: James B. Boulden and Elwood S. Buffa, "Corporate Models: On-Line, Real-Time Systems," *Harvard Business Review,* July-August, 1970.

statistical and mathematical manipulation available in the data analysis phase, and Figure 12–10 details the report generation and simulation phase.

With these standard routines available to be used at will, an analyst might take raw sales data from the business file and smooth them (remove seasonal variations) by either a moving-average or an exponential-smoothing technique. He might then compute seasonal factors, plot the smoothed data with a variety of economic indicators from the economic file, or do multiple regression studies. The final result of his analysis is a forecast which is then an input to the report generation and simulation phase. He may wish to take

FIGURE 12–10

Corporate Financial Analysis

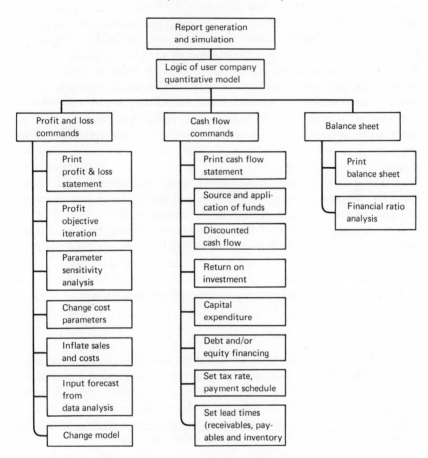

Source: James B. Boulden and Elwood S. Buffa, "Corporate Models: On-Line, Real-Time Systems," *Harvard Business Review,* July-August, 1970.

more than one forecast (for example, expected, optimistic, and pessimistic forecasts) into the simulation phase to see how they reflect on the profit and loss statement, cash flow statement, and balance sheet.

The important fact concerning the data analysis phase is the integrated nature of the general system program, which makes it possible to carry effects computed by one subprogram into another subprogram.

During the next phase—report generation and simulation—the manager can test the different assumptions and ideas he has. This is the part of the system in which businessmen are most interested. Figure 12–9 shows the main kinds of manipulation and output possible in corporate financial analysis using this model.

In the report generation and simulation phase, the forecasts generated in the data analysis phase (and/or forecasts generated externally by field sales managers) are fed into the corporate model. Raising "What if. . . ?" questions of the type mentioned earlier, the manager determines the effect of various events on income and cash statements. The corporate model logic works in conjunction with the general system program to produce reports printed in the form specified by the manager. Thus, the manager can try many alternative sets of assumptions and see almost immediately the effects of the proposed changes, since these models are on-line real-time systems, in which the manager works with a terminal connected to the centralized data processor.

The interactive nature of these models makes them effective decision aids, since the manager can ask his questions and get his answers immediately, while he is in the process of developing his financial plans.

More complex versions of financial simulation models have been developed. For example, both Inland Steel and Potlatch Forest Products Companies have developed such models,[5] as have several oil companies.[6] In business today, corporate financial planning models are among the most widely used computerized management decision-assisting systems.

Longer-Term Strategic Planning

Work is being done on complex computerized models for longer-term corporate planning. For example, one major oil company has done a preliminary design study of such a strategic planning model, since it was a logical extension of the company's work on financial planning models. This advanced model integrates all functional planning within a single computerized model. The following is a summary of the proposed model.

Oil companies are faced with a complex planning problem, since there is a close relation among marketing, manufacturing, and supply and distribution—an investment in any one area often commits the company to compensating investments in other areas to avoid imbalances of supply and usage. Such imbalances have a major impact on profits. For example, too many gas stations in any one area might require the company to buy gas at a premium from an outside supplier, if the company does not have adequate facilities

5. Boulden and Buffa, "Corporate Models," pp. 69-ff.

6. For example, see: George W. Gershefski, "Building a Corporate Financial Model," *Harvard Business Review,* July–August 1969, pp. 61-72; and Henry I. Meyer and Stephen O. Jennings, "Financial Planning Models at Pennzoil," *Management Review,* December 1972, pp. 22-27.

available; and excessive refinery production must be sold off at a discount, if expansion of the company's marketing operations has not kept pace with production expansion.

The purpose of a new model is to provide management with an analytical decision-making tool through which it could test out or "simulate" the effects of alternative plans, in order to project the effect of decisions in one area on other functional areas and eventually their ultimate effect on return on investment. The model is also able to pinpoint any potential supply and demand imbalances within the company and so minimize them by identifying additional investment requirements.

The model focuses on the timing, cost, geographical location, form, and profitability of new investments in each area of an oil company's operation. It can be used to analyze additions, as well as divestments, in the facilities area. To do this, the model stores information on all reasonable supply and distribution product movement patterns, manufacturing refinery capabilities, and marketing alternatives and intentions—both now and in the foreseeable future.

Some of the planning decisions which can be studied with the model are:

1. *Marketing decisions*
   a) Construction of new service stations in established areas.
   b) Construction of new service stations in new areas.
   c) Purchase of existing service stations.
   d) Closing or disposing of existing service stations.
   e) Rehabilitation of existing stations.
   f) Significant departures from current product sales mixes.

2. *Manufacturing decisions*
   a) Major expansion or revision of existing facilities.
   b) Closing existing refineries.
   c) Measuring the importance to the company of new technologies.
   d) Evaluating new crude oils.
   e) Assessing the company's ability to meet continually changing product quality requirements.

3. *Supply and distribution decisions*
   a) Expansion of existing major pipelines.
   b) Withdrawal from participation in existing pipelines.
   c) Participation in new pipeline arrangements.
   d) Changing tanker loading facilities.

These are only some of the planning decisions the model can be used for. The model's major breakthrough is in being able to examine all the functional capabilities simultaneously and determine how they interact. For example, when considering entering a new market area, the model can simultaneously analyze crude supply, refining capabilities, product distribution, and marketing alternatives. The circular problem arising from the fact that the size and capability of a new refinery depends on the market it will serve, while at the same time the size and kind of marketing effort depends on the refinery capability, is thus solved by the computer model. The model is also able to project the changes in manufacturing facilities required by changes in current product mixes in the marketing area. Thus, the model's most important contribution comes in the area of such interacting decisions.

The model is basically a large linear program, with four major sub-models: manufacturing, marketing, supply and distribution, and finance.

The manufacturing sub-model contains detail on all the company's refineries and major processing agreements. Since it is capable of studying interactions among manufacturing, marketing, and supply and distribution, it can estimate the costs associated with various levels of product demands, crude supplies, crude prices, and refinery capacities. To do this, the model includes representations of the size and capabilities of major refinery processes in each refinery (present or proposed) and the significant quality variations which distinguish various crudes and products.

The marketing sub-model is principally a description of demands for each major product in each of the company's geographical areas. The demand description is broken down into four parts: base demand arising from existing marketing outlets, increments in demand arising from proposed and planned investments in new outlets, decreases in base demand resulting from outlet divestments, and large, foreseen, discretionary sales contracts.

The supply and distribution sub-model contains formulas representing processing agreements, product movements from source to market, and product exchange opportunities at either supply points or market areas.

The financial sub-model contains the financial criteria which management has established (objectives and restraints). This sub-model is the integrating aspect of the total model, for it is used to estimate the financial impact of any plan—that is, its impact on earnings and return on investment. Depending on data supplied, this model can also be used to generate any type of financial report in any proposed plan: funds flow statements, balance sheets, profit or loss statements, sources and applications of funds statements, etc.

The integrated planning model requires a considerable amount of data. For example, the manufacturing sub-model needs the following information on an annual basis: crude prices, availability and qualities; yields for each major crude representation; product quality specifications; unit configuration and capacities in each refinery; economics and extent of processing agreements; variable operating cost data for each refinery; yields and capacities of

planned or considered new units in each refinery; unit expansion or moderni-
zation and their planned effects; foreseeable new techniques (new yields or
processes); yield, capital and operating costs of refinery processing units of
various sizes; and financial and economic data regarding refinery assets and
fixed operating costs. A similar amount of information is needed for each
sub-model.

It should be clear from the above discussion that such a model is
expensive to develop and use, and only within the scope of large companies.
For example, development of a model like the oil company one described
above might take four people three years (around $240,000 in salaries and
supporting services), and require extensive computer time ($100,000) and
information services from many operating departments ($100,000). The total
cost, therefore, allowing for estimating errors could run close to $500,000. In
addition, yearly operating costs for maintaining and using the model could
run between $100,000 and $150,000. This high cost accounts for the limited
work done to date by business on these kinds of computerized decision-
assisting information systems.

Larger-Scale, More Fully Integrated
Management Information Systems

The concept of larger-scale, more fully integrated management information
systems was first introduced in Chapters One and Three. As seen in Figure
3–18 in Chapter Three and in Figure 12–11 below, these systems involve a
large, central data bank (or data base) which is used to serve the information
needs of many departments.

In the past, a company most often introduced computer systems into
various segments of its operations piecemeal; and, as management gained
experience with computer systems, the company would integrate more and
more of these systems. For example, a company might first computerize its
inventory control and production scheduling system, later integrating them
with its materials management and sales forecasting systems. The beginning of
such evolution towards more fully integrated systems is seen in the examples
described in Chapter Nine. Normally, then, there are varying degrees of
systems integration, depending on the company's experience with and need
for computer-based data processing and information systems.

On occasion, a company such as Mead Corporation, whose systems development effort is described in Chapter Thirteen, will start with the objective
of developing as fully integrated a system as possible, covering many marketing, financial, and production areas. Mead, however, had had considerable
prior experience with computer systems in their different operating divisions;

FIGURE 12–11

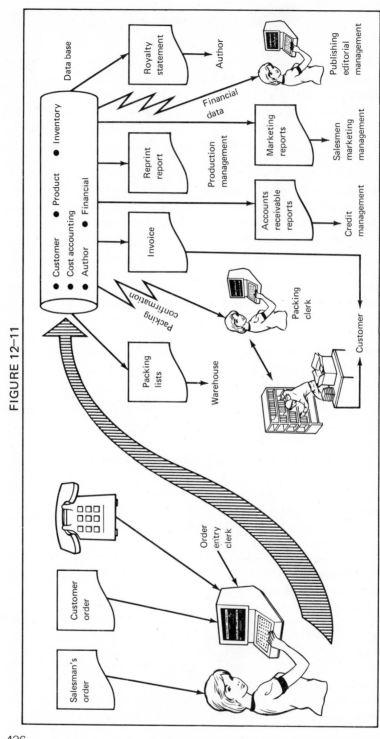

Source: Reprinted from Edward Schefer and Ernest Thompson, "Integrated Systems for Publishing Houses," in *The Arthur Andersen Chronicle*, March, 1971.

and, in developing a new and larger system, the development was still done in stages, one operation at a time, starting with production control. The unique feature of Mead's development effort was that Mead began with the concept of a larger integrated system from the outset: by studying the information and data processing requirements of all operating areas that would eventually be served by the total system *before developing any one particular sub-system,* the problems involved in integrating the sub-systems at a later date were minimized.

Unless such eventual integration is kept in mind from the beginning of the systems development effort, when studying user requirements, major problems may be encountered in later merging the data files, data processing procedures, and report generation of different sub-systems. Where such a total perspective has not guided the development of individual systems, it is not uncommon to have to scrap an entire departmental data system, when the decision is finally made to merge systems serving several different operating areas. For example, in the *Bantom Pharmaceuticals Company* study described in Chapter Nine, the materials management system was incompatible with the inventory management and production scheduling system; because of this, their merger was delayed several years until the development costs of the materials management system (which was a perfectly good system for that operating area) were amortized. An integrated systems approach might have prevented this waste and delay.

It is helpful, therefore, to think of the systems described in Part Two not as separate systems, but as sub-systems of larger data processing systems—and when developing such departmental systems to spend some time during the study of user requirements to explore ways in which each of the departmental systems under study might eventually be integrated with other operationally related systems. Such broader background studies are especially useful when making decisions about the nature and structure of the data file, such as the kind of random access storage (if any) to use, the sequence of the file, the coding of the data entries, and the amount of data to be stored in each file.

The following is a description of an integrated data processing and information system used at a publishing company.

A Publishing Company's System

The publishing business has several distinguishing characteristics: their book products are developed by independent authors; book writing is a highly creative type of work with a long lead time from formulation of the book idea to book completion and production; the business is highly volatile, with side swings in sales of individual books; backlists of standard books provide some stability to the business; and publishing management is slow in accepting changes in business practices, because publishers are often suspicious that scientific modern management methods will stifle creativity.[7]

In spite of the natural resistance of creative businesses to sophisticated computer systems, progress is being made in developing advanced data processing and management information systems for publishing companies. For example, Figures 12–11 and 12–12 show the outline of a typical integrated publishing company system.

In this system, the order processing clerk uses a cathode ray tube (CRT) input device to enter and validate the order information. This entry uses the Customer Master File by matching the customer's name and account number to determine initial credit screening information and shipping instructions. The books ordered are then entered by a title code and edition number, and the Inventory Master File is used to determine the availability and best warehouse location for shipment. As availability is determined, packing lists are prepared for removing the books from stock. Once packing is confirmed, the invoice is prepared and distributed. A receivable is created and the amount of credit available for the customer is reduced on the Customer Master File. If the total value of the order puts the customer over his credit limit, a message is sent to the order processing clerk either to request approval of extension of additional credit or to backorder the over-limit items until payment of outstanding receivables is made, restoring the credit available to a sufficient level.

Sales, inventory, and cost of sales are updated on the Product, Inventory, Author, and Financial Master Files. If the sale causes inventory for a title at a location or in total to fall to a predetermined reorder level, reports are generated to notify management of the need to make a decision to ship from a different location, schedule a reprint, or let the title go out of print. These reports would include a computer-calculated economic ordering quantity for review by management. Most of these actions are programmed to occur automatically in the computer system and require no further manual entry of data, except for such items as packing confirmation. A similar series of events would occur for other transactions.

The schematic flow diagram in Figure 12–12 does not attempt to show all the possible data paths, but simply portrays some of the typical inputs and related processing, master files or "data base" and update processing, and information processing and related outputs that make up the system.

The system benefited the publishing company in many ways. First, it provided many financial management information reports faster and in more

---

7. This section and the reports in it are based on Edward A. Schefer and Ernest B. Thompson, "Integrated Systems for Publishing Houses," *Management Adviser*, November–December 1971, pp. 41-52.

FIGURE 12–12

Schematic

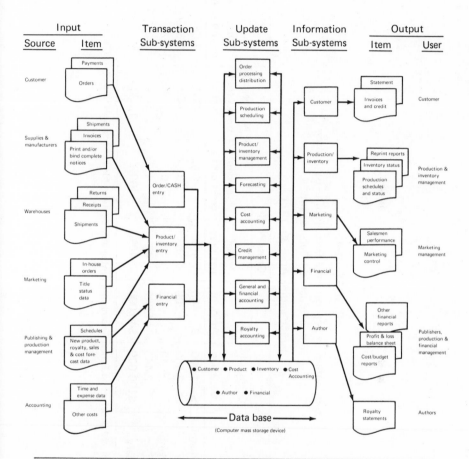

Source: Reprinted from Edward Schefer and Ernest Thompson, "Integrated Systems for Publishing Houses," in *The Arthur Andersen Chronicle,* March, 1971.

detail than before. For example, the system generated profitability reports by book, author (Figure 12–13), and department. In addition, periodic reports on book development and production expenses are generated by book and by department, as shown in Figure 12–14. Through combining data in the files, the computer system could also produce interim profit and loss statements, balance sheets and cash flow statements for the entire company.

Second, manual order processing had been done by a large group of employees, each a specialist with knowledge of certain types of customers

FIGURE 12–13

Contribution to Departmental Gross Profit—By Author

Higher Education Department

Period ending April 30, 1971

Author	Title	Net sales	Gross Profit			Number of books sold (net)	Pub. month	Book number
			Amount	% of net sales	% of dept. gross profit			
Nesredna	XYZ corp. history	$ 1,000	$ 400	40%	1%	200	7-69	492
Nesredna	Door design	2,400	1,200	50	3	400	9-69	571
Nesredna	Ticking & tying	40	2	5	0	14	2-70	451
Author Summary		3,440	1,602	47	4	614	—	—
Department Summary		$100,000	$40,000	40%	100%	1,228	—	—

Source: Reprinted from Edward Schefer and Ernest Thompson, "Integrated Systems for Publishing Houses," in *The Arthur Andersen Chronicle*, March, 1971.

FIGURE 12-14

Work-in-Process Ledger—Trade Department

Period ending April 30, 1970

Book #493—Author: M. Berger—Title: Teleprocessing Made Simple

Vendor	Invoice date	Description	Quantity	Unit cost	Costs					Plant costs	
					Total	Paper	Printing	Binding	Freight	Plate	Pre-pub expenses
Smith Bros.	4- 2-70	Beg. Balance			120	100			20		
Preston Co.	4- 4-70	Engraving								1,000	
		Reproduction								500	
Jones & Co.	4- 4-70	Paper-Text	10,000	.20		2,000					
Cogswell Corp.	4-10-70	Printing	10,000	.15			1,500				
Gerk Co.	4-11-70	Binding	10,000	.10				1,000			
Noll Trucking	4-18-70	Freight							70		
Falk Co.	4-21-70	Art Work									500
Brown Bros.	4-21-70	Fees									100
Total for Month					4,570	2,000	1,500	1,000	70	1,500	600
Ending Balance					4,690	2,100	1,500	1,000	90	1,500	600
Transfers Out:											
—To Bound Stock					4,090	2,000	1,000	1,000	90		
—To Variances					600	100	500				

Source: Reprinted from Edward Schefer and Ernest Thompson, "Integrated Systems for Publishing Houses," in The Arthur Andersen Chronicle, March, 1971.

and books. The computer was able to economically store all pertinent customer information, check inventory status, determine delivery dates and the like—tasks formerly performed by the clerks. The computer system was also able to perform a large number of the clerical functions involved in author royalty accounting and so saved considerably there.

Third, since the inventory planning and control system was fully integrated with the order processing system, currently up-to-date inventory files were maintained. Besides maintaining inventory files, the new system was able to generate such management action reports as the inventory reordering report shown in Figure 12—15, which showed not only when a new printing of a book would be needed, but also the amount needed in that printing (calculated by the computer). One unique report produced by the system was an analysis of book costs and estimates of the price which must be charged to cover those costs (Figure 12—16).

Fourth, the computer system was also able to store data on commitments for new books and, based on this data, could produce tentative schedules of the amount and timing of manpower, production, printing, financial, and other resource requirements. These schedules could then be used in management planning for all these areas. The computer system was also able to help in marketing planning decisions. For example, records of past costs were used to project future costs of similar books; and when this data was combined with market analysis data on the potential sales of the new book proposed, estimates could be made of the projected profitability of the book under consideration. These profit estimates are useful in deciding whether or not to sign up a new book.

Fifth, the computer system also produced control reports used in marketing management. For example, Figure 12—17 shows a report for one salesman. Total result reports could also be produced by department. Analytical reports on demand and costs by distribution channel and warehouse location were also prepared by the computer system and used in marketing management decision making.

The integrated data processing and management information system used in this publishing company is a fairly straightforward integrated financial result reporting, order processing, inventory control and production scheduling, and customer account maintenance system. Such systems, with modifications to suit specific company requirements, are becoming more common in larger companies. For example, the system described at Mead Corporation in Chapter Thirteen (especially Figure 13—1) is basically just a much more complicated version of the system described here, with the addition of production planning and control subsystems.

As seen from the discussion of management tasks in Part Two, while such integrated systems are more advanced and more fully integrated than those

FIGURE 12–15

Reprint Ordering Report
Higher Education Department

Period ending April 30, 1971

Title	Author	Available inventory	Next 12 month forecast	Economic order quantity	Order to be placed by	Bound book available date	Out of stock date	No. months supply	Action code
American history	P. Jones	14,000	20,000	17,500	5-15-71	7-15-71	8-15-71	3.5	1
Anatomy	M. Landesman	22,000	12,000	24,000	No Order			22.0	2
Ticking & tying	A. E. Nesredna	3,000	15,000	10,000	5-1-71	8-1-71	7-15-71	2.5	3

Action code tables:

1 Reprint
2 Excessive stock (more than 1 year supply)
3 Reprint & expedite

Source: Reprinted from Edward Schefer and Ernest Thompson, "Integrated Systems for Publishing Houses," in *The Arthur Andersen Chronicle*, March, 1971.

FIGURE 12–16

Reprint Pricing Report

Higher Education Department

Period ending April 30, 1971

Title	Author	Next 12 month forecast	Economic order quantity	Estimated reprint order date	Req'd selling price—per pricing formula	Current selling price	Action required
American history	P. Jones	20,000	17,500	5-15-71	12.50	10.00	Yes
Anatomy	M. Landesman	12,000	24,000	No order			
Ticking & Tying	A. E. Nesredna	15,000	10,000	5- 1-71	4.50	5.00	No

Source: Reprinted from Edward Schefer and Ernest Thompson, "Integrated Systems for Publishing Houses," in *The Arthur Andersen Chronicle*, March, 1971.

444

FIGURE 12–17

Sales Report—Trade Department

Period ending April 30, 1971

Agent	Period	Number of accounts	Net sales	% dept.	± Budget	Back orders	% sales	Advance sales	± Budget	Returns	% sales	Expenses	± Budget
A. GINZBURG	APR	40	$ 10,000	5%	$ 2,000	$ 4,000	40%	$ 2,000	$500	$ 500	5%	$ 1,000	$ 200
	YTD	40	100,000	4	3,000	5,000	5	4,000	200	6,000	6	8,000	50
E. JACOBS	APR	4	2,000	1	(1,000)	—	—	100	(400)	1,000	50	800	200
	YTD	8	24,000	1	(7,000)	—	—	200	(800)	6,000	25	10,000	900
DEPT. TOTALS	APR	845	200,000	100	5,000	6,000	3	8,000	550	20,000	10	100,000	4,000
	YTD	1,125	2,000,000	100%	50,000	27,000	1%	12,000	700	200,000	10%	100,000	40,000

Source: Reprinted from Edward Schefer and Ernest Thompson, "Integrated Systems for Publishing Houses," in *The Arthur Andersen Chronicle*, March, 1971.

management information systems described earlier in this book, they still serve only a limited range of management information needs. For example, while such systems provide effective management control tools (especially in the financial and production areas), their use in making strategic planning decisions in marketing management is negligible.

These systems nonetheless represent major advances in the systems development area. In developing them, for example, major problems in file construction had to be solved. Through the process of developing these systems, management is learning how to develop even more complex and more fully integrated systems. Management is also gaining experience in dealing with the many organizational problems that are encountered in developing larger-scale computer systems. These organizational problems are discussed in Chapter Thirteen.

Other Examples of Advanced Information Systems

During the late 1960s and early 1970s, not only have companies done considerable work in developing more advanced management information systems; but they have also been more willing to write about their work. The following is a list (with brief descriptions) of company studies, some with disguised names, which are now available from the Case Study Clearing House at Harvard Business School (Boston, Massachusetts 02163). These can be used for further study or for classroom discussion and exercises.

1. *The Eaton National Bank* (#9-171-259). This study describes a basic computerized data processing system used in a bank, the problems encountered in taking full advantage of its capabilities for generating management information, and its impact on operating personnel.

2. *McDonnell Douglass Corporation* (#'s 9-170-008, 9-170-009, 9-170-010). These studies describe the company's information systems and its information systems planning process.

3. *General Systems, Inc.* (#9-170-004). This study describes the sources of information and the systems used for gathering information for strategic planning.

4. *The Polyplastic Corporation* (#'s 9-171-647, 9-171-648). These studies involve preparing a formal management report containing information requirements specifications for a new computerized short-term sales forecasting system.

5. *Carver Consolidated Products* (#'s 9-114-001, 9-114-013, 9-114-014). These studies focus on the problems of designing a computer-based system to assist in inventory control and product distribution

and in marketing management, and the role of management in insuring that effective systems are developed.

6. *Carter University* (#9-171-611). This study describes a feasibility study done in a large public university which was interested in developing an integrated computer-based management information system.

7. *Philips* (#9-171-001). This study describes how the company has organized and planned its massive world-wide computer usage effort.

8. *Airmont Packaging* (#'s 9-171-654, 9-171-655). This study presents excerpts from a sixty-five-page report recommending a comprehensive computer-based management information system, and describes the problems encountered in trying to develop the system.

9. *American Airlines* (#9-170-032). This study describes the uses of American's corporate planning model in general and the uses of the model in planning the Pacific route concession in particular. American's model is a more complex version of the airline planning model described in the first section of this chapter. In American's model, the impact of equipment and schedule changes on average passenger loads and consequently on revenues is also calculated to permit the analysis of the ultimate profitability of each alternative considered.

The reader can obtain these studies by writing to the Case Study Clearing House and asking for them by name and number.

Total Information Systems?

Strictly speaking, it is impossible to develop a total information system for a large business enterprise, since there will always be some subsystems which have only a limited interface with the company's basic management information and data processing systems. For example, information systems for strategic planning are almost always separate systems which do not provide direct input to other company computerized data processing and information systems. Another example is the quality control system developed for the manufacture of the F-111 fighter described in Chapter Nine, which—although it is an advanced information system centrally administered by the computer services division—was a separate subsystem that had very little interface with other computer-based systems in the company.

The term "total information system," then, is used to refer not to an actual system to be developed, but to the scope and viewpoint of systems studies which, during the initial phase, review *all* the information and data flows within a business. Often, as the study progresses, it becomes clear that some of the information flows cannot be efficiently handled by an advanced computer information system. These flows may be processed manually (for example, external market information on buyer motivation used in planning market strategy) and when this information is translated into specific plans and budgets, it would become input into the computer network.

The term "more fully integrated" systems is thus used in this chapter to indicate that companies are examining their management information systems from a total enterprise viewpoint and working towards greater and greater integration of their data processing and management information systems. However, given the state of today's computer technology and management practices, one can only say that more integrated systems will be developed. In practice, then, total information systems are only an ideal conceptual framework, as noted at the end of Chapter One.

Summary
Conclusion

This chapter has described two kinds of advanced information systems: advanced decision-supporting systems, which make use of simulation models, and larger-scale computer-based processing systems, which serve the data and information needs of two or more departments within a company.

Several examples of different kinds of advanced decision-supporting systems were covered. As seen from these examples, while these systems can make a significant contribution to management decision making, they can be expensive and difficult to develop and so are not widely used in business today—with the exception of corporate financial planning models. And even these models are sometimes not used effectively in companies which have them, as is seen in the *Sun Oil Company* study exercise which follows at the end of this chapter.

Larger-scale more fully integrated data processing and information systems, which were also discussed, should be more familiar to the reader, since they are basically extensions of the kinds of systems discussed in Part Two. Most large companies today have some form of advanced integrated data processing and management information system, normally in the order processing, financial result reporting, inventory control and production scheduling, and account maintenance areas.

A manager plays as key a role in developing these advanced systems as he does in developing the systems described in Part Two. Since these advanced systems are more complex, however, so is his role more complex. Not only are there more technical complexities, but very often each manager's requirements must be integrated with those of other managers, increasing the problems of organization and coordination of the systems development effort.

Chapter Thirteen describes some of the problems encountered in developing complex management information systems and how these problems might be overcome.

TEXT DISCUSSION QUESTIONS

1. Describe some of the ways in which advanced decision-supporting systems (based on simulation models) are used in management decision making. Describe an example of one of these systems, covering both its structure and use by management.

2. Describe some of the uses made of advanced computer technology in the advanced decision-supporting systems described in this chapter.

3. What kinds of compromises may have to be made when developing mathematical formulas to represent real-world relationships in simulation models? In what ways do these compromises affect the validity of the models and the results they produce?

4. Describe the kinds of management questions that can be answered using computerized corporate financial simulation models. Describe the limitations of the information produced by such models.

5. Explain why it is so difficult to develop computer-based strategic planning models.

6. What kinds of problems are encountered in developing the data bank (or data base) in larger-scale management information systems serving the needs of two or more operating departments?

7. Discuss how the concept of subsystems described in Chapter One (especially Figure 3–1) relates to the discussions of departmental systems in Part Two and of integrated systems in this chapter.

8. Describe the concept of total information systems. How does it affect management information systems development?

9. Why is it said that a total information system can never be developed for a business enterprise?

Case Study Exercise

The Sun Oil Company (A)

"We have decided to develop a computer-based planning model at Sun over the next few years," Mr. Donald P. Jones, Vice President-Comptroller, said in January 1966. "We feel that such a model might benefit our planning efforts by allowing us to plan more accurately and faster."

"The Project Team was organized some months ago, and we are now ready to make several decisions about the design of the model," Mr. Jones continued. "Quite frankly, this task troubles me a bit since I am not a computer expert. But I realize that, as a future model user, my opinions and not those of the computer experts should be controlling."

"I understand from the Project Team that four basic problems must be resolved. Should we build an optimization model or a simulation model? Should the model incorporate probability distributions? Should the model be largely based on continuous data compilation from the line departments, or should as much information as possible be internally generated in the model? Finally, how detailed a model should we build?"

Company Background

Sun Oil Company, with corporate headquarters in Philadelphia, was a fully integrated petroleum company. In 1965 it was ranked seventy-first in sales, forty-first in assets, and forty-second in profits in *Fortune* magazine's list of the 500 largest U.S. industrial corporations. A ten-year financial summary is given in Figure 12–18.

Sun was active in all branches of oil industry operations, exploration, production, transportation, refining, and marketing. It had, in addition, wholly-owned subsidiaries engaged in shipbuilding, and in the design, sale, and rental of oil well surveying instruments and services. Affiliated companies refined and distributed naphthalene and produced urea, ethylene, and hydrogen.

There were three key features of operations. The first included oil production, transportation and refining. Sun's North American oil production activities were conducted in twenty-three states and four Canadian provinces, embracing an area from Florida to California and from the Gulf of Mexico to the Arctic. Crude oil was transported by pipeline and/or ocean tankers to the

This case was prepared by Peter Lorange, Research Assistant, under the supervision of Professor Richard F. Vancil, as a basis for class discussion rather than to illustrate either effective or ineffective handling of an administrative situation.

company's three refineries: the 151,000 barrel per day capacity refinery at Marcus Hook, Pennsylvania; the 95,000 barrel per day capacity refinery at Toledo, Ohio; and the 30,000 barrel per day capacity refinery at Sarnia, Ontario.

The second sphere of operations encompassed refined products marketing, distribution, and research. Sun's gasoline marketing territory covered twenty-two states, the District of Columbia, and the Canadian provinces of Ontario and Quebec. Industrial products were sold in most of the United States and Canada. Sun's products were distributed through an integrated system of pipeline, tank ship, barge, tank cars, and tank truck transport. Economic and market research as well as associated planning activities were conducted in the home offices.

Foreign activities were the third area of operations. In addition to the United States and Canada, Sun's products were sold in Europe, Central and South America, Africa and the Far East. Most of the oils sold outside North America were delivered in bulk by tankships. Exploration and production activities were conducted through subsidiaries in Venezuela, the Middle East, England, and Australia. Recent oil discoveries in the Persian Gulf and natural gas in the North Sea were adding to Sun's reserves.

Factors Contributing to the Start up of the Corporate Planning Model

"The complexity of our fully integrated petroleum enterprise requires close direction and control from headquarters," Mr. Jones said. "Compared to many other industries our environment is relatively stable and the growth in the demand for most of our products is fairly predictable. Consequently, top management have tended to put relatively more emphasis on short-to-medium-range profit planning while long-range planning generally has received relatively less attention. Also, the timing of certain classes of expenditures has a major impact on the current earnings in oil companies, and this tends to increase the importance of short-term planning." Industry accounting practices, particularly those concerning the write-off of oil exploration expenditures, allowed management to influence reported earnings within reasonable limits so that year-by-year income trends tended to be highly stable.

Mr. Jones continued, "Long-term planning, on the other hand, has been rather informal. Top management has based their evaluation of long-term decisions upon their experience, intimate knowledge of the company's resource capabilities, and an intuitive feel for the oil industry.

"Over the years I have felt less and less comfortable with the fact that we did virtually no formal planning for periods of more than two years. It seemed less and less possible to evaluate properly the effects of long-range capital investments. What would be their effects on future earnings, capital requirements, manpower, and so on? I also felt that we were not paying enough attention to possible long-range effects of the short-to-medium range decisions that took most of top management's attention. In short, we had no choice but to start long-range planning on a more formal basis.

"A specific proposal for Sun to build a corporate financial model came to my attention in early 1965 from Charles A. Pfahler, an Assistant Comptroller. (See Figure 12–19 for Sun Oil corporate organization chart.) A national officer of the Planning Executive Institute (PEI), Charlie suggested to me that Sun and PEI jointly might develop a corporate computer-based financial model. PEI would use such a project as part of their research. He convinced me that such a model might be very helpful, especially in strategic decision making where planning was most urgently needed. I saw two reasons why a corporate planning model might benefit Sun. First, the model might help us in our evaluation of long-term strategic decisions. It would indicate interconnected consequences of a decision in various parts of Sun. Second, the model project would help to create a favorable climate for formal long-range planning. Thus, I saw it as a means to get formal planning started. So, I actively supported the project," Mr. Jones concluded.

Initiation of the Corporate Model

In mid-1965, top management at Sun decided to launch the corporate model development project. Over a period of two to three years the project was expected to cost 100-125 thousand dollars. A steering committee consisting of three upper middle-management Sun executives was appointed with Mr. Pfahler as chairman. While top management was not directly involved in the project, they kept in touch with it through Mr. Jones who communicated with Mr. Pfahler.

A project team was established under the leadership of Mr. George W. Gershefski, Manager of Corporate Economic Planning. The team consisted of six to eight members, generally MBA's with a technical undergraduate background such as engineering, statistics, or operations research. The team was therefore a "general management" one rather than a "specialist" one. From the beginning the team felt they had general encouragement and cooperation from men in all levels of management. In spite of occasional friction and disagreements they felt that line managers were willing to contribute their experience and knowledge of their segments of the company operations.

In the initial phase, the project team undertook a feasibility study, concerned with such problems as what design approach to choose in the subsequent model building phase. The study's results were presented to the steering committee in late 1965, and from there had been brought to Mr. Jones by Mr. Pfahler. The model project had been halted temporarily while decisions were being made about the four design questions. These decisions would establish the project's future direction. Both Mr. Jones and Mr. Pfahler felt that the issues were rather "technical" for their general management background, but they realized that the opinions of top management as the future model users and not those of the computer experts should be paramount as to the solutions to be chosen. However, even Mr. Jones had no clear conception of the model's future uses other than as a tool for aiding top management in their long-range planning.

The Degree of Detail in the Model

To obtain a better understanding of what would be the appropriate degree of detail in the model, Mr. Jones solicited the opinions of various staff and line executives.

Mr. Gershefski suggested that they model the total corporation but with a minimum of functional detail. The alternative would be to consider each part of the company in detail and develop a total corporate model function by function.

> "I feel" said Mr. Gershefski, "that the second approach would be very time consuming. Besides, our model is to be a tool to aid top management in revealing the financial statement impact of alternative operating or investment strategies, determining the need for long-term debt, or assisting in determining feasible corporate goals. Such a tool does not have to be that detailed. So, I prefer the 'tree' approach, not the 'branch' approach."

Mr. Robert \. Smith, Manager of Corporate Accounting, had some doubts about the usefulness of the broad approach.

> "I agree that the model should capture the whole organization, but it must be able to do this with a degree of realism," he said. "I'm afraid the aggregate model will be too unreliable to be useful in, say, developing a documented projection of financial position, or in helping to provide revised financial projections rapidly. Although it involves more development efforts, the model has to have considerable detail to be of any use to us as a tool to aid in budgeting."

Optimization vs. Simulation Model

Another problem was to determine whether to use a case-study model (simulation) or an optimization model. From talking to the project team, Mr. Pfahler got the impression that optimization models automatically identified the best of a set of alternatives to reach a specified objective based on a given set of future conditions. The objective, for instance, might be to maximize profit or to minimize costs. A linear programming model would do this. On the other hand, a simulation model would be designed to project the future, given that a particular alternative would be followed. By examining several cases, each using a different alternative, the model would presumably enable the user to select that case which would lead to the best results. Again people had different opinions about which type of model would be better.

> "Our objective is clear, or at least should be clear; namely, to maximize corporate profit," Mr. Pfahler said. "Hence, let's use optimization since it is the better approach for fulfilling this goal. From reading several articles I believe that the corporate model should be developed from the budget. The budget relationships should be formulated as linear equations, and linear programming should be used to come up with the combination of variables that yield the maximum profit solution. This seems to me to be the most logical, simple, and straightforward approach."

Dr. James S. Cross, Manager of Economics and the immediate superior of Mr. Gershefski, the project leader, favored a simulation model.

> He said, "there is no doubt that simulation techniques should be selected due to the tremendous difficulty in using optimization with as much data as we have. It may be impossible to construct a linear programming model on such a large scale. Also, I seriously doubt that an optimization model could be accurate since the assumption of linearity in the underlying relationships may be unrealistic."
>
> "Even if we disregard the 'technical' difficulties of building an optimization model, I would still choose simulation," Dr. Cross continued.
> "I feel that simulation's ability to help evaluate results from various alternative actions is a major advantage. It allows management to ask 'what if' questions. Also, they are not forced to stick to one specific objective, such as profit maximization. Although I agree that maximum profits should be our ideal goal, I think that Sun has other important goals, such as keeping up sales volume, stable growth, and so on."

Probabilistic vs. Deterministic Model

A third problem was to decide whether a probabilistic or a deterministic model should be constructed. From the project team, Mr. Jones got the impression that a probabilistic model would be ideal for dealing with an operation which might have a great amount of uncertainty associated with it; such a model would project the likelihood of future outcomes of a given decision. He had the impression that a deterministic model, however, would project the result of a decision based on a given set of future conditions.

> "For practical reasons the choice of a probabilistic or a deterministic model depends upon the decision about the degree of detail in the model," Mr. Gershefski commented. "If the number of variables is kept to a reasonably small level, probabilistic techniques might be applied without too much difficulty. However, when large amounts of data are involved, it seems practically impossible to use probabilistic techniques."

FIGURE 12–18

Sun Oil Company (a)
Ten Year Financial Summary

	1965	1964	1963	1962	1961	1960	1959	1958	1957	1956
Revenues—excluding excise taxes (thousands of $)										
Sales and other operating income	$925,243	$838,295	$844,142	$794,026	$775,642	$749,767	$735,697	$721,773	$771,620	$731,412
Other income	16,793	11,802	11,008	10,245	6,651	5,659	10,568	2,259	7,009	2,411
Total	$942,036	$850,097	$855,150	$804,271	$782,293	$755,426	$746,265	$724,032	$778,719	$733,823
Net income (thousands of $)	84,835	68,507	61,216	53,195	49,787	49,273	42,844	32,061	47,492	56,160
Return on revenues (%)	9.0	8.1	7.2	6.6	6.4	6.5	5.7	4.4	6.1	7.7
Earnings per full common share ($)	$5.03	$4.30	$4.04	$3.67	$3.60	$3.78	$3.48	$2.73	$4.17	$5.22
Net assets 12/31 (thousands of $)	$851,203	$784,211	$730,593	$692,697	$654,559	$617,819	$581,704	$550,598	$529,935	$493,195
Return on average net assets (%)	10.4	9.0	8.6	7.9	7.8	8.2	7.6	5.9	9.3	11.9
Capital expenditures (thousands of $)										
Production										
Leases	$ 26,984	$ 20,087	$ 11,975	$ 11,350	$ 13,906	$ 14,243	$ 15,957	$ 16,919	$ 39,993	$ 27,541
Wells and equipment	26,255	22,507	16,846	20,005	20,395	20,009	29,120	17,884	19,728	19,127
Total	53,239	42,594	28,821	31,355	34,301	36,252	45,077	34,803	59,721	46,668
Manufacturing	13,619	9,755	6,172	28,197	21,943	10,070	9,601	6,674	7,917	9,642
Marketing	41,830	42,030	27,760	33,968	27,525	16,264	21,288	18,513	19,058	14,152
Transportation	2,651	2,216	1,097	1,047	988	6,554	16,970	7,759	1,891	7,244
Mining	72,286	7	23	4	6	28	105	25	53	53
Shipyard and others	776	728	667	1,236	5,069	3,937	923	2,908	4,219	217
Total	184,401	97,330	64,540	95,807	89,832	73,105	93,964	70,682	92,859	77,976
Intangible development costs	37,027	32,067	25,874	28,705	30,110	33,490	38,733	30,084	39,961	36,711
Total	$221,428	$129,397	$90,414	$124,512	$119,942	$106,595	$132,697	$100,766	$132,820	$114,687
Expenditures for exploration and development of production (thousands of $)										
Capital expenditures	$ 48,339	$ 32,777	$ 25,217	$ 27,266	$ 29,720	$ 31,038	$ 38,952	$ 31,395	$ 56,113	$ 42,421
Intangible development costs	37,027	32,067	25,874	28,705	30,110	33,490	38,733	30,084	39,961	36,711
Other expenses incl. lease rentals	29,862	29,773	26,846	27,025	28,220	29,732	30,215	32,695	28,428	27,789
Total	$115,228	$ 94,617	$ 77,937	$ 82,996	$ 88,050	$ 94,260	$107,900	$ 94,174	$124,502	$106,921

455

FIGURE 12–19
Sun Oil Company—July, 1968

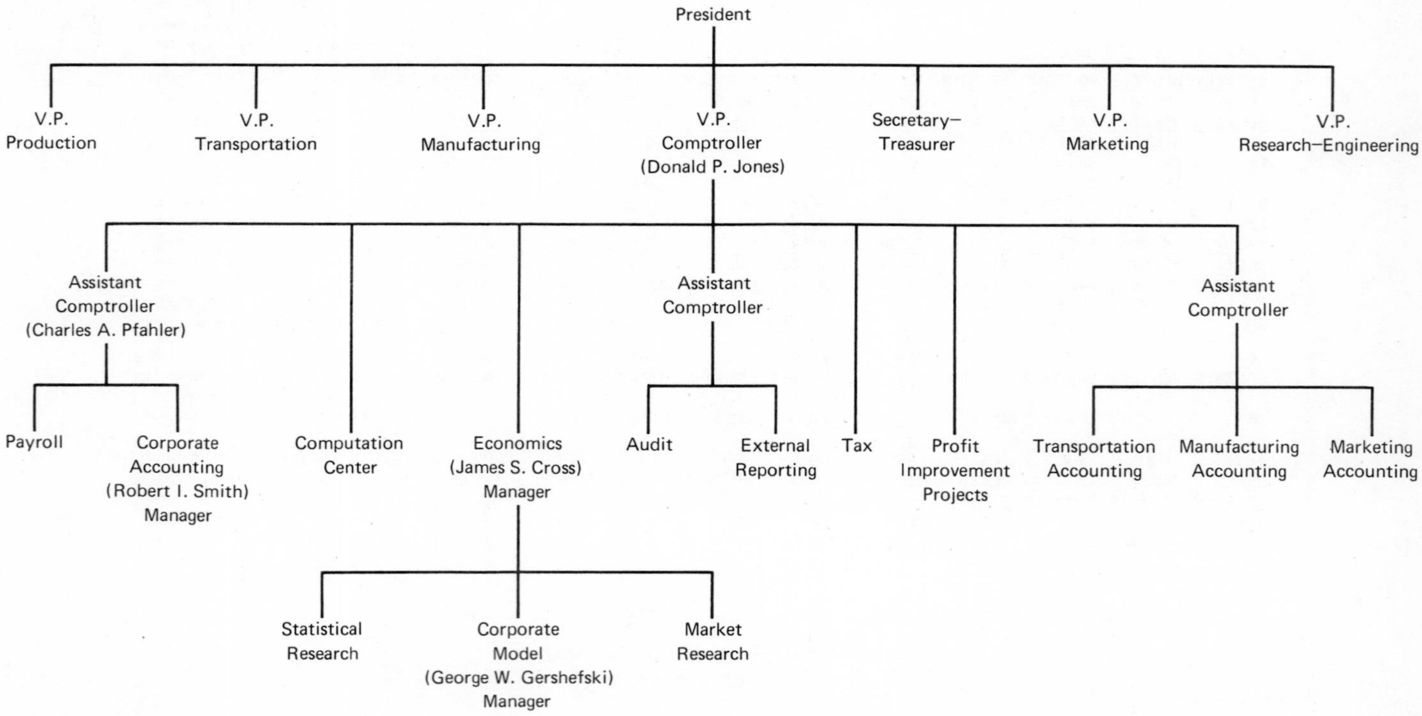

External Data Compilation or Internal Data Generation

The final decision concerned internal generation or external compilation of information for the model. These notions were entirely new to Mr. Jones, but he seemed to grasp the idea that, on one hand, an information compiler would receive, as input, data collected from the company's various departments, would perform the arithmetic necessary to consolidate these, and would develop an over-view of the company. On the other hand, an information generator model would start with a few inputs, and because of its internal makeup, would generate new information on the basis of statistical relationships developed from the historical data base.

> "We will have a much more efficient model if we base it primarily on internal information generation," Mr. Gershefski stated. "In this way we are less dependent on the time-consuming and often inaccurate data collection from the functional departments. Updating and modification of the model is then a lot easier."
>
> "I am worried about asking line people for too much data at this time," Dr. Cross commented. "They could easily get fed-up with the whole idea of a corporate model if we put too many burdens on them. Consequently, a negative attitude might develop if we base ourselves primarily on the use of external information generation. Right now we should try to sell the idea of a model and avoid frictions within the organization."
>
> "I would rather base decisions on model results which I know I can trust since I have provided all the pertinent key data," Mr. John D. Rice, chief planner in the Production Division, said. "I would have less confidence in results based largely on the model's internal information generation."
>
> "When it comes to financial and accounting data, we have to provide the model with those inputs," Mr. Pfahler declared. "It is important that these data be accurate, and that relationships among the various components be portrayed as simply and accurately as possible. Hence, I would be much happier to have the model based primarily on external information compilation."

The Sun Oil Company (B)

In October 1968, Sun Oil Company consummated its merger with Sunray DX Oil Company, another fully integrated oil company headquartered in Tulsa,

---

This case was prepared by Peter Lorange, Research Assistant, under the supervision of Professor Richard F. Vancil, as a basis for class discussion rather than to illustrate either effective or ineffective handling of an administrative situation.

Oklahoma. Sun's sales in 1967 were 1,173 million dollars, compared to Sunray DX's 592 million. The merged company had combined assets of approximately 2,363 million dollars, sales of 1,801 million dollars in 1968, and approximately 29,000 employees. Although both were essentially the same type of company, they complemented each other with respect to sales territories and, to some degree, in terms of special products in their respective lines. The merger resulted in a full integration of the two companies' production and sales. The new joint corporate headquarters was located in Philadelphia.

> "Sun Oil's corporate financial model was suddenly obsolete as a result of the merger," Mr. Donald P. Jones, Senior Vice President of finance, said in March 1970. "The model reflected the structure of the old Sun organization. Because organizational changes resulting from the merger were considerable, the old model is no longer an accurate planning tool. It cannot be economically modified to reflect our entirely new organization.
>
> "We have now overcome the initial problems of combining the two organizations," Mr. Jones continued. "The new organization is stabilizing itself and we can already see what the new company profile will be. We are thinking about developing a new corporate planning model. But, should we do it? If so, is this the right time to start? And, if yes, what kind of model should we build?"

The Development of the Old Corporate Financial Model

In early 1965, the corporate model project team began developing a macro-simulation model of the total Sun organization. (See the Sun Oil Company (A) case for a description of the early model development.) The aim was to create a planning tool to aid top executives in their evaluation of long-range capital investment so the effects of these investments could be seen in the context of the whole company. Using ten to fifteen-year forecasts, the model was intended to help top executives gain a better understanding of where Sun was going in terms of capital investments, growth rates, etc. The model displayed the interrelated effects of the various functional operations, thus permitting management to plan in a coordinated way. The model also permitted management to identify potential trouble spots and, in case of trouble, to evaluate the financial implications of alternative solutions.

The company had chosen a deterministic simulation-type model because it allowed for relatively simple handling of large data masses, it allowed top executives to evaluate the effects of "what if" strategic questions, and it was felt to be more easily explainable to top executives. As an information generator-type model, it applied some statistical relationships to certain input information to generate new information.

By June 1966, the company's model was working. Although top executives seemingly received the new planning tool favorably, they were reluctant to use it as it was intended. This was a disappointing experience for both the development team and the executives who had supported the project.

However, the model development project had created considerable interest in some staff and line departments. The model had been designed to generate as much information as possible internally. The departments had submitted considerable historical and forecasted data to give the model-building team a data base for developing the many econometric relationships. Many department heads complained that the information they were asked to submit did not focus on the typical activities of their departments. Also, some departments disagreed with the results that the long-range model forecasted for their part of the business, claiming that the model was too aggregate to be reliable for planning within segments of the company.

Several department heads, however, perceived the model as a potentially helpful tool, if it could be modified for their part of the business. Many of them submitted their own activity data to replace the internally generated forecasts. The model was especially useful in budgeting, and Mr. Pfahler, Assistant Comptroller, soon saw it as a means of lightening the burden of budget computation. The manager of Manufacturing Accounting and the manager of Marketing Accounting were quick to seize upon it to help prepare and monitor their individual budgets.

Because it was computerized, the model enabled the corporate budgeting department to update the consolidated budget whenever the assumptions used to prepare the budget became outdated. Previously, this had been a time consuming process and had been done only once a year. Top management generally seemed to appreciate this ability to have revised budgets developed.

Thus, the scope of the corporate model project had gradually changed. The time horizon of the forecast was shortened until it corresponded to that of the budget. The model also grew more detailed and was based largely on compiling externally prepared data. "The model was, in fact, used by management in their short-term profit planning and not in long-range strategic planning, the original purpose," Mr. Gershefski, Manager, Corporate Model project, said.

Benefits from the Corporate Model Project

Nevertheless, many members of Sun's management felt that many developments resulting from the original model had been useful to Sun. One was the Marketing/Manufacturing Planning System, developed in 1969. Also, the Monthly Monitoring Model, which predicted an annual income at the end of each month, was an offshoot of the original effort. The detailed modeling of

U.S. and foreign tax codes as applied to the oil industry was felt to be most helpful in dealing with tax problems. The Iranian Sun and Venezuelan Sun models were developed on the basis of the expertise gained from the original project.

> "Apart from the tangible spin-offs from the corporate model project, we got several intangible benefits, which are rather difficult to evaluate," Mr. Jones said. "The model has had a positive educational effect on top management; they are indeed more oriented toward long-range planning. Today we are better organized for long-range planning, but it is of course impossible to weigh the relative importance of the underlying reasons. We have also benefited by having management at various levels acquainted with this computer-based management tool. The pressure to present precise data often forced them to redefine their own information routines. A lot of redundancy and duplication were eliminated. Also, management became 'computer-minded'; they overcame their original scepticism about using the computer for analysis.
> "Clearly, we also gained valuable know-how about computer modeling. Our corporate model team learned from trial and error and they now have a lot of experience. After all, they developed the largest computer based corporate financial model in existence!"

A New Corporate Model?

> "As our new organizational pattern has stabilized," Mr. Jones explained, "managers at various levels have asked for a new corporate model. Top management wants a monthly updated budget. Many line managers would like a new model to help them prepare budgets. These specific requests seem to point in the direction of a short-term, relatively detailed model. But with the present organizational setup and management climate, I believe we would also benefit from a long-range strategic model."
> He continued, "We have to decide now whether to build a new model. In one way the timing is unfortunate since our new organization might not have stabilized itself sufficiently. But our modeling competence is rapidly deteriorating. Mr. Gershefski just left the company to join the consulting profession and the model builders need to be reactivated if they are to continue to stay on top of the problem. So, all the model design questions that we faced in 1966 may be before us again, but first we must decide whether or not to proceed."

Organizing and Implementing the Development Effort

T HE RANGE AND EFFECTIVENESS OF THE OPERATING SERVICES AND management information support provided by the data processing and information systems development activities are affected by the way these activities are organized and managed within a company.

This chapter discusses the variety of ways in which data processing and systems development activities are organized in business, the impact of systems development efforts on business organizations, and the human factors affecting information systems development and administration. The discussion concludes with a review of the problems encountered in specific systems development situations and how these problems might be overcome.

Organization of the Data Processing and Information Systems Development Functions

The frequent placement of computerized data processing departments under the financial, control and accounting areas during the 1950s was a normal outgrowth of the early applications of computerized data processing to automated handling of large clerical activities, such as payroll accounting, customer billing, account maintenance, and the like. Automated record-keeping functions even today still consume the largest amount of computer processing time.

Progress was slow, for several reasons, in putting computer systems to work in other operating areas, such as marketing and production, and in providing management with a broad range of information services. The payoff was more immediate and visible in the financial account record-keeping area. The organizational location of the computerized data processing activities discouraged extension of their applications into other areas. Moreover, the early computer systems had critical storage and processing restraints; and, in addition, there was a limited supply of systems analysts and technicians, which in turn set limits on the new applications which could be developed.

Time and time again during this period, as the author worked with companies on expanding computer applications to other operating and management information problems, the work was pushed aside in favor of more immediate financial accounting priorities. Such priorities were not surprising, since the data processing department was usually under the financial accounting executive, and his interests naturally came first—especially in light of the personnel and equipment limitations and in light of top management priorities.

During the early 1960s, efforts were undertaken to broaden the operating areas and management information needs served by computerized data processing systems. One major step taken to further these efforts was to set up separate data processing (sometimes called information services) divisions, which reported directly to higher management. These departments had systems analysts, as well as programmers and computer operators, and their mission was to serve data processing and management information needs throughout the company. In many instances, where such organizational changes were accompanied by strong and continuing top management support, these efforts were successful, especially in developing applications to operating problems.

For example, the Mead Corporation, one of the larger paper companies in this country, started on a broad review of its data processing facilities in 1960.[1] At the time, these facilities were decentralized and located in several different divisions and operating areas. As a result of a study, data processing activities were centralized in 1962 under a Director-Information Services (who reported to the Administrative Vice President) and the group was greatly expanded, drawing operating personnel from within the company as well as trained technicians from outside. In addition, work was begun on ways to expand data processing applications, especially in the paper production and customer service areas. In 1964, the systems study group recommended development of a total information system, as shown in Figure 13—1, and top management approved the project proposal.

During the subsequent period of systems development, Mead made major advances in using their computer for production process control, and, by 1966, they were a recognized leader in this area. While they had also developed sales support data systems (order entry, customer billing, etc.) and financial reporting systems, it was recognized that greater management information support was possible in this area. The systems group thus began work on advanced data retrieval systems to be used by sales management, systems which would take advantage of the technical advances in computer storage and processing capabilities during the mid-1960s. These new systems enabled salesmen, for example, to give customers more accurate delivery dates on a more current basis, since the sales management information system was linked with the production scheduling and inventory management data systems through on-line, real-time communications systems.

The ability of Mead to use its data processing facilities first to service a wider range of operating needs and subsequently to provide more effective management information support was attributable in large part to the orga-

---

1. *The Mead Corporation* (Boston, Mass.: Harvard Graduate School of Business Administration, 1966); Thomas R. Prince, *Information Systems for Management Planning and Control* (Homewood, Illinois: Richard D. Irwin, Inc., 1970), pp. 331-350; and various company publications.

FIGURE 13-1

Total Information Planning and Control System

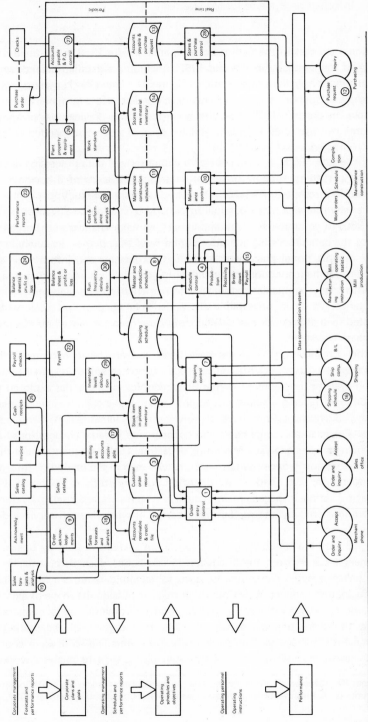

Source: Reproduced with permission from Thomas Prince, *Information Systems for Management Planning and Control* (Homewood, Ill.: Richard D. Irwin, Inc., 1970), p. 336, 342, 343, and 349.

465

nizational changes in the data processing area. Figure 13—2 shows the organization of the company in the mid-1960s, including a detailed breakdown of the information systems organization (Figures 13—3 and 4). Top management also showed support for the systems development effort in many ways: for example, in the mid-1960s the Director-Information Services was promoted to Administrative Vice President and his area of control expanded (Figure 13—3 compared with Figure 13—2).

By the late 1960s, the concept of a computerized data processing department as a systems support organization serving all areas of a business was fairly widely accepted. As seen in the Mead Corporation study, the evolution of this new role was made possible in part by technological advances during the 1960s in computer systems, and in part by major changes in the organization of the data processing and information services activities. Even where the actual organizational placement of the data processing and information systems development functions remained within the financial accounting area, as it has in many companies today, this new orientation and viewpoint gained acceptance. While in principle the broader role concept has been widely accepted, actual progress has been slow in developing advanced management information systems.

Other organizational changes have been and are being tried to further emphasize the "user" orientation so needed for successful management information systems development. James Bieneman, for example, has explored the possibility of placing systems analyst groups under the operating departments served.[2] Such suggestions have already been implemented in many companies. For example, some personnel departments in large corporations have their own systems analysts. Marketing departments also frequently have their own information services departments, as was seen in the marketing information operations described in the *Enright Company* study in Chapter Seven, where marketing management information systems were partially developed and administered by the marketing department's information services division.

In light of the broad range of information systems needed by operating managers (as seen from the discussion in this book), such an organizational shift makes sense. A marketing manager, for example, requires a wide variety of information support, much of which may be outside the scope of existing data processing operations. An information coordinator and administrator within the marketing department is able to integrate all the marketing department's management information requirements and so develop coordinated supporting information systems. By having systems analysts working

---

2. James N. Bieneman, "Bridging the Gap Between Data Processing and Operating Departments: A Fresh Approach," *Management Adviser,* September—October 1972, pp. 17-20.

FIGURE 13-2 Plan of Organization (December, 1965)

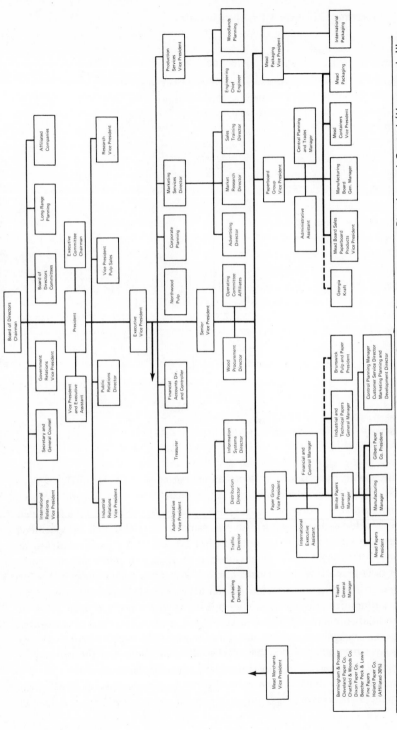

Source: Reproduced with permission from Thomas Prince, *Information Systems for Management Planning and Control* (Homewood, Ill.: Richard D. Irwin, Inc., 1970), p. 336, 342, 343, and 349.

467

FIGURE 13–3

Administrative Vice President
Plan of Organization
(June, 1966)

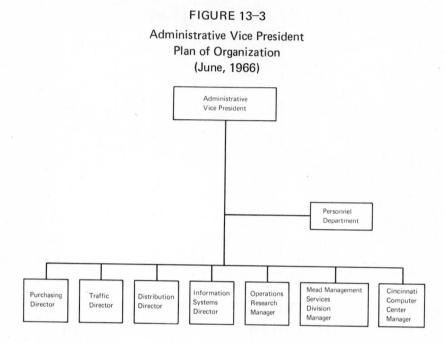

Source: Reproduced with permission from Thomas Prince, *Information Systems for Management Planning and Control* (Homewood, Ill.: Richard D. Irwin, Inc.), p. 336, 342, 343, and 349.

directly under the marketing department, better use can be made of data processing facilities in meeting marketing management information needs, especially in new information support areas—such as developing strategic planning information systems. At the same time, marketing management information systems development will not be limited by (and restricted to working within) existing company data processing capabilities. If the company's data processing department also has a systems analyst responsible for working with marketing systems, he can insure coordination and integration of marketing management information systems with other company information and data processing systems. The author has worked with several marketing operations where responsibilities for the systems development work are divided in this way between the marketing department and the company's centralized data processing department, and it proved quite effective.

Organizational changes then can make a major contribution to effective management information systems development. Such organizational changes

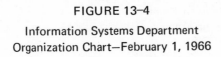

FIGURE 13–4

Information Systems Department
Organization Chart—February 1, 1966

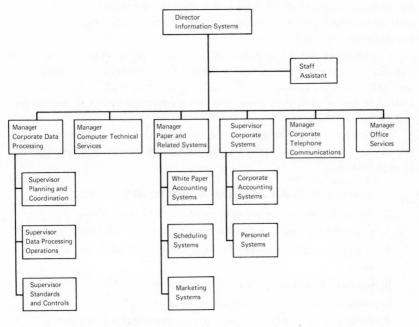

Source: Reproduced with permission from Thomas Prince, *Information Systems for Management Planning and Control* (Homewood, Ill.: Richard D. Irwin, Inc.), p. 336, 342, 343, and 349.

are needed for several reasons. First, there is a natural resistance to change within an organization and, unless sole responsibility for systems development is given to a separate department, adequate attention may not be given to systems development. Second, there is an enormous knowledge gap between operating managers and computer technicians which cannot be bridged merely by telling each to learn more about the other's area. Third, systems studies often lead to an in-depth reappraisal of a company's entire organizational structure and to readjustments in that structure. Unless specialists are assigned to these problems, and are given the time to adequately study them and the authority to examine all areas affected by the change, systems development may be haphazard.

These and related organizational behavior questions are discussed in the following sections.

The Impact of Systems Development
and Implementation on Company Organizations

Information systems development has had a far-reaching impact on the internal organization of individual business enterprises and the decision-making processes within them.

In organizing the components of a business to achieve its objectives, traditional business organization theory has emphasized the relationships between people by focusing on the tasks to be performed, the job positions related to performing these tasks, and the appropriate authority and responsibility for each job position.

In *Management Systems,* McDonough and Garrett[3] give some of the principles of organization that show the traditional, people-oriented approach to organization:

1. Be sure that adequate provision is made for all activities.
2. Group (departmentalize) activities on some logical basis.
3. Limit the number of subordinates reporting to each executive.
4. Define the responsibilities of each department, division, and sub-division.
5. Delegate authority to subordinates wherever practical.
6. Make authority and responsibility equal.
7. Provide for controls over those to whom authority is delegated.
8. Avoid dual subordination.
9. Distinguish clearly between line authority, functional authority, and staff relationships.
10. Develop methods of coordination.

These principles clearly focus on the person-to-person relationships within an organization, and on the physical and functional departmentalization of the business unit. The commonplace block-diagram organization chart reflects this concept. Such relationships are, of course, important in thinking about organizations, but overemphasis of these relationships can obscure the information and communication links so vital to effective decision making within a corporation.

When changes are introduced within the traditional organization structure, new departments or units are normally added or new responsibilities are given

---

3. Adrian M. McDonough and Leonard J. Garrett, *Management Systems: Working Concepts and Practices* (Homewood, Illinois: Richard D. Irwin, Inc., 1965), p. 9.

to existing departments. Sometimes these additions or changes are made to meet new business needs, sometimes to take maximum advantage of an individual executive's particular combination of talents, and sometimes merely to adjust to the personalities of individual executives. Such a fragmented development process almost invariably leads to some decrease in the effectiveness of the decision-making processes within an organization.

The systems approach helps avoid this problem by focusing on the dynamic interaction and intercommunication among components of the system. The systems approach forces a manager to look upon his business organization as an information network, with the flow of information providing the decision makers at various management levels with the information needed to make decisions of all types. The information systems viewpoint thus subordinates the separate units or departments of a business to decision-making information and communication networks. Understanding this difference is fundamental to understanding how the systems approach has affected business organization.

When introducing a computer system or system change, many companies tend to approach the changeover in the traditional way—piecemeal, department by department. Such an approach only reinforces the fragmentation and disruption of information and decision-making systems.

Instead, as most companies sooner or later discover, before a major decision concerning computerization is made, management must step back and re-evaluate the entire flow of business—not merely the individual operations being computerized—in order to isolate the major decision-making areas, their interrelations, and the information needed to make these decisions most effectively. In other words, the systems approach has proved in practice to be the best one.

For example, in a medium-size mail-order business which was changing to computerized order processing and information handling, the first inclination was to write programs in steps (first for marketing, then for order processing, billing, inventory control, and so on) for each of the components or departments currently operating in the company.

It soon became apparent that this was not the best approach. At this time, management directed the systems group to study the nature of the business in which the company hoped to be engaged within the next five years, and the environment in which the company would operate.

The group next constructed a chart of the flow of the business operation, starting with the coupon-advertisement offering the product and asking for the order, and following the customer's order through processing and billing until the product is shipped, the merchandise restocked, and the bill paid. For each phase in the flow chart a supplemental list was made of the significant planning, control, and operational decisions necessary to manage that phase well. The information needed to make these decisions and the form in which this information was needed was then determined.

Only after the above studies were completed was a decision made as to how to proceed with systems development. While not the primary purpose of this study, the study of the company's business and the decision-making processes within that business provided a useful basis for restudying the company's organization. As a result of this reappraisal, the actual organization of the operation was restructured around the picture of the business which had been developed in the systems study.

The diagram of the restructured organization may have looked to the casual observer like the traditional organization chart of the former organization, for there were departments for marketing, order processing, billing and credit, product procurement and inventory control, and liason among all these operations. But the changes made to bring the organization into line with the newly perceived operational and decision-making needs of the business were significant.

Pockets of personal power had been wiped out, and antiquated reporting relationships had been drastically changed. Major adjustments had been made in the daily interworkings between departments and in the groupings of functions within each department. For example, advertising was now a marketing department, order processing now included customer service, and product procurement and warehousing were combined. In other words, what is commonly called an "authority" organization structure had given way to a "systems" organization structure.

The re-evaluation of the company's organization structure growing out of the systems study showed that the organization had not grown dynamically with the business but was a conglomeration of old operating procedures, compromises made to accommodate personality differences, and the like. Although the changeover was painful for many people, it revitalized the operation.

The mail-order company cited in the above example was fortunate. In spite of the organizational difficulties arising from using the systems approach, the company profited from it. Many companies faced with the introduction of computerized systems or systems changes have taken the easy way out. Instead of starting with a thorough re-evaluation of their businesses, they have computerized their operations piecemeal without regard for total business systems. Many problems can be created by not using the systems approach; for not only can it hinder development of effective management information systems, but it may also leave out-of-date and ineffective organizational structures intact.

Human Factors

As seen from the preceding discussion, management information systems development efforts have an impact on the people within a business organization, as well as on the company's organization structure. At the same time, human factors have an impact on these development efforts.

Because computerized systems are often new to many people and affect such a wide range of company operations, there is often resistance to introducing computerized systems and the organizational changes which sometimes accompany them, as there is to any major change within an organization. Introduction of such systems can require changing decision-making practices, learning new techniques, and establishing new working relationships. All of these are time-consuming and disruptive, and, consequently, they breed resistance. The degree of resistance increases with the size and the timing of the changeover.

Resistance to computerized systems can take many forms and affect systems development and use in a variety of ways. At the management level, such resistance may arise from fear of loss of authority or control over the operations necessary to performing one's job, as in the *Midwest Apparel, Inc.* case study at the end of this chapter. Or, it may arise for personal reasons— for example, from a fear of being passed by or of failing. Whatever the cause, resistance at the management level can hinder the development of the system itself, as well as its effective use, as is seen in the company studies described in the following section and at the end of the chapter.

Resistance at the worker level arises in situations involving computerization of operations performed by workers. Since most management information systems are part of data processing systems with operational applications, such worker resistance can have an impact on management information systems development, as is seen in the *Avco-Everett Research Laboratory (A and B)* case studies at the end of this chapter.

The publicity given to technological displacement caused by the introduction of computerized data processing systems in many companies reinforces the concern many people have about losing their jobs to (or being replaced by) computers, and so increases their resistance to these systems. Even though study after study has shown that *overall* employment increases when computers are introduced in most cases, each person nonetheless faces the problem of whether or not he will be given the opportunity to upgrade his skills, or sometimes whether or not he will have the capacity to take advantage of such opportunities if they are offered. As was pointed out in Chapter Two, therefore, some attention must be paid to the way changes are announced, and the training and retraining opportunities offered, if resistance to new management information systems (and any accompanying organizational changes) at the management and worker levels is to be overcome.[4]

It is fairly common for managers to fail to anticipate the people problems which will arise in introducing a new computer system or to plan steps to overcome these problems, especially where management wants the conversion completed quickly. *The City of Dalton* case study at the end of this chapter describes some of the problems which can arise in such situations. In that situation, insufficient time was allowed for training personnel and for preparing for the new system. Instead, management personnel tried to fit in the extra work around the jobs they were already doing, and understandably the people involved simply were not able to handle the work load.

A phased (gradual) participative approach has proved useful in helping to overcome some of the human problems encountered in implementing new management information systems. Since this approach involves managers and other systems users in the systems development work, such an approach enables not only a gradual orientation of users to the new system, but also draws upon their knowledge in shaping the system to meet business needs.[5] The *Avco-Everett Research Laboratory (A and B)* case studies at the end of this chapter contain an example of how in one situation a gradual approach to introducing a management information system was used to overcome anticipated organizational behavior problems.

The continuing development and use of management information systems requires both managers and computer technicians to acquire new knowledge and skills, in learning computer techniques on the one hand and learning management jobs on the other. Such integration of computer systems with the management job thus requires new interdisciplinary and integrative man-

---

4. For further discussions of individual and organizational resistance to change, and ways to overcome it, see: Paul R. Lawrence, "How to Deal with Resistance to Change," *Harvard Business Review,* January—February 1969, pp. 4-12; Tom Burns and G. M. Stalker, *The Management of Innovation* (London: Tavistock Publications, 1961); David R. Hampton, Charles E. Summer and Ross A. Webber, *Organizational Behavior and the Practice of Management* (Glenview, Illinois: Scott, Foresman and Company, 1968); and Garth N. Jones, *Planning Organizational Change* (London: Routledge and Kegan Paul, 1969).

5. For further discussions of the use of the participative approach in managing organizational change see: Larry E. Greiner, "Patterns of Organizational Change," *Harvard Business Review,* May—June 1967, pp. 119-130; Richard Hoffman and R. W. Archibald, "Introducing Organizational Change in a Bureaucratic Structure," and Raghu Nath, "Dynamics of Organizational Change: Some Effects of a Change Program in a Client System," *Academy of Management Proceedings,* December 26—28, 1968, pp. 25—36 and 51—66; Ben Miller, *Managing Innovation for Growth and Profit* (Homewood, Illinois: Richard D. Irwin, Inc., 1970), pp. 243—257; and Tom Lupton, "The Practical Analysis of Change in Organizations," *The Journal of Management Studies,* May 1965, pp. 218—227.

agement training. Books such as this one, and the courses in which they are used, represent one method used to bridge the knowledge gap between managers and technicians. The participative approach to organizational change, and the new approaches to organizing data processing and systems development activities described earlier in this chapter, are other ways.

A situational approach to behavioral management[6] can help guide a manager in identifying potential behavioral problems which might impede the development and use of management information systems and training in behavioral management can provide some insights into ways in which these problems can be overcome. But such training can only provide tools and techniques, and increase one's awareness of these problems and of how others have solved them. It cannot substitute for the learning gained through one's own experience.

As is seen in the following section, information systems development situations are dynamic, and the personalities and organizational environment involved in each situation varies. While there are guidelines for dealing with the behavioral factors involved in management information systems development, then, there are no pat formulas for success. Rather, each manager must work to learn through his own experience how to use available behavioral tools and techniques to create more effective management information systems.

Planning and Developing an Information System: Guidelines for Overcoming Some Typical Problems

This section describes the experiences of several companies in developing computerized information systems.[7] All of the companies were of moderate size, under $70,000,000 in annual sales. In each case, a large portion of the business was done through direct-response selling—that is, selling a product or service through an advertisement or mailing piece which asks the customer to write directly to the company to order the item advertised. The products these companies sold through direct-response advertising ranged from maga-

---

6. Robert J. Mockler, *Management Decision Making and Action in Behavioral Situations* (Austin, Texas: The Austin Press, 1973); Robert J. Mockler, *The Business Management Process: A Situational Approach* (Austin, Texas: The Austin Press, 1974): and Robert J. Mockler, "The Situational Theory of Management," *Harvard Business Review,* May–June 1971, pp. 146-154.

7. For example, see: Robert J. Mockler, "Developing a New Information and Control System," *Michigan Business Review,* March 1968, pp. 13-19; Robert J. Mockler, ed., *Putting Computers to Work More Effectively in Business Publishing* (New York: American Business Press, 1969); and Robert J. Mockler, "The Control Job: Breaking the Mold," *Business Horizons,* December 1970, pp. 73-77.

zine subscriptions and book club memberships to phonographs and television sets.

As they grew, each of these companies saw the need to convert to up-to-date computerized data processing and management information systems.

The Decision to Develop a New System

In each company the development of the new system began in the same way: top management decided to install a new computer to process orders, to maintain the file of customer names for billing and re-promotion, and to generate planning and control information reports for management.

In no case was there a formal feasibility or cost study which compared the existing and the new systems, and which determined whether or not a new system was needed and how much time and expense would be involved in developing a new system. Formal feasibility studies were not conducted because each company's management already seemed to have made an instinctive commitment to a new computerized system. This attitude seems to be typical of many small and medium-size companies that have not had extensive experience with computers.

The first problem common to all the companies studied, therefore, was the lack of a thorough preparatory or feasibility study. Fortunately, in all instances the economy and efficiency of an updated, high-speed, computerized processing system proved beneficial to company operations.

Preparing for the Systems Study

The actual systems development study was begun in the traditional way: a group from the systems analysis section was appointed to develop a systems proposal and subsequently the actual system for the new computer. Then all the operating managers affected by the new information system were notified that the study was to be undertaken and were asked to cooperate.

Corporate management gave verbal support to the project, but did not appoint a corporate executive (or other responsible manager) to head the study group and, in fact, attended few of the group's meetings during the year or so spent developing the new system.

The second problem, therefore, was the lack of top management guidance, support and, most important, participation in the systems development work.

The Changing Scope of the Initial Study

Because no feasibility study was done, the exact scope of the systems development study, and the time and effort needed to develop a new system, were not clearly spelled out from the beginning. In retrospect, it seems that management thought of the project as writing a program for a new computer. Only as the systems development group delved deeper into their study did the scope of the undertaking expand into a true company-wide operations and information systems study, which was what management finally determined they really needed and wanted.

Through the study group's efforts, management came to realize that no judgment about where a computer can be used effectively and economically is possible until the operational and decision-making processes within the company, and the flow of information needed for decision making, are studied and defined.

Because no one had expected the project to be so complex, it had to be significantly modified as it progressed. The confusion, resistance and waste of time and money this caused could have been avoided by defining the mission broadly rather than narrowly at the outset. Then management could have either provided the time, money, and manpower needed to do a complete job, or lowered their sights and settled for a system of more limited scope.

Therefore, the third problem, a composite one, was the failure to understand that a broad background study of the company's business flows and decision-making processes was needed, ignorance of what such a study entailed, and the failure to provide the people, organization, time, and money needed to do a complete study.

The Initial Phase of the Study

Because at the outset the project was narrowly defined as a computer program-writing project, the systems group first examined each of the individual operational areas being computerized. As the work progressed, however, the group found they needed to do more background work before they could understand these operations, and they began exploring in more depth such factors as:

1. The general nature of the business and the markets within which the company operated.
2. The company's entire business process, from order receipt to customer payment.
3. The kind of information needed for decision making at the various critical points in the business process.
4. The timing and format of the information needed.

The businesses being studied were mail-order selling operations. Sales or inquiries were solicited by mailings, by magazine or newspaper coupon ads, or by radio and television commercials asking for customer orders. The products sold ranged from $500 television sets to $2 gift merchandise and magazine subscriptions. Sales were solicited from former customers, from the general consumer market, and from customers served by other divisions of the company. Most sales were on credit, but lower-priced merchandise was frequently sold on a cash-with-order basis. The companies were, therefore, retailers, and all of the functions normally handled in a retail store would have to be handled by the new system.

Once the general nature of the business was defined, the systems group looked at the internal flow of business. Orders and payments were received in the mail room. Payments were sent to the collection section, which deposited the money and credited the payment to the customer's account. Orders were sent to the order-processing section. If the order was from a customer in good standing, it was processed; if not, it was sent to the credit department for clearance or rejection. Once the cleared orders were processed, the products were shipped and customer billing began. In all, five operating sections were involved:

1. Product procurement, including warehousing
2. Marketing
3. Accounting and financial analysis
4. Fulfillment: order processing and file maintenance, including billing
5. Credit

As the systems group extended their study, they found how little they knew about the areas other than order processing and how much they would need to know to develop a sophisticated system to meet operating and management information requirements in all these sections.

The systems study group encountered some problems when they began the necessary detailed study of each of the five areas. Although they had been told to call upon all sections involved in the study, no one person in each operating section was designated to help the study group and no executives from the operating departments were appointed members of the study group. Since the systems group was part of the fulfillment (order processing and file maintenance) section and since they could obtain little assistance from the other four sections, they naturally tended to create a system designed principally for the fulfillment area, a system which would only secondarily serve the information and operating needs of the other sections.

At each company, it was necessary for a corporate executive to intervene to resolve the problem. At one of the companies, for example, the marketing manager met with the systems group, saw the potential deficiencies of the new system being developed, discussed the problem with them, and recommended expanding the study group to include a representative from each operating section. Four operating managers were then appointed to the group. A timetable for completion was developed at the same time.

Only at this point, therefore, was the true breadth of the new system officially recognized. What had originally been basically an order-processing and file-maintenance system now became a total data processing and information system, and the group was given the manpower needed to complete the project successfully.

Prior to this step, the scope of the project had been limited, not because management wanted it to be limited, but because they had not provided the mechanism or organization to implement a broader study. The fourth problem, therefore, was that representatives of each operating section were not made part of the original study group and so did not participate in the systems planning work.

Defining Information Needs

The next step in developing the system was to have each operating section define its operation, the kinds of decisions it made, the information needed to make these decisions, and the form in which that information was needed.

This was not a simple task, especially when defining management information needs. First, the operating managers were reluctant to spend the time needed to define their requirements. Each felt that he knew his job and that describing it in a report would be a waste of time, since he did not understand the importance to the project of his systematically defining his management information requirements in detail. In addition, he felt that he would now be reporting to the systems analyst, although he had been told that the analysts would be reporting to him and doing the detail work. Second, a systems analyst needs considerable skill in interviewing in order to draw out information about future and ideal needs, for operating managers tend to describe the information they now get, instead of what is required to make good decisions.

Again the corporate executive closest to the study was forced to intervene. He explained that a periodic review of job objectives and functions was good business practice and normal, that the systems group was working for the operating managers but that only the operating manager knew his area well enough to define its needs thoroughly, and that the new system was a wonderful opportunity to relieve operating managers of a considerable amount of detail work and to obtain better reports for them, in more readable form and on a more timely basis. However, the price to be paid over the short run was that each operating manager would be required to devote time and attention to the project. If the operating managers did not give such time, they could not justifiably complain later of not having up-to-date and complete data processing and information services, or of not having the information in the form needed to make decisions quickly and easily.

The fifth problem, therefore, was getting a clear definition of the operating and information needs of each of the operating and management areas that would be served by the system.

Balancing the Information Needs of Each Operating Section

Because of the lack of direction from top management and support from the operating managers and because of the systems analysts' training in machine processing, it was difficult for the systems group to maintain a "total system" perspective and to be objective in balancing the needs of each operating group in developing the new system.

While ideally the systems analyst is supposed to have the perspective to view an entire business system objectively and to pull together all aspects of an operation, there is no guarantee that he will. The systems analyst is often a trained programmer. Because of his background and training he often tends to be machine-oriented and to think in terms of machine processing efficiency, rather than of operational decision-making needs. Like the sales manager, production manager, and financial manager, then, the systems analyst has a functional bias.

The ability to view an operation objectively and in its entirety is not an exclusive characteristic of any particular functional area in a business. It is a characteristic of effective management. Any good manager, in any functional area, should be able to maintain a broad, comprehensive, objective viewpoint.

In the companies studied, the problem of maintaining a balanced viewpoint was further complicated by the fact that the systems group in a mailorder operation is part of the fulfillment operation. Where compromises had to be made, therefore, the group tended to accommodate either machine efficiency or the efficiency of the processing system for the fulfillment area.

As a result, operating managers came to believe that the information needs of their areas—whether product procurement or marketing—were considered secondary to the needs of the fulfillment area. However, these managers were not willing to devote the time needed to help shape the new system to their own needs. The systems group wanted to be objective, but in the absence of sufficient guidance from top management and from operating managers, they naturally concentrated on satisfying the needs of those areas they knew best: fulfillment and computer processing.

The situation at this point become very confused. For example, the marketing section wanted the fulfillment section to make daily manual tabulations of customer orders received by media and to report them daily to the marketing section. This would enable the marketing section to make quicker decisions on the profitability of promotions, and so whether to continue or repeat them. The systems group immediately reacted negatively, for the request would require adjustments and delays in the order processing system. In other words, the systems group revealed an unconscious bias towards creating the most efficient fulfillment system possible, even at the expense of the operating and management needs of other operating sections.

The same kind of problem arose when the credit manager asked that certain credit checks be built into the system, when the marketing manager asked that the billing envelopes be enlarged so that he could enclose promotional material in them, when the product procurement manager asked for an on-line perpetual inventory sub-system, when the financial analysis manager asked for a returned merchandise count by promotion, and so on.

The situation fortunately did not get out of hand; for, in all these cases, objectivity was supplied by the informal intervention of a corporate executive, who knew systems, understood all the operations affected by the system, and was well-liked by the persons working on development of the system. It was this executive who prevented the systems group from fashioning the parts of the system to suit machine efficiency exclusively and arbitrated the compromises necessary to create a balanced system that served the needs of all operating areas. It was he who filled the gap left when top management failed to become directly involved in the project.

The sixth problem, therefore, was maintaining objectivity and balance in the new system.

The Final Determination of the Costs and Performance Characteristics of the New System

Not only did management underestimate the costs and complications of developing the systems, they also underestimated the costs and performance characteristics of the final systems. Fortunately, even though the costs of the final systems were higher than anticipated in each situation, the savings under the new systems were sufficient to justify their installation.

However, modification in the design and size of the new systems occasioned sizeable delays. In all cases, the computer system originally ordered turned out to be too small. The equipment order was changed, delays resulted, and management had to adjust to increased costs. The machine hardware configuration (that is, number of drives and printers, storage capacity, and computer specifications) also changed and its final form differed considerably from that originally proposed. Management also had to adjust to some basic changes in the system performance. It was found, for example, in one situation that the new system could not substantially decrease order-processing time, and that it could provide only a modified on-line inventory control.

While some changes are inevitable, a more complete feasibility study would have reduced the number and size of these changes. The seventh problem, therefore, was making a commitment for the new computer before completing a detailed study of costs and the computer configuration needed for the new system.

The Organizational Impact of the New System

The systems development programs at the companies studied led to major changes in the organizational structures of the companies. As a result of these studies, attention was shifted from what each department had done in the past—that is, which department had handled what functions—to the operations and management jobs that were needed to run this type of business successfully.

Some personnel with narrow outlooks saw the studies as a threat to their positions. And they were right; the studies made it obvious that certain changes in the organization were needed. Other personnel, however, realized that a business is dynamic, and that internal changes are constantly needed to meet changing market conditions and improve operating efficiency. To these persons, the new system represented an opportunity, not a threat.

While the adjustments came easily for some, for others who were not prepared for the changes and resisted them, the adjustments were painful. Some pockets of bureaucratic resistance were wiped out, for a number of departments were eliminated and their remaining functions were put under existing or new departments. For the most part this was healthy, but in the process some valuable people were unfortunately lost. With proper foresight and planning, these people could have been retained.

The eighth problem, therefore, was not anticipating the changes in organization structure and the dislocations in personnel that would be occasioned the new system, and not developing plans and educating personnel to meet these changes.

Other Benefits Derived from the New Systems

A number of other benefits resulted from the systems development efforts in these companies. In addition to a thorough re-evaluation of corporate goals and the interaction of the various functional operations needed to achieve these goals, a considerable amount of coordination and education occurred. A spirit of cooperation gradually developed as operating personnel found that their ideas were needed and used. In turn, the interchange helped to educate operating personnel in the problems of other operating departments, and provided them with insight into management objectives and policies, both for the coming year and for the longer term.

Such coordination and education benefits did not happen by chance. They came about because, in administering the later stages of the systems development, management took the time to listen to ideas and follow up on them, and to communicate corporate policies and the rationale behind them. Where operational deficiencies were found, they were not made a cause for reprimand. Rather, the problems were explored to find their causes; and means were developed to prevent their recurrence.

As a result, a well-knit operating and management group emerged from the systems development effort. Operating and management personnel had a common purpose. They knew what was expected of them and what the major problems of the business were. They knew that they had the freedom to innovate and make mistakes, and that their suggestions would be considered. Most important, they knew why they were doing their job and how it fit into the rest of the company's operation.

All of these side benefits of the systems development projects could have been lost, if time and attention had not been devoted to cultivating them.

Summary Guidelines

Managers cannot expect everything to go smoothly in developing a new data processing and management information system, but they should not use this as a rationale for tolerating unnecessary inefficiency. Information systems development is a relatively new area, in which many managers lack experience. Clearly, performance in this area can be improved, and this discussion has attempted to establish some guidelines for improving management information systems development programs on the basis of the experiences of the companies studied.

These guidelines may be summarized as follows:

1. Systems development should begin with a feasibility study.

2. A corporate executive (or other responsible company manager) should be appointed to head the systems development group (where the system being developed affects a major segment of a company's business), and he should participate actively in the work. Control points should be developed, where top corporate management can participate in and demonstrate their support of the project.

3. The scope of the project should be defined early, so that management will have realistic expectations as to what the systems development

program will accomplish and will know how much work will have to be done to fulfill these expectations. Adequate time, money, and manpower must be allocated for the project.

4. The study group should include a manager from each operating section affected by the new system, to insure the direct involvement of these areas in the project. Deadlines for each stage of the project should be set, to insure the continuing involvement of all parties.

5. Time should be taken to develop an adequate definition of the major decision-making areas within the business system and of the information needed for effective decision making in each of these areas.

6. Balance and an overall company perspective should be maintained in the new system. Extreme care should be taken to see that no one functional area dominates the structure and development of the system.

7. The final commitment for machinery should be withheld until a very precise idea of what is needed has been formed.

8. Major changes in organizational structure and major dislocations in personnel will occur, and plans and programs should be developed for making these changes and dislocations as painless as possible. This includes educating everyone concerned in what is happening.

9. Time and effort should be taken to realize the education and coordination side benefits possible from a systems development program.

10. The study should result in the preparation of a formal report listing all findings, conclusions, and recommendations.

The companies examined in this study had alert, bright, and realistic management. Although there were problems, once they were recognized, management took the necessary steps to resolve them. These steps could, however, have been taken earlier in the systems development efforts, thus avoiding many of the problems. Instead of false starts, which made the normal activities required to develop a system seem like problems, each step could have been conceived of positively, as a necessary activity in the normal development a new data processing and management information system. In this way, there would have been fewer negative feelings about the projects and less time and money would have been lost in carrying out the development efforts.

A Summary Overview:
The Systems Approach at Work

The approach to management information systems development, as outlined in Chapter Two, includes three major activity areas:

1. Diagnosing situation requirements, developing the concept (or structure) of the information system needed, and analyzing existing information and data systems.
2. Developing the information system.
3. Implementing the system.

The success of any management information systems development effort depends on organizational and behavioral factors, both in developing and implementing the system and subsequently in using it effectively to carry out the management job.

While the preceding chapters in this book have concentrated on the earlier phases of the systems approach, situation diagnosis and system development, and not considered in any depth the organizational and behavioral aspects of systems development, implementation and use, these aspects are equally important. This chapter has discussed some of the ways in which organizational and behavioral factors can affect systems development efforts, and how behavioral roadblocks can be overcome.

Organizational changes and innovations have proved useful in many companies in facilitating management information systems development. By giving greater autonomy to the data processing and systems development departments, by organizationally linking management users and systems technicians, and by involving higher management in development efforts, performance in this area can be improved.

Major systems development efforts have in many companies had an impact on company-wide organization structures, as well as on the organization structure of the data processing area. This chapter discussed how these changes evolve from the situation diagnosis and systems development studies, and how they can be anticipated. In addition, the discussion covered other organizational behavior factors which should be considered in management information systems development.

Introducing consideration of user (manager) needs early in the systems development effort helps keep human factors in mind throughout the effort; in addition, it encourages user participation in the development effort, and so can help improve the system itself and reduce resistance to its introduction and use. Not surprisingly, systems technicians often resist each user involvement, both because it takes time and because it invariably leads to adjustments in the system design and to compromises which make the system, from a technical viewpoint, less perfect.

Where such a user orientation does not guide management information systems development, major problems inevitably arise. Lack of user participation can lead to poorly designed systems, extensive reprogramming, delays and added costs, ineffective use of the system, disruption of interpersonal relationships, and, at times, the junking of an entire system. At the same time, however, it is not always easy to obtain the cooperation and participation of operating managers in the systems development project—even though these managers seem to realize that the system is being designed to help them and that, if they do not participate, the final information systems may not be to their liking.

One of the reasons for this is that many managers do not know how to participate or are unfamiliar with information systems technology. The purpose of this book has been to introduce managers to data processing and information systems, the systems approach, and the ways in which a manager can participate meaningfully in information systems development.

Part One first introduced the reader to the nature of management information systems and the general systems approach. This discussion was kept fairly general, since it was designed for a manager or potential manager who was not familiar with the subject and who was not planning to become a systems technician. Next, the mechanics of data processing systems were reviewed in detail, and the reader given some insights into how these systems (which are the basis of modern management information systems) are developed by systems and computer technicians.

Part Two of the book discussed developing information systems in several basic business management areas. While actual systems were described, the emphasis in these discussions was on the manager's role in these efforts— defining his information requirements, based on an analysis of his job and his decision-making needs, in a way that would be useful to the systems technician. There are many ways for a manager to describe his job and its information requirements; the task here was to learn how to describe his requirements with data processing, storage, and reporting restraints in mind.

The final part of the book dealt with more advanced management information systems areas, as well as with the problems involved specifically in organizing and implementing information systems and more generally in putting the systems approach to work in actual business situations.

Putting the system approach to work is not a simple matter of following a step-by-step procedure. As seen from the examples cited in this chapter, individual personalities, the specific organizational environment, business conditions, and management attitudes and philosophies can all affect how the development effort is carried out.

Some companies have made considerable progress in overcoming these organizational and behavioral roadblocks to successful management information systems development. For example, by the 1960s Mead Corporation had had sufficient experience with computerized data processing systems to have developed an effective organizational approach to systems development, an approach which worked largely because of active management support. Other

companies, such as the mail-order companies described in the preceding
section, evolve such an approach only after much trial-and-error, as they
wrestle with actual systems development projects within their individual work
and management environment.

As was pointed out in Chapter Two and reemphasized in this chapter,
then, while the systems approach is easy to grasp in concept, considerable
management skill is needed to put it to work, first in developing the system
itself, and second in implementing and using the system. These skills can be
developed through reading and practice exercises, such as those provided in
this book. But practical experience is also a necessary ingredient of this
learning process, especially because organizational and behavioral factors have
such an important impact on the outcome of systems development efforts.
Hopefully, this book will make that learning experience more meaningful and
productive.

TEXT DISCUSSION QUESTIONS

1. Describe some of the ways in which data processing and information
   systems development activities have traditionally been organized in business. Discuss the ways in which these organizational patterns do and do
   not facilitate management information systems development.
2. Describe some organizational innovations which have been tried in an
   attempt to facilitate development of more comprehensive and sophisticated management information systems.
3. Discuss the ways in which systems development projects have affected or
   can affect the organizational structure of a company's entire business
   operation.
4. Describe some of the behavioral factors which can affect management
   information systems development, and the ways in which they affect it.
5. Discuss some of the major problems encountered in gaining manager (user)
   cooperation in management information systems development efforts, and
   describe some of the organizational and other methods used to encourage
   manager participation in these development projects. Refer to the text of
   Chapter One, as well as to this chapter, in answering this question.
6. Discuss the nature of the knowledge gap between managers and systems
   technicians as they affect management information systems development,
   and some of the ways in which that gap can be closed.
7. Based on your reading of the company studies described in the chapter
   and in the following case studies, discuss the ways in which the systems

approach described in Chapter Two and throughout this book has to be modified in putting it to work in actual systems development situations.

8. Describe some of the practical roadblocks encountered in actually developing management information systems. In what ways might the roadblocks described in the *Guidelines* section of this chapter be considered typical (or not typical) of systems development efforts in other companies you are familiar with.

9. Outline the guidelines given in the chapter for putting the systems approach to work in actual business situations. Describe the ways in which these guidelines could be amplified or modified based on your reading or experience.

Case Study Exercises

Domby Publishing Company (see end of Chapter Two)

Assignment

Identify the nature and causes of the resistance to the new information system in the editorial department. Discuss ways in which this resistance might be overcome.

The City of Dalton [8]

The City of Dalton is a municipality of approximately 35,000 people situated twenty-five miles due west of Houston. Each year, the city receives from the accounting firm which conducts the annual audit of the municipal books, a list of recommendations for improving the procedures and methods used in performance of the various financing and accounting functions. In the recommendations made following the 1963 audit, the accounting firm suggested that serious consideration should be given to adopting electronic data processing equipment to handle utility billing, tax statements, and other accounting functions. According to the accountants' report, utility billing and tax statement preparation and collection were becoming burdensome tasks. Clerical errors were frequent, resulting in considerable time being spent each month in an attempt to balance utility bills to the general ledger. Based on the city's

---

8. All names, dates, and places have been changed in order to disguise the identity of the city involved. This case was prepared, as a basis for class discussion, by Mr. Donald L. Caruth, under the direction of Professor Frank M. Rachel, Ph.D., University of Dallas, Irving, Texas.

projected growth rate, the present billing machine system would be woefully inadequate in a relatively short time. Therefore, the accountants' report recommended that a formal study should be made of the various types and costs of electronic equipment and systems available.

Impressed with the necessity of taking action to remedy a potentially serious problem, the Dalton City Council, in the months immediately following the receipt of the audit report, held meetings with representatives of several computer-manufacturing companies. However, it was not until July 25, 1965 that the City Council made the decision to rent from Generamic, Inc., a model KX2100 computer.

At the time this decision was made, no one in the city organization below the level of the City Council had seen the chosen computer system in operation. In fact, Generamic had only two KX2100 systems in operation and both of these were in the New York area.

Generamic indicated to the city that it would furnish representatives to work during the initial phases of installing the new system. However, it would be the city's responsibility to select personnel to work within the system and to carry on the operation once a degree of success had been achieved by the system. The determination of the organizational structure to be used in regard to the new system was left solely to the city. A firm delivery date of May 26, 1966 was established by the manufacturer.

Almost immediately after the decision was made to install the EDP system, Wilson Wyscuf the accounting department manager, submitted his resignation effective August 31. The chief accountant, one of the finance director's main subordinates, is responsible for the performance of all accounting work performed in the city organization. The position also entails the supervision of several accounting clerks and related personnel. Two days before Wyscuf's departure from the organization, the decision was made to promote Alfred Neuman, an administrative intern, to accounting department manager. Neuman had been working in the accounting department as a temporary machine operator and had gained some knowledge of the city's accounting procedures. Although he had no academic background in accounting or previous experience in supervision, Neuman was felt to be the logical choice for the position because he was the only full-time male employee in the department.

While working as administrative intern, Neuman had been pursuing a degree in marketing at a local university. Because he was able to take the necessary courses at night, he felt that his promotion would in no way interfere with his academic endeavors and he would continue to work toward his degree.

Toward the end of August, Denton Ashburn, the Director of Finance, decided to test all of the accounting department employees in order to determine if any possessed the necessary aptitude for computer programming. The tests were given September 13, and of the thirteen people tested, only four made satisfactory scores on the test. These included Ashburn himself, Alfred Neuman, and two part-time employees who were students at the university. One of the students indicated to Ashburn that he had no desire to learn to program; the other stated that he would "give it a try."

During the next several weeks, no further work was done toward preparing for the computer installation or training personnel, because of the heavy seasonal activity in the finance division. During September and October of any year, the employees of this division are normally busy with three specific tasks. The first of these is preparing, printing, assembling, and binding the city's budget document. This activity must be completed by no later than September 20, so that copies may be presented to the City Council in time for final approval before the beginning of the new fiscal year on October 1, 1965. The second job of major proportion is preparing and mailing tax statements for the year. This process must be completed in time to mail the statements to taxpayers by the end of September. The third and largest job is the annual fiscal closing which is started as soon as possible after the ending of the fiscal year. The 1965 fiscal closing was complicated by two factors: the lack of experience of the new accounting department manager and the preparation for an upcoming bond sale. During 1964 the voters had approved the issuance of both revenue and general-obligation bonds. The date set for the sale of these bonds was December 15. Therefore, it was imperative that all closing procedures be completed as rapidly as possible so that the books could be turned over to the independent accounting firm for audit and certification before the bond sale. The accounting department completed all of these tasks by November 8.

During the third week of November, Generamic put a KX2100 system on display in its Houston offices. Anxious to get a look at the equipment which the city would shortly install, Ashburn, Neuman, and Tom Anderson, the university student who had expressed some interest in working with the system, journeyed to Houston to attend a special showing of the equipment. At this showing, Generamic representatives impressed upon Ashburn the need for getting the city people who would be programming the system enrolled in the company's programming school as soon as possible. Ashburn decided that initially he and Neuman would attend the training sessions. The starting date for the two-week programming school would be January 10, 1966.

On that date, Ashburn and Neuman commuted to Houston to begin training. The bulk of the training provided by Generamic consisted of a series of recorded lessons accompanied by programmed learning text materials. Returning to Dalton after listening to tape recordings for the third day,

Ashburn suffered a heart attack and was rushed to the hospital. The initial prognosis was that Ashburn would be unable to return to work for a number of months. However, he expressed a desire to renew his training when he was able.

With Ashburn now out of action, greater responsibility fell upon Neuman. It was immediately apparent that he would be unable to attend the rest of the training sessions. Arrangements were made to secure the tapes and other materials from Generamic so that Neuman could continue the training in his spare time. However, because he was attending classes at the university three nights a week, his time was severely limited.

After several weeks, Russell Clinton, the city manager, decided that with no one in a position to provide over-all supervision, guidance, and coordination to the work of the various departments of the finance division, problems might arise which would lead to unnecessary difficulties. To prevent this, Clinton appointed Adrian Long, the director of public works, to serve as interim finance director.

In early March, the city was notified that Generamic's advanced programmer training institute would be held in Houston the week of April 4. This announcement came at a very inopportune time for Neuman. Not only was he struggling with a heavy load at the university, while continuing to work on his programmer training materials, but he was encountering problems and long hours in his job as chief accountant. First, it had become obvious that the city's account numbering system, which made liberal use of alphabetic codes, was unsatisfactory for conversion to an electronic system; thus, the numbering system had to be revised. It was further decided that this period of conversion from one numbering system to another would be the most logical time to rearrange the ledger of accounts and realign the meter book routes. This process involved a considerable amount of overtime work by all employees of the accounting department. Secondly, March 31 is a quarter-ending date. Because the city manager is required to present a quarterly financing report to the City Council, the books must be closed as of the end of March and financial statements prepared as soon thereafter as possible. This activity occupied the greater part of Neuman's available time during the week prior to the advanced programmer training institute.

On April 4, Neuman began attending the training sessions. To his dismay, he soon discovered that all of the other attendees were programmers and EDP managers from firms which were converting from smaller Generamic computers to the new KX2100 system. All of the training material and discussions were therefore oriented to people having extensive backgrounds in EDP.

The representatives of Generamic were themselves somewhat dismayed to learn that the City of Dalton did not have any of its computer programs prepared and ready for testing. They were, of course, aware of the finance director's illness, but felt that the city should have, nevertheless, been able to make more progress than it had.

The week following the training institute, Denton Ashburn returned to work on a part-time basis. At the same time, the university student who had indicated an interest in working with the computer, quit his job with the city. Ashburn indicated that as soon as his doctor would allow him to return to work full-time, which was expected to be the middle of May, he would like to continue with the programmer lesson series. However, because May was also the month in which the following year's budget had to be prepared, most of Ashburn's time during the remainder of April and the first part of May was devoted to gathering and compiling budget requests as well as preparing statistical analyses. But, despite this workload, Ashburn was able to resume listening to the recorded instruction tapes on May 20.

During May, Generamic's representatives began to lay groundwork for the scheduled arrival of the computer on May 26. An initial order for supplies was placed and discussions were held regarding how best to program the city's utility billing and payroll procedures, the first areas selected for computerization. On May 15, Generamic informed the city it would be unable to meet the scheduled delivery date due to complications which had arisen in the manufacture of the KX2100. No definite revised date for delivery was given, but September was held out as a possibility.

On June 15, after a long and tiring day at the office, Denton Ashburn collapsed at home and died. After the initial reaction to this sudden tragedy had subsided somewhat, thoughts turned to the main goal of the next few months which, as far as the finance division was concerned, would have to be the continuation of those items of work that were normal and those for which deadlines were most pressing. The responsibility for keeping things on an even keel fell to Alfred Neuman.

After hurriedly searching the market for a new finance director, Russell Clinton selected Trevor Watson, who, because he was between jobs at the time, was able to report for work on July 1. Although Watson was thoroughly experienced in municipal administration, he had no previous experience with EDP and was also unfamiliar with the type of organization used by the City of Dalton.

One of Watson's first acts was to create a Data Processing Department which would be responsible for all activities connected with programming, installing, and operating the new computer system. This new department would be on the same organizational level as the accounting and purchasing departments and would be directly responsible to Watson. Watson appointed Neuman as manager of this department. Neuman's departure from the accounting department created a vacancy which was not filled until October when George Taylor was hired as accounting manager.

During the latter part of July, Johnson Howard, Generamic's customer support representative, arrived in Dalton to assist with the computer installation planning. Finding that the city had no one available for programming on a full-time basis, Howard elected to do all of the initial programming himself. Much of this initial effort was concerned with converting the city's utility rate schedules into a billing program, a task which proved to be far from simple. During this programming period, it became evident to Howard that the internal storage of the KX2100 Central Processor would be utilized to the hilt by the calculations necessary in the billing programs for the city's 13,000 utility accounts. Due to this factor, Howard found it even more difficult to construct the required programs.

On September 15, the long-awaited computer arrived. For several days thereafter, technicians from Generamic's Houston office conducted routine tests of the equipment.

The work routine in the finance division did not bear too many interruptions at this point because it was now back to the busy September-October period of frantic activity. In contrast to the previous year, there was no upcoming bond sale; however, the only person in the entire division above the clerical level familiar with the annual fiscal closing process was Alfred Neuman. Therefore, most of Neuman's time was spent in supervising and performing the closing activities, while simultaneously attempting to train George Taylor. Neuman's work in the accounting department was finally concluded on November 15, at which time he was again able to turn his thoughts back to the installation of the computer system.

Shortly after the end of September, Howard decided that it would be a good idea to try for conversion of the city payroll system to a computer operation in order to produce checks for the November 15 payroll. Generamic had a payroll program in its software library, and Howard felt that with a few "patches" to the program to accommodate special features of the city's payroll, conversion could be accomplished in short order, and it was. Out of the 365 payroll checks produced on the first November run it was necessary to void and remake 29 of them. In Howard's opinion, this represented a high degree of accuracy for the first live run of the payroll program. Probably the best result of this first payroll run was the demonstration to all concerned that, with proper design of input data and programs, the computer could be made to do beneficial work.

As time went by after November 15, most of the efforts of Howard and Neuman were directed to planning the details of the utility billing system's related routines. Of primary concern was the design of a utility bill form.

Howard, with his technical orientation, tended to be most concerned about the speed of processing and the mechanics of auxiliary operations such as printing. Neuman, more oriented to the governmental aspects of the project, tended to worry about such things as the potential effects on public relations of generalized name abbreviation policies or of failure to present a separate itemization of sewage and garbage charges on a printed bill.

During December, Clinton and Watson became more and more concerned about just when the actual runs on utility billing would be made. Several target dates had been established by Neuman, and several postponements always followed the establishment of these dates, so that at any given time the target date was roughly nine months away. The major reason for the continued delays lay in the large amount of time required to prepare data inputs on the 13,000 utility accounts. The gathering and producing of this data in a machine-usable form was complicated by the necessity of entering alphabetic data such as names and addresses into a basically numeric system. The only people available for this translation function were the clerks in the accounting department and they could only be spared from their regular duties on a part-time basis. Both Howard and Neuman suggested that more people were needed for the conversion period, but, unfortunately, such a need had not been foreseen during the time of the budget preparation and consequently no allotment had been set aside for extra help.

After struggling along short-handed for some time in an effort to convert to the new computer system, Howard and Neuman were pleasantly surprised when one of the two clerks who had been producing utility bills on posting machines announced that she would be terminating her employment the first of March. It would have been futile, at this late date, to train a new billing clerk to perform what would become an obsolete function. The alternative, as Neuman saw it, was to get a large enough amount of the utility billing on the computer so that a single billing clerk could handle the remaining accounts until total conversion was achieved. Neuman approached Watson with the possibility of doing this, and Watson readily agreed. The vacant position was therefore transferred to the Data Processing Department, thus giving this office its first employee.

In the meantime, preparations were made to produce computerized bills for the first cycle of customers. The process was started on March 19 and, by working around the clock, it was possible to get all of the bills in the mail by the afternoon of March 21, 1967—several months after the original test target date for the first production. But, at long last, the system was fulfilling one of the functions recommended for conversion by the city's audit firm in 1963.

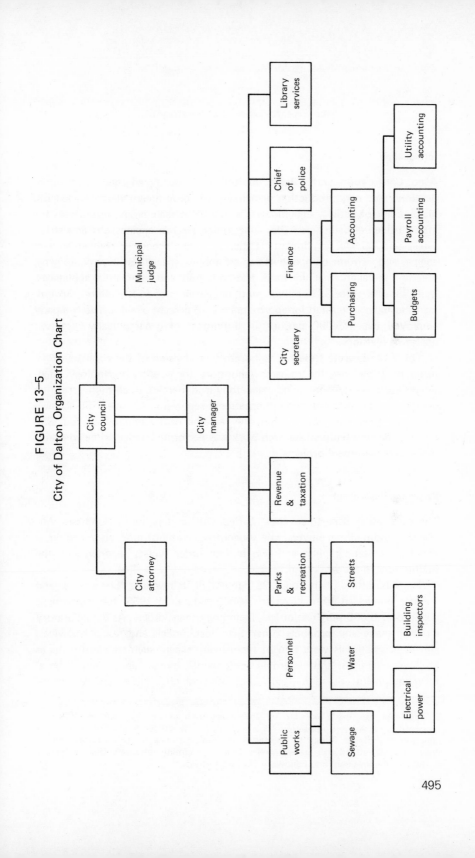

FIGURE 13–5

City of Dalton Organization Chart

Avco-Everett Research Laboratory (A)[9]

Introduction

Avco Corporation was a large, multiplant company engaged in research, development, and production principally for government defense agencies. Major fields of activity encompassed space flight technology, nose cones for intercontinental ballistic missiles, electronics, aircraft engines, airframe structures, and missile components. Other activities produced civilian aircraft engines and airframe components and assemblies, specialized farm equipment, precision metal and machine parts, and household and commercial appliances. In 1958, sales were $283 million, with net earnings of $11.6 million. Government business accounted for approximately 75 percent of sales. The company employed over 15,000 persons in a number of geographically dispersed operating divisions.

The Avco-Everett Research Laboratory, a division of the company organized in 1955, was the research laboratory for re-entry technology, high-temperature gas dynamics, and magnetohydrodynamics. In all these areas, the laboratory had established an international reputation for scientific achievement and pre-eminence. In 1958, the research center employed about 350 persons. Substantially all research work was performed under prime contracts linked to government projects.

Purchasing Department

The purchasing department was staffed with a director of purchases, Mr. Harold Bloom, three buyers, one subcontract administrator, an expediter, a secretary, a stenographer, and two to four order typists depending on the fluctuations in the work load.

The laboratory spent about 25 percent of its revenues for materials and services purchased from close to 3,000 vendors. In 1958, the department issued over 6,000 purchase orders, including change orders. As the laboratory did not make any products other than test models and research devices, almost no materials were bought repetitively except such standard items as fasteners, electrical and electronic components, metals, and general laboratory equipment. Standard items were stocked on a "min-max" inventory control basis. There was an exceptionally large variety of nonrepetitive and often highly specialized and exotic materials, parts, and equipment bought for each research program, accounting for the relatively large number of active vendors and purchase orders. Approximately 10,000 different items, many of which were stocked in quantities of as little as one or two, were carried in inventory at a value of approximately $300,000. Withdrawals of about 150 different items from inventory were made each day.

Since the laboratory undertook most of the research work for the government on a cost-plus-fixed-fee basis, the government exercised close technical and administrative control over the work and the supporting activities of the laboratory, including procurement. The government defense agencies requested regularly extensive data on the execution of research contracts awarded to the laboratory.

In 1958, Armed Services Procurement Regulations were issued requiring from prime contractors a report on vendors to the Department of Defense (DOD) four times a year. DOD maintained comprehensive records of "debarred" and "ineligible" bidders on government work and regularly advised prime contractors of companies to be removed from their respective vendor lists.

To meet the manpower requirements for the typing and the updating of these bimonthly reports on the laboratory's 5,000 vendors, Mr. Bloom decided that an additional full-time clerk-typist would have to be added to the staff. His order typists, he knew, were unable to prepare and maintain such lists, because the volume of order typing was already creating bottlenecks and leading occasionally to considerable overtime. Furthermore, he anticipated that DOD and other governmental agencies sooner or later would require from prime contractors detailed information on the distribution of purchase orders to large and small vendors, by states, and, possibly, by regions within states. Mr. Bloom recognized that such demands would necessitate the employment of additional personnel.

Mr. Bloom thought that, inasmuch as the preparation of the bimonthly vendor list was unavoidable, the purchasing department should derive as much benefit as possible from such a compilation. One immediate benefit to his department could be achieved by combining two operations on this job: (1) the preparation of the list of vendors and (2) the preparation of a directory of vendors by product category for department use. The current practice of his buyers in selecting sources of supply was to depend heavily on their individual notebooks, card files, and similar records for the names of previously used suppliers. This practice was particularly used on orders and subcontracts for items and materials awarded at infrequent intervals. He knew also that these individual records were incomplete, not always up to date, and not readily available to the department.

In considering his needs for the ever-increasing governmental reporting requirements, Mr. Bloom's first reaction was that this was the opportune time to introduce EDP to the purchasing function.

Mr. Bloom had gained a thorough knowledge of electronic data processing equipment through buying computers and peripheral equipment for the laboratory's scientific computing work. Shortly after the formation of the laboratory in 1955, he had begun to buy outside computer time, as the center had neither the qualified personnel nor the time to set up and operate a computer system. Within two years, however, the funds spent on outside computer time had reached proportions making it imperative for the laboratory to acquire its own equipment. An order was placed for an IBM 650, two key punchers, an accounting machine, a sorter, a verifier, and a printer. During the waiting period of 12 months for the computer, the laboratory with the help of an outside computer consultant trained the key punch operators, programmers, and computer technicians to form the staff for the scientific computer center.

In the process of buying outside computer time and negotiating contracts with various computer manufacturers, Mr. Bloom had read extensively on the subject of EDP and had visited a number of companies with computers in operation, including some with EDP systems for purchasing. Thus, he not only was aware of the potential assistance EDP offered to procurement—particularly in providing buyers with better decision-making tools, in the form of vendor performance reports and analyses, not available from manual record systems—but also he was anxious to apply what he had learned about EDP to certain procurement functions in his department to determine if purchasing performance could be improved. He was very much impressed with an integrated system used in the purchasing department of a large oil refinery, which carried nearly 10,000 stock items maintained on a "min-max" basis. This EDP system scanned past purchases to compare price and delivery as the reorder point for an item was reached, printed out a purchase order with an economic order quantity, compared invoices with receiving reports, and printed out a check for payment.

But as Mr. Bloom began to think about a "total systems" approach within the setting of his laboratory, several problems became apparent to him. One problem was that, lacking any degree of repetitive ordering as in a mass-production operation, a switch to a totally automated system would not decrease personnel cost appreciably, if at all; and a justification for using a computer for his department on the basis of direct cost savings alone would be impossible. A second was that, except for himself, no one in his department had any knowledge of, or experience with, mechanical or electronic data processing machines. In fact, he recalled that on several occasions some of his buyers had implied satisfaction with the fact that the laboratory's purchasing activities were, in their view, so nonrepetitive and nonroutine in nature that EDP would not be applicable. A third problem was that any automation of any function of purchasing would have to be preceded by a thorough and time-consuming systems analysis, whereas the need of making adequate provision for new governmental reporting requirements was immediate.

In thinking about a manual preparation of the vendor lists, Mr. Bloom was confronted with the problem of increasing administrative costs by hiring at least one additional clerk-typist, while there was already a great deal of pressure exerted by management upon each department to keep strictly within budget limits. By contrast, the use of EDP in his department would be something entirely new, so that the cost of this alternative might be more easily accepted by management than an increase in the department's man-power. Since the laboratory already had a computer and the necessary data input and output equipment, he believed that he would be in a very advan-tageous position, in that he would not have to justify the buying or leasing of any equipment but argue merely for a time allotment on the laboratory's IBM 650. Also, he was convinced that the Department of Defense, from the viewpoint of vendor performance control, material cost control, and prompt and complete compliance with governmental data requirements, would look favorably upon the laboratory's use of EDP in purchasing and that this would be helpful in future contract negotiations with government procurement officers. Furthermore, it occurred to Mr. Bloom that the argument *against* automating the purchasing function, namely, the great amount of time required for training, systems analysis, systems design, and conversion, could easily be turned around. Just *because* of the significant time element in-volved, steps toward installing an advanced EDP system should be initiated immediately before the rapidly expanding volume of purchasing reached a point where his department would be rushed headlong into it.

Summing up the situation, Mr. Bloom believed three alternative courses of action were open to him: (1) He could hire an additional clerk-typist for the initial preparation and subsequent periodic updating of the vendor list. (2) He could confine the use of existing IBM equipment to the preparation and updating of the vendor list *and* the buyers' directory. (3) He could use the new data requirements of the Armed Services Procurement Regulations as a basis for full automation of all routine procurement steps.

For the first alternative, Mr. Bloom estimated that total costs for a clerk-typist, including salary and such fringe benefits as life, health, and accident insurance and retirement pension, would be $75 a week, or $3,800 a year. But this employee would also be able to assist in order typing, reducing overtime cost for this activity by as much as $1,700 a year.

For the second alternative, he estimated that the costs of preparing and updating the vendor list and the buyers' directory six times a year with IBM equipment would be as follows:

Development of coding system and setting up organizational procedure (1 staff man for 4 weeks full time and supervision by the materiel manager)	$2,100	
Punching and verifying 5,000 cards (IBM 026 key punch)	1,000	
Total nonrecurring costs		$3,100
2 sortings 6 times a year (IBM 083 sorter)	$ 600	
2 listings 6 times a year (IBM 407 accounting machine)	600	
1 additional set of print-outs 6 times a year	300	
Punching and verifying 300 additional cards a year	60	
Total recurring costs		$1,560

For the third alternative, without having detailed studies of what would be involved in automating routine procurement functions (excluding receiving, stores, and payment of vendor invoices), Mr. Bloom estimated that operations cost for the purchasing department would be increased by at least $30,000 a year. This figure did not include the nonrecurring expenditures for systems analysis, systems design, programming, costs of personnel training, and conversion costs. Although he knew that automation would reduce administrative cost for purchase order typing by as much as $8,000 a year, through use of Flexowriter equipment, he thought that the major justification for computerizing the routine purchasing work in the department would be the availability of detailed, up-to-date, follow-up reports and purchase performance reports to his buyers and expediter. These analytical tools, he thought, would significantly improve his buyers' decision-making capacity and ultimately result in substantial material cost savings. Mr. Bloom was convinced, however, that assigning financial values to such improvement in the laboratory's purchasing function would be extremely arbitrary and that it would be difficult to base a decision to automate on projected cost savings alone.

Avco-Everett Research Laboratory (B)[10]

Avco-Everett Research Laboratory, a division of Avco Corporation, was primarily engaged in advanced space flight research and development work for government defense agencies.

---

10. This case was made possible by the cooperation of the Avco-Everett Research Laboratory of Avco Corporation. It was prepared by Jurgen Ladendorf under the

In 1958, the laboratory's director of purchases, Mr. Harold Bloom, wondered how his purchasing department could best comply with a new requirement under the Armed Services Procurement Regulations calling for the submission of a bimonthly list of the laboratory's vendors to the Department of Defense (DOD). Mr. Bloom believed there were three alternative solutions from which he could choose: (1) prepare the vendor list manually, requiring the employment of an additional clerk-typist, (2) prepare the vendor list mechanically by using some of the laboratory's automatic data processing equipment, or (3) use the new data requirements by the Department of Defense as an opportunity to computerize the laboratory's routine purchasing functions. (See the Avco-Everett Research Laboraoty (A) case.)

First EDP Application

Mr. Bloom rejected the idea of preparing the required vendor list manually. Although he believed that such an approach had some merits from the viewpoint of short-term costs, it offered to him no satisfactory solution in the long run, since any further, yet unforeseen data requirements by DOD or other government departments would quickly lead to further additions to the clerical staff.

The establishing of a comprehensive EDP system for the procurement function was also discarded by Mr. Bloom for the time being. He believed that, in the interest of maintaining the laboratory's favorable relationship with the Defense Department, compliance with the new Armed Services Procurement Regulations should be both immediate and complete; however, automating routine purchasing activities was estimated to involve approximately one year of system analysis and design work. Thus, Mr. Bloom concluded that the introduction of an EDP system into purchasing was not the answer to the specific problem faced.

In giving preference to the alternative of limiting the use of automated equipment to the preparation of the vendor lists, Mr. Bloom was guided by the comparatively low costs of operation and by the expectation of prompt availability of the lists and of the buyers' directory. He also was influenced in his decision by the fact that his staff lacked familiarity with EDP. In this regard he recalled a conversation with the purchasing director of another company in which the latter spoke of a 90 percent turnover of personnel following the installation of an integrated EDP system in that firm's purchasing department. Mr. Bloom was convinced that a gradual introduction of EDP to his department, together with provision of ample opportunity for his staff to participate in a switch to EDP, would avoid such personnel difficulties. He realized that the automated preparation of vendor lists would entail the development of a vendor coding system for use with punched cards, and he believed that this would provide an opportunity for his staff to gain some familiarity with punched card work.

With the assistance of his buyers, Mr. Bloom set up 49 broad commodity categories covering all types of materials, supplies, and services bought by the laboratory. If a vendor provided materials in more than one category, the single item supplied in the greatest quantity served as a criterion for placement of the firm into a commodity category. In addition to a product category number, each vendor was assigned a set of numbers indicating the company's name, principal office location, and size of operations as measured by total work force. Next, approximately 5,000 punched cards were prepared and procedures established for their continuous updating. By early 1958, the purchasing department was able to obtain at any given moment current lists of vendors in alphabetical order, by product category, by region, and by size of company.

In addition to expediting the preparation both of DOD data and a comprehensive supply-source index for the buyers, the general use of the vendor code instead of the full name and address, according to Mr. Bloom, cut the time spent by buyers on filling out requisitions to be transcribed by the clerk-typists into purchase orders.

Subsequent Developments in Procurement

Following the initial application of punched cards to vendor listing, several years went by in which no further use of automatic data processing was made in the purchasing department. During these years, the laboratory experienced a rapid increase in research contracts. By 1962, the laboratory, which by that time employed slightly over 700 persons, spent about 25 percent of its $10 million annual revenue for materials and services purchased from close to 5,000 suppliers. The purchasing department's work load increased accordingly, and despite the addition of several buyers and clerks there was little time left for matters outside of pressing day-to-day purchasing activities. "Being of relatively small size, we simply did not have any people to whom we could have assigned the job of mechanizing some of the purchasing work," commented Mr. Bloom, and then he want on to say, "Furthermore, there was practically no time left on the IBM 650 after the scientific computing work, payroll, and accounts receivable had been processed. The machine was used to its limit."

In 1962, four developments revived the issue of computer utilization in the purchasing function: (1) The complexity and volume of purchasing had continued to grow at a fast rate, and it became apparent to Mr. Bloom that his buyers needed more timely and more comprehensive information upon which to base their buying decisions. (2) The volume of purchase orders had grown to a point where delays of up to three days in confirming verbally placed orders had become fairly common. (3) In order to achieve improved interdepartmental coordination, Mr. Bloom had been appointed materiel manager with the result that, in addition to purchasing, subcontracting, and expediting, he was charged with the responsibility for receiving, traffic, shipping, and inventory control. (4) The IBM 650 had been replaced with an IBM 1401, which was a larger and more versatile machine.

The delay in order confirmation, according to Mr. Bloom, was serious and required immediate attention. "Material ordered by telephone was coming into the receiving department before purchase orders for the material had been typed; consequently, the receiving department had no documents to enable checking and routing the material into the laboratory," said Mr. Bloom. "This put real stress on our procedures for the handling of incoming supplies and created a great deal of confusion. By 1962, we were writing about 1,000 purchase orders per month, using two girls full time and several girls part time. When we fell too far behind, I brought the full-time order typists in on Saturdays."

Associated with the heavy work load for the order typists was a high labor turnover rate. Mr. Bloom commented, "During the past year, I hired so many girls for the job that I cannot remember the names of half of them. Some got married, but most of them said I was working them too hard and that they were typing themselves crazy. And each time we hired a new girl we had to start the training all over again. I wanted to do things right. So, in the description column of our purchase orders, for example, I wanted to see the noun first. As an illustration, when we ordered gloves, the order read, 'Glove, rubber, grey, size 3' and not '3 pairs of size 3 grey gloves in rubber' or something like that. And to train these girls in the proper nomenclature took a great deal of time. Also, they needed training in reading requisitions, in which the buyers frequently used abbreviations of technical terms. As the work load increased, and since I could not hire more full-time personnel because I had reached the limits of my budget, turnover increased; and, consequently, the number of errors in the purchasing orders climbed tremendously because of less and less experienced order typists. These errors caused a big headache, not only for the purchasing department, but also for the accounting department in paying invoices."

In addition to these problems, Mr. Bloom had become concerned over the time and effort that went into the preparation of an annual report to management containing detailed statistical analyses of the purchasing department's work. This report included such information as the dollar value of purchase orders by month and year, classification of purchase orders by size, number of purchase orders by month and year, number of purchase orders by buyer per month and per year, number of vendor calls and vendor interviews, number of blank orders and total dollars spent on, and number of releases issued against such orders, material cost reductions, volume of purchase orders submitted to and approved by DOD, dollar value of purchase orders by product category and by vendor, and number of shipments received by month and year. In 1961, the materiel manager's secretary had spent three months gathering and preparing data for this report.

As Mr. Bloom set out to find solutions to these problems, he decided not to explore the possibility of increasing the purchasing personnel. He believed that, while it might be feasible to eliminate bottlenecks and delays in the typing of purchase orders through the hiring of a sufficient number of clerk-typists, the problem of personnel turnover and errors in the manual preparation of purchase orders could not be solved in a manner that would justify the increase in wage costs and administrative overhead. But a more important consideration in rejecting this alternative to EDP was Mr. Bloom's desire to increase significantly the quantity and quality of information for the buyers' decision-making as well as the speed with which this information would be available to them. "Even if I added 20 clerks, I could not get the kind of daily open order status report, with a weekly summary, and the kind of monthly buyer activity report that I had in mind," explained Mr. Bloom.

While Mr. Bloom found it relatively easy to choose between improving the department's existing manual data processing system, on the one hand, and a further utilization of the laboratory's existing computer installation, on the other, he was far less certain (1) in what way and (2) to what extent to computerize the procurement function. Mr. Bloom became particularly concerned with the question of whether to take the "total system" approach or the "hardware" approach. The "total system" approach would apply EDP to the laboratory's entire procurement cycle from the creation of a purchase requisition through the ordering, follow-up, and receiving process, to accounting distribution and vendor remittance. The "hardware" approach, on the other hand, would mechanize only portions of the procurement cycle, being confined largely to routine *purchasing* activities and perhaps not even involving a major change in existing methods, procedures, and organization.

Mr. Bloom thought that the recent combination of purchasing, receiving, traffic, and inventory control under his responsibility offered a good opportunity to develop an integrated EDP system. But at the same time he was aware of the fact that such an "optimum" system would require a large amount of system analysis, in order to define in detail the operating characteristics of the laboratory's procurement cycle, and would most likely lead to fundamental changes in forms, procedures, and policies. He also knew that such projects as automatic comparison of vendor invoices with receiving reports and purchase orders, or automatic printing of checks, would require extensive reprogramming of the accounting function, a function that had just been reprogrammed following the laboratory's switch from an IBM 650 computer to an IBM 1401 computer. "In fact," said Mr. Bloom, "even our coding system already in use would not be compatible with the system used by the accounting department."

Another problem that in Mr. Bloom's view had a bearing on the issue of total vs. partial EDP system was the lack of any significant repetition in the laboratory's material requirements. The lack of repetitive buying favored a continuation of manually prepared requisitions thus eliminating an integral part of a total system, such as the one he had examined in another company (see Avco-Everett Research Laboratory (A) case).

As in the first application of automatic data processing to purchasing four years earlier, Mr. Bloom again wondered about the impact of an integrated system on his personnel, particularly in stores and receiving. Because of their experience with EDP in 1958, Mr. Bloom expected no resistance from his buyers, although he was not sure whether he could expect the same attitude from the rest of his purchasing personnel. "If there were no other considerations involved," he said, "I think I would prefer a minimum-area approach, converting one or two routine functions at a time."

Of primary importance to Mr. Bloom were the economic aspects of a switch to EDP. Whether such switch be on a system-wide basis or follow a minimum-area approach, he believed that the use of the laboratory's computer center for purchasing could ultimately be justified only through an increase in the laboratory's net profits. But at the same time he believed that a reliable economic analysis, comparing revenues and costs, was nearly impossible to achieve because of the difficulty involved in measuring the "revenues" of an EDP system. The materiel manager thought that this was particularly true in the laboratory's case, where improvement in the buyers' decision-making through an improved information system was a more important objective than a reduction in purchasing-order processing costs.

Moreover, he believed that the difficulties met in attempting to appraise the possible effectiveness of data processing (in terms of costs, accelerated record production, and improved quality of the data made available) were compounded by the absence of a detailed design of a system that might be suitable for his needs.

Mr. Bloom believed that, for the purpose of cost analysis, the following items were relevant: costs of (1) system analysis, (2) system design, (3) programming, (4) conversion, (5) equipment, and (6) personnel. Mr. Bloom estimated that, if he decided to take the total system approach, approximately 18 months would be absorbed by the analysis, design, and programming work and training of personnel. The total cost would be approximately $135,000 (including salaries and administrative overhead for a two-man systems analysis team, made up of a procurement expert and a computer programmer; fees for an outside computer consultant; costs of introducing EDP to the personnel affected by a switch; and costs of training punch card operators). Mr. Bloom was at a loss to determine the costs of conversion (i.e., expenses incurred during the period from final program testing to discontinuance of the existing processing system). He estimated that the charges by the laboratory's computer center to the purchasing department for the use of equipment would be in the vicinity of $20,000 per year and that the costs of additional personnel, consisting of a part-time programmer and a computer operator, would be close to $15,000 annually.

As an alternative to an integrated system, Mr. Bloom considered a limited system in which the typing of purchase orders would be automated as much as possible by use of a Friden Flexowriter. The information contained in the purchase orders could be fed to the computer system, stored, and processed for analyses and reports on such items as order status, purchase commitments, vendor performance (price, quality, and delivery), and lead times. This system would exclude the receiving and inventory control functions and would not be linked to the laboratory's accounting setup. Mr. Bloom calculated that a two-man team could perform the pre-installation work in about 12 months at a cost of approximately $65,000 and that total costs of operation would absorb about $30,000 annually, including rental fees of approximately $7,500 per year for a Flexowriter.

As in the case of an integrated system, Mr. Bloom found it easy to estimate the savings in clerical costs but regarded it as difficult to assign numerical values to the ultimate effect on the laboratory's material costs of previously unavailable decision-making information and of such operational improvements as elimination of order typing bottlenecks, reduction in purchase order errors, and reductions in late deliveries.

Although Mr. Bloom was convinced that it would require much less persuasion to sell management on a step-by-step approach rather than on the idea of an integrated system, because of the differences in time, costs, and uncertainties, he believed that any advantages of the former approach were at least partially offset by the need for substantial reprogramming if stores and receiving were to be linked up, and compatibility with the accounting system were to be achieved, at a future date. Mr. Bloom was convinced that such link-up would take place within two to three years.

Another problem with which Mr. Bloom became concerned was the question of who should carry out the required systems analysis, design, and conversion work. He believed that a decision in this area, however, was much easier than one on the question of how much of the procurement function to include in the EDP system at one time. The materiel manager thought that the procurement man of the systems analysis team should not only be intimately familiar with the functions and operations of procurement but also should have some basic knowledge of computers and electronic data processing, whereas the EDP man should be an expert on computer systems and programming techniques and, in addition, possess a working knowledge of the procurement function. Mr. Bloom believed that both men preferably should be recruited from within the laboratory.

Midwest Apparel, Inc.[11]

The Midwest Apparel, Inc. is a large manufacturer and distributor of men's and women's apparel. It was founded in early 1900s, and has grown steadily in its size and sales volume through the expansion of its market and acquisition of many factories, supply units, and distributing firms. In the middle of 1950s the company owned nearly 40 plants located in southern and midwestern states, producing men's shirts, suits, slacks, sport coats, overcoats and top coats, and women's suits, coats, shirts and blouses. The sales volume was about $150 million at that time, achieved by the distribution of Midwest products to many company-owned stores, subsidiaries, and independent chains, department stores, specialty shops and other retail outlets throughout the United States and several foreign countries. The general office is located in a large midwestern city accommodating all central administrative offices which planned and controlled the company activities in all functional areas.

Despite the steady growth the Midwest had achieved in the apparel industry, the company was experiencing serious production planning and controlling problems in the middle 1950s. Up to that time, it had kept the long established tradition of good customer service; a sales executive once commented, "We want to always keep enough stock in all styles and sizes to provide ready and prompt services for all our customers." Under this general policy, three departments in each of three operating divisions[12] worked closely to perform production planning and control functions. The Merchan-

11. Prepared by Professor Hak Chong Lee, State University of New York at Albany. Copyright, 1964, by the School of Business Administration.

12. The Midwest Apparel, Inc. was originally founded by the merger of three apparel firms each manufacturing and distributing men's and women's lines. In this merger, all factories of the three companies were brought under the centralized control of Vice President in Manufacturing. However, each of the three companies maintained within the Midwest organization a separate operating division carrying out decentralized sales and production planning activities (Figure 13–6).

dise Department selected different styles of men's and women's apparel, estimated future sales of each style and size, and placed production orders for each style. The Specification Department determined the quantities of different materials necessary to produce the orders placed by the Merchandise Department, and the Production Planning Department scheduled the orders into factory production. Each division maintained independent Data Processing Departments equipped with punch card machines which processed limited sales and production data once a month for the exclusive use of each division.

As the consumer demand in the apparel industry was becoming more complex, with more frequent changes in style, the company was faced with a significant amount of shortage or obsolescence in the stocks of textile materials and finished goods. Such waste in production resources and loss of sales opportunities, because of the rapidly changing styles, was critical to the Midwest whose main objective was to maintain the leadership in sales volume in the apparel industry where the competition was becoming increasingly tight. The mounting clerical cost in its general office added a problem to the profit squeeze to which the company had been subjected since the late 1940s.

Mr. Thomas, the President, was concerned with the situation in 1955, and asked three executives to form a committee and initiate a thorough study of the existing company procedures for style design, materials purchasing, and production scheduling. After several months of intensive study with the service of an outside consulting firm, the committee recommended the installation of an electronic data processing system with the belief that it would significantly improve the existing conditions. The committee estimated that the use of electronic data processing would not only eliminate a great number of clerical employees, but also prepare more frequent, timely, accurate, and complete market and production information (commonly known as "merchandising" reports by the company officials) to the management which would use the information to exercise closer and more frequent control over materials purchasing and production planning in accordance with changing market conditions. These were expected to bring clerical savings and a reduction of mark-down losses from the obsolete materials and finished goods.

Two reputable electronic data processing machine suppliers were interested in Midwest's problems. They both confirmed the feasibility of "merchandising" applications, and further proposed an expansion of data applications into payroll operations to increase the clerical savings to a considerable degree. The I.B.M. Corporation offered its 705 model on a rental basis, along with services for the local training of programmers, the actual programming of computer applications, and the on-the-spot testing of the programs in the computers at the general office. The Remington-Rand offered its Univac computers on either rental or purchase basis and all other similar services offered by the I.B.M. However, at that time, Remington-Rand was to train programmers in New York City and test the programs in a large midwestern town located near the general office. Both suppliers provided Midwest with savings estimates expected from "merchandising" and payroll applications (Table 13–1).

While the President and the committee members were seriously considering the installation of computers, there was a sign of resistance at the division level. Mr. Frederick, a member of the committee, thought that the company should consolidate all division punch card machines into a central data processing department for computers in order to realize the maximum savings possible with both "merchandising" and payroll applications. Other members of the committee argued, however, that considering the feeling of resistance toward the computer installation, it might be better to leave the operation of

FIGURE 13–6

Partial Organization Chart of Midwest Apparel, Inc.

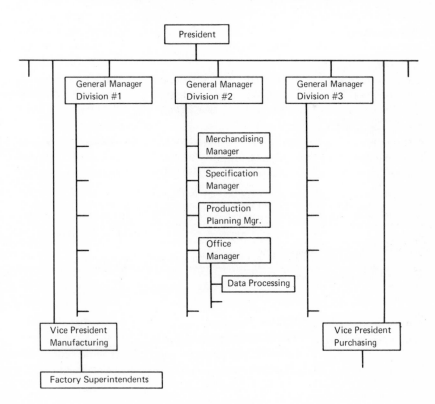

TABLE 13–1

Comparison of Expected Annual Net Savings
under Different Alternative Conditions

	Initial expenditure[a]	Additional annual cost[b]	Annual savings[c]	Net savings
"Merchandising application				
Decentralized input*				
I.B.M. rental	$ 97,100	$674,400	$592,400	–$ 82,000
Univac rental	107,600	NA	NA	NA
Univac purchase	207,600	NA	NA	NA
Centralized input**				
I.B.M. rental	$ 97,100	NA	NA	NA
Univac rental	125,600	NA	NA	NA
Univac purchase	245,600	NA	NA	NA
"Merchandising" and payroll				
Decentralized input*				
I.B.M. rental	$114,100	$707,200	$890,500	$183,300
Univac rental	107,600	664,900	890,500	225,600
Univac purchase	207,600	649,800	890,500	240,700
Centralized input**				
I.B.M. rental	$114,100	$833,900	$1,229,400	$395,500
Univac rental	125,600	898,400	1,229,400	331,000
Univac purchase	245,600	839,500	1,229,400	389,900

* Each division operates punch card machines for input data into computers.
** All division punch card machines are combined into a central data processing department.

(a) Include costs of computer room construction, programming, training programmers, freight in, and spare parts inventory of $100,000 (in the purchase situation only).
(b) Include the payroll for computer personnel, rental or amortization of computer and additional equipment cost, power and supply cost, and maintenance and spare parts expenses of $44,000 (in the purchase situation only.)
(c) Include savings from personnel reduction and elimination of some existing equipment. About 60 employees are expected to be released from "merchandising" application, and over 200 from "merchandising" and payroll combined.

punch card machines at divisions and only integrate them into the computer functions for any data applications that may be adopted.

As the committee members lacked complete accord for specific action, the President called an Executive Committee meeting to reach a final decision.

Questions—Midwest Apparel, Inc.

1. Explain in detail how the problems in the Midwest Company came about. Consider all factors including organization, policy, market, technology, competition, etc.

2. In your opinion, should the company install an electronic data processing system?
    (a) If your answer is yes,
        (1) Which machine system would you choose, and why? What are the factors supporting your decision? Are there any other considerations or assumptions you ought to make to qualify your decision?
        (2) What data applications would you recommend for the computers, and why?
        (3) What would you prefer, centralized or decentralized division input? Discuss advantages and disadvantages under the two different conditions.
    (b) If your answer is no,
        (1) Why would you oppose the installation of computers?
        (2) What alternative courses of action would you propose instead?

3. Assuming that you have 1½ years before actual delivery of computers, what general programs and activities would you formulate to prepare for the particular kind of system that you desire (Question #2a) to operate?

Accounting, 7, 93–120
  cash flow forecast, 113–15
  cost, 103–6, 111, 129–32
  defined, 93
  profitability, 109–13, 137–39
  responsibility, 106–9, 132–37
Advanced management information
    systems, 9–10, 410–49
  examples of, 446–47
  planning, 411–35
    airport facilities, 411–14
    corporate financial, 426–32
    manager training, 425–26
    marketing, 414–24
    strategic, 432–35
  supporting systems, 410
Advertising management information
    systems, 158, 172, 176–85,
    222–26
Airmont Packaging, 447
Albert Sidlinger Company, 174
American Airlines, 447
American Institute of Certified
    Public Accountants, 93

Application systems, (see
    Operational systems), 8

Bajar Industries, 129–32
Balance Sheet, 7, 96
Bantom Pharmaceuticals Company,
    318–23
Barker Company, 132–37
Batch processing, 79–80
Bedrock Products Company, 222–26
Bieneman, James, 466
Binary code, 57–59
Boulding, Kenneth, 12
Budgetary systems, 98–103, 126–29
  advertising budgeting, 180
  capital budgeting, 115
    proforma, 98–99
  sales budgeting, 173–74, 213–14
Budgeting, 8

Capital budgeting, 115
Carter University, 447
Carver Consolidated Products, 446
Cash flow forecast, 113–15

Computer systems, 53, 276, 283, 435–46
  assembly, 68–72
  batch processing, 79–80, 317–18
  decision-making applications, 80–81
  program, 72–74
  real time, 80
  simulation, 397, 411–26
Concept design, 23–30
Condor Foods Corporation, 335–38
Corporate management, 7
Correspondence Schools Unlimited, 218–22
Cost accounting, 103–6, 111, 129–32, 266
  job-order, 104–6
CPM, (see Critical path method)
Critical path method, 9, 361, 365–70
Customer service information systems, 158–59, 189–96, 226–31

Data bank, 75–79
Data processing systems, 10, 46–81, 437–46, 462–69, 483–84
  components of, 46–47
  computer (EDP), 53–64
  converting to management information system, 74–75
  development, 64–74, 435
    computer assembly and program, 68–74
    documents, 66–68
    file design, 68
    systems description, 64–65
  manual systems, 48–51
  organization of, 462–70
  punched card system, 51–53
Design of information systems, 5–6, 22, 23–30
Deterministic decision, 384
Distribution management information systems, 158–72, 185–89
Dodge, F. W., Corporation, 210
Dupont Corporation, 361

Eaton National Bank, 446
EDP, (see Data processing systems)
Enright Company, 200–210

Facilities management information systems, 265, 302–5, 335–38
File design, 68
Financial information systems for management, 115–19
  supporting information systems, 95–115
Financial management information systems, 7, 92–120
  planning, 426–32
  long term, 432–35
Forecasting, 157
  distribution facilities, 186
  sales, 8, 162–65, 210–14, 414
Frequency distribution, 287–95, 392–93
Fully integrated systems, 447–48, 495

Gantt chart, 270–73, 360
Garrett, Leonard, 470
General Dynamics Corporation, 323–27
General Systems Incorporated, 446
Gizmo Novelty Company, 214–18

Handpower Company, 314–18
Hardware, 74
Harvard Business School, 446
Hughes Aircraft Company, 308–14
Human factors, 30, 473–75

IBM, 5, 52, 58–60, 63
Implementing information systems, 32–36, 470–75
Income and asset reporting, 120–26
Income statements, 7, 96
Industrial engineering, 264
Information needs, 479
  balancing, 480–81
  defining, 479–80
Information requirements, 3–4
  defining, 3–4
  structuring, 27–29
  translating into information systems, 4–6
Input, 13, 47–48, 53–54, 66–67
Integrated management planning and control technique (IMPACT), 362
Integration of management